SHEFFIELD HALLAM UNIVERSITY
LEARNING C
COLLEGIATE C
SHEFFIELD S

102 064 962

D0351735

...SASTER:
...Politics of
...World Transformation

Sheffield Hallam University
Learning and Information Services
Withdrawn From Stock

OP Purchase
8 SEP 2012

AVOIDING SOCIAL AND ECOLOGICAL DISASTER

THE POLITICS OF WORLD TRANSFORMATION

*An Inquiry
into the
Foundations of
Spiritual and Ecological
Politics*

Rudolf Bahro

Revised, abridged edition
*Translated from the German by David Clarke
Edited by Palden Jenkins*

GATEWAY BOOKS, BATH

First published in 1994 by
GATEWAY BOOKS
The Hollies, Wellow,
Bath, BA2 8QJ. U.K.
with a new Introduction by Rudolf Bahro
Translated by David Clarke and checked by Robert Schumann
Edited by Palden Jenkins

Copyright © 1994 Gateway Books

This work is a revised and abridged version
of a work first published in German in 1987
by K. Thienemanns Verlag of Stuttgart as
Logic der Rettung: Werkmann die Apokalypse aufhalten?

[an unabridged English language version of which
is available from Gateway Books as
A Strategy for Human Survival
ISBN 1-85860-001 4]

Distributed in the U.S.A. by
ATRIUM PUBLISHERS GROUP
11270 Clayton Creek Road,
Lower Lake, CA 95457

No part of this book may be reproduced
in any form without permission from
the Publisher, except for the
quotation of brief passages
in criticism

Cover design by Studio B of Kirkbean
Text set in Plantin 10 on 12pt by
Oak Press of Castleton
Printed and bound by WBC of Bridgend

British Library Cataloguing-in Publication Data
A catalogue record for this book is
available from the British Library

ISBN 0-9446551-71-5

SHEFFIELD HALLAM UNIVERSITY
ux
304.28
BA
ADSETTS LEARNING CENTRE

Contents

An Outline of the Theses of the Book

Our civilisation has created and is rooted in what Lewis Mumford has called the Megamachine. This machine, in whose actions we all participate, and whose basic goals of more, faster and bigger are rooted in our souls, feeds on and is hostile to the natural order, which it is destroying at an accelerating rate. We are approaching a precipice of self-annihilation which will result from the degradation of the natural order, to the point where it can no longer support the Megamachine. This is the Apocalypse.

The Apocalypse is not fore-ordained, but if it is to be avoided we must stop the Megamachine and then dismantle it, building in its place a new civilisation which respects the supporting capacity of the earth's biosphere and is compatible with a healthy and thriving natural order.

The recognition that the Megamachine, or 'treadmill of production', is destroying the biosphere has been with us for some time, and was one of the main reasons for forming the Green Party. But the first (1982) political attempt in West Germany to stop the Megamachine and turn things around failed, because people were not willing to countenance and accept the fundamental life-style changes entailed.

And the changes needed are indeed sweeping. Bahro documents the way in which humans and their artifacts in West Germany are now impacting the natural environment, by the extraction of raw materials and the throwing back of wastes, at a rate which is ten times higher than it was 100 years ago – the time at which the rate of extermination of species began to increase exponentially. Today a species is vanishing every day, and by the year 2000, if Megamachine growth continues at its present rate, a species every hour. Thus, if the apocalypse is to be avoided we must almost at once reduce our impact on the natural environment to what it was 100 years ago. This entails the acceptance of a material standard of living which is only one tenth of that which we now enjoy. Not surprisingly, therefore, essential proposals to make such radical changes in policy were dismissed as being economically and politically unacceptable, and the Green Party was co-opted into the political mainstream, with its restrictions.

So now, Bahro tells us (writing in 1987), we are five years nearer the precipice. The time has come to make a new attempt, digging deeper and recognising that it is the basic psychological structure of Western humanity which blocks the way to an ecological politics, and that this structure must change before the necessary practical policies will have any chance of acceptance.

The first section of the book is concerned with economic and industrial growth as the main danger. Free-market liberalism, socialist state planning, and the plan-market economy of Japan are the same in that they all aim to maximize Megamachine growth. Only early Gandhi-Mao agrarian-type movements show any promise of being able to live within ecological constraints, and they are being joined by ecological splinter movements originating in conservative and socialist camps, in particular the 'Ordoliberalism' of Kurt Biedenkopf and the 'fundamentalist' wing of the Greens. These are examined in detail. Collectively they might be able to form a 'rainbow coalition' for an ecologically responsible politics.

The second section of the book examines the 'logic' of self-extermination; of the unremitting and ever-accelerating growth of the industrial system. This is traced back to its roots in Western philosophy and psychology, and is seen as rooted in the human genotype itself and in a series of structures arising from it; patriarchy, the European cosmology, the dynamics of capitalism, and the Megamachine; all leading to exterminism – which culminates in disaster or in human transformation. A separate sub-section is devoted to each of these structures. The industrial system cannot be managed or controlled for its undesirable side-effects; it must be removed completely and replaced by something different, resting on a new psychosocial foundation.

The third section is concerned with the 'logic of salvation' and demands a thorough reconstruction of the foundations of human subjectivity. Dangers here are the pessimistic conviction that nothing can really be changed, and addiction to the status quo. We have reached the point where the most important political discipline is the seeking out of truth about ourselves. This means inner work of a kind to which we are largely not accustomed. What is needed is an 'anthropological revolution', a jump in the evolution of the human spirit, the grounding anew of society on the basis of powers of consciousness which up to now are not revealed or unfolded.

'Exterminism', is a deformity of the human soul; a set of attitudes which, while normal at their time of inception, have grown pathogenic by lasting too long. Our civilisation now brutally opposes three of its peripheries; the dispossessed outsiders, the natural environment, and our own internal nature (especially its feminine side). The Western psyche has become so injured and tender that it cannot stand much interaction with others. Money and the power it brings comes to the rescue, making possible the security of today's 'free but solitary' individualism. Since the demand for security is insatiable, money and power constitute one merged expansionistic syndrome, a major driving force of the Megamachine. Magic and megalomania have been with money from the start, and its pathological effects will only vanish when the human being heals him/herself from within.

At this point Bahro's thesis rests heavily on the 'psycho-historical' work of the Swiss mystic and cultural philosopher, Jean Gebser (1905-1971) who set forth his ideas in *The Ever Present Origin (Ursprung und Gegenwart*, 2 vols, 1949, 1953). Gebser argues that the history of civilisation is the unfolding of consciousness, a process which proceeds by mutational leaps, each leap ushering in a new consciousness structure. He documents five structures of consciousness:

The first of these is the Archaic, in which the human consciousness has not yet differentiated from the rest of nature, and where there is no sense of separateness and no sense of time.

Secondly comes the Magic period which emerged about 100,000 years ago. This was the period of the hunter-gatherer, during which language was evolving. During this time a sense of our separateness from the rest of nature achieved an insecure existence. Life was still driven by emotion and instinct, the sense of time being little more than an awareness of the passing present.

The third, or Mythic, period emerged perhaps 20,000 years ago, and was made possible by the maturation of language, the telling of stories, and the ability to organize larger societies around ideas set forth in myths. Thus emerged the earliest towns and agricultural systems. Language made possible the conceptualization of past and future, giving us a cyclical time sense modeled on the recurring seasons. The Great Mother was the main mythical figure of these apparently peaceful civilizations of the Mythic period.

The fourth, or Mental period emerged during the last two millennia B.C., and brought with it an intensification of the human determination to transcend nature. It was male-dominated and warlike, at war not only with neighboring states and empires, but also with nature, with the feminine, and with the life of inner impulse. This period saw the birth of the major world religions, teaching that life should be lived according to religious and ethical principle rather than inner impulse. It developed a linear time sense, time having both a beginning and an end. For many centuries it was dominated by the monastic ideals of prayer, intellectual effort, work, and mortification of the flesh. After the Renaissance this tranformed itself into the ascetiscism of scientific research and the Protestant ethic; the continuing insensitivity toward nature permitting the building of the industrial system. At the end of the period the deep frustrations resulting from the denials of body, nature, and feminine led to the violence and cruelty of concentration camps and two world wars.

The fifth or Integral structure is emerging today and is characterised by a relinquishing of the rigid hold of rationality and linear time, and a re-assimilation of the feminine, the natural and the impulsive. It permits the recovery of awareness of earlier consciousness-structures and of the Origin, and has a new form of time-awareness in which past and future are contained in a timeless present, the achievement of which brings serenity and freedom from driven-ness. This structure of consciousness is characterised by a preference for frugal and contemplative values and a concern for the health and integrity of all life.

These structures of consciousness, although unfolding in time, do not supersede each other but are all contemporary. Whether consciously or not, all structures are present and active in each one of us.

Accepting this scheme, Bahro argues that whether or not we are able to move from the logic of self-annihilation and embrace the logic of salvation depends on how rapidly a critical-mass of the population can achieve the integral structure of consciousness, for without this we will be unable to renounce our addictive attachment to the Megamachine. Although the emergence of the Integral structure of consciousness is a spontaneous occurrence, the process can be speeded by contemplative practices, the nature of which he discusses at length.

The fourth and last section of the book is concerned with how the political and economic transition is to be made, how we shall make the journey from politics-as-usual to an 'eco-politics', which puts the health of the biosphere at the top of its agenda and operates according to the principles and values of the Integral structure of consciousness.

The transition is likely to occur via the emergence of two 'great coalitions': the coalition of political and economic forces of inertia, and a new alternative coalition for a 'rainbow society' in which political tendencies of all kinds combine, unified by the spreading awareness of environmental threat and a gradual growth in understanding of the values of the emerging structure of consciousness. The interaction of the two will likely bring about a re-institutionalisation of society which, among other things, will establish the Integral mode of consciousness as the social norm and offer all members of society the opportunity to acquire the skills needed to reach this level.

David Clarke, Bellingham, WA.

*I dedicate this book
to the memory of
Ulrike Meinhof,
whom I have admired
and in whose suicide
I do not believe.*

*Her soul, torn this way and that
between love and hate
has, in a different form,
been at my side
whilst I wrote.*

*What I believe is:
she would today
have been able to write
in this spirit
were she still alive -
and had achieved freedom.*

*Whoever
dares not to know
that the whole is the false,
cannot for a moment
argue with her.*

Overcome the walls!

Rudolf Bahro

INTRODUCTION
A new social foundation

Two years after publishing *The Alternative* in 1977, and as a result of it, I landed in West Germany. Two years after publishing *Logik der Rettung* (the original German version of this book) in 1987, I became once again a citizen of East Germany, forgiven of my political sins, and made a speech, at the same time as the Berlin Wall collapsed, to the last party meeting of the Social Unity Party. I spoke for the entire half hour on a single theme, starting with the idea of 'state-aided cooperatives'. I spoke about the possibility of introducing a politics of the ecological turning-point in what then was still the German Democratic Republic.

Since the greatest part of the industry in GDR had been ruined by the world market, and since of the remainder three-quarters would not be worth the millions which conventional environmental protection would cost, there was bound to be immense unemployment by any reckoning.

"Good!" I said, the question then is this. "What can we do to close the gap, in view of the shrinking and modernising of the remaining industry and the enormous need to catch up on infrastructure-maintenance arrears?" The need is not mainly for social policy or emergency help, but rather to turn the emergency into a virtue! What was needed was to create the starting conditions for an 'eco-social' sector of society. I am talking about *communitarian subsistence economy* as an alternative, not least to the disastrously nature-destroying agribusiness. This concept of subsistence has as its goal a style of life which withdraws itself from the capitalist market and interest mechanism.

If it really is clear to us that the name *Titanic* is suited to the ship in which we are travelling, then salvation is to be found, if at all, not in some sort of 'ecologising' on the boat, but rather in quite a different direction, which lies close at hand. This is to build new lifeboats, using the energies of the tourists and the materials of the lost luxury liner. It is not an agrarian-commune escapism, but a path which leads out of an economy driven by money-making and towards a subsistence economy.

The prolonged psychological and social crisis in the now-colonised ex-GDR paradoxically offers extremely favourable conditions for relevant experiments: an excess of liberated forces, people and materials.

The real question is whether this opportunity will be matched by a sufficient number of East Germans who find in themselves the spiritual readiness, courage, responsibility and creative power to exploit it.

Since after a time at least half of the population will either be unemployed or not meaningfully employed, even very fertile land will, acre by acre, fail to find access to the market, and thus lie fallow. Buildings, machines and tools of considerable value today have only scrap value to those who yesterday worked with them country-wide and made a living at it.

As often happens in 'peripheralised' regions, selective 'redevelopment' creates fewer work places than the number of previous living possibilities which fall away. Also, damage to the regional culture and inner peace resulting from the disappearance of no longer lucrative structures challenges us to look for an all-embracing alternative to structure the social order. Its kernel is contained in the formula: *places for living instead of work places*, or *living-working-places*. Developed on a larger scale, this would be something new.

Such an alternative, which has prospects only if comprehensively conceived, will most certainly not proceed from any colonialistic reversion to capitalistic circumstances, and it is just as unlikely to be created by state intervention. It can arise only when a large number of people associate together to do it. The recent East German situation makes room for precisely this need.

In the meantime, caring for the unemployed millions will become more expensive than anyone dared to think. Here the state must play a role, which it can fulfil only if the money is there. Could not at least a part of the billions used be used in such a way that support-costs are reduced, that an equivalent value is created, that culture is maintained, that support payments transform themselves into help toward helping oneself, and towards self-reliance? In the best case, these funds could help the creation of self-sustaining new forms of living!

And now no lesser person than Kurt Biedenkopf, whose views I thoroughly examine in this book, and who is now Minister-President of the new state of Saxony, says *Yes*. He and his co-workers are acting from wider-reaching motives: the project has become publicly plausible and thus politically an acceptable subject for discussion.

The situation is now this: provided enough people come together, who have thought the thing through and are willing to accept responsibility for making it ultimately self-supporting, the state government of Saxony will help to get it started. It will do this administratively and financially – and recent events have shown that the government is serious in its intentions. Wherever the will to develop a new lifestyle arises, there is a way forward. In view of this it is clear that transformation does not have to fail on account of material privation. If it does fail, it will be on account of inhibited self-confidence. Already, a great number of people are looking at this possibility practically, and some of them are ready to make a start.

The modern age has separated people from the earth and from work materials, so that the individual cannot secure a subsistence without the mediation of a 'job'. This separation is among the driving causes of world destruction, and greatly increases the difficulty of taking over responsibility for our daily actions in the social work process. It must be overcome. People who possess neither land nor working materials, and who cannot and do not want to make a profit, must be enabled to choose anew their form of subsistence, under the protection of the political order. Today this is a need which is grounded in much more than social politics.

Clearly, the ecological crisis requires objective public support in favour of this reversed direction. Pragmatically, this amounts to levelling a path to subsistence by means of subsidy, and there are concrete models for this. For the reader of this book, it should be clear that the real meaning of such initiatives is perceptible only beyond the economic-ecological perspective in the narrower sense. It requires a social framework for the practise of a different set of beliefs, one which transcends original egoism. Its ultimate goal is the cultural capacity for giving society as a whole a new foundation.

What is Green Fundamentalism?

When I came over to West Germany in 1979 after two years' imprisonment, the result of my criticism of Soviet and East German socialism, I turned at once (to others' surprise) to a new party which was then coming into existence – the Greens. Carl Amery, one of the founders of political ecology in Germany, had indeed identified me as a 'closet Green' before I came: this was because the entire closing section of my book *The Alternative*[1], advocated that the East should abandon growth-competition with the West, stop confusing human emancipation with maximum satisfaction of material needs, and should unilaterally disarm, to compel the West to pursue a peaceful path. Both ideas expressed the tendencies, articulated in West Germany by the Greens, toward neutralisation and overcoming the bloc structure.

Owing to the sensational circumstances, far more copies of my *The Alternative* were bought than read. Many people who had heard on TV of my arrival in the West were disappointed: in spite of my collision with East German authoritarians, I did not fit into the East-West *either/or* mould, believing that changes would be needed in *both* parts of Europe[2]. Yet the reforms in Moscow since 1985 far exceeded anything which I would then have considered practically possible, and filled me with great hope for developments in many countries.

I left the Greens in the middle of 1985 because they had become a different party from the one I personally had wanted. Although they had remained loyal to the idea of *ecopax* (an alliance of forces for peace and ecological awareness), the drive for reform and the sharing of power led them to convert their original capital into the small change of daily electoral politics.

I, too, am responsible for the Greens' development. Among other things I ought to have given a definitive outline of my fundamentalist position earlier – which I intend to do now. Most of what I have said is in scattered publications, and much has only been expressed verbally. The theoretical context which I am about to elaborate is very hard to bring within the framework of a party exposed to the need to amass power, and to the associated need for pragmatic compromises.

I don't deceive myself into thinking that I could have prevented the Greens crystallising out as an adapted reformistic party of the Left, exploiting environmental protection as a profile-building theme, exactly as the other parties do. This development was clearly unavoidable: the Greens could not escape the challenge of the threatening catastrophe, and were well-attached to the metropolitan environment. Above all, organisation into a party did not further the mission of the ecological turning-point, but caused a turning-away from it.

I have continually used the term *'fundamentalism'*, even though I am not particularly happy with it. This concept has unfortunately become associated with superficial and demagogic debate about political 'responsibility' (to play the political game formalistically) or 'refusal' (not to play it), or with building coalitions or not building them. As a consequence of this its real meaning has been altogether obscured.

What is *fundamentalism*? At the beginning of 1984 I would have answered: in the *outer* sense, it puts ecology before economy, and long-term matters before immediate and short-term ones. In the *inner* sense, it must be a policy which has spiritual drive and makes moral claims. A policy of radical change in the *Metropolis* – the nations of the 'developed' world – begins with a readiness for self-transformation, even self-surrender, of the bourgeois individual.

Parliaments are not the place to decide whether fundamentalism can ever prove to be constructive or destructive: fundamentalism refers to *attitudes*. In other words, *the dynamic of the industrial system can only be stopped in external reality when its motivation has been broken up*. Fundamentalism in this sense was never a *wing*, and was hitherto never more than an intermittent mood in the party. However, it touched every single Green *'realo'*[3].

In the course of his research into world history, Arnold Toynbee made generalisations concerning what happens when civilisations disintegrate, and what mechanisms recur in the resulting crises[4]. He spoke of decay and disintegration in society and in the soul. On this he based his characteristic and useful concept of the *proletariat*, which is different from the Marxist one in use.

Toynbee argued as follows: when the leading minority in a society stops being creative and is merely *seen* as leading (thereby forfeiting its inherent right to lead), the entire non-leading majority feels and becomes progressively an 'internal proletariat'. The true mark of a proletariat is thus neither poverty nor humble birth, but rather *its sense of being robbed of its ancestral heritage and its full place of residence in a society* – and the resulting feeling of resentment. A proletariat defined in this very all-embracing way is compatible with the ownership of material means.

Toynbee showed that if the creative power of the ruling minority even partially remains, it contributes a *philosophy*, and officials who have been educated in it build up a *universal state*. In our case the universal state is the entire organisation of the Western or Atlantic Metropolis, with supra-national bureaucrats and businesspeople at the head. However, the internal proletariat creates a *higher religion* which often, as in the case of the Christianity which arose in Rome, has its origin in a different culture, and evolves into a *universal church* which strives for transformation into a new culture.

From the point of view of the Englishman Toynbee, it is not surprising that so many people such as Native Americans and Tibetans are now helping in the evolution of European and American spirituality – they constitute his '*external proletariat*'[5]. Naturally outside traditions, such as the Native American, will flow into the new spiritual synthesis, alongside sources *within* the culture – not least of all that of Christ freed from 'his' church. Something quite new must come into existence, because now, for the first time in history, we are really concerned with the *whole earth*. At the same time patriarchy is decaying, so that a new male monotheism, hostile to the senses, has become impossible.

The life-germ of the next social order is not economic, but *spiritual*. The spiritual renaissance, in the end, will turn out to be a rise in consciousness, and not a regression. I call it the '*ecopax-formation*' (another possibility is the 'rainbow society'). This renaissance is not yet a river, but is already active in many streams and rivulets. The many new sects (Christianity began as a sect!) are definite indicators – they have much to do.

It would be difficult to explain why a new political party such as the Greens had, from the beginning, a spiritual component – admittedly for the most part bashfully disowned. The Greens were clearly a grouping on the far side of the anti-religious enlightenment, and were seen by the establishment as the most dangerous tendency, the root-cause of the fundamentalist tendencies within this enlightenment, and a movement about to overrun everything. In the *ecopax* movement the Greens cannot overrun everything, since spirituality is its essence.

Putting a Stop to the Megamachine: The First Attempt

At first glance everything seemed quite simple. We can no longer continue with over-large cities, over-size factories, chemical agriculture, concrete schools and vast hospitals, and the whole pentagon of power derived from money, computers, bureaucracy and the military, all over the earth. Yet we are so pitifully dependent on it all, and we tell ourselves so every day, and regard the situation as devoid of a way out. What else remains for us except to go ever more deeply into it? We have also noticed that environmental protection is also beside the point. The misery in the world is not made less by an 'Africa Day'.

Hoimar von Ditfurth's book *Let Us Plant a Little Apple Tree: the Time Has Come*[6] was a best-seller for two years. The author wanted to reconcile us to the fact that we must all die anyway. In the meantime the word got around the 'chattering classes': "anyway, everything is going down the tube". Or *could* we change our lives to such an extent that arming to death and destructive industrialising stop? We could indeed do this, but do we *want* to? Isn't it comfortable to have accountable officials whom we can accuse of not doing enough, even though we haven't authorised them to do anything decisive? For that, of course, would cut into our own flesh. We would rather carry on as usual: what else is possible?

If we really dared to *want* it, we could quite quickly have a government, or better, a social order, with which we could save ourselves, in spite of all hindrances. But we still lack the decisive precondition for salvation, the *will* to turn things around. How few of us were so bold, after Chernobyl, to demand the immediate closing down of nuclear power stations! This is why the existing mountain of proposals on the agendas of governments – every one of us has something to contribute – are deemed 'not feasible'.

In the early 1980s, carried along by the rise of the *ecopax* movement and the Greens in Germany, I still thought that irreversible progress toward the Turn-around could be made at the first attempt – if only the issue could be stated radically enough! I reprint here a few passages from a text for German radio which I wrote then and which, for me, still constitute a valid first statement of what I am now about to argue more closely[7]. I had been asked at that time: *What is peace?*

It is, according to my reply,

that ideal state of affairs in which people avoid violence against each other – even indirect and covert violence – in which each person can develop him or herself to the level which the time makes possible. This implies both freedom and justice. It also implies a balance in interpersonal relations.

At first glance this goes too far. Wouldn't it satisfy us just to know that we would not be killed by atom bombs or even 'normal' tank grenades? That the annual death rate by starvation of children in the southern hemisphere (14 million in 1981) would not exceed the annual casualty rate of World War II? That we will not run out of oxygen to breathe in the near future?

But can we avoid these things, if we just carry on as before? We have shown the whole world what and how much we like to have. How can there be a good outcome if ever more people on our finite earth follow our example of continually using, destroying and poisoning more per capita? We are bound *to collide with each other and with nature.*

We don't like to hear it when somebody says: "There have always been wars..." Nevertheless it is only too true. If World War III is to be avoided, if half of humanity is not to sink into absolute misery and a large number die of starvation, if the terminal collapse of the environment is to be averted, then we must *lift ourselves above the hitherto-acknowledged laws of human history.*

First we must learn – all of us, not just the military – that to seek for security *is not the same thing as to seek for* peace. *Those who seek security mistrust others and take protective measures, which in turn feed the mistrust of others. It is obviously due to the politics of security that we are now sitting on a nuclear powder-keg. This is supposed to deter the other side. A politics of* peace *would take away the deterrent or minimise it, and trust that the threat would go, or at least be reduced. He who lumps together the politics of security and peace deceives his hearers. Up to now, the politics of security have been the politics of suicide.*

But to refrain from building the newest rockets, or even to want to remove the whole structure of armaments so that they don't remove us, is no longer enough. Whoever wants that much and no more will not succeed. You can't conquer the Hydra by cutting off this or another head, as long as its inner forces continually produce new heads. If we want to rip open the belly of the monster so that it really dies, we must first of all know its name.

It is our industrial system and our industrial life-style. We have not achieved it by accident. It is our cleverness in altering nature to the ultimate limit which now discloses to us the cloven hoof. Originally we had great success with the work of producing our own food supply. Since then we have repeated the experience at ever higher levels according to the Olympian formula, "Higher, wider, faster, better!" And above all things, "More and more!"

Here in Europe we have found the non-plus-ultra, *the style of economy with the sharpest drive and the most frightful efficiency, and we are so proud of it...*

This is so much at the root of all the growth curves (which since 1750 have no longer grown imperceptibly as they did earlier, but suddenly point sharply upwards) that there is little sense in referring any particular arms production back to some particular profit interest. To do this is valid, of course, but there is much more at issue. Up to now people who wanted to solve everything by expropriation were in no way thinking of stopping the Megamachine. The relationship to capital is not the ultimate cause, but only the most recent means of expansion. It is simply the highest branch on the tree of human methods of production, and it will prove quite impossible for us to reject it twig by twig.

Peace demands that we begin our civilisation altogether anew, and that we stop the source of competition for scarce material goods. This we should do by referring back all material consumption and production to what is needed to achieve an approximately equal basic minimum satisfaction of natural needs. Goethe had his Faust say: "Our view of the Beyond is blocked: foolish is he who turns his squinting eyes in that direction... To the proficient, this world is not inscrutable". Thus he let him who would ascend the mountains drain the swamp. What now, since we have finished this task?

It seems the only prospect open is beyond, above, inward, *and of course toward* other people. We must thus concentrate ourselves carefully to use our cleverness in this *direction, because it is terminally dangerous to continue making so much change in the natural order, to heap up knowledge, and make fortunes doing it.* Halt! No further! *Every new capital expenditure, not just those in rockets, is at the same time both devilish and fatal. Peace begins when we take our hands away from the work which most of us daily perform. Admittedly we would be occupied for a time with demolition and reconstruction.*

Do not the majority give up hope because they are afraid to exert the resistance of which they are easily capable? Afraid more of the everyday risk than the ultimate *risk? Think of the days of the resistance against Hitler! How little would the citizens of this land have to risk, in order to achieve very essential changes! It is not even necessary to practise civil disobedience. He who won't risk anything at the present time either doesn't know or doesn't want to know that the coming of the apocalypse is extremely probable, unless we reckon with it in all earnestness and behave accordingly.*

We must find the way out, and we must seek for it so unconditionally that if the worst comes to the worst the fault will not be ours. We cannot deceive ourselves that the dove on the roof will be easy to catch. All we know is that, this time, the bird-in-hand will be absolutely useless to us. What we want to achieve is like trying to stop an avalanche from within that avalanche. Anybody who could observe this process from the outside would see the avalanche slowed and stopped as if by an invisible hand, shortly before it struck.

This would be against the laws of the inert mass of concrete and steel which surrounds us. It can thus only be achieved by an exertion from within consciousness, out of our souls – an effort so intense and involving so many people that it would be without parallel in history.

We must have a vision, like the exodus from Egypt inspired by Moses, and like the first Whitsun after the Resurrection – both combined into one, spreading through the whole of humanity, and beginning in the rich countries, especially Europe. For we were the sorcerer's apprentice who first summoned the broom, and everybody copies us. It is here that the vicious circle has its centre of gravity, and our continent is the most vulnerable.

I believe that this Turn-around is possible, because humanity feels itself threatened in a way which triggers the instinct of self-preservation. Thus arises the primitive instinct, present in everybody, to trust to one last, most extreme alternative, however uncertain – because nothing else is left. The resolve can occur suddenly, tomorrow or the day after, in millions of people, and thus overnight widen the horizon of the politically possible. There will be no lack of small and moderate catastrophes to remind us of the nearness of the day of reckoning.

In anticipation of this day of resolve, I propose that each individual, both alone and in his immediate circle, cultivate the sense of restlessness and readiness for the general change in consciousness. Let us withdraw not only our votes from the Great Machine and its servants. Wherever possible we must altogether stop playing that game, *and we must gradually incapacitate everything which runs in the old direction: military installations and freeways, nuclear power stations and airports, chemical factories and large hospitals, supermarkets and factory-like educational institutions...*

Let us reflect how we can feed, warm, clothe, educate, and keep ourselves healthy independently of the Great Machine. Let us begin to work on it, before it has total control of us, concreting us in, poisoning us, suffocating us, and sooner rather than later subjecting us to total atomic annihilation.

The task is still the same. Since everything is carrying on as usual, our situation is now – supposing we don't want to stop reckoning backwards from a foreseeable final bang – several years nearer the precipice. We conceal this from ourselves nowadays with 'business as usual' or new record statistical peaks.

I see things in a somewhat different way now, not factually but in a spiritual sense. In my earlier answers I talked then as if the victims would not awaken by themselves, but would have to be awakened. "It is always Gethsemane, always everyone is sleeping"[8]. In the meanwhile the dangers *are* being noticed. But there is among the public a very great absence of earnest reflection on what we could do if disarmament negotiations and environmental cosmetic programmes fail us. There is also a lack of closer examination of what is insufficient, unable any more to support anything or save anything – and why.

Allegedly this leads to resignation. Yet first a proper despair concerning all attempts to cure symptoms (rather than causes), and concerning all proposals aiming at less than a cultural transformation, will awaken us from within.

The Aim of the Book

I am only secondarily interested in the things we *could* do, even though I shall once again elucidate, with necessary sharpening of definition, what the emergency demands: getting out of the large Megamachine and the small car, furthering unilateral military and industrial disarmament, and re-equipping to suit the needs of a heap of fairly independent eco-republics which look different to the Republic of Germany, the European Community, or NATO, but which nevertheless yield an international authority for justice. If we don't want to take a good hard look at all this, then we may as well say that we want to die.

However, when we speak of *the environment*, we are wanting to alter something external, to ascribe to the external the character of ultimate cause. This, however, is really *within* us. As if the bomb right from the beginning were not our own creation, and as if we didn't know this just as well as Einstein, who finally said, after so much preoccupation with physics, that *the real problem is the human heart*.

At the present time the ecology/peace movement has again become an undercurrent. It will regenerate itself and radicalise by making contact with innumerable spiritual streamlets which came into existence independently of it. Many have taken up these spiritual paths because, earlier, they were despairing of purely political practice – fixed, as it was, on objects and enemies to be fought. The *ecopax* movement will all come back and then be much stronger, even politically, than on the previous occasion.

A reason for this is that it will spill over into the ranks of the scientific and bureaucratic sectors. A split within their ranks will be decisive in determining whether the death-spiral can be halted *in time*. Without betrayal and defection in the laboratories and control-rooms, the new movement within these sectors cannot be brought to take a stand. Then on the other hand a paralysing deadlock can only occur if there is discrimination against the *challenger*-logic in the population. The revolt over ecological resource-exhausting indulgence will coincide with a splitting of the secular church of Science and its priests of all ranks, as in the last Reformation in Europe.

Meanwhile nothing is more important than to expand and deepen the mental and spiritual bases of the ecological and peace movement. They must be dominant in the future when the movement again becomes active; for it contains the source of power and continuity. All those who are touched by the idea of a new age beyond the industrial Mega-machine have a certain responsibility to bring about a meeting of the ways, which will neither allow nor make necessary the development of a 'psychocracy' – an organisation of squads of soul-tamers. We will come together on a new basis and form a network not only as big as one nation, but crossing boundaries – and yet it will not be a political organisation of the old sort.

It is now obvious that there is no short and direct point of entry into an ecological politics. The deep psychological structure of western man stands in the way. Politics and everything to do with it is only the last latch-key to open gates, which must first be unbolted in quite a different way. The fact that today the idea of *environmental protection* has gained general currency blocks for the moment *ecological* thinking, because ecology and environmental protection are confused with each other. It will still take society a few years to wake up to the fact that environmental protection merely serves as decorative panelling for the wide path to Hell, and does not indicate a new reconciliation with the earth.

For this reason I am not writing this book about *ecological politics*: I am writing about their *fundamental principles or foundations*, about their spiritual context, and about how the roots of the catastrophe – and also the possible salvation – lie in the essence of humanity. Only if we start here can we find a radical and, in the true sense, *fundamentalist* answer. The bomb, Chernobyl, the misery in the world which increases as our civilisation spreads, are all mere beginnings, even if inescapable. We must follow the logic of self-destruction right back into the *human heart*, because *it is only there that the logic of salvation can make its start*.

What we *do*, what we are doing to ourselves and to all creatures, can only have its roots in what we *are*. If we now see that our existence as thinking beings is causing a disturbance of the harmony of the world, of the balance of nature, then this can have no other cause than the confusion of our spirits and hearts. More precisely, whatever the circumstances which may have caused this bewilderment, we must first of all not look at circumstances, but at *ourselves* as the root, as the decisive point of origin of all our vicious circles. How can we turn human energies away from all the false work in factories and offices, from all the suicidal daily activities?

When I speak of the *logic* of self-extermination and of salvation, I am first of all making the assumption that there is an 'implicit' or 'enfolded' Order, a body of natural law in the Cosmos and on our planet, and that this order extends into us as a basis of behaviour. We can therefore always know as much as is necessary in order to adapt ourselves. Words such as *logic*, *logos* or *Tao* (being in harmony with the Great Order, in nature and society) refer to the possibility of human access to this ultimate ground or origin, to its unfolding and effectiveness. Our behaviour needs to conform itself to this awareness, even though it is inaccessible to reason. In this direction alone lies the balance we seek. Here lies the cyclical economy underlying evolution.

In the *logic of self-extermination* the arrow of evolution, conquest and expansion has torn itself loose from the cycle of eternal recurrence and turned itself more and more against the Origin. We don't preserve, but exploit as we proceed. "In the world you are afraid", it is written. The ego, especially the masculine ego, seeks to compensate for this by the pursuit of power and the politics of security. In this way, stage by stage, always internally and externally at the same time, we have created this suicidal civilisation, none more extreme than ours, the white man's Empire.

It is easy to underestimate its evil: putting the bad things in the garbage but the successes into storage, in order to hang on to them. Our civilisation is, however, *wholly wrong*, and thus the *logic of salvation* begins with the readiness *to let go of everything* – including our treasures, above all money-making and its techniques, and our particular form of competitive democracy – which is also part of the noose around our necks. And the logic of salvation ends with our giving up our highest treasure, the Doctor Faustus in us which is always ready to renew the pact with the Devil (Goethe's "Highest happiness of children of earth is still personhood")[9]. We destroy the world to make ourselves a name, in order to take the path which "does not founder in aeons".[10]

Between a beginning and an end of a logic of salvation lies the field of the *politics* of salvation, the field of a new-order politics, a politics of reform. The content it receives will depend on the atmosphere which forms itself in the pre- and trans-political sphere.

In view of the intention to combine spirituality and politics, my book has two interwoven strands, an inner and an outer line of approach to the problems of a Turn-around movement.

It is the inner line which is decisive. So far the main emphasis is on the *logic* of self-annihilation and the *logic* of salvation – by these I mean that we should be aware of the deep effect of both the power of self-destruction and the power of healing, in a culture. If we lack this awareness, we exhaust ourselves dealing with symptoms, and accumulate merely disappointments, because the old logic 'will not give way at the first push.

We must understand the thrust with which the industrial Mega-machine forges ahead, and thus the kinetic energy of the impulse it commands. Also we must know how much we are caught up in the very avalanche we would like to arrest – truly no conventional assignment! The initial conceived solutions we may have are completely useless, since they are based on models of behaviour, derived from class-struggle, to determine how big a slice of the pie each gets. We need to invent a different mechanism to get us toward social justice: the present one internally heats up economic expansion and externally exploits the rest of humanity, life, and nature as a whole. *The immediate task is to gain understanding and not rush madly into the next plan of action.*

Yet the outer line, or external strand, must not result in a plan of measures to be taken, but rather in *axioms and principles of a politics of salvation*, and in questions about the institutions which such a politics would need. Truly there is no shortage of occasions for action – the dams are everywhere beginning to give way – but we lack an approach which would get us out of the patchwork of the *status quo*. Formulae remain thought-experiments, unrealistic in application, as long as the great majority, in spite of all nagging, is still willing to put up with the plagues of Egypt. At least verbally, measures to *protect the environment* look like good business, but they fall far short of the needed *ecological* reform of root and branch. Yet the time for a politics of ecological transformation will indeed come.

It will probably begin as a kind of conservative revolution, for which the needed political strength has not yet accumulated. The reorienting process which this will bring in traditional major parties will be more important than the evolution of the Greens. Therefore I leave the Green *realpolitik* on one side in order to examine the most soundly-based conservative contribution towards fitting environmental protection into our economic and social constitution – to which socialist parties have nothing of equal value to offer.

Two schools of thought exist within conservative circles: one takes a header into the next wave of technological innovation, while the other would like to install a logic of damage-limitation and use it to turn around the whole old institutional set-up. The latter 'ecological market economy' would not really withstand the catastrophe, but if it were to be consistently carried out more would be learnt from it than from any other *realpolitik*.

It would come to grief. *Any* strategy which is limited to economics and politics would come to grief. While the Megamachine quite obviously cannot be stopped by public demonstrations of opposition, at the same time neither can legal or governmental intervention, however necessary they may be in the short run. We must withhold nourishment from the Megamachine – human energy – rather than discipline it by defensive battles from below and regulatory measures from above.

Yet what shall we do with social energies, which have hitherto been channelled into changing the world by social action and the making of things? Certainly we will need activity to set up a new order to adapt us to the limited natural context of the earth. But very little activity can or should be converted into production. So it is actually a far-reaching re-dedication of the human energy-supply from deep within individuals, on which we can still place hope. This has to happen from the ground up, not just from those reservoirs of surplus energy which can no longer find an outlet. It comes from the original tendency of life-energy itself, which strives for a joyous expression.

On closer inspection this means *spirituality* (as opposed to materialism). It means a reorientation of our energies from predominantly outer to predominantly inner activities, from material object to personal subject, from construction to communion.

Without spiritual perspectives, the *ecopax* movement will be unable to free itself from the logic of self-extermination. Its heroes will lie dead on the stage in the last act. This is not to say that all we have to do is accustom ourselves to a little bit of euphoristic positive thinking, so that everything will fall back spontaneously into its place. To develop the logic of salvation, we need to recover access to the oldest human wisdom – going back to the Old Stone Age, when people lived and celebrated the basic circumstances of their existence and their place in the Cosmos, still to a great extent free of the deforming ballast of later cultural specialisation and alienation. Above all things, we must learn to direct our awareness to ourselves, rather than to the world we have created. We must also remain ongoingly conscious of the connection between inside and outside, for everything is within us, and we are in everything.

In the new age scene it is customary to reassure ourselves that we are one with the clouds, the trees, the rocks and the animals. Correct, we are all part of the trees and the trees are a part of us. But it is equally important for us to recognise – according to the same logic! – that we are also part of the Megamachine, and the Megamachine is part of us.

Today's adepts drive the *Monte Verita* in automobiles they identify with
more strongly than they do with trees.

A political attitude which could save us begins precisely at the point
where we clearly see our co-responsibility for self-destruction. It is
human social behaviour as a whole which makes the difference between
an act or omission which is harmful or furthering to life. *The most
important political discipline is thus the seeking out of the truth about
ourselves.*

The fall of the Wall

For a brief period of a few weeks in November and December 1989,
West German society had, across all its political camps, hoped that the
breakup in East Germany might bring about a transformation in the
whole of Germany. This meant that deep in its unconscious it is
altogether clear that capitalism, which euphemistically calls itself the
'market economy', is not the solution, but one of the most obvious
aspects of an absolutely insoluble problem, which one could call the
dilemma of the modern world.

And meanwhile, this society is sleeping more soundly than ever.
Before the mirror that the East German demand for symbols of affluence held before its eyes – from Japanese entertainment electronics to
Mercedes cars – it could have been horrified by the prospect latent in
the hope that our insane standard of living could be available for
everybody. Instead of this it allowed itself once again to be deadened by
Pyrrhic victory, believing the message that the Western World was the
best of all possible worlds.

What is the cause of this inclination to sleep? The Berlin novelist
Theodor Fontane once wrote that the modern world is founded on the
ego, and will founder on it as well. The western post-war world is a
golden nut constructed around the material needs of this ego-centre,
and is hollow inside – or rather, as the Gulf War has once again shown,
it is much worse than merely hollow, for its kernel is as black as Hell. Is
it not easy to recognise that the hellish machine which the westerners
turned loose on the Iraqis was planned, built and set going in Hell?

For this reason it is also high time for the perception that the healthy-
healthy talk and the esoteric new age advice channelled ever more
expansively from the 'other world' is all nothing much more than empty
chatter and is anything but illuminating. 'Totally relaxed in the here-
and-now' is a motto misunderstood as permissiveness toward lazy self-
satisfaction and pleasure in the beloved ego, and is not comprehended
as a challenge to unilateral personal disarmament and the relaxing of
our vain defence works called 'personal identity'.

The entire therapy and meditation business is reducing itself to just

one more late-Roman luxury, if it does not emphasise the responsibilities and obligations for a comprehensive new foundation of society.
So I will close by placing nakedly in space a sort of Islamic proposition –
borrowed from Fichte and concealed in this book – in order to explain
the essential starting-point for a politics of salvation: *God alone is, and
outside God is nothing.*

NOTES

(1) *Die Alternative. Zür Kritik des real existierenden Sozialismus* (Köln, Frankfurt, 1977), translated into English by David Fernbach as *The Alternative in
Eastern Europe* (London: Verso, 1981).

(2) *Ich werde meinen Weg fortsetzen. Eine Dokumentation*, 2. erw. Auflage (Köln:
Frankfurt, 1977).

(3) *Realos*: the *'realos'* were the contrasting wing to the *'fundis'* in the Green
party, advocating *realpolitik*. *Realpolitik* is the pursuit of pragmatic realities and
material needs, rather than ideals and morals.

(4) I refer here to Jonas Cohn's introduction to Toynbee's *Gang der
Weltgeschichte.*

(5) An *external proletariat* lives outside the economic system (for example,
'barbarians' or colonised peoples), while an *internal proletariat* lives under it (for
example, internal less-privileged classes).

(6) *So lässt uns denn ein Apfelbäumchen pflanzen. Es ist so weit.*

(7) Bahro 1982, p91ff.

(8) Blaise Pascal, *Geist und Herz, eine Auswahl aus dem Gesamtwerk* (Berlin,
1964).

(9) Goethe in *Westöstlicher Diwan*, Buch Suleika.

(10) Goethe in the last act of *Faust II*.

Part One:

MAPPING THE SITUATION

1. The situation as I see it

What is exterminism?

In order to furnish a basis for resistance to rearmament plans, the visionary British historian E P Thompson wrote an essay in 1980 about *exterminism*, as the last stage of civilisation[1]. Exterminism doesn't just refer to military overkill, or to the neutron bomb – it refers to *industrial civilisation as a whole*, and to many aspects of it, not just the material ones – although these are the first to be noticed. It made sense that the *ecopax* movement in Germany began not with nuclear weapons, but with nuclear power stations, and seemingly even less harmful things. Behind the various resistance movements stood the unspoken recognition that in the set of rules guiding the evolution of our species, death has made its home.

Thompson's statements about the "increasing determination of the extermination process", about the "last dysfunction of humanity, its total self-destruction", characterise the situation as a whole. The number of people who are damned and reduced to misery has increased unbelievably with the spread of industrial civilisation. Never in the whole of history have so many been sacrificed to hunger, sickness, and premature death as is the case today. It is not only their number which is growing, but also their proportion of the whole of humanity. As an inseparable consequence of military and economic progress we are in the act of destroying the biosphere which gave birth to us.

To express the exterminism-thesis in Marxian terms, one could say that the relationship between productive and destructive forces is turned upside down. Like others who looked at civilisation as a whole, Marx had seen the trail of blood running through it, and that "civilisation leaves deserts behind it"[2]. In ancient Mesopotamia it took 1,500 years for the land to grow salty, and this was only noticed at a very late stage, because the process was so slow. Ever since we began carrying on a productive material exchange with nature, there has been this destructive side. And today we are forced to think apocalyptically, not because of culture-pessimism, but because this destructive side is gaining the upper hand.

19

I would like straight away to emphasise that the problem ultimately
does not lie in the perversions and associated monstrosities of Ausch-
witz and Hiroshima, in neurotic lust for destruction or for human or
animal torture. It lies in quantitative success, and in the direction that
our civilisation took in its heyday. This success is not at all unlike that of
a swarm of locusts. Our higher level of consciousness has furthered
development, but has had no part in determining scale or goal. In
general the logic of self-extermination works blindly, and its tools are
not the ultimate cause.

For centuries the problem has remained below the threshold of
consciousness for the vast majority of people. In the *Communist Mani-
festo*, Marx and Engels evaluate the capitalistic preparatory work for the
desired classless society:

> *Through the exploitation of the world market, the bourgeoisie has given a
> cosmopolitan pattern to the production of all countries. To the great
> dismay of reactionaries it has pulled the national basis out from under the
> feet of industry. The age-old national industries have been annihilated
> and continue to be annihilated daily. They get pushed aside by new
> industries, the introduction of which becomes a life-issue for all civilised
> nations.*
>
> *These new industries don't make use of domestic raw materials, but
> process raw materials from the remotest regions, and their products are
> used not only in the land of their production, but equally in all parts of the
> world. In the place of needs which can be satisfied by domestic production
> come new ones, which demand for their satisfaction the products of the
> remotest lands and climates. In the place of the old national and local self-
> sufficiency and isolation comes traffic in all directions, and a dependence
> on all sides of nations upon each other...*
>
> *By means of enormously increased ease of communication the bour-
> geoisie draws all nations, even the most barbaric, into civilisation. The
> cheap prices of its wares are the heavy artillery by which all Chinese walls
> are shot down, by which the most stubborn barbarian xenophobia must
> capitulate[3].*

As we see today, this is written on account of civilised worker-interests,
and is a clearly 'social-imperialistic' text. The concern is with the
proletarian take-over of businesses in this civilisation, and social-
democracy, or even more the trade unions, and the legitimate heirs of
this programme, to whose basic cultural themes they adhere un-
brokenly.

Wolfram Ziegler has developed a scale which measures, with brilliant
simplicity, the *total load* we are placing on the biosphere, in order to

bring about the 'good life' or 'standard of living', and on this basis to defend the 'social peace' of the rich Metropolis, which is certainly being ever more strongly threatened by ecological panic[4]. Ziegler's starting-point is that the decisive lever in our attack on nature is the use of technically-prepared imported energy. The poisoning and destruction of nature is bound up with this material throughput, with the putting to work of our energy-slaves.

For this reason Ziegler takes the amount of energy used per square kilometre per day and multiplies it by a 'damage-equivalent' for the amount of matter-transformation, and impact on nature, in each region. In this way he arrives at a figure for the load on the biosphere measured in equivalent kilowatt-hours per square kilometre per day. This figure is far in excess of the raw energy use because the toxic and noxious effects are factored in. Today in Germany we are impacting the environment to the extent of 40,000 KWh/km2/day [103,600 KWh/sq mile/day] with real energy use alone – that is, without reckoning in the damage factor. This is about ten times as much as it was a hundred years ago.

Exactly a hundred years ago, the rate of dying out of biological species began to increase exponentially; as a result of which in the mid-1980s a species vanished every day, and by the year 2000 this will have increased to *a species every hour*. We are monopolising the earth for our species alone. We began this with the geographical surface, which we don't only reduce in area, but divide up to such an extent that ecotopes lose their wholeness, and the critical number of individuals of any species is reached, such that they cannot share the same living space.

Ziegler has calculated that in Germany the total weight of our bodies averages out at 150 kg per hectare [134 lbs per acre], while all other animals including birds weigh only 8-8.5 kg per hectare [7-7.5 lbs per acre]. This excludes the domesticated animals we exploit, which account for a further 300 kg per hectare [267 lbs per acre] – however they don't belong to *themselves*, but to us. In addition to this we have at least a further 2,000kg per hectare [1,780 lbs per acre] of technical structures for our transport systems alone, and the lion's share of this is taken by the automobile.

Even though we no longer feel any natural solidarity with the rest of life, we nevertheless depend, for our biological existence, upon the species-variety of plants and animals. Our 'anthropogenic' technical monocultures of 'useful' plants and animals are perhaps the most persistent instruments of suicide that we use. The dying off of species is the most fundamental indicator of the general exterminating tendency: the overgrowth of the industrial system has pushed it to a galloping rate.

For Ziegler a load of about 4,000 real KWh/km2/day [10,360 KWh/

evolution.

The following brief story of Easter Island, which Hermann Remmert published in the periodical *Nationalpark*, serves as a warning:

In about 400 AD the Polynesians came to Easter Island, which may well be the loneliest island in the Great Ocean. They settled in, felled trees, built villages and temples, and evolved with their simple celts a remarkable technique of stonemasonry, creating the famous stone figures which they set up round the island near their villages and harbours. They felled yet more trees, increased their numbers, and began to make war among themselves as their numbers grew too great. The temples were destroyed, built up again, destroyed again, and the forest was annihilated… The Europeans discovered a remnant population of about 500 people when they first set foot on Easter Island. The island was by this time a treeless steppe, and the remnants of what had once been over 20,000 inhabitants lived in caves and practised a cruel bird-cult and cannibalism.

Subsequently the population increased again a little (in spite of the slave trade); dogs, cats, and sheep were imported (and wiped out the poultry brought in by the Polynesians), and from 1900 to 1950 the island was one enormous sheep farm (with about 60,000 sheep)…

Today three species of land birds live here, imported from South America. Nobody knows what the exterminated trees were. Are the crickets, wasps, butterflies, lizards, native? Nobody is able to say. A Stone Age culture destroyed its own living space, and emptied this once rich bird island. The Stone Age humans didn't live in harmony with their homeland, and destroyed it, just as we are doing.

The Maoris of New Zealand burnt the forest down and annihilated some twenty-three species of giant kiwis, and many other species as well. Large areas of New Zealand are denuded of trees – the work of humans who settled before the white man did. The people who settled America advanced behind a girdle of terror, the zone of 'overkill' as we say today. Thus came about the poverty of mammalian species in North and South America. The annihilation of the forests in the Mediterranean region, the destruction of life-support in Norway (attributed to the wanderings of the Vikings), the Bronze Age destruction of the oak forests in North Germany (which created the Luneberg Heath) – all this shows us that whenever they could, humans have destroyed their living space. They never tried to be members of a stable ecosystem. No, looking to the past gives us no help. The notion that primitive humans lived in harmony with nature is a pious fairy-tale.

It can be of help to us, in our terrifying situation, to study the path from the missing link to homo sapiens. *Otherwise Easter Island is a model of our world, and a terrible one at that: from about 20,000 people the*

population sank to about 500 – through war, cannibalism, and disease.
Today we can determine the causes with frightening exactness. We know
what is at issue and we see the dangers.

We have but two choices: voluntary renunciation of the world, or the
terrible spectacle of renunciation a la Easter Island (if we are so lucky)...

The recipe for self-extermination and our mental attitude which makes
it unavoidable have been typically demonstrated by the editor of the
conservative *Wörmser Zeitung*, in two lead-articles about the Chernobyl
catastrophe: we must be more careful than ever with atomic energy, but
since we need it for our standard of life, we must "in future also live in
the shadow of the bomb and in the neighbourhood of the atomic pile".
The standard of living for which we compete among ourselves must
have priority over life itself.

We are all participants in exterminism. Clearly the behaviour of
humans, though correct according to a wide variety of customs and
laws, suffices to bring about the collapse. For this reason no order can
save us which simply *limits* the *excesses* of our greed. *Only spiritual
mastery of the greed itself can help us.* It is perhaps only the Prophets and
Buddhas, whether or not their answers were perfect, who have at least
put the *question* radically enough.

Everything which has been said about domination, exploitation and
class-war as the *ultimate* cause of expansion is false, even though these
factors play a part. Social contradictions admittedly are accelerators and
strengtheners of expansionism, but only because of human predispositions, which constitute its uniqueness and glory. *Why* the human being,
especially the westerner, destroys life instead of serving it, is the key
question. Even if we doubt whether the impulse to salvation arises *out of*
danger, those who don't see the danger and its cause cannot even
awaken, let alone give an answer of any sort.

The products and symptoms which make us anxious, and which first
made the ecological movement turn to environmental protection, are
really only pointers to deeper-lying causes. And even if, acting on the
'polluter pays' principle, we want to make people responsible for a
particular production-process liable, the death of forests nevertheless
confronts us with a complexity of causative factors, such that we are
most unlikely to track down the causes while we are paying attention
only to specific pollutants and polluters.

According to all appearances the industrial system has crossed a final
carrying-capacity threshold. Exterminism could clearly be seen in the
two world wars, preceded by the development of the industrial system.
As far as the natural order is concerned, there are hardly any peaceful
production methods left. It is thus very clear where we stand.

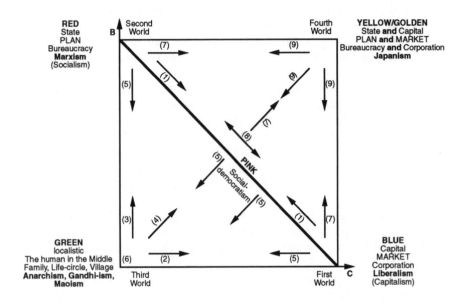

Galtung's World-Schematic

Johan Galtung, a Norwegian researcher into peace and evolution, invited me early in 1983 to a seminar in the Berlin College of Science. We had a wonderful discussion, and I was very pleased with the striking methods he used to describe various styles of social evolution. Until 1989, whenever I wanted to make my fundamentalist position clear, I went back to Galtung's 'five colours' (blue, red, yellow, green, and pink) and 'four corners' (corresponding to the first four colours)[5].

His 'value-free' world-schematic of the Cold War situation made it very easy to find one's way about in an adversarial political landscape which was being rearranged by the eco-crisis, then by the 1989 changes in the political map of the world, and which, at the time of publication, have not yet formed into a clear picture, except that the Soviet bloc has ceased to exist, and the new arrangement of nations is still sorting itself out. Below, I shall firstly explain Galtung's schematic, and then I shall add comments pertaining to the changes which have taken place since 1989.

The most important explanations:

The four corners represent 'pure principles', considered in each case as an ideal type: *Blue* was the Western; *red* was the Soviet; *green* was that of 'under-development', and refers to traditional societies[6]; *yellow* (or golden, not to be racist) was that of the Japanese and Asia-Pacific rim 'Tiger' or 'Dragon' economies. *Pink* in the middle was social-democratic, 'Swedish' in principle. Decisive here is the diagonal B – C or better C – B (because at C lies the centre of gravity, and the blue pole had the most powerful influence on it). This is the 'diagonal of modernisation', of the modern society.

This is above all the *diagonal of destruction*, and I want to single it out for emphasis. It represents the reality of the *industrial Megamachine*, which has been superbly defined by Lewis Mumford[7]. This reality forbids our entertaining any 'project of modernisation', because nothing could come of it except extermination, *the mass-extermination of life-forms of all species*. This main axis connects the 'blue' market-fixation (*economism*) of the West with the 'red' state-fixation (*statism*) of the Soviet-Chinese sphere, and the extremes meet each other in the social-democracies. Seen from the Soviet perspective, these looked capitalistic, but from the US perspective, they looked socialistic. Yugoslavia was perhaps the country located nearest to the middle of this axis.

Galtung used arrows to indicate:

1. The tendency of East and West to converge. Here are firstly the social-democracies, and then the 'first-and-a-half' world;

2. Western aid for countries of the third world, in order to draw them into an obedient underdeveloped position at the capitalistic end of the main axis;

3. Eastern aid for these countries, in order that they could take an analogous position at the socialistic end of the main axis;

4. Social democratic aid, in order to make the undeveloped position possible for third world countries, drawing them towards the 'pink' convergent position on the main axis. Incidentally, in my opinion Galtung over-estimated the autonomy of these 'pink' factors – this was demonstrated in the post-1989 tendency for these countries to align with the blue corner, rather than creating a new non-aligned focus of their own.

I find Galtung's comment about aid to developing countries very relevant: it was a way for countries with a strong ambition to world influence to be successful. They needed to get themselves allies and markets; to enhance the value of their own systems; to impress others with methods they themselves knew and had mastered best all of these without having to consider the poor and oppressed. In any case there existed a broad consensus that aid-givers were 'modern' and 'developed': they landed somewhere on the main diagonal. This was the 'development' doctrine.

Meanwhile there are dissidents:

> 5. *A green wave, made of people who break off from some point on the diagonal, because they had had enough of the whole plan/market logic, enough of the whole modernising project; they were looking toward the values of the dark green corner – Iran under Khomeini was an example;*
>
> 6. *Then there were people in the third world who accepted their own pole not only as realistic but as desirable, and they defended it – they didn't want to be 'developed'.*

Finally there was the yellow (golden) pole. According to Galtung it lay off the main axis, because in the Land of the Rising Sun and the Tiger economies integration, not opposition, between plan and market prevails. I feel the threat of exterministic overkill from this pattern – to which not only the Japanese belong. In any case the Japanese example caused:

> 7. *a suction which affected Gorbachev in Moscow, which affected others in all other countries of all colours[8];*
>
> 8. *a frustration about the pulling and hauling between the poles of planned- and market-economy on the old diagonal – affecting particularly many Islamic and Pacific rim states;*
>
> 9. *finally in Japan itself perhaps a collapse of its own success, which could lead to developments in every conceivable direction – why not in a direction crossing the west-east axis (not an attractive axis from Japan's point of view), and moving in the direction of green, or more likely 'rainbow'?*

Galtung was of the opinion that all five models (blue, red, golden, green, and pink) worked badly. Green, indeed, is better than the others, but it produced poverty, even if misery was avoidable. The pink model was better than the other three, but it shared aggression against nature, the spiritual dimension, the local level, and stayed involved in the arms race. So he sketched a zone in his scheme called 'rainbow': removed from sides, corners, and from the main diagonal. Here we could find *bright blue*: something like a non-monopoly market society. Bright green in the sense of 'small is beautiful'. This was also his 'open window for development'.

It is my opinion that, in Germany at least, many people would already like to go there. If only it could be done with full comfort and full security! If only there were a guarantee that the bear wouldn't get wet while washing its fur!

Interestingly enough Biedenkopf specified roughly the same goal in his *New Look of Things*. Coming from the blue direction, his thought

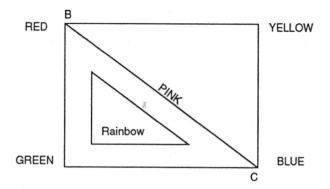

moves away from the diagonal of destruction and towards the green, into the triangle 'rainbow'. On the other hand there was minister-president Späth, who wanted to break out from the diagonal in exactly the opposite direction: vehemently towards the golden.

The Iron Curtain falls

Some years after its first German edition of 1987, this book ought to be largely out of date. For isn't almost everything different since the Berlin Wall and its symbolism fell? And it fell, moreover, because the giant Soviet state had exhausted itself to death! The Soviet Union is no more.

Even so, I maintain that from the ecological perspective little has changed. This perspective was indeed much more prominent in the East bloc, where environmental destruction cried to heaven. In the former German Democratic Republic (East Germany) the victorious west has to deal with old burdens, the inherited burdens of a regime which notoriously and almost malevolently failed to protect the environment. This was because the struggle for self-assertion in economic competition with the superior opponent, a competition long since lost, left neither materials nor energy to spare for this task – a useless one, seen from the viewpoint of productivity.

But the all-German perfection of the automobile-society intensifies the contradiction between humans and the earth far more fundamentally than did the failure of the eastern bureaucracy, and at the 1992 Rio conference on the environment incompatible things such as 'environment' and 'development' made it once again fully clear that western civilisation is the decisive cause of environmental disturbance. The enormous ecological destabilisation everywhere else in the world is primarily a symptom of western structural penetration into 'indigenous' social and natural conditions.

Now the attempt to introduce in the former East Germany, the apparent achievements, the reactive standards and norms of Bonn-style nature and ecological management and environmental protection will take at least ten years, and cost millions upon millions. In addition to this the point of view which permitted environmental matters to be treated in this cosmetic manner has lost further in credibility since the collapse of the East bloc. The thousands of millions spent on 'environmental protection' represent *additional* energy and material turnover, especially when they are built into the Megamachine. They are work-protection for the industrial system itself, and as such have an anti-ecological effect.

All that the weaker eastern variant lacked was the means and the knowhow by which the west repressed awareness of where the journey is headed – namely *nowhere*, but not the nowhere of William Morris. In the usual view of experts, the annoying thing about nuclear reactors of the Chernobyl type is not their general nature as offspring of a highest-risk technology invented by us, but that they conceal so badly the nature of the whole situation. Misuse and human failure in the case of such reactors make all too obvious the irresponsibility of the *use* of a technology which, instead of depending on us happily-fallible humans, must depend on robots – which we fallible humans want to programme infallibly.

No, the collapse of the East bloc made no contribution to overcoming the ecological crisis, which is the fundamental crisis of white world civilisation – even if taken up successfully by the golden corner, the Japanese and the Tiger economies. On the contrary, it sharpened it up. If we extrapolate the German rate of automobile use, the Chinese will quickly want approximately 700 million private cars which by comparison is their 'due' – and along with them, the corresponding infrastructure. In Siberia, the *Departure from Matyora* (Valentin Rasputin's report about the annihilation of trees, villages and islands in the name of energy-production) will accelerate, but under another banner. From Germany to the Pacific Ocean the white *homo conquistador* is only now finally unleashed and would like to accelerate away as quickly as he decently can.

Is Galtung's world-schematic no longer valid, because the 'red' corner of the 'development'-hungry second world is no longer there? Possibly Galtung would change the form of expression, but there is really no essential need to make changes. The red corner stands for the *principle* of central planning, for the state-supported direction of economy and society which, under the pressure of the western lifestyle, it practices more or less in all 'underdeveloped' countries.

For the 'red' structure was from the beginning far more *statist* than socialistic, and served the safeguarding, by means of state power, of a path of development which, whatever example you choose – whether that developed under Stalin and Mao or under the Persian Shah, or even under Franco and Pinochet – was determined by an envious comparison with the western standard of life. And this was just how Galtung characterised it. The very transition drama from Berlin to Vladivostok shows that the capitalistic world market ruins any 'under-developed' economy and landscape much more certainly than did state plans – by means of which the people could let themselves be cared for after a fashion, as long as the ideological boundary, protected by rockets, could be kept impervious.

And in the rich countries themselves the market economy has sunk to the level of professorial illusion. For example, in Germany a good half of the gross social product goes to the government budget. Moreover, the planning principle in the major western nations progresses all the more clearly and more urgently, the more these nations constitute themselves as a besieged fortress against the rest of humankind, and against the ecological crisis. In a sense their trade unions and associations are not in fact idealistic, but in reality 'red', and thus constitute the 'pink' in the middle of the axis of world destruction, in the scheme which I took over from Galtung.

As far as I can see, the diagonal of destruction characterised by statism-economism is not coming out of balance, regardless of what happens with the red corner. Whatever is advancing in the direction of green (the third world) to golden as 'development', needs to be accom-panied by state measures of all kinds on a large scale, including arms build-up and terror from above – because of its tendency to annihilate body, soul and nature. The provisional final victory of western de-mocracies does not, for those newly-blessed with pregnancy by this system, lead directly to democracy, for they see themselves as exposed to an all-embracing colonialism of a far more effective sort than the 'socialistic' one – a reality which the Islamic and Pacific rim nations are now bringing into focus.

Where the Megamachine is historically at home and got its start, it is hard to outbid totalitarianism, whatever may stand printed in the constitution. And if West Europe instead of the Far East should win the race – which I find hard to believe possible – it can only become an inferior golden to the Japanese-Chinese sphere, as a result of European Community bureaucratic jaundice and sclerosis. The dissolution of the Soviet system in the name of 'western values' leads to anything except a turning away from the diagonal of destruction.

'Blue' and 'red' in any case each contains the other inside itself. The red corner is simply the shadow of the blue, and can hardly vanish without the blue vanishing also. It even seems to me that out of the western 'victory' there comes an unavoidable tendency to 'eastifying' the West (something which in SW Europe is matched by a 'north-Africanising') – something subliminally feared by many people in the former West Germany.

Now that vigilance in the face of the external enemy, which functioned as an ideological brake, has fallen away, statism in the West will be all the more certainly internalised. The 'Confucian' Chinese and Vietnamese, incidentally, at the other end of the diagonal, are attempting the same thing in reverse: to the extent that the policy of Deng is being followed, they are internalising economism in order to safeguard statism.

Even in my *Alternative* (1977) I was of the opinion that the Russian revolution *de facto* had an anti-colonial 'development' perspective. As a civilising phenomenon it was not really autonomous, but over-determined by western competition. Aitmatov, the Soviet-Kirghiz poet, had denounced Moscow as an agency of western civilisation because of the inner cultural destruction resulting from competition over satellite countries. Yet even today's Russia is a long way from embracing real economism. For a long time there will remain at least a 'red' shadow.

The loss of statist guidance, not replaceable by capitalist market-mechanisms, makes itself devastatingly noticeable, internally and externally – all the countries previously covered by the Soviet imperium have temporarily become half-colonies of the West. Even the assimilation of East Germany, a country only slightly 'underdeveloped' – although ruined by competition with the West, which had completely destroyed the old structure – has been so expensive that the victor tightened its belt and fears for the stability of the Deutschmark.

The collapse of real socialism has a number of other consequences, especially a degree of emancipation for the Janus-faced western model. But my whole book rests on the insight that we can no longer continue to give priority to individual achievement and the struggle for social position, when confronted with the question as to whether planetary nature can endure the stresses which the final competition amongst us will place on it.

Having said this, the collapse of the Soviet empire and the victory of the West has only one advantage, though an important one: there are no longer any second-order causes of world destruction which can serve as excuses. We will no longer try to convince ourselves that, for example, displaced small farmers are to blame because they burn every last stick of wood, or destroy the ancient Amazon forest acre by acre. *We* are the guilty ones, with our white man's empire, and it is no longer possible for us to conceal this fact by laying the blame on some evil neighbour or other – unless, of course, we start blaming Orientals in their successful adoption of our military-industrialism.

The shameless media-manipulation during the Gulf War did not succeed in concealing 'convincingly' that *we* are empirically the strongest motivating cause behind Saddam Hussein or his like. Mr Bush and his comrades-in-arms were, on account of this orgy of killing and its predictable consequences, the first candidates who belong before a tribunal. Europe should take thought about itself, and Germany, even if it means going it alone, would do well to pull out of NATO, and even out of the European Community, in order to cease supporting such atrocities as are being committed in such places as Bosnia.

Germany already lives in enough abandonment by God and its own friends. But in the United States, the propeller of exterminism seems to be turning a few knots faster. In view of the obscenity of the 'just war' against our sorcerer's apprentice Saddam Hussein, all I can think of to say about the western world and its figureheads on the television screen is that it is the 'last outpost of barbarism'!

The mad caesars of Rome behaved in this way creating a 'new world order'. Our nature- and world-condition cannot possibly be entrusted any more to such strategists.

Under such administration – and in which western country is it basically better? – the progression of the logic of self-extermination is unavoidable. Details – such as the attitude which the US administration took at the Rio environmental summit – are almost marginal. Even so, Bush's argument that to set limits to the level of industrial world destruction would be unacceptable because it would cost *jobs* lets us draw conclusions about the stupidity of our form of civil society, which lives by such a policy.

We citizens of the White Empire – and Americans are merely in the lead – are responsible for a style of life which carries genocide, biocide and ethnocide to the remotest corners of the earth. In view of this, the question of changing the political structure seems more relevant than ever. It is now also clearer that the emergence of such a changed structure is a *cultural question* in the widest sense, far more than just a question of the political culture or class itself.

If no other structure of consciousness apart from the 'normal' one is spreading itself around and gaining power, it is hopeless to wait for an institutional constitution which is adequate to overcome it. Perhaps even we, who are ecologically relatively enlightened, are too lazy and sleepy to produce that charisma without which there will be no turn-about in the mass consensus, in favour of a politics of salvation.

Turn-about in the Metropolis

Galtung's sketch was immediately defective to me, in that he only indicated the ideal zone, the 'window', saying nothing about how we should get there. When we reflect how little people like extremes, whichever the corner, the proposal can naturally be made cheaply if it is done in pastel colours. Let the rainbow idyll live!

While I was in the Berlin College of Science I added a sketch to Galtung's scheme, which would display the dynamics of a fundamentalist Green movement. These dynamics operated on the *other* diagonal of the scheme, on the *development-axis* between the green and golden poles. In this way I arrived at the accompanying diagram.

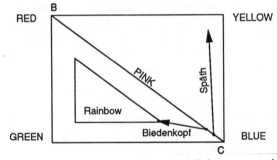

The rainbow society is naturally the 'other republic' or an association of 'other eco-republics' which Greens and Alternatives have been wanting. Those forces which push off from the blue-red diagonal in the direction of industrial breakthrough will admittedly bring about a different kind of republic, one which will be established somewhere between Huxley's psychedelic *Brave New World* and the atomic state described by Robert Jungk. It would be more than just a totalitarian state: a totalitarian *society*. In reality the whole blue-red diagonal was moving itself in the direction of the super-industrial breakthrough, which would be flanked and concealed with ecological modernising.

In this scheme then were blue and red, the 'security partners' of the East-West conflict, as well as the 'social partners' of the internal class-conflict, by all distinction first and foremost accomplices of *one* overarching system, the *industrial system* or *industrial civilisation*. It was *one* two-headed dragon – which, from 1989, began merging as one. At the time I pointed out why in the East the socialist and communist attempts to break out of this system didn't succeed. Now Peking as well is building 'according to the capitalist pattern', at least economically.

Today it is not a question of whether capital conquers work or the other way round, but of whether we succeed in disengaging *this whole suicidal formation*, and recovering the human energy and existence which have been invested in it.

Johan Galtung has written a fine little book, *Self-Reliance*, which states that the international solution of the boundary crisis depends decisively on whether (in my sketch) the movement out of the green corner and the movement for a Turn-around in the Metropolis meet together socially where I have indicated – in a world-wide rainbow

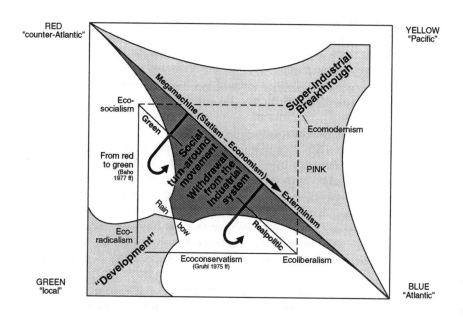

RED "counter-Atlantic" ... YELLOW "Pacific"

Eco-socialism

Megamachine (Statism – Economism)

Super-Industrial Breakthrough

Green

From red to green (Baho 1977 ff)

Social turn-around movement

Ecomodernism

Withdrawal from the industrial system

PINK

Rain

bow

Eco-radicalism

"Development"

Exterminism

Realpolitic

Ecoconservatism (Gruhl 1975 ff)

Ecoliberalism

GREEN "local" ... BLUE "Atlantic"

society patterned on 'small is beautiful'. A drawback of the scheme is that it does not show that we can also hope for a Turn-around movement in Japan and the Tiger countries, similar to ours.

If the super-industrial breakthrough in the Metropolis succeeds, the future ten-plus thousand million people in the third world would unavoidably strive towards a higher standard of living. This would mean that our demands and capacity for damage would be multiplied by a factor of between 10 and 20. Ultimately they would all want to have cars like ours – which we would under no circumstances do without, but rather modify with catalysers, at the same time as we turn to new, 'lighter', technologies. Even political solidarity such as the Left so much loves would become pure hypocrisy, if the friends of all possible liberation movements do not bend their energies to the task of securing the disappearance of the Atlantic model, the Megamachine.

Dumping the industrial system does not imply dispensing with every kind of industrial product. In the event of a Turn-around, the microchip does not *have* to be left behind, even though it is obvious that *on the diagonal of destruction* it unavoidably becomes a weapon in the hands of Big Brother.

From the point of view of the conventional concept of development, the Turn-around movement *appears* to be regressive, to the extent that it appears to run 'backwards' through the green-golden axis, in the direction of the Stone Age rather than that of biotronics. This impression arises because we have *humanly* identified ourselves, right down into the deepest levels of the psyche, with the materials and tools of domination of nature. Only from the viewpoint of productivism and technomania, characteristic of business society, do hunters and gatherers look like Stone-Age people, the ancient Egyptians as members of the Bronze Age, or the Greeks as members of the Iron Age.

For me the rainbow society is not characterised by any particular *type* of technology, but only by its exclusion of means which are hostile to life. Here, of course, are included installations and systems which are too big and complex to be made humanly adaptable, controllable and justifiable. I do not imagine the alternative as lying somewhere between Stone Age and high tech. Whatever we may use for materials and tools, we may *under no circumstances* evaluate them positively on this scale, but only negatively – that is to say by excluding practices which attack the balance of nature.

Contrary to appearances, machine-smashing or Luddism is not the same as radical, fundamentalist ecology. We wouldn't object to the automobile if it didn't murder so much life, both directly and indirectly. Similarly, the Turn-around doesn't start with abolishing things which affect only *symptoms*. What we may not do is grant a veto-right against our long-term survival interests to any kind of technical, social or cultural achievement. Anybody who opens the discussion by demanding a guarantee that the iron lung shall be retained is not interested in the changes which salvation requires! Yet to make this assertion does not imply that the iron lung must be abolished at any price.

Do we understand Buddha's parable of the burning house, which Bertold Brecht[9] made use of in the anti-fascist struggle? When the roof was already in flames, people asked the Buddha:

What's it like outside, is it raining,
Is the wind blowing, is there another house out there..?
And the Buddha answered: "Really, my friends,
To him for whom the floor is not yet so hot that he would gladly
Exchange it with anybody else rather than stay where he is,
I have nothing to say".

Let us return to the social movements which I have symbolised by the fat arrows. I use the term *movement* in a historical sense. It refers to developments in consciousness which, whether or not they are led by an active minority, are so widely distributed in the population that practically every man and woman participates in them. Even the strategists of the super-industrial breakthrough have covert rainbow-fantasies.

Originally I had carried my earlier vision of an ecologically-reformed association of East German 'alternative' Communists in revised form over into the West German Greens. For I did not yet have the party-political fixation behind me. When I said in 1979, "Red and Green go well together", I didn't mean to indicate the position which today is labelled *eco-socialist*, where the Greens are often only hangers-on. As a result the newly-drafted 'reconstruction' programme aims to overcome firstly unemployment, secondly poverty, and only thirdly the destruction of the environment. What I had in mind was a new integration on Green basic principles.

I soon recognised that it is nonsense to want to salvage and carry into a new age the pattern of *any* ideology originating in the industrial age. It is not clear how a morality dominated by progress could today give us the support we need. My path is described in the title of a book of auto-biographical interviews published in England: *From Red To Green*[10].

However this does not mean rolling up hedgehog-wise in the eco-radical corner. What floated more and more before my mind was a social breaking-out from the diagonal of destruction into the rainbow triangle, the vision of a *spiritually-based Turn-around movement, an exodus from the industrial system*. With this idea I terrified the Greens just before the 1983 federal elections, in which they needed to secure minimum 5% of the votes. At first I looked upon all this mater-ialistically, as if the immediate task were to propose an economic alternative to the Megamachine. As I was soon to learn, that is a trap, because psychological preconditions and readiness must ripen up, otherwise the finest eco-villages are premature, and come to grief indi-vidually on the old ego-structures of the pioneer.

I regarded the Greens from then on as an auxiliary force, useful for masking this social Turn-around movement as it takes off. On the one hand they could guarantee it the necessary time for its full unfolding, by delaying the ecological catastrophe and lessening the danger of war. On the other hand they could support and protect it politically, legally, financially and territorially as it makes inroads into society. For this purpose they could not establish themselves definitively on the system-diagonal, but only show up there as partisans, conceiving themselves as an instrument of take-off. Finally I exerted myself to hold open the decision 'in or out?' I wanted to accost travellers fairly coercively, and finally learnt from this that something must be wrong with my own political attitude.

Certainly the direction for a political force of the kind I had imagined was already written in a broader historical sense, and even so the Red-Green illusion burst of its own accord, without any interference from me. But when it came to the shape this force should take, my thinking was structurally conservative, being still too fixed on the party model. In the foreground was the fact that the Greens were not equal to their task, because they were unable to achieve even a provisional integration of the currents relating to the rainbow project. But was this provisional integration possible?

For it to have been possible, the exodus would have to have been spiritually-willed, for the integration is only thinkable on the axis of this Turn-around movement, that is to say politically *aiming at* the eco-radical corner of the rainbow triangle. In this way the Green party would have retained significance. The socialist eggshells here and the liberal ones there would, it is true, not have been extinguished, but subordinated, and the tension between goal-field and reality of Green intervention in the social process would have held out and been made fruitful. Yet no autonomy can be achieved by the addition of ideologies of the bourgeois age fitted with an *eco-* prefix.

NOTES

(1) Edward P Thompson, "Exterminism as the Last Stage of Civilisation", in *Writing by Candlelight*, London 1980.

(2) *MEW* Band 32, S. 32f.

(3) *MEW* Band 4, S 466.

(4) In the periodical *Ökologie*, no. 26, 1984. His statements correspond with the reference to the structural destruction of the soil and its far-reaching consequences which Gernot Graefe gives in his essay "Die fehlenden Bindeglieder zwischen Pflänzenwürzeln und Kolloiden im Boden" ["The Missing Connective Tissue Between the Roots of Plants and Colloids in the Soil"]. Inquiries about the manuscript should be directed to the Forschungsstelle fur Bioenergie der Österreichischen Akademie der Wissenschaften, Donnerskirchen, Burgenland.

(5) The sketch I give here comes from an unpublished manuscript of Galtung's which I have before me.

(6) See Marshall Sahlin's book *Stone Age Economics*.

(7) In his book *The Myth of the Machine*.

(8) Where, of course, they are directly facing the gold-yellow. Now William Irwin Thompson, who wrote the fine book *The Time Falling Bodies Take To Light – Mythology, Sexuality, and the Origins of Culture* (New York: St Martin's Press, 1981), has published *Pacific Shift* (San Francisco: Sierra Club, 1985) in which he stands squarely in this slip-stream; he must have forgotten some of the things he said in his earlier work in order to assume now that the next, Pacific, phase could be more successful than the previous Atlantic one, if only we alter a few thought-structures, while technologically things proceed precisely in the old direction.

(9) In *Hundert Gedichte*.

(10) Rudolf Bahro, *From Red To Green, Interviews with New Left Review*, translated by Gus Fagan and Richard Hurst, (London: Verso, 1984).

2. The answers others are giving

Here I shall review the major thinkers in this field in Germany, who have their parallels amongst thinkers and politicians in other countries – although it is worth learning from the German situation, inasmuch as eco-political thought has been developed and focused more than in many other lands, even though the facts and arguments are much the same internationally.

Timid High-Tech fix-it Imperialism

It seems to me that the 'damage-limiters' (such as Kurt Biedenkopf) have drafted the most interesting answer to our problem. Before getting to them I want to turn first to their polar opposite, the 'high-tech fix-it' school (such as Lothar Späth[1]). It is particularly important to me to distinguish clearly between the two, because there are ways of perceiving (or mis-perceiving) their concepts, in which they can be seen as almost identical.

The critics of Späth's book *Wende in die Zukunft* (*Turning Toward the Future*) generally speak of 'Späth-Kapitalismus' [late capitalism – a word-play in German on Späth's name, the German word *spät* meaning 'late']. But this emphasis does not uniquely characterise him. One may just as easily speak of damage-limitation capitalism (Biedenkopf), of pink-capitalism (Wolfgang Roth), or even of social-democratic capitalism (Lafontaine). The economic structure is automatically given a new name by anyone who wants to create a *realpolitik* of any sort. The immediate issue is the *sort* of politics envisaged.

The secret of the 'high-tech fix-it' position lies in the frightened ego of the developed world. It wants to encounter the rest of the world well-defended, and today the chosen defences are scientific-technological. The object of concern is an *empire on the defensive*. Because Europe and North America are threatened by merciless competitors, they must hold their place by means of their productive capacity. Otherwise their affluent citizens, fighting over the distribution of an ever-shrinking pie, would break each other's heads. The high-tech school would like to react *positively* to our late-Roman situation. They would like to stabilise

39

it with·competition rather than with limes and legions (even though they don't say anything about wanting to abolish the military, the accent is on *technical* defence). Out of fear for the inner peace of our white man's imperium, they want to lead us in one last advance, with scientific war-songs accompanied by the resounding voices of robots. It is in this sense that I speak of *imperialism*.

The 'pink' social democrat Peter Glotz has a very similar concept, if just a little less technomanic. In his 'work of bringing things to a head' he seeks to construct a sort of collective Augustus of the Left, and asks himself: what must a politics look like to the imperial centre, the colonialistic Metropolis of the world? For him this is to be achieved through the same nimble risk-capital, accommodating contractors, scientists and engineers, as in the case of the high-tech school. The only difference between them – one of point of view, not substance – is in their approach to social questions, for both politicians, because of their party membership, must from their different angles exert a pull on the trade unions.

The high-tech school sees quite correctly that social democratic competition for the throne is not the main issue for them. But he who has the better cards for 'turning toward the future' will also automatically make better tricks. So they are competing for power *inside* the conservative political establishment. For we in the developed countries are surrounded by a world of enemies: we are still at least as powerfully besieged by developing outsiders as is our dear earth by science-fiction challengers in the galaxy.

"While we in Germany absolutisé goals, harden up our standpoints and reject other solutions as imperfect, the world around us is developing economically and technically, with breathtaking speed". Nations are formulating long-term common perspectives, while state, science, economy and society form a "broad consensus"[2] for their attainment. So says Herr Späth, of the high-tech school.

It sounds quite modest, but at an earlier time the same style of thought resulted in a Tirpitz [Alfred von Tirpitz, 1849-1930, built up the German fleet before World War I]. Now this death-loving combative spirit is disguising itself as 'technological structural transformation'. It is exactly such motives which drove the Reagan Administration to proceed with its plan for the arming of space, called SDI. If technical re-armament comes too late, this (according to Späth) threatens "loss of credibility, the increase of uncompromising fundamental criticism, and the splitting up of political cultures in such a way that the fragments are no longer able to talk to each other"[3].

Späth's book assumes right from its beginning that the law of action is a function of the logic of things – a common business-conservative viewpoint. We *must* build the 'information society', because the idols which we have fashioned for ourselves out of science and capital demand it as the expression of their most recent stage of self-development.

"The technical structure-transformation together with its political, economic, social and cultural effects are the kernel" of the *social* blueprint which this technocratic approach has. High-tech conservatives clearly place the human being at the *end* of this chain of effects, which they·regard as unavoidable: as the last creative variable in our *adaptation* to the unavoidable. Anybody who wants to avoid this is pushed aside on moral grounds. High-tech conservatives have no inkling of the monstrosity of their demands.

How familiar! This is also the ethos of the now-tarnished, collapsed East European five year plans! Except that in East Europe, they could claim mitigating circumstances, prescribed for them in the logic of the inescapable consequences of superior geo-political competitors. The techno-conservatives borrow this logic. Where they only have to worry about the comforts of governing, those in the East had to worry about the continued existence of their Leviathan – as long as they could not give up the race for 'parity' with the West. All that is now gone, and the Soviet bloc has now joined the West in its own game.

In latter years there was uninterrupted talk about the 'merciless imperatives of the world market' which determine who will survive and prosper, and secondly, talk about who can share the consumer lifestyle. In a commentary in the weekly newspaper *Spiegel* of June 1986 titled *We Conquerors of Space*, the Prague paper *Rude Pravo* was quoted: "The death of the Challenger crew is the human price of progress which humanity must pay for being so bold as to explore the secrets of space. In this sense it is with justification that the Challenger tragedy has moved people deeply all over the world"[4].

Incredibly Lothar Späth actually believes that it is still possible today for a western society in ecological crisis *to be inwardly-reconciled, in that its will to self-assertion, without any correcting of the psychological drive which lies behind it, could be oriented towards technological matters,* instead of, as earlier, to military-fiscal and geo-political ones. On the domestic political front his thesis is that "the new technologies lay an obligation, derived from both reason and conscience, on all peoples who can apply them and develop them further, actually to do so"[5]. In reality this is a psychological programme of civil war, because it challenges an opposing fundamentalism almost to the point of building barricades. But he doesn't seem to have even an inkling of this.

Fully blind to himself Lothar Späth closes his book by harking back to him who, on a bright midday, hoped for the homecoming of the gods. He quotes, as if the words were his own, from Hölderlin's

Hyperion: "How the feuds of the living are the dissonances of the world! Reconciliation is in the middle of quarrel, and all things which are divided achieve union again". Against this another poem of Hölderlin comes to my mind, one in which he left the last line incomplete; his *Prayer for the Incurable*:

> *Hurry, hesitant Time, and bring them up against nonsense:*
> *Otherwise you'll never show them what their sense is about.*
> *Hurry, and wholly undo them, appall them with visions of Nothing:*
> *Otherwise they'll never know just how de-natured they are.*
> *Never will these fools reform until they begin to feel giddy,*
> *Never recover their health save in the stench of decay.*[6]

Serviceable Spirits – the Greens

Naturally Späth's *Turning Toward the Future* includes the respectable intention of protecting the domestic environment, as background to the expedition. He has contracts to place for environmental protection, and helpers are welcome. They must just fit themselves in. Ivan Illich[7] has already described with penetrating insight the kind of knife-edge such a 'turning' is moving along:

> *It could be the case that technocrats are given the job of leading the masses along the edge of the cliff. That is to say, they would have the task of establishing multidimensional limits to growth just short of self-destruction. Such a suicidal fantasy would keep the industrial system going at the highest possible rate of production. From birth to death the whole of humanity would be locked up in a permanent school on the world scale, treated in a huge world-wide hospital and attached, day and night, to inexorable communication channels. To want to introduce an era which is both hyper-industrial and ecologically feasible means accelerating the destruction of the remaining components of the multidimensional balance of life.*

There is already an elite preaching the anti-growth orthodoxy. Up to now it aims at the limitation of goods production and not of supplying services. Then comes the key passage:

> *If the population is tempted to accept a limitation of industrial production without calling the basic structure of the industrial society into question, it would be compelled to give more power to the bureaucrats who specify the limits to growth, and deliver itself into their hands. Consequence: the stabilised production of standardised goods and services would make convivial production, even if it were possible at all, even more remote than the industrial growth society.*

And this bureaucratic exploitation of the ecological crisis is already under way. The industries that wouldn't be seriously affected by this take the precaution of opposing it with anti-bureaucratic arguments and volunteers, without any obligation to do a better job of environmental protection, allowed to do things according to their own rhythm. They survive their social contribution in spite of all complaints about the high cost of labour. In protecting the environment some branches will earn well, and others will be able to pass the costs on without the raised prices cutting them out of the market, because the competition must also undergo eco-modernising. And should it really get too expensive, it is possible to get the production done somewhere else.

Above all it will be necessary to move into new areas which are 'greener' and more attractive from the start. It is the Japanese solution: the mixture of coerced internalisation of costs (the 'polluter-pays' principle) and obliging and concessionary insight on the part of large corporations. It will install itself to the extent that time is gained to write off the old plant. And so the route taken, immediately beneath the threshold of direct self-destruction, will be exactly what Ivan Illich had feared 14 years ago: treading a parallel to the abyss.

Jöschka Fischer, in his admirably blunt way, announced this quite openly as the goal of green politics[8]. He appealed to the giants of the German chemical industry, Hoechst and Merck, as well as to the trade unions, asking on the one hand for something to be done for minimum necessary acceptance of industry by the population, and on the other hand for safer work-places – for example about commitment to production processes which produce less waste and are more environmentally tolerable. He said, pointing to California and Japan (with their more drastic regulations), it could hardly be the case that Hessen as an industrial area would have to suffer stricter tolerance tests. A modernising of Germany without ecological clean-up and protection "would make life in this country so intolerable that only with a very short-sighted perspective could we do without ecological correctives".

Very nice. He wants to lay the tracks not one, but five metres away from the top of the cliff, in order to test his conception "of the extent, within this late-capitalistic industrial society, to which an ecologically-determined structural transformation can really be achieved, through the application of politics, the mobilisation of affected citizens and governmental action, without bringing the system itself into question".

Such a minister is eligible to be the darling of the nation *and* industry. What did Illich say? If one bestows on the people a limitation of industrial production *without* calling into question the basic structure of industrial society, convivial production retreats still further into the distance, if it is even still attainable. But from here on this is exactly what the Greens are good for. Fischer and others have delayed the progress of ecological enlightenment for a while in the advanced sectors of social consciousness. They were active in that shaded corner of the small eco-political rectangle which, in my scheme of system-diagonals, points in the Japanese direction. Whether they wanted it or not, this was decided at the moment they began to work with the power-apparatus which, at least up to now, has long been programmed to adapt the Megamachine to the environment and the environment to the Megamachine.

In the 1980s the debate within the Green party shrank almost to an exclusive discussion of bourgeois sociology and political theory. The remnants of Marxist terminology and analysis did little of significance to change this. Since Marxian socialism in its essence belonged to the industrial diagonal and would rather seek union with big corporations than pull out of the industrial system, the eco-socialist corner offered only a small amount of formal resistance to the '*Realo*' wing, which carried the state with it. If the Green party were to side with big labour against big industry, it would further developments on the diagonal of exterminism, whatever the secondary advantages.

It would have made much more sense from the point of view of *realpolitik* to have driven the officials of the main political parties into environmental protection. Relief of specific problems merely saved them the trouble of learning. To take away the environmental department from the Megamachine is either naivete or seducibility or – simplest of all – the returning home of a strayed citizen-youth into its social environment.

The Green party then took the position of the shaded triangle: an alibi for our environmentally-desolate society. And those who held to the hypotenuse in the rear were called '*Fundis*' (fundamentalists) only because they didn't want to turn the Greens *directly* into a sister party of the Centre-Left main parties. Yet the *Fundis* in the Greens were just as unimportant as the radical Left, even if they did sometimes win elections to boards.

Meanwhile there was a continuation by the *Realos* of the Sindelfinger 'reconstruction program'. In order to be above all suspicion, the Greens expressly assured us that they didn't want to pull out of the industrial system, but just to 'reconstruct' it. Only "those modes of production, consumption, and waste-removal which are extremely (!!!) harmful to the environment must be discontinued". Congratulations! I said in 1984 that the Greens appeared to be in the process of preparing themselves for a next and last restoration of the imperial centre. Now this is cleared up. They were in principle just as imperialistic as any other established party.

The Limiting-ORDO

'Ecological modernisation' with robots in the lead completes the spiritual impoverishment of the Right, and eats up the remains of the values which they campaign with. 'Information society' is a name of the extremest alienation! We will subordinate ourselves to our mental tools, and become excellent at communication with machinery and our nature-abstractions. The courage for inter-personal openness and mutuality, the strength for warmth and love, will perish still further. Even children will achieve a form of maturity which is accustomed to the cold.

Can the conservative camp fall ecologically into line? Not, of course, without a break in continuity. It will not come from the corrupt political conservatism with which we are familiar – unless somebody lights a fire under them, and that *somebody* would not be these institutions themselves. It might be something like the fire of a true Reformation among the people, which could get its start from anger about the commerce in ecological indulgence.

Still less is this readiness likely to come from Red or Red-Green eco-reformism. Firstly they deny the existence of spiritual capacities which fuel true ecological politics. They are still wedded to the rationalistic Modern Project and want to cure the terminal functional defects of this with more of the same medicine. Secondly Red-Green reformism is pledged to achieve material equality within the rich Metropolis, as a *precondition* for any ecological action – so that until the Day of Judgement there will always be *something* which has priority over ecological action. Thirdly, if this Red-Green group were to achieve a place in government in coalition with the coal, steel, concrete and computer segments of the Centre-Left, it would be out-maneuvered by the *de facto* Great Coalition of technocrats coming from both popular parties, of the Centre-Left and Centre-Right.

The 'damage-limiter' Biedenkopf contrasts with this background. Unlike Lothar Späth, he understands that our basic situation is a *crisis of limitation* – he has been a critic of growth since the middle 70s. Material expansion "overtaxes our ecological base and thus exposes us to an existential danger"[9]. He shows a sensitivity for thinking in categories which respect the scale of nature, and which certainly are in no position to support our far-reaching expansion. His orientation is toward preservation and not fitness-training.

Where others speak of 'turning toward the future' or of 'different progress', we could characterise Biedenkopf's book as 'a new order for the limitation of the economy'. Even more, in view of the erosion of society from the state to the individual, a sickness for which no Black Forest clinic has a remedy, he knows that it will gradually become urgent to introduce a new order which primarily helps not 'the economy', 'the welfare state', or 'the environment', but before all things the otherwise inevitably-destructive human being.

When, in his prologue, he takes 'unchanging values' as his basis, he apparently means anthropological values, because in the same breath he perceives us as being in such an upheaval that we must "for this reason re-examine basically the most important assumptions and values of our culture"[10]. By this he doesn't just mean a re-evaluation of sexual relations[11], a tray-full of hospitality-gestures for people climbing in and out of the male structure.

While others, when they say 'ecology', mean only 'environmental protection', because they've no idea there is any difference, Biedenkopf, when he talks about environmental protection, frequently means ecology. He understands that our way of doing things is on the whole too massive, hefty, heavy, violent and complex. But he doesn't accentuate this very sharply, because he doesn't want to give his Centre-Right clientele too crude a shock. After his later electoral defeat he could afford to feel freer.

His vision extends beyond the boundaries of his own country. The "worldwide extension of European economic forms, even to countries which lack the necessary pre-existing cultural conditions" brings into existence a mass demand which compels a more extensive, and ecologically even more destructive, repetition of the process that West Europe has gone through in the last 150 years. Meanwhile we have reached a point at which "material expansion has not only threatened the ecological balance of our planet, but has permanently endangered it".

Remarkably, Biedenkopf gives no attention to checking this process at its *periphery*. He does not, for example, lament the population explosion, because, unlike doomsters, he knows that it is primarily a consequence, and only secondarily a contributory cause, of expansion. He is much more concerned to refer the danger back to *European* developments since the Renaissance. And he is absolutely clear that things cannot go on like this any longer.

He sees the cause as lying in the "expansivity of our thought *and* the carrying-over of the results of this thought into the material sphere, into the production of goods and services, and into affluence and material fortunes"[12]. Supposing it is the case that the *first* cause really lies in *thought*, which is politically-pragmatically understandable, he adds, not altogether consistently: the *critical point* is not just the extension of knowledge in all these dimensions, but rather the *application*, the "*carrying-over of possibilities into reality*".

Decisive then is the nature of the drives which are concealed behind this carry-over, and whether or not they can be disconnected. It is certainly theoretically right that we are not *compelled* to do all the things that we *can* do, hence it would seem feasible to take aim at the *application* of knowledge as the ultimate cause of material expansion, while leaving out the expansive *acquisition* of knowledge. The advantage of this is that we are spared a discussion about the ever more problematic 'freedom of science'.

Yet from the beginning of industrialisation, up to the present, this disconnecting has never happened, and today science is regarded – and financed – as an 'immediate productive force'. This is a development which could assert itself along two parallel tracks of social will-to-power: on the one hand that of the self-assertive ambition of the scientist himself, and on the other hand that of corporate profit. Thus the security of the connection is cared for from two sides at once.

In his all-embracing *Critique of Scientific Reason*, Kurt Hübner[13] even speaks of the *fusing together of science and technology as the law of the modern*. The concern is less and less to achieve a precise mirroring of the laws of nature, but rather "exhaustively, systematically, and without constraint, to explore the realm of technical possibility". This matches the corresponding pioneer psychology:

> *Thus is evolving a new type of human, who has never previously existed in this form:* the inventor. *He is educated in science and has so far in this respect a theoretical orientation; his interest is in the systematic process of inventing, rather than any particular invention; economic, social and political interests are not decisive for him, and are often just used as excuses; but he is nevertheless dominated by the will to get his prototypes into production, even to the point of forcing them on to his environment. We find this constitution in all great inventors, from Leonardo da Vinci through Papin, Huygens, Watt, Trevethick, Niepce, Daguerre, Nobel, Edison and others, up to the present, where as a rule the team has replaced the work of the single individual.*

If the self-realisation of the scientist is a driving-force, capital is just as powerful a facilitator and driver. Material expansivity has the economic form of capital accumulation! In no way is it a real goal of science to "lighten the drudgery of human existence"[14]. Spirit and money both readily walk over corpses for the purpose of achieving their own growth.

Unfortunately the ORDO-liberal school, where Biedenkopf had his education, has tacitly assumed that the *internal dynamics* of these torrential rivers of science and capital are necessities of nature, and is thus only concerned to contain them by strengthening their banks. And a

direct consequence of this is the *way* in which Biedenkopf has arranged
the limitation problem for legal and political access: one must arrange
the competitive system so that its expansion is limited, without disturbing competition itself. Stated more precisely, policy is supposed to
refrain from boosting growth, so that it does not reduce production.

Ecological Market Economy

So the watch-word here is *ecological market economy*. The immediate
meaning of this is that in environmental protection policy the damage-
limiters refuse to use methods of government intervention, which they
don't like anyway because of their heritage of ORDO-liberalism. Meanwhile the reformist Green ex-minister Fischer confirms that the complex tug-of-war in the struggle to limit environmental damage serves
mainly to bring about an enormous increase in the size of the bureaucracy. And whatever the Minister for Environment is called, there
is at his back no real national sovereign body which can stand up to
powerful economic interests.

Concerning the impact of the industrial system, it is swings and
roundabouts, whether I would rather see regulation by the government
(*statism* or *etatism*) or regulation by the market (*economism*). It by no
means follows automatically that, because the bureaucratic alternative
has failed, we would have more luck with the market economy. Nevertheless, seen from within capitalist economics, damage-limiters seem to
me to be right: if industry must be made to internalise the cost of its
impact (the polluter pays), this is done better *with* than *against* the grain
of business economy. An industry can then, assuming the existence of a
coercing mechanism, minimise costs within its undertaking, and absorb
the impact tax which damage-limiters have in mind. This can be
reckoned against the expenditure for installations or whatever is needed
to reduce the damage. Industry can then find the most advantageous
way forward within its own planning horizon.

As to the coercing mechanism, damage-limiters make no secret that
when they say "less state" they mean a *stronger* state. The state shall not
exhaust itself in guerrilla warfare over taxes, shall not have to strike
here, there and everywhere because of date-deception, obstruction and
the bargaining-down of quotas, but shall establish regional-maximum
values of the total impact enforceable by the field of social forces. These
'politically-established shortages' must, by means of impact certificates
which the polluter will be forced to acquire, be translated into economic
pressure. That is to say, whoever will contribute to the permitted total
impact must pay a tax by means of which the total impact will sink,
always a little ahead of the technical state-of-the-art and the routines of
putting it into practice.

This is, as far as I can find out, the best idea for achieving *system-immanent damage-limitation*. Damage-limiters can in no way demonstrate that the market will nevertheless *not* destroy nature, or that a 'non-expansionist competitive economy' is possible. But at least I can comprehend Biedenkopf's thesis that the market would 'govern' nature better than the state with its policy of interventionist environmental protection[15]. It all depends on the political struggle over impact tax, its magnitude, and the determination of total impact.

But where are the empirical limits of such an 'ecological market economy'?

Firstly, we can proceed with certificates only on the basis of sources of danger that are *known* and *establishable*. In a situation in which specific instances of damage (as in the case of formaldehyde or CFCs) are only established decades later, and in which their cumulative and combined effects can only be guessed at, we would be playing a dangerous game. The forests will be dead before the licences for countless suspicious factors have been sold – a process suited only for the tour along the edge of the abyss which Ivan Illich talks about.

Secondly, the principle, even if it is presumably more effective than bureaucratic methods, has a psychological drawback: *it sells permission to pollute*. As a consequence, this marginal-value method has come to be regarded as inadequate and illegitimate. 'Politically-determined scarcities' based on this principle legalise the untenable tactics of making compromise deals with nature. "Don't cover it up, *protect* the environment" – but we can't do it in this way[16].

Are peak values the main problem? Dioxin is best understood as an indicator of the *basic impact* of the industrial system, but it has become too great. Damage-limiters put hydrocarbons on the negative list. But when will we have rid the world of them by means of certificates? The chemical industry impacts the biosphere *as a whole*. Quite apart from whether or not they can be replaced by 'soft' methods, *whole lines of production* must *immediately* be closed down. Into the indefinite future, the capacity for investment should primarily be directed to removing the environmental damage which has already been done!

In the logic of Biedenkopf's reflections, the establishment of scarcities could indeed be extended and made more radical. On the one hand – in opposition to the entire labour theory of value, which sets at zero the value of the contribution of nature – resources should be taxed to such an extent that even the most expensive hourly wage becomes once more affordable. On the other hand *every* emission, *every* waste-product, must be *progressively taxed from zero upwards*, in private households too.

Precisely because there is *no* zero impact, *no* economy of perfect recycling, it must be rigorously insisted upon, using these means, that the use and degradation of nature be *minimised*. Every waste and every impact must appear as a cost of production.

Yet even this modification would only hold the consumption and degradation of nature as low as possible per *unit of production*. And the limit of the capacity of *any* market-economy solution is reached at that point where it becomes a question of limiting the *volume* of production, *the market itself*. Or is there a possibility of building the limits of nature into the market economy so that production shrinks, not just temporarily but permanently? The production of cars for example? Is it thinkable, by means of the market, not only to compel the production of environmentally-benign cars, but also to prevent the total number of cars worldwide from growing to 21 thousand million (based on the present rate of car-ownership in Germany)? Scarce environmental goods would sooner or later grow more expensive even for those competitors who are the worst environmental sinners. But *all this cancels out!* The rising cost of land has never been able to halt the building-up and concreting-over of the landscape.

It seems to me that the damage-limiter Biedenkopf's *intention* is more radical than the measures allowed by his theoretical framework. He leaves the reader confused as to whether the issue is really the limiting of growth, or only the preventing of further stimulation of it. What, in our economy-obsessed society, is the meaning of 'dynamic balance'? His solution to these questions relates to factors *internal* to the economy, and is in no way primarily concerned with the balance between society and *nature*. The ostensible goal is 'limitation of expansion', but the ORDO-liberal position only contemplates mechanisms for *regulation* of expansion.

Certainly it is a good thing to switch off the auxiliary motor. But does the pressure of need, do supply and demand *in the form of expression and in the dimensions they have acquired after centuries of expansion*, belong to the natural order? Are they compatible with the overall balance of the earth? From the point of view of *The New View Of Things* the whole post-war society, whether democratic or centrally-controlled, has been unjust to the natural order. Further, is it not the case that the idea of ORDO, under the name of social market-economy, has been used to restore an economic principle to which the warning signal had already appeared, through both world wars?[17] Isn't the temporary victory in the after-war period, called the economic miracle, more disastrous than military defeat was?

Thus the ORDO idea only offers the new opportunity which Biedenkopf ascribes to it, if it can break the fetters with which it is fastened to the diagonal of destruction. The boundary idea urgently demands values such as individuality, initiative, self-realisation – the positive essence of freedom – and they no longer should be bound together with entrepreneurship in the fields of profit and prestige-oriented material research, invention and production. The values mentioned need, in the interests of freedom, to be ruthlessly self-critical toward the expansive and aggressive subjectivity which clothes itself in profit and invention.

A Conservative Revolution?

So far I have ignored the fact that the damage-limiters consider the idea of *order* to be stronger than the drive to accumulate, even though they give no evidence for this. Is it really possible to put the brakes on capitalism with a politics of order? I find it hard to do anything but laugh at such an idea as an Office for the Control and Supervision of Cartels.

Yet Biedenkopf's teacher Franz Bohm wanted a "ruthless removal of the power of the private economy" and a "de-privatising of the then remaining market power". According to all appearances this was meant seriously. How various are the attitudes which can be taken to the capitalistic reality!

Whoever is convinced that you cannot get the better of capitalism with order-politics confronts a contradiction: if, for example, the 'social responsibility' of property is unenforceable because it runs counter to the system, how is it then that we have been demanding from the state that it shall enforce the 'polluter-pays' principle, and in actuality something like an ecological, perhaps even a 'social-ecological' market economy?

In the centre of his *New View of Things* Biedenkopf introduced an expression which is very ancient, from which one can get a great deal more mileage than he in fact does. It is the Roman sounding concept of ORDO. He intends with this to introduce into our social affairs something like a 'naturally' pre-existing order, or to attempt to model our society on some kind of Platonic idea or form of 'correct' arrangements.

As far as I can see his critics have accepted nearly all he says, but have treated this centre-piece disdainfully as whim or caprice. And yet this gives his scheme its conceptual strength! Everybody has some sort of notion of an order-politics. Moreover, such notions are continually put into practice. But that somebody should defend the notion of an *idea* of order! There is the greatest degree of agreement that a disorderly muddling around with uncontrollable problems is the only thing which is 'do-able', and nothing else is wanted. Almost all people fear having to lose something because of some over-arching new order, and they react with anxiety even when the proposal is laid out in the most liberal and democratic manner possible.

The social-democrat von Dohnanyi detected religious overtones in Biedenkopf's proposal: "The grail is called ORDO", he states[18], and he rejects any social-ordering force which is not part of the struggle for a share of the great cake, as unacceptable for 'social democracy'. It would amount to the attempt "*by means of an alien compass*, to steer a sure path in today's complex economic and social world". In opposition to this he pleads for the *status quo*: "There is no appetising substitute for the balancing of interests in the power-struggle between groups and parties".

Remarkable. The Social-Democrat will not admit any factors outside those of economics and capitalism. He rejects the limitation idea of the Centre-Right because it takes its departure from an element which is alien to the logic of capital. Thus 'pink' as a political principle doesn't offer even a hint of ecological policy.

All those who find much of interest in *The New View of Things*, but prefer to dismiss the order-thought as caprice or old hat, miss the heart of the issue; and at a later date they will probably be amazed at the strength of this starting point. Also to be led by an over-arching idea will, in the foreseeable future, begin to pay off in a new way. Damage-limiters see the overall social problem from the point of view of the ecological crisis, and see it as a challenge to create order; they want to tackle it from an Archimedean point lying outside the machinery of the economic system, a point which, from the point of view of *realpolitik*, still has to be created.

For the first time somebody in the Centre-Right confronts the ecological crisis conceptually, by the way in which the 'environmental crisis' is approached. Still more, Biedenkopf is the only politician who does not allow other concerns (employment, social problems) to get surreptitiously exempted from the necessity for limitation. What he is trying to outline is nothing other than an *ecological transformation-government*, and he is doing it with great urgency and, within the framework of his premises, consistently.

Initially the ORDO concept is neutral in content and fits any social conditions. It can be summarised as the willingness to comply with certain non-arbitrary regulations, regardless of what it is at the moment which needs regulating. Human nature can adapt itself to such a wide variety of conditions that it is impossible to derive from it a specifically human purpose. So the ORDO concept initially expresses no more than the intention to set and enforce norms. It is permeable to well thought-out content leading to reform projects, capable of being government policy, such as might be acceptable to the mentality of the conservative majority. An ecological transformation is quite impossible without the *factor* of a conservative revolution, and of course just as impossible if the impulse to do it gets bogged down in it.

Even back in 1977 somebody who had studied the long waves of technical innovation[19] wrote under the chapter heading "Change of the Order; Order in Change", that the relevant new social-organisational adaptations

> still belong in the government period of restoration leaders, iron chancellors, or autocratic regimes, which, from the conditions of instability of technological stalemate of the time, were called into office. This was the case in the epoch of Metternich, Bismarck and Hitler, and was no coincidence. Clearly the socio-economic evolution took a path of conserving change: innovations which impacted the rules of the order could, in the past, only be introduced by people who were rooted in tradition and whose conservative inclinations were beyond doubt. They could only become influential in periods in which forces of conservation were in the ascendant.

If this is the case, it matters which conserving forces we might adopt, while keeping an unwavering eye on the chief competitors on the world market. This time the social peace of the rich countries shall be achieved, not with concrete, but with microchips. And in this process the environment will only be watched to the extent necessary to make sure nothing gets out of control. The likely speed of the journey to Hell has shown itself as a question of habituation. The citizens only want to watch TV and read the paper, while the government cares and acts.

As long as identifications with the western 'democratic industrial society' do not fundamentally break up, the project of a an ecological transformation as a conservative revolution, in spite of its limits, remains the most promising.

When I make use of the concept of the conservative revolution, I do not mean the specific state of mind which established itself under the same name in the foreground of Hitlerism. For a long time now, from Luther through Stein and Bismarck and up until Hitler, Germany has been the country of the conservative revolution. To the extent that Hitler genuinely belongs in this series, we have been burnt enough, and so we don't need to be scared by the project. Both market economy and democracy must become negotiable – this does not mean they must be abolished, but it does mean that we must clearly recognise how very deeply they are enmeshed in the logic of self-extermination.

'Moor the Boat to the Bank!'

As always: on the positive side we can say that damage-limiters take up the issue precisely at the point where conservative forces, after Hitler's breakdown of 1945, were ready for some heart-searching, and initially wanted something more than just reconstruction and the economic miracle – namely a damming up of capitalism, illusionary as that may have been. The application of the ORDO idea to the relationship with nature, to the ecological crisis *is* new. This is exactly the issue today: to make ecology, the relation between humans and the entire earth, between society (species) and nature as a whole, into the fundamental pivot of a new politics of order.

Order originally means something different from the 'peace and order' of the police president. Biedenkopf shows this in his insightful position on the right to demonstrate[20]. He does not reduce order to the state executive, but refers it back to the field of the fundamentals of justice, and even to regions of the pre-political, the social, and the ethical. And first to be transmitted and established are the 'natural' elements of order, that is those given in the essence of human nature itself.

As far as *method* is concerned I am fully in agreement with this position. The ecological crisis compels us to go back this far, and perhaps even a step further, to the point where we raise the question as to whether there is a contradiction between the order of 'human nature' and natural or cosmic order. Every economics is dependent upon *human beings*, and regards them only from the point of view of their social interests, which are automatically opposed to a balance with nature. The system which we and the natural order together comprise, the cosmic and earthly framework of our existence, is basic, and yet does not for this reason have a place in the fundamentals of economics, law, and so on. Why it does not is hardly ever asked, although it is normative in the *highest* sense, being concerned with the kind of economy humans ought to have in order to express their *mission*[21].

Those who talk of the reconciliation between economy and ecology as if it were some sort of *compromise*, as if they were dealing with two *equally-ranking social sectional interests*, have simply no idea what they're dealing with. In 1983 a wise old Japanese woman found the following child-like parable, showing the extent to which we can be mistaken about our need to act in accordance with naturally given priorities. This woman, Rynju Tamo, writes:

Imagine millions of ants in a little ship made out of a bamboo leaf. The ship is nearing a waterfall – but they don't notice it. It seems they even have no idea they are travelling in a boat. These ants, who would work together if they understood their situation, are on the contrary divided by hate, malice and greed, and are obsessed with intrigues and quarrels. And they continue in this way even though once the boat reaches the waterfall it is the end of all of them, friend and foe alike...

Now they are afraid of war and are worried about the use of nuclear energy. And in truth, both are serious problems. But are they aware that they face far more urgent problems? The peaceful times, in which we could afford to get distressed about something like the danger of war, already belong to the past... Dangers of war and of nuclear energy are problems of the kind which only concern the ants among themselves – problems confined to the little boat; they are independent of the main problem, which is that the little ship carrying the ants – whether they are in a state of peace or a state of war – moves unswervingly closer to the waterfall. Although it is hardly possible, even if the world were to become war-free, the whole of humanity would still be progressing day by day to its doom...

The important thing is to 'moor the boat to the bank'. By the bank is meant the eternally unchanging 'cosmic order' (from which we have distanced ourselves, otherwise we would not be moving in the boat toward the waterfall – R.B.)...

To get to know this cosmic order precisely and to arrange our lives accordingly means 'mooring the boat to the bank'; living life according to the 'cosmic order' as the greatest and most important directive has, with very few exceptions, never been realised in the politics of the world.

Inasmuch as we fail to give the course of human life, based on this overriding directive, a great change in direction, 'falling over the waterfall into the abyss' will only be accelerated, never mind what forces we may call upon.

'Superficial' characterises the striving for the welfare of humanity alone, 'true' characterises making the whole community of existence and the prosperity of the entire creation the basis of action. Naturally the 'superficial politics' which we have had up to now is also necessary, but must now unconditionally be managed in accord with 'true politics'. Precisely the realisation of 'true politics', which gives the direction for 'superficial politics', gives to humanity today, standing on the threshold of the abyss, the basic principle of rebirth.

There is nothing in particular to say against this order of things, adapted as it is to economic interests, if it is bedded in this 'true policy', of 'mooring the boat to the bank'.

Richard Wilhelm, translator of *I Ching*, made a note against the hieroglyph for 'The Well': "We must go deep to the foundations of life. All superficiality in the ordering of life, if it leaves the deepest needs of life unsatisfied, is as inadequate as if we had made no attempt at order at all". The economy, even where it one-sidedly dominates and occupies the whole, can for this reason not be the primary datum of a new crystallisation. For regulating competition is a derivative, 'superficial' problem, the discussion of which is intrinsically meaningless. There *can* be no success in a new attempt to regulate 'at least this basically important sphere of the economy'.

The real decision is thus anthropological – and more precisely spiritual. And since in reality humanity and the earth have grown together to be *one* system, the basic decision is also ecological.

Hence we must seek to recognise the *one* economic order which is required of us if we are to continue to exist. It must essentially be based on human capacities which are yet to unfold, rather than on the average behaviour which we can already see. Without an evolutionary jump, without a change in behaviour arising out of the awareness that direct striving for advantage will be the death of us, there is no possibility of achieving a saving new order in which the economy is only a part, and never the foundation. We must choose a new economy if we are to overcome our undignified dependence on the world-wide supermarket.

Almost everywhere in the world people still want a Megamachine which nevertheless doesn't destroy anything, and they don't want to know that they can't have one. The only serious answer is to remove the 'development' model. This model imposes self-destructive standards of value worldwide, because it is bound up with the infrastructure with which we have covered the earth, and from which we cannot escape.

To do this we have to create a consensus. Even if a functioning expansion-free market economy *is* possible, for it to exist something must first happen to our needs and to the profit motive. We must stop being fixated on the economy, and rid ourselves of the security-philosophy which reflects our spiritual dependence on the Megamachine. Otherwise no way of ordering ourselves into the economy will amount to anything. The incentive-dynamic itself is the problem, not the damming it up from outside.

The internal political struggle of the many interest groups and property owners is indeed only a limited segment of this encroaching great disorder now displayed by the world system. The state as ordering power, and the group of interests which quarrel among each other for its skin, belong to the same 'false whole'. The defect in this false connectedness is irremovable because it is rooted in quite a different matrix, in a much deeper stratum of humanity.

ORDO – Against the Dynamics of Motivation?
In contrast to the natural order, a legal order and laws, right from their beginning, do not have the status of a first cause. They are rather *reactions to disturbances in the great order*. Lao Tzu, who had quarrelled about this with Confucius, understood the real course of events in this way:

The great Tao got lost –
goodness and uprightness came into existence.

Cleverness stepped forward –
the great hypocrisy came into existence.

The clan was torn up –
the feeling for family came into existence.

The state fell apart in chaos –
the loyal minister came into existence[22].

This compensatory status of the 'loyal minister' is one of the oldest and deepest truths about state and law, and from it one can understand the practical dependence of law on its executive, however much we would like it to be the other way about. But this we may only credibly demand if we understand the disorder thus established as a state of the world-in-its-entirety and, above all things, when we *want* to overcome it. Whoever wants to refer back this disturbance of the ORDO, this absence of the *Tao*, merely to error and false concepts, conceals the rift in the world instead of earnestly embarking on the task of healing it.

'Ordo-liberalism' wants to leave the individual a free hand in all activities, all initiatives, even all expansion, and to interfere as little as possible in their fields of action: a free market economy! And then to this free play of forces, wherever it could have a harmful external effect, an *external* limit shall be set, which shall guarantee *fairness*. Humans are seen as having an intrinsically uninhibited, *by nature expansive thrust from within*, and an opposing retarding and channelling agency operating inwards from the *boundary* of the market system.

If fair competition aimed at the best possible satisfaction of needs were the normal condition, we would have no impulse to get the state to intervene. Even I am of the opinion that the power-logic of market forces was not foreseen in the 'plan of the world'. But all market idealists who insist that all that is missing is the correct concepts and legal consequences are still making the same mistake for which Lao Tzu had criticised Confucius.

Where Confucius wanted to save something by customs and mores (stronger than laws in organic societies), Lao Tzu saw only the degree of degeneration which enabled such an effort to appear sensible. Richard Wilhelm interprets:

Far-reaching internal untruthfulness had eaten away all relationships, so that externally human love, justice and morality could still appear as high ideals, whereas greed and love of possessions had poisoned everything internally. Under such conditions every attempt to produce order only increases the disorder. Such a sickness cannot be helped by externally-applied remedies[23].

In the same spirit Max Kaltenmark renders a passage of the 38th Saying in such a way that the *ranking* of the *order-producing* virtues of government during the *falling-off* from the Great Original Ordering and its principles of operation becomes clear:

When we have lost the Tao, *we rely on the* Teh *(power). When we have lost the* Teh, *we rely on our humanity. When we have lost our humanity, we rely on justice. When we have lost justice, we rely on rites. Rites are only a thin veneer of loyalty and trust – and the beginning of flagrant disorder*[24].

All this indicates that we cannot be satisfied with the building of regulations from outside. Something must happen with the misguided driving energy itself, which makes itself disastrously felt in all manifestations of our civilisation. External corrective measures of that descending rating will be necessary, but at the same time they will lack proper justification unless these measures will be part of an attempt to start a new order which is *fundamentally correct*. Only if we look solely at the economic level can it seem that all we have to do is limit the avalanche of accumulation which is rolling materially over the earth.

NOTES

(1) I refer to Späth's book *Wende in die Zukunft, die Bundesrepublik auf den Weg in die Informationsgesellschaft* (*Turning Toward the Future, the Federal Republic on the Way to the Information Society*), Reinbek, 1985.

(2) *ibid*, p13.

(3) *ibid*, p12.

(4) *Spiegel*, June 1986.

(5) Späth, *op cit*, p151.

(6) Translation by Michael Hamburger in *Friedrich Hölderlin, Poems and Fragments* (Cambridge University Press, 1980) p609.

(7) Illich, p175ff.

(8) In an interview with *Wirtschaftswoche* on January 10th 1986.

(9) Kurt H Biedenkopf, *Die neue Sicht der Dinge, Plädöyer für eine freiheitliche Wirtschafts- und Sozialordnung*. München, Zürich, 1985, p43.

(10) *Ibid*, p45.

(11) The key passage here shows clearly the direction in which Biedenkopf's utopia is to be found, and it also shows clearly that the idea of limitation must be an inner need:

Emancipation means the regaining of the natural *role of the woman. But not 'natural' in the sense of a pre-imprinted 'naturalness' through obsolete modes of thinking; but as an ordering force of society, mainly in the primary group. The time of doubt, of questioning, and of measuring, the time when matter and spirit were in confrontation, the time during which humanity dominated nature, was a time which corresponded mainly to the characteristics of man. The time of renewal of the context of the whole, the rediscovery of the organic unity of nature, the decentralising of life in small living circles, the time of dynamic balance between people and between humanity and nature, and the time of the rediscovery of the family and householding as the place where people discover their identity; all of this is more accessible through the characteristics of* woman. *She is more readily able to reunite humanity and nature. For her the natural emotionality of human beings, as it is seen by the traditional exact sciences, is not irrational because not measurable and 'objectifiable', but reasonable... A new understanding will arise between representatives of the 'rational' and women, who re-discover for us in a politically relevant fashion the 'emotional' and the access to the natural ordering elements of human society (p50 of his book).*

So it depends decisively on the 'primary group', in particular on their importance in social cohesion, their real power equipment, that is, the freedom they have to dispose of the lion's share of the means of their reproduction, not least of the education and socialising of children, which now is so completely subjected to the technocratic principle. For women to be able to influence the whole cultural climate in this way, these primary groups must be among the basic units through which the whole society, right up to the world level, is more powerfully determined than by all other social forces. No dependencies in the other directions were called for. No 'higher levels', no specialised institution or activity may exempt the human and the natural from their responsibility. The 'freedom of science' and the 'free market economy' must abandon their Mephistophelian cock-feathers, because they are notorious for the colonising way they treat this region of life.

(12) Biedenkopf, *op cit*, p46.

(13) Kurt Hübner, *Kritik der wissenschäftlichen Vernunft* (Freiburg: München, 1979), p364f.

(14) Galileo, in Bertold Brecht's work of the same name.

(15) Biedenkopf, *op cit*, p436.

(16) Biedenkopf himself mentions the physics expert and economist Georgescu-Roegen, whose life work, going beyond Marx and Keynes, centres on demonstrating that human production fundamentally and unavoidably cuts into the basis in nature of our existence and, according to its character and extent, shortens to a greater or lesser degree the life-span of our species on the blue planet.

(17) Old Testament, *Daniel* 5, 24-28.

(18) In *Spiegel* 44/1985.

(19) Gerhard Mensch, *Das technologische Patt. Innovationen überwinden die Depression* (Frankfurt: 1977) p266ff.

(20) Biedenkopf, *op cit*, p201ff.

(21) Even Biedenkopf's teacher Eucken must have reached his position as a consequence of other dimensions than his national economic theory for the 'social market economy'. Why, for example, did he speak out *for* a structure

which is oriented towards the highest profit, or in his generalising terminology towards "highest possible net gain", and towards continually increasing consumption? Finally he talks about the Christians of late antiquity (p221 of his major work), who "at that stage did not earn unlimited amounts, but only (wanted) to satisfy a constant and modest level of needs, in order to win time for divine services and prepare themselves for the City of God (...). Bound up with this was the idea that 'the highest possible net income' should no more be the target, but the 'best possible provision of goods' (...)" What a difference in the human image! That was not a business society! And why, under *such* auspices, should the market have compelled growth? The people were hardly exposed to competition and provided themselves continually with the same goods. Expansion comes in fact not from exchange, from the market as such, but from the need to have.

Are then the two orders, the 'Christian' order of today and the Christian order of that time identical in the light of the idea of ORDO? Couldn't it be the case that *in principle* we *cannot* win in the face of God-Nature, by striving to achieve the highest possible net gain? According to Christ at any rate the following belongs to ORDO: "You cannot serve two masters, God and Mammon". And again: "You should not build up for yourselves treasures on earth, for where your treasure is, there also is your heart". And this was already valid *before* the ecological crisis.

(22) Lao Tzu, *Tao Teh Ching*, 18th saying.

(23) Lao tzu, *Tao teh king – Das Buch vom Sinn und Leben*, translated and with a commentary by Richard Wilhelm (Düsseldorf and Köln, 1979) p16.

(24) Max Kaltenmark, *Lao tsu und der Taoismus* (Frankfurt, 1979), p91.

3. Who can stop the Apocalypse?

The News Has Arrived

Only a few years ago we had to justify ourselves for thinking about an apocalypse at all. The atom bomb seemed to belong to quite a different kind of threat – we knew in advance who was to blame and we could easily deceive ourselves about our share of responsibility for the arms race. Ecocide could be regarded as nothing more than an ideological epidemic. The indicators of the real danger of catastrophe seemed hardly worth a glance, unless to refute 'scare talk'.

A person who considered the apocalypse possible was dubbed a pessimist, even though in reality s/he is the optimist. The motif of the apocalyptic vision is the conviction that there may still be a *chance*, provided we realise that disaster is probable if we continue with our habitual life-routines. "What can serve us as a compass? The forecasted danger itself". This idea of Hans Jonas is not an adequate motivation – because we need to anticipate positive joy from a change if we are to make the effort to achieve it. Jonas talks of a 'heuristic of fear'[1]. We humans are led by fear in other matters, especially the fear which makes us avoid causing one of our everyday fuses to blow. Thus the challenge is to *reorder our fears*, so that they stand in a proper relationship to what we want to avoid.

On the Left a spurious additional anxiety was obstructing this. Many regard the subject of apocalypse as dangerous in itself. The lid of Pandora's closed Box springs open whenever the ecological crisis is recognised in its full magnitude. This crisis does not proceed from an external enemy against whom we could take aggressive action!

The very same people who painted a grim picture of the nuclear first-strike could, the next moment, behave as if taking it seriously would be in poor taste. If, in the *ecopax* movement, we fear that people could again behave badly, were we to introduce the idea of apocalypse into policy, then we are firmly stuck in the trap of our history. And then, if by a series of mini-reforms we proceed uncontroversially toward the catastrophe, the eco-dictatorship *will* come.

Meanwhile, expressing dislike of the apocalyptic argument sticks in the throat of the 'enlightened' critic, because the reality of the logic of self-extermination is making itself all too clearly felt. In recent years the social climate has drastically changed. But while the apocalyptic vision is basically optimistic, leading towards things being turned around, the mass of humanity responds in the most unconcerned fashion, saying: "Well, that's really something which nobody can prevent".

Since ancient times nearly everybody has been regarded as guiltily implicated in the apocalypse – not just the king and high priests. Even the most hard-boiled layer of blame suspects he is a participant and jointly responsible: it is thus not so easy to interpret good and bad to one's own advantage. Resistance against new understanding is rooted in dislike of a seemingly unreasonable demand to change accustomed ways of life. One can accommodate oneself to a danger, once it has been denied: it's more comfortable this way. It is for this reason that the doomster Hoimar von Ditfurth's book is a best-seller. It gives scientific and metaphysical justification to this popular feeling.

For did not the author dedicate the book to "the all too many people who still don't want to believe it" – namely, that it is a question of the terminal crisis of western civilisation, which threatens to drag us all into nothingness?! This insight has popular appeal, which is rewarding, businesswise. The strongest thing in Ditfurth's book is the first part, which says nothing new, but, as in the Dürer woodcut, brings together the riders of the apocalypse on a fixed page. It is by means of the extermination of species that he reveals to us the pace with which the decline is already proceeding. In the mirror of this we should recognise ourselves as Satanic, in terms of our effect on all other life forms.

Beyond this he sees only emergency exits, which are not really exits at all. That we do not use them, which he complains about, is insufficient to prove that nothing can be done. He regards, for example, the reorganisation of arms to serve only defensive purposes as being an open barn-door, but it might just as well be a tiny back-door if it opens on to the same abyss. The American Star-Wars insanity of the 1980s *was* 'defensively' motivated. And it can be just the same with the application of the 'polluter pays' principle, as long as the idea of industrial mass-production remains unchallenged.

Von Ditfurth also thinks we shouldn't be so *childish* as to want unilateral military and industrial disarmament. In no way does *he* want to be taken for such a childish person! He is much more afraid of being ridiculed than of being killed by the bomb. On the other hand he is not afraid of making himself morally questionable by regarding population growth – anywhere but in Europe! – not as a symptom of evil but as the 'root of all evil'.

So the news has come that we are destroying ourselves, both accidentally and by design. At the same time it has become clear that moderate, 'mature' recommendations do not get at the pervasive psychological structures behind this destruction. Von Ditfurth offers a new method of dealing with this news. He says that human beings are totally incapable of saving themselves because they are defective.

The brainy animal has created for itself an environment to which its genotype is not adapted. Apparently our genetic 'loading' means that our brain only functions in a correct fashion in the *natural* environment, and it doesn't suit us to leave the natural world behind and climb into a space-capsule. Herr von Ditfurth considers it abnormal that while we fail as helpers in the environmental process, we also want to play the role of the computer-assisted good Lord. It never occurs to him that we could cut back our ambitions to an area and scale which we are fully equipped to handle.

He sees us foundering because we are not able to master the work of our heads and hands, work which we have made into our idols. Lost in the labyrinth of knowledge, he does not question the origin of the calamity, comprehensible as it is: what is really driving us to make things which assert themselves against us? The fault cannot lie in our cellular equipment, which we share with the animals, if fear of death seems to be leading us to embrace death.

What nonsense to assume that it is the organs of perception that are our real problem, rather than the hubris which brings us not to make good use of them, and the falsity with which we drive ourselves into the future. The westerner regards Buddha as defeatist because, after examining the human condition, he came to the conclusion that we should renounce the extent to which we affect the external world. But ultimately it is our eager activism which is much more defeatist: we don't *want* to do anything about all those things we have done.

Hope, Because We Are It

There are situations in which one is at the mercy of everything, in which one is completely dependent on luck and grace – birth, death, and a number of others. Ice ages, floods, earthquakes, volcanic eruptions – the forces of nature do not need any help from us, but they are getting it in this technical modern age, since many of the catastrophes are made by us. But war, hunger and the poisoning of the environment have nothing to do with what, from our narrow perspective, appears to be the arbitrariness of nature, let alone the arbitrariness of our own nature. It clearly has to do with the *natural law* with which our species began, with its capacity for conscious mastery of the world, and its deficiency in self-control.

I refer to this inherent law-abidingness when I speak of a *logic of self-*

extermination and a *logic of salvation*. These things need be understood by the people who have assumed leadership in the blind alley of mega-technical civilisation.

Even so, Germany is one of the first countries in which the majority has opened itself to the insight which Hiroshima revealed: not only that we *could* wipe ourselves out, but also that we're *doing* it. *At least subliminally, most people know this.*

And yet we carry on living just as we have been doing. While we are not behaving with free will, we are not behaving against our own will: that is, we are behaving as if we *wanted* to wipe ourselves out. As always, we are trapped in our habits and fears, in the inertia of our minds and hearts. Over many years we have fashioned an external prison out of the diffuse material of these habits and fears, a great heap of external constraints and dependencies, into 'material constraints' which say to us: "you can't behave any other way!".

Many object to this 'we' talk. They persist in claiming to have found the chief sinners in the corridors of power, and their accomplices among dim-witted neighbours and colleagues. Our eyes are still mirrors of the world, not mirrors of the soul. We direct our senses inward more rarely than ever (the new movement for meditation is barely beginning). We see causes only on the outside. It is others who are aggressive and threatening. All we have to do is defend ourselves. It is those 'above' who are the militarists and the destroyers of the environment.

The safety-needs and comfort-needs which *we* have, these are *due* to us. We readily conceal the fact that we still agree with Caesar, who said "if you want peace, prepare for war". To build defences is a matter of course. And in truth the automobile is no longer a luxury. Goethe going to Italy in his carriage, *that* was luxury!

The peace movement and the Greens meanwhile have paled into insignificance: the peace movement has not said that we should stop defending ourselves and thinking in terms of enemy-images, but only that for our safety we need *more reasonable* armaments. And the Greens, while they have engendered much environmental awareness, have certainly not been able to offer an alternative, because they have not dared to say that survival with the industrial system is impossible. We have become habituated to horror stories. With surprising speed politicians have learnt to find environmental protection enormously important, but only up to the extent that the voter has also done so.

If things carry on as they are now, in another generation we shall have finished our work of converting such nations as Germany into one single city. But will we be unable to conceal from ourselves that we must begin primarily with ourselves – not just with arms, or 'arms conversion'? Shouldn't we really also be able to *save* ourselves, if we want to?

Would we really have to have these governments, these military blocs, these lethal industries, if we really didn't want them? Who is it really who has poisoned earth, water and air? 'Them' alone? The Rhine is dying because no resolve arises in *us* to have a revolutionary *ecological* government, not to speak of an eco-pacifistic revolution in our daily lives – for which we would have to put ourselves under pressure. But we still have quite different worries, such as maintaining our involvement in those things which occupy the time in our daily lives. We have set ourselves up psychologically so that all necessary actions and self-limitations will repudiate just the freedom we are talking about.

Perhaps the most hopeful thing in this drugged atmosphere in which we are relentlessly driving on, is that we no longer have the escape of making others responsible. A glimpse: still higher than Hoimar von Ditfurth's book on the best-seller list was the *Ganz Unten*[2] report. It brought the message that it is not the fault of Turkish 'guest-workers' if the conflict between 'work and environment' gets continually worse. [Wallraff, a reporter, worked for a time disguised as a Turk, and described his experiences in this book, *Right at the Bottom*. – tr.] This is new in Germany: no dagger thrust, no Treaty of Versailles, no Jews to blame, not even 'the Russian' as a real threat – we ourselves really are the trouble.

Perhaps the reason we haven't yet found a *will to salvation* in ourselves is that we are confronted by an impossible tangle which we can't unravel. The logic of the ecological crisis must become very clear in our awareness and must speak to us irresistibly: "There is no point from which you cannot be seen. You must alter your life" – as in Rilke's 'archaic torso of Apollo'[3].

So far as I understand it, *we can remove the sentence hanging over us only when we are ready to acknowledge our self-annihilating practices, in full recognition of their closeness to our most intimate being. When enough of us risk doing this, we will create the necessary 'critical mass' for a social chain-reaction. Then, the energies we are now investing in catastrophe could save us.*

Anthropological Revolution
Never mind the conservative revolution: what we really need is an *anthropological revolution*, a jump in the evolution of the human spirit. This has already started, preliminary notice of it having been given in the 'axial age' of Buddha, Lao Tzu, Plato, Christ and Mohammed. By an anthropological revolution is meant the grounding anew of society on the basis of powers of consciousness which up to now are not revealed or unfolded.

As the result of a social evolution based on ego-competition, we have reached a point at which natural evolution threatens to go wrong. Yet our institutions are structures erected to benefit ourselves at the cost of the whole. If this is the case, then we should not ask what sort of institutions would match our natures – the ones we already have match our natures all too well! Only after a jump into a new constitution will humans create and support institutions which correspond to human nature in a wider sense, in that they also pay attention to humanity's place in nature as a whole.

Biedenkopf writes that we are free to choose our institutions. In what sense? We are certainly not the first to have this freedom. So why has a non-antagonistic constitution never been chosen? Further, he is not talking about the freedom of each individual so much as the freedom of the political actors to offer something to all the others, to set something up. For a great deal would have to change in each individual before the mass of individuals could meaningfully choose institutions.

Meanwhile, for Biedenkopf, the 'nationally-constituted society' shall mobilise the 'political energy' for a reorganisation[4]. Social structures are human creations "to the extent that they are shaped by justice, law, or the power of the state – that is, by the experts in these fields". To *these* people then falls the task of making clear to everybody, that it "is not *human beings* who must change, but the social and political structures which we have created for ourselves"[5].

People can remain in their subordinate position! The initiative comes from the constituted political realm. Yet the whole structure of this realm is based on the logic of expansion. I will not dispute the fact that *some* of the initiative must come from this realm. Not *all* the energy invested there functions in conformity to the overall pattern. Nevertheless it is a very clear, very European contrast between 'inner' and 'outer': "It's not the people, but their arrangements".

In this way 'damage-limiters' can distance themselves from the 'educate the people' moral sermon of structural conservatives. It is right that structures take their form from people, and should not continually make excessive moral demands. I endorse the alternative "morality of renunciation or structural renewing of society"[6] for the reason that renunciation-motivated small sacrifices lead towards a necessary order of size. We must bring about a degree of defoliation, crumbling and thinning – on ourselves.

But doesn't the 'structural renewal of society' demand *more* subjective readiness for a Turn-about than the appeal to a morality of renunciation? There is no *internal* way in which a new decision about first principles could be wrung from a conventional party and the bureaucratic apparatus. Here are entrenched those resistances which are otherwise distributed diffusely throughout society: when necessary they can summon all the forces of social inertia behind them. Unless state-actors and the *public* mutually fire each other up, all reform will be a dull performance, and the matador will contract tuberculosis from the stage-scenery dust. Envious competitors for power need only put on a show of revolt by the subordinate and the stupid, and for this people really don't need to change.

All the forces with which we have to reckon are forces of *consciousness*. Institutions are objectivised forces of consciousness, congealed part-aspects of our cultural existence. We *always* have to deal with people, even when we want to produce change through re-adapting institutions. Only in this case we deal with people more indirectly. It is with our *own* consciousness as reformers that we must deal, since we want to dig a new channel for the consciousness of others.

The thesis that it is institutions which have to change, not people, is firstly a consequence of the tacitly-pessimistic assumption that people would not themselves be able to change. Secondly this thesis entails a programme of revolution from above, and touches exactly that aspect of the conservative revolution which I have earlier referred to as being especially German.

This *aspect* will be indispensable. But if it predominates we do not get beyond an eco-Bismarck. The revolution will only be a further structural adaptation *within* the exterministic European project; it will remain a 'Green' Restoration of the old powers.

So where do we make a start? Do we begin the re-ordering with the state and law, or, in accord with our *priority*, with the self-changing individual? Do we start with the dead or with the living spirit?

To confront the ecological crisis – something human nature is equipped to do, but nevertheless requires that it be fitted and anchored into the cosmic order – requires a critical approach to human ways of behaving. From a social point of view these ways are altogether 'natural', but in the larger context they are opposed to nature. In the end, for example, the competition among researchers in a military laboratory to find the most devilish idea for annihilation is altogether natural.

Is it not the foundation-stone of the structural-conservative world-picture to reckon with human beings only 'as they are', and not 'as they were intended to be'? The proposal that law, not the state, is the centre-piece of society *can* only succeed as an aspect of a general revolution in consciousness. Indirectly, Biedenkopf confirms this himself:

Even today it is hard for our thinking to assume that there can be a natural and legal order in which the human being develops freely. The connection between order *and* state, *that is between* order *and* command, *is deeply anchored in our thought*[7].

As long as this subordination holds, the finest of institutional reforms will simply modernise the ruling class. Such reform can alter nothing of the basic structural violence which lies in our Megamachine, in our dependence on the supply-system. One and the same governmental action can have a very different or opposite meaning, if it was initiated from above, or actively wanted by the population.

In a power-determined society almost everybody would like to be a monopolist. It needs a conscious decision, a swimming against the stream, if one is not to be taken in by the pull and push along the scale of power-powerlessness. We are driven to become 'capitalists of power', whatever the coinage in which the accumulation takes place. Economics, science and politics are just the predominant arenas of struggle. Here we bump up finally against the eternal circle in which the ordo-liberal argument is trapped. Power is there, but it shall not work in the manner which lies in *its* 'order', *its* being. Squaring the circle.

Isn't it obvious that the best way to approach order, or ordering, is with an examination of the *power* question? Not in the usual sense of the flux of power between one monopolist and another, but in the sense of the dissolving of *power obsessions*, setting up an order which will remove them and block them at birth. For once power is present in concentration, it is of little avail to attack it with laws or a hundred policemen. If we are unsuccessful in building a society which can domesticate and educate the will-to-power, then everything will carry on as before and all the old problems will return.

Biedenkopf counts on the churches, on Christianity. But why not the *person* who is capable of salvation? If it is true that Christ lived and was a man, then we have at least an indication that the 'anthropological revolution' is possible, as the Catholic liberation-theologian Johann Baptist Metz[8] named it in the context of Marcuse, and Christologically interpreted it. In our reflections about ORDO we should begin, not with the fall of Adam and Eve, but with the symbol of the resurrected Christ, which the Holy Ghost gives to *all* humans.

In terms of church history, this was the real Reformation: Martin Luther, with his fixation on original sin and authority, missed it completely. Last chance for an established Christianity?! I'm sceptical. As far as I can see, churches are as little capable of such a transformation as states. But the idea, coming for example from Joachim di Fiore, Francis of Assisi and Master Eckhart, achieves once again meaningful content, both within and without, in Christian or foreign garb.

We cannot save ourselves with normal behaviour and 'sound popular instincts'. The reactions triggered by terrorists, by the Falkland Islands war, the Gulf War or the bombing of Libya demonstrate such instincts: these behaviour-potentials for fear and resentment, available for recall, aggression and self-distraction, are only waiting for an occasion, or any designated enemy. We are exploitable by every manipulation of our inner super-powers, however fraudulent. This shows humanity to be prisoner of a psychological mechanism which not only makes a Turn-around unlikely, but even blocks simple understanding.

Sages, prophets, illuminati and saints have shown for 2,500 years that humans can lift themselves above this style of being and mode of consciousness. I don't suggest that this is about to happen in a wide-spread fashion – nobody knows what is going to happen. But there is no other possibility for salvation except to jump into a more aware mode of being-in-the-world, and to behave in accordance with it. So many questions could become answerable, if only we make the inner resolve that they *must* be answered. The path to the answer is our own trans-formation. We could resolve to overcome a number of disorders of human nature, hitherto regarded as incurable – not just second-hand, through a Christ or a Buddha.

Ever-stronger alienation from the primal source of life is the fate of the civilised human. In *Prologue in Heaven* Goethe has the Lord say to Mephistopheles, as he leaves the task of seducing Faust to Mephi-stopheles' discretion, "Divert this spirit from its primal source"[9]. Even less than Faust do we reach the point at which the Spirit of the Whole, or the Spirit of the Earth, speaks to us. We rarely achieve happiness-of-being or at-oneness with the whole of existence. This foundering in the attempt to find our way back through our activities, drives us to pseudo-magic, to the accumulation of power and money, and to the exchanging of substances with nature, instead of self-development. The method of Mephistopheles: "Dust shall he eat, and with pleasure".

Thus the ecological crisis is one of the last opportunities, but also the greatest, for achieving a new human articulation. Until now even radical minorities of the most various kinds have hardly earnestly attempted this. Now things are getting serious. Not just the danger, but also the lack of compensatory offers could drive us forward. The linking back to the original source would organisationally hinder us from destroying the earth. We don't need to control things from the outside, which is unlikely to be crowned with success, but we would have the regulator within us, in accord with that divine trust: "a good person in dark distress is well aware of the right path".

No Higher Being Is going to save us – so what Is Spirituality?

The word *salvation* stands in twilight. Although the verb 'to save' indicates activity, *salvation* is more readily associated with the passive meaning of *being saved*. A *saviour* is a person who acts on behalf of other people or other things. Salvation customarily has a passive object. In the conventional religious context, and often in the political one, the saviour comes from above, a redeemer to creatures who can't help themselves, and are dependent on him. The descendants of Alexander the Great in Egypt frequently appended to their names the title 'Soter', which means 'saviour'; and some took just this name alone. It was an era of addiction to salvation.

Until our century we have repeatedly experienced how much heroes and saviours, to whom we ourselves have gladly turned for deliverance, get in the way when they have the assignment of liberators. Especially heroes, who must prove themselves to the world, belong to the same logic from which they would deliver us. Basic to the apocalyptic perspective of civilisation is both the heroic ego and the mechanism of corruption, which will not stop working unless every ego gets free from its *cramp*, from its *compulsion to pursue pleasure*. With this goes the requirement that we stop projecting expectations onto a leader – we then no longer have to hold ourselves to expectations.

If we avoid the half-baked atheism which throws the baby away with the bath water, there remains what revolutionaries sang about in their 'International':

> *No Higher Being will save us,*
> *No God, no Caesar, no Tribune.*
> *To redeem ourselves from misery*
> *Is something which only we can do.*

In view of the ecological crisis we need to take back into ourselves all these symbolic forces. We need to internalise the sovereignty which confronts us in these symbolic figures. Then the symbols themselves – God, Caesar, Tribune, Master – can be helpful personal forces. The urge to reject them arises because of the fear of becoming dependent on them as fetishes.

Wilhelm Reich said a great deal about this in his *Murder of Christ*; how an unhealthy system of mutual blocking arises between a person who attracts the salvation-expectations of submissive souls, and these souls themselves. As Christianity arose, collectivistic behaviour-structures were still dominant, and the collective ego was stronger than the individual one. The masters and prophets of the axial time from Buddha until Christ were very advanced in individuation. The less individualistic their self-understanding was, the more they felt themselves socially responsible, so the more they fell into the role of the mass-leader – a role in which they were bound to come to grief, because they brought about a new dependency.

We should not, on account of our relatively powerless church, let ourselves be prevented from dealing uninhibitedly with religious phenomena. Representations of God have never been more than aids to the creating and stabilising of attitudes to the relation between ego and human world, and between human world and nature. The ultimate source of religious (not ecclesiastical) authority has always been a joyous inner encounter with the pre-personal and trans-personal ground of existence, from which we differentiate into our separateness and individuality.

What does *spiritual* mean? It can mean either mental [in German *geistig*] or spiritual [*geistlich*], but it is helpful to distinguish between the two. Together with body (sensation) and soul (feeling), mind (thinking) is a given and *intrinsic* part of being human, but in its basic existence it does not yet have a spiritual accent. Thought and the application of understanding is a mental, not yet a spiritual, activity. Spirituality only occurs in the case of "the mind which is aware of itself" (John Eccles[10]), which then usually experiences itself as ego or self, not only in its uniqueness as this particular consciousness, but also as an instance of consciousness as a whole.

All humans have the capacity for spirituality. To actualise it requires that we make use of our central nervous system as a unified organic whole. It is a function of whole communication and communion with the world, with the not-I, with the deep structure of universal life. It is the quality of complex, uninhibited, living contact beyond the boundaries of the ego.

The medium of spirituality is *intuition*, the integrating function of the right cerebral hemisphere. In decisive moments of our lives, it is from here that our experience of the world must come, if we are to experience ourselves as unified with the whole. If the left hemisphere, dominated by analytical reason and its cultural externalisations, continually takes charge, the intuitive mode of integration into the world-whole will be subordinate and under-developed.

This goes against the original structure of our psychological control system: the archaic mind (spirit) *is* spiritually guided, and it is still the magical and mythical spirit, even though increasingly hemmed in. Except that the modern mental-rational mind blocks connections back to it, overthrowing its leadership instead of updating and qualifying it. Only in exceptional cases, such as that of Einstein, does the Great Integration succeed.

Our ego regards itself as an objective observer standing opposite the world and explicitly separated from it. It is an abstract authority which has agreed with itself that spiritual components must exist unacknowledged. Science, in the positivistic sense, always approaches its object from outside, but spirit works invisibly from within. It is the leading light and pattern of inner self-activity in the whole of evolution.

If now the *human* spirit self-consciously and reflexively makes contact with this guiding aspect of the universe, it is straight off and *intrinsically* in its element, however much it places itself 'opposite'. Within it are the pattern-, information-, organisation- and structure-aspects of the Cosmos, a written-in law-abidingness and order-function which is not only given, but also conscious. From the objective mind (of cosmic intelligence) to the subjective, self-conscious human mind, consciousness completes something like a circular track, so that it seems to get further from its origin and to tread in alien opposition to it, the nearer it gets back home to it.

For the intellect it may seem, right up to the end, like the fable in which Achilles cannot catch up with the tortoise. But beyond this embarrassment, for those who can break through the wall erected by alienated understanding and its social safeguards, reality will again become self-evident: that our psyche is part of an all-embracing field of consciousness, so that differences and oppositions between the single drop and the whole ocean fall away. Or, as Meister Eckhart said, there is *within* our soul a crossing-point between self and universe, a 'little spark', a 'municipality', where the ultimate ground of God or nature and that of the soul are one and the same. How could it be different, if the Cosmos is a unity?

It makes no great difference whether we are 'materialistic' or 'idealistic' *monists* – that is, people who are convinced of the unity of the world. Engels said that the unity of the world consists in its materiality. In this he unhappily raises into prominence the inertia aspect of the whole, and logically compels us to admit that the psyche also is material. And Lenin's concept of 'objective reality' is even more neutral. 'Pure spirit' would not exist any more than 'pure matter', 'pure energy'. These are all abstractions which refer to *aspects* of the *universe*, the *one* Cosmos[11].

Mircea Eliade points out in his *History of Religious Ideas* that the *holy*, not God, is the subject-matter of these ideas: it is a permanent element of the structure of consciousness and not a past stage of its history. "Through experience of the holy, the human spirit has come to know the difference between what has revealed itself as true, powerful, significant and meaningful and the opposite – the chaotic and dangerous flux of things and their accidental and meaningless rise and fall". So this would be one of the most elementary methods for us to order the Cosmos, with respect to the needs of our species, and to reconcile the two. For arbitrary projections will be of no use to us.

We are dealing with psychic realities and their objective counterparts. When I touch upon religious things, I do so in this sense. I acknowledge no personal God the Father, and therefore obviously I don't acknowledge Christ as his son, but as a prophet, a Buddha. We can speak of the Godhead in the same sense that we speak of the Spirit of the Whole, which we share, and with which we can establish a conscious connection penetrating deep into our Origin[12].

Einstein experienced as crucial the question of whether or not the universe is friendly. I can imagine that he didn't want to see this question answered analytically. If we shoot it up with rockets it can't be friendly. The question can only be answered normatively: we must move ourselves into the position of friendliness, and that means joyousness. We must exert ourselves with grace, if only to survive. We must make life so satisfying that we can stop being warriors. We must carry out some *preliminary work* in psychological demilitarising, and we mustn't idealise the fighting aspects of existence in a deep cultural revolution.

At the moment two immediate, diametrically-opposed points of departure toward spirituality are struggling, in each of us. In our tradition, an ascetic-restrictive, *Apollonian* attitude dominates, and gives rise to ethics of responsibility and frugality. The conservative ecological posture doesn't understand that it is adopting a major part of this very same world view, internalised since the time of the Old Testament, which has led to exterministic accumulation and cultural cruelty. The other point of departure is hedonistic and friendly to the body, directed in *Dyonisian* manner towards the abundance of life, corresponding to an elysian ethic of a well-disposed, happy consciousness: lovers readily and spontaneously practice the 'golden rule', not to do unto others what you would not have done to yourself.

Spirituality is re-emerging today as a body-friendly discipline, and this means that we want to base our integration into the world-whole upon the wisdom of our *whole* organisms, not merely on the intellectual function, which has its centre of gravity in the left cerebral hemisphere. Naturally, intelligence is itself a spiritual component, but it has become the servant of its own alienation. Materialism means the defeat of living work and living spirit. Up to now it has proven useless to use philosophical reason as a corrective for an intelligence fallen victim to quantity, because discursive thought is altogether too bloodless and remote from *Eros*. It wants to sublimate all sensuality to the level of the rational, scientific ego.

It is true that the human organism has its focus in the large brain – we are the brain-animal. For this reason our structural balance is at the same time basically endangered. The greatest risk is the desire to subordinate the human body to the brain, with the notion that it is 'ordered in relation to' the mind-organ. From the evolutionary point of view our precarious short-term specialisation as brain-animal has need of a counter-balance. I find significant what Dürckheim learned in Zen: that we can only avoid being thrown out of balance by the head if we have our centre of gravity in the middle of the body, in the *Hara*. It is not a question of thinking less, or in a more concentrated and clearer fashion, but of our connection back to the bodily centre and our grounding in the earth.

Pure thinking makes us melancholy because the truth it stores up for us is dead. It tends to bring gloom and depression to the whole of the psyche; in its one-sidedness it is unavoidably an unhappy companion. If our cognitive capacities do not constitute a bottleneck, thought no longer functions to enlighten us. The problem for us is *how* in future we shall employ our powers of abstraction, and it demands a culturally-binding solution.

All cultures have religious foundations and are rooted in the solution of basic human problems. For this reason no new culture can be built on the idea that religion is a 'private matter'. This is a principle which emerged from the collapse of Christianity in the late Middle Ages, and which is understandable in this context. What a misunderstanding, to see the 'freedom of the children of God' threatened if this bourgeois-individualistic principle of ultimate existential abandonment is questioned!

In view of the seductive and extortionate pull which existing circumstances exert on the solitary psyche, salvation depends on those who possess enough strength and individuality to withdraw, and to base their attitude on a substance within the self not exhausted by adaptation and fitting in. The masses of atomised, non-autonomous individuals who desire nothing more than to survive and cope and enjoy their remaining days, are *unable* to find a way out. Self-discovery is the necessary precondition for emancipating oneself from the Mega-machine, and this attempt to find oneself unavoidably leads to an experience of communion around which a new culture can crystallise. Every human genotype is unique, something which 'western' culture has brought out more clearly than any other. Yet we live in the know-ledge that we are all one – which is in no way anxiety-provoking, but rather a cause of happiness.

For this reason the politics of *salvation* does not begin with *politics* in the usual sense, but with the practice of a dogma-free meditation which will be friendly to the body, liberating to feelings, and schooling to thought. New cultures have always emerged from such inner spaces in which subjectivity assumes a *pattern*, because of which there should be salvation – in which spheres of life arrange themselves, in time to display the pattern themselves in ethical and material matters.

In the course of history there have often been leaps in consciousness.

Yet in each case the preparation took time, and we have no way of knowing how much time. For this reason something must always be done to accommodate the *delay*, the *days of grace*. It is one thing to seek the 'standpoint of the Godhead' in meditation, where the distinction between good and evil is not only inapplicable, but is also seen as one of the causes of evil. Yet it is part of reality that the power-complex which pushes toward extermination approaches this same Godhead.

Insofar as a million Buddhas are unable to meditate away the massive momentum resident in the movement of the Megamachine, we can't disregard politics. The Aztecs sent their strongest and most effective medicine men to stop Cortez. Their powers bounced off the western ego of this hero. In the concrete honeycombs of the Megamachine, in its Pentagon, its bank skyscrapers and its laboratories, is concealed a plenitude of people with the armoured hearts of the Conquistador. As long as even a third of the personnel of the Megamachine continue to do what they have been doing up to now, the collapse is certain, however the rest of the population spend their time.

Groupings, 'good guys' and 'bad guys', although fortunately not so rigidly separated as they might imply, really exist in every heart. It must and will result in a phantom battle, not *in front of* police-defended gates, but *within* in the nodal points of research and production, management and business, education and politics, dependent on the psychological power-relations in society. In order to reach the ecological turning-point, necessary just for the lifting of the death sentence, the *ecopax* movement must concern itself with the state, at the institutional level.

It is a question of *how*, not of *whether*.

The answer to the question of how will vary greatly, depending on whether or not we start with the deep structure of our ecological crisis, and see it as a dilemma rooted in the *design of our civilisation*. Up to now we have always used crude and direct methods – rockets, nuclear power stations, dioxin – which sustain the dominant structures and lead too readily to confrontation along the old fronts. Yet this also has achieved more than *just* an institutional hardening up.

Even so the shift in thinking can only spread through *persons*, not functionaries. Only human beings who exert themselves and develop a morally partisan awareness (not warlike) can, when such an hour comes, give a new direction to the regular structure, if the consensus for it has been subliminally prepared – as for example in the former Czechoslovakia in 1967-68 and 1989.

NOTES

(1) Hans Jonas, *Das Prinzip der Verantwörtung* (Frankfurt, 1979), p7f.

(2) Günter Wallraff, *Ganz Unten* (Köln: Kiepenheuer und Witsch, 1985).

(3) Rainer Maria Rilke, *Werke, Auswahl in zwei Banden* (Leipzig, 1957); Vol 1, *Gedichte*, p194.

(4) Biedenkopf, *op cit*, p47.

(5) *Ibid*, p48.

(6) *Ibid*, p191.

(7) *Ibid*, p107.

(8) Johann Baptist Metz, *Unterbrechungen*, (Gütersloh: 1981), p34.

(9) Tr: George Madison Priest, *Britannica Great Books*, v47.

(10) John C Eccles and Hans Zier, *Gehirn und Geist*, (München, Zürich: 1980).

(11) *Materialism* versus *idealism* is a most highly conditioned battlefield (conditioned by the abstractionistic phase of development of intelligence). Marx's historical materialism has particularly turned itself against the unconscious ego or interest-shy subjectivistic insanity of the psyche. From the point of view of humans, whose 'top-heaviness' is an even more basic given fact than is the risk bound up with it, it is certainly more sensible to see the unity of the world in its spirituality, that is to bring into prominence the cybernetic or intelligence aspect of the universe. For Marx too, change in consciousness preceded change in the world; and how could Lenin, in spite of his tendency to slip back into a dualistic and mechanistic world-view, make precisely 'awareness versus spontaneity' (the latter alias inertia, structural-conservative hold-out of spirit) the pivot, as soon as it was a question of forming the Party as an instrument of intervention?!
Historical materialism is a part-truth, and is shut up in itself particularly because it does not take *human beings* with their body-soul-spirit unity as the tectonically important 'most material' factor lying behind all historical achievement. If we put the emphasis on its alienated forms – forces and conditions of production – , we subordinate consciousness to the factors of inertia. It is the dilemma of Marxism and quite specially of its slipping into the logic of capital, that it sees this alienation of artificiality, which radically stultifies us, as basic, and then looks for ways to overcome it. So *de facto* it hasn't brought it to Lucifer. The attitude of rebellion was predetermined to get bogged down in the 'trade union' workers' movement.

(12) Ken Wilber, in the 14th chapter of his *Halbzeit der Evolution* [literally 'Half Time of Evolution' – a translation of his *Up From Eden, A Transpersonal View of Human Evolution* (Boulder: Shambhala, 1983) – tr.] gives a closer survey of the stages of development – from the psychic phenomena of Shamanism through goddesses and gods to Goddess and God, and finally beyond these personifications to the Godhead as eternal ground of the universe – in which for us this intuitive totality can be experienced, if we turn our sensibilities inward.

Part Two:

THE LOGIC OF
SELF-EXTERMINATION

4. The Machinery of the Rationalistic Demon

History is Psychodynamics

How can we make the motor of the Megamachine stop of its own accord? A constraining order operating from outside cannot stop material expansion – at best it can only slow it down. What sort of forces carry the capacity for cultural and institutional renewal, and how can we imagine them taking shape on a social terrain so heavily over-occupied?

These are the two intimately-related questions which remain open after Part I. Here in Part II I shall not yet get down to a direct search for answers, because the cogency of the answer cannot be seen until the whole problem is fully understood. As long as we have not followed material expansion back to its ultimate roots in the human condition, and have not seen the social terrain of a Turn-around from *there*, we will only be able to think of short-circuited, restrictive and repressive solutions. For this reason it is not my intention to deal with the above-mentioned questions – how we could *exercise self-limitation* and how we could *institutionalise* it – until we deal with the *politics* of salvation later in the book.

For the moment my theme is the *logic* of self-extermination. I want to deal with the context of expansionism-exterminism, and to expose their deep formation. If the things we can do are to look plausible, the analysis I propose is necessary.

We are not only *captured* but also *biased* by our exterministic civilisation, in spite of all our efforts to avert the evil. It is possible to be trapped in the affairs of the dragon during the greater part of our activities and reflections, even if we are not employed in weapons production, or even if we are unemployed. For example, resources for life-maintenance, and to sustain a desirable minimum standard of living, would rapidly become scarce should the Metropolis dispense with its weapons.

The more tightly the horsemen of the apocalypse hang round our necks, the more we are inclined to plunge into panic activities, reminiscent of locking the stable door after the horse has bolted. But the despair which sooner or later overtakes us is healthy. As soon as possible we ought to be asking what is inadequate and why, what won't work at all, and what is counterproductive and speeding up the journey to Hell.

In his theses on the philosophy of history Walter Benjamin relates this bad dream:

> *There is a picture by Klee called* Angelus Novus. *It depicts an angel who looks as if he were in the act of getting away from something at which he is staring. His eyes are wide open, his mouth agape, and his wings stretched wide.*
>
> *The angel of history must look just like this, his face turned to the past. Where a chain of occurrences appears before us, there he sees a single catastrophe which heaps up pile upon pile of ruins, thrusting them up to his feet. He would love to linger, wake up the dead, and repair the damage. But a storm is blowing up from paradise which has caught in his wings, and is so strong that he can't close them again. This storm is driving remorselessly into the future to which he has his back turned, while the heap of ruins before him mounts up to heaven. This storm is what we call progress*[1].

The human being is not just this angel, driven from paradise. It is he also who is heaping up the ruins, he who makes the storm. Even the dear God, who blows him out of paradise, also sits within him. *History is psychodynamics.*

The logic of self-extermination is a deformity of the human soul. Our suicidal means, our technical and social structures are not natural in basis. Concrete is not material in the sense that rock is. It is only in *culture* where we fail, and culture is a *second* nature created by us. It is the part of our human and psychic existence which still haunts us.

Empirically it is all too true that *being*, especially *social being*, determines our consciousness; that we are a construct of these conditions, as Marx once taught. This is the truth of our downfall. This is the framework of the logic of self-extermination. It teaches us to say Yes to that dialectic of forces and conditions of production that should have given us the material basis of freedom, but which instead has brought us the Megamachine. The material process of life, the practice of making things, this heaping up of wreckage, which we allow ever more closely to determine our existence, is the spiral of death. This human being, with this interest in material things as the core of his material existence, is lost.

Yet when we let ourselves be seduced into taking all the material symptoms for the thing itself, we experience only *how* we are destroying *Gaia*, the life-carrying layer of the earth and her atmospheric covering.

But *why*? If we don't understand that, we apply our technology, pregnant with death, with merely technically grounded corrections for any errors.

Did anybody not suspect that the cause behind the causes must be connected with an ambivalence in our natural constitution, and the social psyche and organisation that corresponds with it?

The truth is annoyingly simple, and has been repeatedly stated by sages, prophets and poets, and chewed over by pessimistic conservatives and the voice of the people, so that we don't trust ourselves to accept it – all the more because we fear the consequences. Consequences which are not dealt with in the solutions of any traditional political party, where earlier values have always conditioned contemporary ones. The ecological crisis is a sickness of the human spirit, of our collective psychodynamics.

Luise Rinser, in her diary *Singing in the Dark*, takes as her point of departure a passage from Rilke's *Duineser Elegien*, raising the 'scary question' whether our 'ecological work' is not a misunderstanding; whether in our attempt to save material things we are not "standing stationary on the threshold, blindfolded". Naturally we must now save and protect material things – but our knowledge that they are in trouble is the result of feedback information. We must look fate in the eye ourselves, at the impulses and purposes with which we possess and use the world.

Ostensibly the purpose of guided nuclear missiles is the destruction of the 'hardened' targets on the other side. This lies quite a distance from a whole cascade of ever deeper and more all-embracing claims concerned with world domination. But why do people and their associations fight over such goals and purposes? For what original and basic need is this necessary? Perhaps for food, clothing and shelter?

True, we have created an economic order in which, apparently, we can only go for the maximum possible profit if we are not to be in danger of losing our whole investment. But why have we set it up this way? There are many out there who lose out in the total game. Here in Germany, because of the events of 1945, an especially large number of 'sharks' originate in the lower classes, in the people. If there are profiteers, it is because there is capitalism.

But earlier the profiteers, who in those days were civilisation-building pioneers, established capitalism as a finally-discovered method of production suited to unlimited monopoly.

> *The man must go out*
> *Into hostile life,*
> *Must do and strive*

And plant and work,
Finagle and grab,
And bet and weigh,
To capture joy.
Alongside flows the endless gift,
The warehouse fills with precious wares,
The rooms extend, the house grows large.
And within, in charge,
The modest wife... [2]

In short, we must seek fate within ourselves, without respecting our noblest characteristic, that Faustian insatiability and hungering after the unattainable. Lewis Mumford has said about our industrial Mega-machine:

> *The human insufficiency of that system has grown in direct proportion to its technical efficiency, while its present threat to all organic life on this planet turns out to be the ultimate irony of its unqualified successes in* mastering all the forces of nature – except those demonic and irrational forces within man which have unbalanced the technological mind[3].

Up to now, even the *ecopax* movement has not faced up to this. It is, however, the basic question, that which in the end is meant by the *logic of self-extermination*.

Obviously this rationalistic demon functions in a way which is anything but rational. Only means and procedures considered singly are rational, not the motives in using them. 'Demon' after all signifies a partial force, which asserts itself against the whole and then becomes a dysfunctional destiny. In this sense the whole of western science and technology is demonic, from its innermost energetic thrust.

Every scientist, technician and businessman is aware of this demon, which is really the driving force in him, even though on the surface his concern is with knowledge, construction or money-making. But to *recognise* something is not to *know* it.

In this Part II, going from the level of exterministic symptoms downwards, I want to emphasise five more structures, that is six altogether, which lie under each other in the logic of self-extermination. As in the case of geological formations, it is a thrust from below which builds them up. Each higher stratum is an expression, a modulation, a specialisation, a result of transformation, of the ones below. Collectively they are the machinery of the spiral of death, the machinery of the rationalistic demon.

As I have said it primarily represents a subjective force, a pattern of consciousness. That it manifests itself in a social form and then in a technical form is secondary. This machinery is on the one hand history, but on the other hand its elements are present in the here and now. That is to say every day each one of us more or less intensively lives and reproduces:

- *exterminism* – as the negative total effect of historical psycho-dynamics;
- the *industrial system* (see Chap. 5);
- the *dynamics of capital* (see Chap. 6);
- the *European cosmology* (see Chap. 7);
- the *patriarchy* (see Chap. 8).

We are nourishing the fatally-destructive tendency which, as exterminism, achieves the upper hand over the constructive tendency. We are doing this with the extraordinary powers of our species for which, following Christopher Caudwell, I use the expression *genotype*, another word for the 'human condition' (*conditio humana*). This concept contains the idea of the individual uniqueness of each human being.

For me, the tectonics of doom, the logic of self-extermination, is accommodated by the following scheme:

Exterminism

↑

Industrial System
(megamachine)

↑

Dynamics of Capitalism

↑

European Cosmology

↑

Patriarchy

↑

Genotype
(human condition)

Or, if you want to draw it as a spiral rising upwards to a perspective of salvation, to an answer from a genotype which is itself under pressure from exterminism, it looks like this:

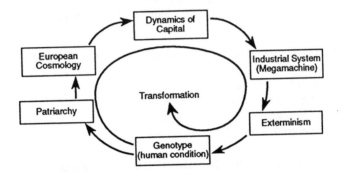

The genotype in particular, of course, always enters anew into the formative process, so that the movement is as follows:

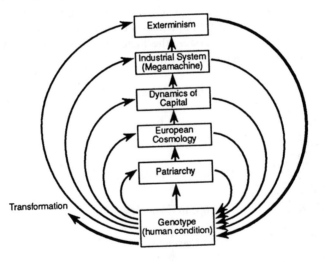

Exterminism is both the manifestation and also the essence of our destructiveness, and we must know about its architecture in depth. If at this point I retrace the causal chain, my purpose is to make us aware of the traps from which we must free ourselves. Because even when playing roles which look non-conforming on the surface, we share so many things which are taken for granted in our culture, so many basic attitudes interwoven with its decay, that the first step of liberation is to make ourselves soberly conscious of them.

Are We For or Against Life?

A friend of mine wrote to me, saying that I should not talk of the *logic* of self-extermination and of salvation, but simply about the choice between life and death. Yet this would mean eliminating just that question which particularly occupies me. Is it clear which of our opinions, feelings and ways of behaving serve *life*, and which serve *death*? Even the atom bomb was justified as protecting life. And the blacksmith making the weapons for a warlike tribe may have thought and felt in ways more bound up with death than does many a manufacturer of contemporary weapons. Whole cultures, for example the ancient Japanese or the Aztec, were more 'necrophile', more in love with death, than we are. The ancient Egyptians devoted the best part of their strength in building burial pyramids and cities of the dead, yet their culture demonstrated its viability for thousands of years!

There are attitudes today which appear to be in league with death, yet these same attitudes would at other times have been unrecognisable as death-related. That people eat meat, for example, was in archaic times altogether part of the order of nature. Only with the coming of organised hunting did this begin to disturb the balance of things, so they created taboos to mitigate the damage. At the present time we are not endangered by our cruelty, but by our consumption multiplied by size of population.

Erhard Eppler writes very correctly that it is "doubtful in the extreme whether our ancestors had an especially beneficial attitude toward nature". But: "People simply lacked the power to damage nature to such an extent that they themselves could be endangered by their actions. There were no chain saws..."[4]. Yet in themselves these chain saws have absolutely nothing to do with a subjective death wish, but on the contrary with the desire to survive at any price.

What sort of energies drive the spiral of death? Least of all the weak energies of those who, early in life beaten and trodden down, are sometimes 'dead' decades before their physical end. And the routinised carrying on with things on a low flame, which is also a form of death, explains just as little, even though the production lines depend upon those who live like this.

It is much more illuminating for us to see how geniuses – from Leonardo to Einstein – have been continually busy building the war machine. *Why*, since the beginning of civilisation, have humans invested ever more *creative life-energy* in murderous and suicidal cultural activities? Perhaps, instead of some longing for death, is it not much more likely the flight from death that is driving us toward it?

It seems to be the case that denial of life, love of death, and preoccupation with dead things appear to dominate our civilisation, if we look at it from the viewpoint of results. Erich Fromm (1977) has written a whole book about the hostility to life we unconsciously carry within ourselves. Some characters are totally dominated by cruelty and the passion to destroy. But why do they achieve key positions more frequently and more effectively than formerly? Why, with the progress of civilisation, does this potential become ever more successful?

Right at the end Erich Fromm, in praising Bertrand Russell, pointed out that his love of life, his capacity for "joy... because all is there in abundance," today is a rare quality[5]. If this is so, then no exhortations and incantations to love life will be of any use. The fountain of happiness is there, but it is covered over. Fromm says further:

> The feeling of being attracted by death is a phenomenon that is deeply rooted in a culture which is more and more ruled by bureaucratic organisations of big corporations, governments, and the military, and in which humanly produced things, apparatus, and machines play the major role. This bureaucratised industrial state has the tendency to transform human beings into things. It would like to replace nature by technical equipment, and the organic by the inorganic[6].

Indeed, from birth onward, via toys, television, school, the street, until the workplace, our lifetime is over-occupied with artificial objects. Our attention, mostly in the case of men, is turned away from living things. Measured by the tempo of our social and technical processes, the clock of life moves too slowly. Bertold Brecht states in one of his poems: "And I contemplated Nature with impatience"[7].

But: is this necrophilia and impatience a *consequence* of the Megamachine or its cause? Is not the Megamachine itself rooted in a culture which had long ago opened the sluices leading in this direction? We may look back into any earlier time we please, before technical civilisation took the upper hand. Yet it is even there that it must have begun. The self-blocking of the evolutionary process must at least have been latent there. Ethnology has discovered native American civilisations which could be an example for us now: the same Iroquois whose medicine wheel can teach us something practised the most cruel torture against their enemies.

Biophile and *necrophile*, furthering life and hostile to life – the expressions include much more than meets the eye. The Megamachine doesn't just function in a death-causing way, it *is* death-oriented. Products like the unintentionally cancer-producing formaldehyde or dioxin are more characteristic of our dilemma than the production of things deliberately intended for destruction.

Already our technical catastrophes are costing more human sacrifices than did wars up till the last century. Even automobile traffic brings about hecatombs of voluntary sacrifices. We accept the most various exterministic effects with approval. The trap of big investments, into which science, technology and capital have led us, 'compels' us to carry on, because *we* have acknowledged 'civilising' values and set them above the basic functions of life. Thus after Chernobyl no nuclear power stations were closed down, even though there is now little active consensus for them, but only a resigned toleration.

Six kilometres away from my home town of Worms stand the two blocks of the Biblis nuclear power station. With the probability attached to technical accidents, some hundreds of thousands of people here live under the threat of an inescapable catastrophe in 'zone A'. Yet Germany has a reserve capacity for generating electricity far exceeding the collective output of the nuclear power stations. Closing them down is an impossibility only legally. The only conclusion is that the overall government of super-complex industrial society is insane.

Yet the social-psychological mechanisms bound up with this insanity are only too normal. Really to stop them would require extraordinary kinds of behaviour in official political circles. And it was improbable – granted the existing structure of human consciousness and culture – that the building of nuclear bombs or power stations, or any other 'useful' technical monstrosity, could have been suppressed. At the present time genetic research and technology is also turning out to be unstoppable. It is programmed into our culture. The lobby, the interest-cartel involved, didn't create this pattern of behaviour: it simply followed existing patterns in the usual way.

From motives which have absolutely nothing to do with any 'longing for self-extermination', we keep firmly to a habitual way of doing things. This way turns out to be suicidal, although it was never meant to be. There can be no more apt example than that of smoking. Smoking didn't originate out of a desire for death, and those who smoke do not as a rule do so because they *want* to die. The addiction is simply too strong. The logic of self-extermination has nothing to do with any metaphysical mystery.

I want now to quote a Green who is *for* life, yet he, through his identification with a habitual style of life, embarks upon a course such that he can only be *against* it. The politician to whom I refer is familiar with the factors of ecological catastrophe and its real dimensions and knows how much pressure the Metropolitan model exerts on the third world.

The theme was the future of the city, the large city of Bremen. City and civilisation are synonyms. Mumford's great study of this subject shows it as one of the major aspects of the global catastrophe. According to United Nations estimates (mid-1980s), the rural population during the next 40 years will remain more or less constant at something under three billion, while the urban population will increase almost two and a half times, from 2.1 to 5.3 billion by 2025.

The stress on the earth cannot possibly let up if this trend is not reversed, because the city consumes far more per head[8]. By reference to Gilgamesh, the oldest human epic, William Irwin Thompson (1985/1) showed how the small walled-in Mesopotamian city of Uruk set humans in opposition to nature, even if only because the city makes for humans 'quite different worries'; we see this again in Socrates' alienation from nature, in the context of the Greek *polis*.

Yet Ralf Fücks said, in his introductory remarks to the opening of the Congress 'Green Future for Bremen' in 1985:

> *Before all things we should be concerned with future proposals for living and working in the city: somewhere on a scale between Rudolf Bahro's call for pulling out of the city, that ecological sink of iniquity, and the soulless science fiction visions of a completely artificial high-tech City, shining with chrome. Most of us would feel little warmth for either of these extremes. Basically, we want to have both: nature-experience in the city, the trusted quarter as neighbourhood section, solidarity of community on the one hand, and at the same time the colourful, noisy and contradictory mixture of cultures and lifestyles on the other; a heaping up of wares and services. We need space for improvisation, for own-work, for uncontrolled things – and at the same time it would be nice if the urban infrastructure, the great welfare arrangements, would function. We acknowledge the increasing alienation and isolation of people in the big city, and yet we do not want to renounce the big city as giving the opportunity for distance and anonymity[9].*

And this lies somewhere 'in between'? In this context 'nature experience in the city' and 'solidarity of community' will remain material for speeches on the part of urban culture associations. Both are seen as possible – and have been desired as long as there have been cities. None of it has anything to do with the crises of ecology and civilisation, or with a minimum of protection for the future. 'It doesn't hinder us from living as we are accustomed – and even somewhat better!' The whole congress rested on taking for granted the continuance of the city as it is and as it shall be[10].

Even in the rich Metropolis, all that has been achieved is a *surrogate* for happiness and liberation. Even so, these surrogates are experienced as great achievements. The destructive factors of individual consumption, for example the automobile and vacation tourism, are associated with freedom. The *preconditions* for general emancipation, as understood in the 19th century, have in fact been achieved. There exists – even if it is now breaking up – a welfare and social state for the great privileged minority of world history, for the lower classes of the capitalistic centre. 'Democratic industrial society', despite the gap between ideal and reality, is the best of all existing worlds, from the perspective of our immediate wishes and habits.

Since the coming of modernity we have hoped that wealth and social security for all would bring about human emancipation, through the progress of material production, science, machinery and organisation. If socialists hadn't also expected general freedom and happiness from these things, the social tensions of the 19th century would not have dissolved so extensively. The same hope exists today, in threshold third world countries whose own resources and circumstances, together with the world market, hold out a faint chance that they might catch up with the 'good life' of Washington, London, Paris or Frankfurt.

This factor of internal emancipation should not be denied. The more so since we can make it the starting point of a stock-taking and Turnaround – if we made use of the current economic position to make changes, rather than to entrench ourselves defensively in it. But the civilising process which has prevailed up to this point brutally opposes the fundamental demands of three 'peripheries', which industrial society exploits and destroys: the 'external proletariat', most people in the third world; external nature; and our own internal nature, especially its feminine side. And in spite of the consequences for physical health, Metropolitan society would be able to tolerate the alienation for quite a while yet, even though it has increased in all these areas.

The threat from nuclear militarism, the poisoning of nature and destruction of landscape outside one's own back door have, at least in Europe, been able to break through the repression. Probably the threat that the happiness of affluence could not be cashed in, and that the fullness of life could easily be militarily destroyed, is a stronger goad than the ecological crisis. Up to now at any rate the defence-reflex outweighs resentment against the price of security.

After the imperial collapse, the population of the city of Rome spontaneously dropped to a low point of 25,000 inhabitants – it had once been one million. My demand was initially nothing more than a provocative formulation directed against *identification* with the city. So the Greens were compelled to consciously acknowledge that they think in 'city of Rome' terms, because the debate in their field grew so intense that they were forced to lay their cards on the table. And behold, they are not Green! For the vast majority the big city is unquestioningly taken for granted. "We want to have both" – to have the cake and eat it.

But this caricatures itself.

I do not think that the way to dissolve untenable conurbations lies *via* such debates. The 'paved street' mentality is already fairly worn. Like the Christians in late Rome, it is possible to live in the Metropolis without identifying with it: this mainly means not letting external material compulsion determine the inner scale.

If anything in Rome interested the Christians, it was free space for the other kingdom which should come afterwards. Spiritually they worked themselves more and more free from Rome. I once said that we should practise non-engagement with the city. We should not compete over the question of an alternative city plan concerned only with a more attractive arrangement of the centre. The ecological perspective leads away from this structure, and requires not just the loosening up, but the dissolution of such conurbations, symbols of the whole industrial Mega-machine. Even Bremen is much too big. It needs to dissipate itself extensively into the surrounding region of Lower Saxony. What I mean is, it should be *conceived* in this way, at least by the 'Alternatives', who are at liberty to be interested in free space in the city. But they could also set the city aside.

NOTES

(1) Theodor W Adorno and Walter Benjamin, *Integration und Desintegration* (Hannover: 1976), p39f.

(2) Schiller, *Lied von der Glocke*.

(3) Lewis Mumford, *The Myth of the Machine, The Pentagon of Power* (New York: Harcourt Brace Jovanovich, 1970, p378.

(4) Erhard Eppler, *Wege aus der Gefahr*, Reinbek: 1981, p119f.

(5) Fromm, 1985, p48ff.

(6) *Ibid*, p54.

(7) Bertold Brecht, "An die Nachgeborenen", in *Hundert Gedichte*, p307.

(8) *Mediatus*, 4-1986, from the Starnberger Forschungsinstitut fur Friedenspolitik.

(9) Grüner basis-dienst, Heft 4/1986, p3.

(10) A little while ago I received a gift from author Ulrich Linse, a little book about the history of the ecological movement in Germany, in which by quotation he encounters another 'realist', the green-seeming Josef Huber. Linse (1986, p8) states that after the first shock of the eco-crisis "it took some time before the obvious was spoken out (in particular in the case of Huber): 'there are alternatives within the industrial society, but no alternatives to it'." But here the industrial *society* is already a social system which is *determined by and dependent upon industrialism*! So we define for ourselves the industrial alienated society as precisely one which no longer has the choice of emancipating itself from the rule of its energy and machine slaves. From the anthropological and spiritual point of view it is hard to accept that the human being would remain an intellectual functionary of the Megamachine.

5. Society as Megamachine

What Is the Industrial System?

We can give up the idea of constructing a picture of the industrial system based on the logic of self-extermination. There are always people who deny or doubt that we are really proceeding towards the waterfall, or even steering in that direction. This attitude leads to the kind of environmental protection which confines itself to dealing with specific problems at specific points – and to the pursuit of 'new social movements' (*anti*-this and *anti*-that) which germinate groups of environmental protectionists. So both sides pursue the same goals, and a ministry is duly set up. Disregarding all rear-guard actions for the saving of time by capital reflux, even industry has accepted the idea of environmental protection in this limited sense.

Everything looks very different if we add up the growing potential for danger and reduce it to a common denominator. The industrial society itself becomes the problem, and what look like avoidable dysfunctions become *symptoms* of exterminism, directly curable only with great difficulty, thanks to the self-destroying logic of industrial civilisation. These symptoms are *appearances* of a deeper-lying *level of being, level of causation*, and I call the syndrome of causes with which we have to deal, along with Lewis Mumford, the *Megamachine* – more exactly the *modern industrial* Megamachine.

The industrial system is in no way identical with the use of particular tools and machines for making work lighter and shorter. For example the mills of the Middle Ages are classed in England under 'industry,' and even today the English still sometimes call their factories 'mills'. A mill serving a couple of villages has a completely different social effect to a modern food industry, which can compel the whole agricultural economy to dance to whatever tune it chooses. The little dam for the mill-wheel still let the brook be a brook. Since ancient times there has been industry in Asia and Europe. But there was no industrial *system*, no society shaped by industrialism.

Industrialism is not primarily the power station, steel, concrete, computer and freeway, but the total social complex which Mumford called the modern Megamachine. It is above all a *power* complex which affects everything[1]. This power complex is the soul of the whole, with capital as the spider in the web, which has created for itself a national governmental superstructure infinitely different from the ideal of the liberal night-watchman state, as it was in the dreams of the bourgeois Enlightenment. Our most modest tools have become dependent components of this whole, which appears to be alien and independent of us – the more so since for the most part we can no longer use the tools with skill.

The crux of the matter does not lie in the striking extremes, intentional instruments of destruction and risky technologies, even though we must comprehend such things as signals. Life cannot stand the *basic load* which industry lays upon it. It is ultimately with the Mercedes and washing machine detergents that we do the damage, rather than with bombs, nuclear power stations and dioxin – these swords of Damocles which we have suspended above ourselves. A private dwelling full of comforts necessarily confirms the whole worldwide infrastructure – including the need for armaments, because in face of monstrous differences in standards it is a threatened luxury.

I have a few more remarks about basic load. I want to recall the inventory of Ziegler mentioned in Chapter 1, and especially his indicator of energy-use per square kilometre, which turned out to be at least ten times too big for the continued existence of the biosphere. What does it mean concretely if for example we think of the transformation processes it makes possible in the large-scale chemical industry?

In the conservative *Wörmser Zeitung* a series of articles appeared about ground-water in the Rhine-Main district. The water is being acidified by chemical production to a depth of 200 metres, an effect which can never be removed. Secondly soil, air and vegetation were poisoned by 60,000 tons of solvents annually, produced, sold and made available for our general use by BASF alone. The third article dealt with agricultural chemicals which destroy the productivity of the soil and spoil foodstuffs: the concentration of nitrates alone in the soil has increased tenfold in the last hundred years. And the conclusion reached by the series? We should increase the size of control authorities, and their monitoring capabilities.

We talk about a 'post-industrial society' and about 'qualitative growth,' because our leading activities have moved in this direction. But by its new technologies the industrial system brings additional vastnesses of earth under concrete to the already over-industrialised countries of West Europe, North America and Japan, rooting up the last natural forests, while at home the artificial forests are poisoned, decimating the species-variety of life, and warming up the atmosphere, disturbing its climatic processes.

Since industrialism is imposing itself on the total population of the planet, each single human being multiplies his or her demands, without gaining anything by doing it. On the contrary: the person who goes to buy groceries at the supermarket, and who up to that time has been a member of an agrarian community, is more threatened by hunger than before, and involuntarily comes to depend on the agricultural industry – an industry known for consuming more energy than it produces. And wherever it occurs, governments celebrate economic growth as a success! Everybody more readily buys a new car. The spiral of death has appeal, and we are so far removed from a natural sense of danger, that we interpret what is patently dangerous as if it were safe. The parasite is very happy at getting larger chunks to eat out of the body of its host, and proudly compares its growth with its equally nit-witted competitors.

The Megamachine really is not the same as the concept 'industrial system'. Firstly, we may think of the world-wide scientific, technical and informational substructure, subdivided into nations, uniting the great units of production, today more important than the market for maintaining the integrity of the whole. It is not only the streams of finance and transport and the cables for the corresponding communications that belong to the Megamachine, but also the education centres, mass media and bureaucratic apparatus.

Back in 1968 Erich Fromm summarised the general result to which Mumford came, when he analysed the modern Megamachine in the following way:

> He means a new form of society which differs so radically from hitherto-existing society that the French and Russian revolutions pale in comparison to this change: an order in which the whole society is organised like a machine, and in which the single individual becomes a part of the machine, programmed by the program given to the whole machine. People are materially satisfied, but they stop deciding, they stop thinking, they stop feeling, and are directed by the program. Even those who run the machine are directed by the program.[2]

The industrial system is more than a composite of plant, communications and institutions. It is identical with industrial *society*. It is the integration of all human forces and activities, which are indeed the actual substance of all its outward appearances. What was once true for the machinery of the single factory, that the worker was a subordinated part of it, is now true for every citizen of industrialised society. The single human being is carved up according to its subordinate functions: he or she belongs to the Megamachine as a television watcher, counted among the quota of people who switch on, no less than among the quota of those who install the sets. And even the big banker is a *servant*, a *functionary* of the flow of capital and the laws that govern it. The

Megamachine has, for all practical purposes, apportioned our entire daily lives among its various aspects. Freely conscious participation – there *is* such a thing – exists only like the gods of Epicurus, devoid of meaning, in the 'between worlds', an irrelevant place.

The Megamachine falsely turns around the social life process. If we really want to create a new order, the first job is to decide a standpoint. Do we want to accept the existence of the Megamachine, its demands on us, and its psychological anchoring, as the norm determining us? Do we want to order things from the point of view of the spider in the web – or do we want to choose a vantage point outside the Megamachine? In the second case we may not take industrial society as an inescapable reality – *even though* it is the result of following the line of least resistance, the natural consequence of our history and the constitution of our consciousness up to now.

The Megamachine shouldn't be adapted or reconstructed, but left alone, or better still dismantled – preferably by those who have felt themselves bound to industrialism to the end. If we are going to have an encounter with the Megamachine, we must do it from the point of view that the *entire* industrial development has violated the limits of the natural order in its course and form of regulation.

However, the colonising of individual existence isn't rigidly determined, and in western countries it appears to be more flexible than anywhere else. But the principle is reliably installed, and mere rebuilding is *quite unable* to make any difference. This Megamachine is the direct subject of exterminism, and to the extent that we are still integrated with it, the taking of the most reasonable attitude on any single point makes no significant difference. It is totally anachronistic to talk of democracy when we are simply dealing with *aspects* of the Megamachine. To want to build up a force of environmentally-friendly police and get rid of water guns – well, who thinks this is enough to be occupied with at this level!?

The Megamachine is an alienated machinery moving according to its own laws, laws which are not directly dependent on us. In view of its magnitude and world-wide interlocking, there are only two possible solutions. Either we draw ourselves back from it, in that we dissolve it, and newly constitute social life down to its material fundamentals, or we assemble ourselves on the peak of the structure and find there a new consensus about how to deal with it. In this case the question would be, which constitution of society and consciousness do we need in order to be able to govern our civilisation from a central world point?

In practice it is the local level *and* the world level which will be decisive, and it is the nation state which must be abolished. *Think globally, act locally* – this embraces both in thought and action the regulatory structures which will be essential, if only because we *must* establish world-wide limits in population and consumption per head. In other words, what would an authority have to look like to be able to govern the world as a just manager of Mother Earth and of the cultural patrimony? How would it function socially, and how could it be made possible psychologically?

Can't we escape? Or don't we want to?

Up to now very few ecologists have understood that exterminism is the quintessence and not just an 'undesirable side effect' of the industrial system; and the Greens with their 'reconstruction of the industrial system' haven't even begun to understand. Even when they have the necessary education or erudition at their disposal, most people do not take the trouble to grasp the essence of the situation. People have always been intensely identified with their social household effects, and we have internalised ours as a value system, and confirm its demands while making only small deviations in our roles. People don't at all want to know what the industrial system is, and thus they easily yield to their *active interest in its inescapability*.

In recent years most of the *ecopax* stickers have disappeared from automobiles. Is this because the movements have waned or because the incompatibility between the medium and the message has been recognised? If we think things through to the end, even the dove of peace is out of place on a car. We won't get rid of the tanks if we're not prepared to risk the automobile, and if we don't get rid of tanks, then nuclear bombs won't vanish either. We can parade in front of the barracks and demonstrate against bomb trains – often without distancing ourselves from the whole to which it all belongs.

The politics of environmental protection makes no contact with the basic consensus of the 'developed' peoples. These are called humanism, progress, freedom and democracy. We have established our interest in these *ideologies* against the foundations of life, such that exterminism is built into our *ideals*, our highest values.

The consequences of cutting this umbilical cord are indeed far-reaching. Not least it will require taking leave of a whole world-view in which liberalism and socialism were in agreement: the idea of general emancipation achieved through the *surplus production* of a world-wide association of workers.

Once, when I was departing from Mexico City, a communist friend there revealed to me, as if pregnant with meaning, the idea that the process of 'development' everywhere in the world means the rise of the working class, until ultimately the whole of humanity becomes working class. Yet because of the enormous smog the highest mountain of the country, Popocatepetl, can no longer be seen from his city, even though it is quite close. He had also shown me the transition zone between the Metropolitan centre of the city with its 'visible population' of 4 million and the slums with their 10 million 'invisible population'. In this seamy area the upwardly-mobile working class strata live in wood and corrugated-iron huts, people climbing into beat-up old cars found in scrapyards and not good enough for the second-hand car dealer. Opportunities here for the car industry!

I was mixed up in all this, having flown by plane to Mexico. The model is from Europe. The Green representative Willi Hoss, organiser of an opposition trade union in Daimler-Benz, flew to Brazil and instructed the workers in the auto industry there about the wage-differentials between Stuttgart and Sao Paulo. So, in which direction is the historical process going, if the already-privileged Brazilian auto workers reach the Stuttgart standard with the firm's model-of-the-year car? It was the message of the Metropolis which he had spread there, even if he had somewhat heated up the class war *within* the firm, and made the manager angry. There is no better way of carrying the logic of self-extermination around the world than to further the interests of the auto workers!

Back in 1959 Günther Anders wrote about normal work, production and usages as if they were crimes:

> *Since the mere existence of our products is already 'action', the testing of conscience today can no longer just consist in listening to the voice in our own breasts, or the voiceless principles and maxims of our work and our products, and we cannot make the change retrospective. This means doing only work that has defensible effects, as if they were the effects of our own direct actions, and it means only possessing those products whose existence 'incarnates' such defensible action, such that we can accept it as our own action.*[3]

We can no longer be responsible for *anything* that we make or use in the framework of the given structure of civilisation. We certainly show ourselves as being morally stupid when we combine car manufacture with direct military production – as Daimler-Benz recently did – but this does not make the difference between innocence and guilt. According to the criterion which Gunther Anders gives, I shouldn't be using the electric typewriter at which I am now sitting! A repair firm which I recently had need of stuck a little label on the frame, according to which the firm specialises in 'computer systems and text systems'. The civilian typewriter carries with it preparations for star wars. Big money, *one* of the unifying media of the Megamachine, is the same in all channels.

I am not less guilty with the groceries from the supermarket than I am with my typewriter. So now I buy my stuff in the organic shop, a small step with noble symbolic meaning, and also an important benefit for the body. For quite a number of reasons – without elevating vegetarianism to a religion – I have given up eating meat. Such acts anticipate something new, yet they loosen up the old context to an extent which is hardly noticeable. We have to make the start with ourselves in this way, but at the same time we must not lose sight of the fact that our oil heating still functions and that the whole machinery is unlikely to stop until the last drop of oil has been burnt – unless we do something.

The popular sorting-out of the achievements of civilisation – good things into the pot and bad things into the garbage – does not lead us far. Within one and the same culture the good and evil things are bound up together to a far greater extent than we like to admit. The partial apocalypses which we are increasingly organising for ourselves, are the unavoidable result of a collective condition. Exterminism comes to the surface and makes itself evident as a set of murderous lesions, but as holistic medicine teaches us, we must be dealing with a general meta-bolic disturbance, and behind the metabolic disturbance is concealed a defect in psychic regulation.

Earlier attempts at solutions fall victim to such a way of looking at things, a way which reality itself is forcing upon us. Even the most conservative socialists are learning that it would accomplish nothing to become owners of the means of production and the infrastructures of giant industry; syndicalism would change nothing; even the late Friedrich Engels had regarded self-government on 'battleships' as an illusion. Even the idea of this binds people spiritually to the factory system. Instead of orienting them towards overcoming the factory system, this idea recaptures them to work with the system.

For example, the whole idea of 'arms conversion' is an escape and a flop. Civilian industrial mass-production, even in environmental tech-nology, is no more peaceful than that of the military. It is not the single discovery that is devilish, not the single product, not even the auto-mobile in itself, but the whole context, never mind what aspect of it may at any time be calling attention to itself! 'Military conversion' is nothing but pastoral care to bring about a tolerable functioning of the industrial society; it is nothing more than the achieving of a little distance *in* one's identification with it.

If 'arms conversion' is typical of a critical left-wing identification with the Megamachine, market-idealism is typical of a critical liberal-conservative one – as far as problems of control are concerned. The market is the original and immanent control mechanism of the Mega-machine, and up to now at least this much is clear, that *expansivity*, a *non-household type* of economy, is managed better by the market than by planning. The conscious plan continually knows too little about the spontaneous process of production-needs, which is beyond our control.

Liberalism and anarchism warn against state-intervention. But this is a helpless ideological fidgeting, because today market and plan are just two complementary modes of perception for an *intrinsically* totalitarian reality. The market mechanism has absolutely nothing to do with freedom – on the contrary! Whoever can picture a *conscious* socialisation in the alienated form of universal nationalisation, can only yield to the automatism of market regulation. We are dealing here with 'under-developed' economies which are only shadows of our own, confronted with the external pressure of the world market.

For better or for worse, humanity is at the mercy of western market mechanisms, not the socialist planned economy. We have reached a point of dramatic contradiction between the gain in freedom of movement by many isolated single individuals and the conditions of survival of humanity. To trust oneself to the market means to trust to the current carrying one to the waterfall, on the ship of the Megamachine logic. In the last analysis it is the market mechanism which leads to destruction.

NOTES

(1) Mumford's life's work on the megamachine and the city presents the material with which we are concerned in a way not to be found in any comparable text (consider, for example, the compilation called *Global 2000)*. I can scarcely imagine that even a Lothar Späth, if he were to withdraw for a week with the classic book *Myth of the Machine*, could afterwards contribute an idea like the 'information society' with good conscience. Mumford does not make his impression by means of any accumulation of horrors, but with the genesis and structure of modern industrial society, the self-exterminating logic of which he researches with precision, and refers back to the human being. I cannot give myself to summarising Mumford's work, which has the same significance for the ecological movement that the achievements of Marx did for the workers' movement. But it is a foundation which I rely on, and I am certain it will stand firm, even if certain conclusions with which I take issue might turn out to be questionable. Whoever discovers this can develop the beginning which Mumford has given us in different way.

(2) Fromm 1985, p152f.

(3) Günther Anders, *Endzeit und Zeitwende, Gedanken über die atomare Situation* (München: 1972), p35ff.

6. The Capitalistic Impulse

The Autonomous Dynamics of Capital

This is the next link, if we want to follow the causal chain of exterminism down to its roots.

Far more people are ready to hold capitalism, rather than the industrial system, responsible. Capitalism is variously understood – ranging in the 19th century from Marx's *Das Kapital* to Wagner's *Ring of the Niebelungen*. Yet hardly anybody disagrees that competition to make the largest possible profit exceeds every other motive for economic expansion. In no other civilisation has this drive for money become such a central power as it has in ours.

It is, however, not the ultimate or most basic drive. It is indeed true that at the moment capital is the most powerful driving force of expansion. The industrial system is a *capitalistic* industrial system. The Megamachine is driven by capital[1].

It is the *principle* of profit producing capital investment that carries us over the brink. If we are to curb expansion, if we want to stop something, then we must first fully understand this driving force as something autonomous, something independent of the good or ill will of the capitalist.

If we are unable to bring the avalanche of accumulation to a stop relatively quickly, then all the other more basic and inward things will come too late. As was said about armaments and nuclear energy: either we get rid of these military and 'civilisatory' weapons systems, or they will get rid of us. But this is far more true of the Megamachine's social structure and its unparalleled expansionist economics. Capitalism is more than the special profit-making striving of this or that group of undertakings.

This brings me back to Kurt Biedenkopf's 'ecological market society'. Only in the present context does it become clear what, apart from ideology, the market-or-planning debate is all about. In the autonomy of market events our own powers have made themselves independent of us. In classical philosophy and up until Marx this was called 'alienation'. Now, *if* this autonomous, alienated, economic process

99

operating by objective laws is to comply with ORDO, with *its* nature and not human nature, *then* we need nothing more than a competitive order improved along the lines of green principles. But what happens if we refuse to acknowledge the rights of this economic deluge, refuse to abandon our partial power to it or to just the centre part of it? What happens if we subordinate economics altogether, down-grading money to the level of an instrument of exchange and calculation?

Let us remember: by concentrating on the (intrinsically blameless) market *mechanism* and its exploitation, Biedenkopf, as a 'damage-limiter', removed practically all attention from market *forces*, or more exactly the forces *bearing on* the market. The satisfaction of needs disappeared behind the exchange of use-values, and with it disappeared also *the main motive behind market organisation: gain*, the increase of money. The person who has something to offer, the person who needs something: these two subjects characterise the flea-market and occasionally the weekly market. Yet even the simplest supermarket is not opened on their account.

In the case of market competition the satisfaction of the needs of the consumer is only the means, never the *purpose* of the establishment. The merchant, the chief actor in the marketplace, is concerned to achieve the highest possible monetary winnings. The changing of money into wares and back again generates more money, and later, when production is carried out right from raw materials to the finished product, the final marketing process is but a subordinate function of the whole capitalistic reproduction process, bringing in an increased amount of money. In the end the lion's share of demand comes under the control of capital, which secures for itself the return on big, long-term investments – not only in the arms sector.

When I speak of the merchant, I am referring to the regulative principle which he introduced in the past, and exploited for the amassing of power. Leaning on money, he introduced a shift in the centre of gravity from concrete to abstract values – from the regulation of the social whole by traditional authority to the mediation of the synthesis through individual competition. The first industrial revolution, which already contained the exterministic tendency, was the result of an *unleashing*. Although the modern period from the Renaissance onwards was concerned with *human* emancipation, this turned out to be mainly an emancipation of *money* or the *money owner* – from all those considerations which in traditional society stood in the way of profit-making (for example by prohibiting usury, the charging of interest).

Today merchants themselves are subordinated. Modern society is controlled by *finance-capital* to a degree which the most influential merchants and financiers of past societies would never have dared dream of. Our job is to learn to see this plutocracy, which has colonised almost the entire process of everyday living. This colonisation is the logical end-station of the road which began with the rise of money and production of goods.

Under money-economy conditions, production for the market is a power calculation, and a very systematic one. Were the inventors of the pure market-economy people who never get tired, or wrong in imagining an ideal market of bidders with equal chances, in which only quality and cost price, or productivity and the genius of the 'right nose' determine the outcome? For market idealists power has a very distorting effect. If it must be a feature of the market, because increasing the amount of money is the decisive drive of the actors, other actions must be taken as purely corrective steps in order to stop the expansion.

It is *capitalistic behaviour* itself which constitutes the capitalistic market – behaviour of a kind which, among friends, one would be ashamed of – the action of buying to sell more dearly, dealing to make profit. And behind the profit motive stands the power motive. Historically, the market emerged as a new all-embracing arena for the power struggle. It is the *circus maximus*, and money is the elixir of upward mobility for the energetic plebeian, who in this way can socially challenge traditional ruling forces (the aristocracy).

ORDO-liberalism takes the position that the power problem is conceptually *added on*. It regards monopoly-capitalism as a path-determining impulse which distorts the ideal-type assumption of perfect competition. In this situation power-fighters armed with money are the protagonists who first constituted the market in its evolved form. Economic power-struggle is the *essence* of market events.

I share Mumford's view that capitalism is not a modern phenomenon and should not be quickly reduced to the appropriation of surplus work – Marxism one-sidedly concentrates too much attention on this. Mumford understands by capitalism:

> the translation of all goods, services and energies into abstract pecuniary terms, with an intensified application of human energy to money and trade, for the sake of gains that accrue primarily to the owners of property, who ideally are prepared to risk their savings on new enterprises, as well as to live off the income of established industrial and commercial organisations.[2]

He pulls three things to the front: *monetarising*, or the tendency toward the total marketising of life, *commercial profit-orientation* as the dominant feature of the human image, and *capital turnover* for extended reproduction. Included is the uncoupling from nature and primary production, which is typical for industrial and commercial activities.

It creates a furore in world history, and is a fundamental offence against the good society, when merchants, who carry out their transactions from the point of view of *quantity* and *exchange value*, get hold of the law of the evolution of species. When this happens, balance is bound to be lost. All archaic orders with their hierarchies of castes (priests above warriors, both above merchants, and all three above farmers and craftsmen), which emerged out of the natural evolution of tribes, were 'more right' than the order we have.

Where warriors and their king rose to the top – as in the conqueror state instead of the original theocracy – and the 'brahman' principle no longer remained as a balancing influence, the culture lost its balance and inclined toward death. More than one Germanic tribe disappeared in this way. But if this shift proves destructive to the theocratic constitutions, how much more destructive is the victory of merchants. Money as ultimate reason is worse than the ultimate reason of kings, the sword – even though it is so much more democratic.

The manna of the priest, the sword of the warrior and the money of the merchant – all are means to power. At the current level of human evolution we cannot escape this: it has grown to be part of us. But money should have ruled the world less than the sword. Right from the start money has the character of a weapon operating at a distance, exonerating the culprit.

In the market economy and the constitutional state, no voice is raised, for example, against taking blood from starving Indians in Bolivia, Columbia or Haiti for a tiny payment and selling it again at many times the price in Europe or USA. The victims should be glad that they can prevent dying of starvation at the cost of a little blood, or even of their lives[3]. But the indicting power of such information is easily lost because the money used is unidentifiable, and those purchasing the blood do not have to know anything of the context.

While manna, like the sword, remains tied into a traditional order, capital has always sought to free itself from its servile role. At the present time the market is becoming a stage for this exclusive determinant of fate, which drags production, science, technology, art, everything, in its wake.

My main concern is to make knowable the *spirit* of capitalism as a formative force in our culture – we are more deeply bound up with the money-economy than one would expect. Only too often criticism directs itself merely against 'tumours', mistaking them for normality[4]. Money appears to be formative in the style of our rationality and science, with their object-dominated and manipulative characters. Coins, bits, concepts, individuals, work-force, atoms, quanta of all sorts – all our world models and behaviour models stand under the *predominance* of these abstract units, which allow themselves to be accumulated to an infinite degree. Very pertinently, the Brazilian ecologist Jose Lutzenberger said that our culture is worse than rationalistic, and that we should call it *abstractionistic*[5].

With the coming of capital a means to power, resting on the principle of expansion to infinity, thrust itself into the middle of society – a means of power which, in the form of interest and credit, has created instruments enabling it to function as a perpetual motion. Mumford points out the parallel with Ziegler's index of destruction, kilowatt-hours per square kilometre per day:

> When human functions are converted into abstract, uniform units, ultimately energy or money, there are no limits to the amount of power that can be seized, converted and stored. The peculiarity of money is that it knows no biological limits or ecological restrictions. When the Augsburg financier, Jacob Fugger the Elder, was asked when he would have so much money that he would feel no need for more, he replied, as all great magnates tacitly or openly do, that he never expected such a day to come.[6]

This inherent absence of moderation has been emphasised repeatedly from Thomas Aquinas to Marx, as being a characteristic projected into humanity. Clearly, as Mumford says at another point:

> The idea that there should be no limits upon any human function is absurd: all life exists within very narrow limits of temperature, air, water and food; and the notion that money alone, or power to command the services of other men, should be free of such definite limits is an aberration of the mind[7]

Yet this mental disturbance is programmed objectively in capitalism, and as a consequence the whole social process rests on the principle of commercialism.

Money is the *universal drug* with which we multiply our tendency to overthrow the balance of nature. For this reason an *economic* society *with the money-making drive at its core* cannot be saved. It doesn't permit any independent ordering power to arise, because it itself dominates the entire field. All it ever wants is to have its craving stabilised. Mumford confirms this:

> The capitalist scheme of values in fact transformed five of the seven deadly sins of Christianity – pride, envy, greed, avarice, and lust – into positive social virtues, treating them as necessary incentives to all economic enterprise; while the cardinal virtues, beginning with love and humility, were

rejected as 'bad for business', except to the degree that they made the working class more docile and more amenable to cold-blooded exploitation.[8]

Capitalism is not an order of society, but a power principle which dominates the varying forms of society, and has done so ever since the invention of money. The modern 'western' social order has taken this power-principle as a collective designation, because no other civilisation ever let itself be governed by this to the same unconditional extent as ours, which has placed capital in its central constellation.

It is not so much a question of introducing a different use and division of money, as of eliminating it altogether as power and control centre of the historical process. Otherwise we shall be killed by our 'godly trash' (as South American Indians called gold), slaves of it as we are.

We would not have had such a tumorous outgrowth if money had a significant meaning only for those who are concerned with its accumulation and concentration, investment and management. "On money hangs indeed everything, for money strives", said Goethe, and by 'everything' he means 'everybody'. We are so deeply involved in it, that this alone is enough to make us retain capitalism.

Money and Freedom

The reason why we are so very hung up on money is that we are so inescapably dependent on it. It is on grounds of *freedom* that we *prefer* this money-mediated dependency to other dependencies. For example, we prefer it much more than private property, for property ties us to community obligations, whereas money brings to the individual a great many 'freedoms from'. It makes it possible for us to withdraw from society, to the point of being asocial; it makes possible behaviour of a kind which lacks regard for others. In general to 'buy ourselves free from' takes precedence over the will to exercise freedom 'for something'. Uncoupling is more important than self-realisation. By now it is impossible to determine whether money first alerted us to this possibility or whether it exists for the sake of it.

We might not have enough money (because it stands as symbol of psychic insatiability), and therefore we may want to improve the world, alter its money arrangements or its money distribution. But money as an institution is the structural basis upon which western individuality grew up. It is an achievement in form to which all members of civic society can lay claim. It is not at all identical with individuality or personhood, but something specific which goes beyond these.

Personality is something whose existence rests on the assumptions of economics. The citizen is only possible as an *independent* individual (independent of nation, tribe, local control, family group, and currently, authorities), if the social context is mediated in a different way from that of concrete personal and collective power! Money first made possible the constitutional state, equality before the law, even the declaration of human rights as such. Only on the basis of a money economy could the absolutist king Frederick II of Prussia declare that religion is a private matter: each may seek salvation in his or her own way.

All this is made possible by money as a regulating mechanism, which binds individuals into the total social process without direct coercion, and above all things without personal or collective arbitrariness. The invisible hand, the market mechanism, together with an inbuilt drive to exploit all that is 'not-me', especially nature – these things appear to allow us to compete for an ever-higher material standard, for the 'greatest happiness' – and this is the secret of the deep consensus on which capital rests.

In a prosperous capitalistic society the majority is positively identified with money as an intermediary and a promise, in spite of resentments against big money, interest and inflation. The possession of money is associated with freedom. Anti-capitalistic opinions do not generally go beyond this. Otherwise the 'free market economy' would not have been able to hold its own as an ideology – political developments leading to the world wars, and economic developments leading to despotic Mega-machine progress, have been grounded all along on this principle of financial guidance.

The ideal of not needing the polity any more, because we can carry it in our pockets as money, still causes excitement in all traditional societies, where the individual would like to free himself for an apparently higher level of ego-evolution. With the emancipatory impulse which the money economy always carries along with it, it allures people in the underdeveloped countries and former Soviet bloc. Money is insufficiently recognised in this role, because it is concealed by the fact that it always 'works' *as capital*, driving the merciless world market.

The objective ambivalence of money is the basic script, according to which exterminism and emancipation intertwine with each other. We are dealing here with a contradiction which is built into human nature itself, which certainly is not solved like a cancer operation on the outer tumour of money, without attending to the inner conflict which gives rise to the cancer.

All basic ideas about a 'natural economic order' are false to the extent that they do not recognise that once subsistence needs have been met, human beings immediately begin to produce instruments of power which they use against each other. Division of labour and exchange cannot be regulated 'naturally', but only against a background of the self-regulation of the human condition, and the overall social order which predetermines the goal and status of the economy, and also limits its autonomy.

Power and money constitute *one* expansionistic syndrome, which derives from the context in which they came into existence. Money thus has a function it cannot be cured of, unless we suppose that the human being were to heal *himself/herself* in this respect, through a veritable withdrawal-cure, through a psychotherapy in the grand style, or through a religious *metanoia* – by means of which s/he tames his addiction and greed, not just psychologically, but also institutionally.

Human beings have always created institutions, in order to shore up their unstable constitutions. And it is clear that emancipated money would actually be destabilising, or more exactly *mania-stimulating* and *addiction-producing*. It is the abstract blood of the demon, which keeps us possessed in a very real sense, and not only permits, but also compels us to utilise instruments of murder and suicide. Thus theories of money reform stand in colossal disproportion to the tap-root of the problem, which can hardly be touched by the technical proposals of their new orders.

To see money as alienated from its purpose, the moment it is used in a power-seeking and exploiting way, is to stand reality on its head. Right from the beginning money had an *autonomous* logic which was never directed toward those purposes which, in the spirit of an 'original moral economy', it could have obeyed. At the beginning of the history of money the most prominent thing was the human need for recognition and adornment[9]. More exactly money turns out to be an invention of the patriarchal spirit:

> The possessions of adornment out of which money evolved did not arise from (female) attractiveness-enhancing adornment, but out of (male) dignity and rank adornment: the woman invented the adornment, the man made money from it. (Further) the striving for validation leads directly to the point where all those who by natural standards are disadvantaged seek for new tokens of differentiation.[10]

To this end money is the ideal means, for it can be traded for absolutely anything: power, property, prestige, personality. Nowhere does this achieve more pointed expression than in that scene from Shakespeare, which Marx also made use of in *Das Kapital*, where Timon of Athens, digging for roots, hits upon the 'damned earth', namely upon yellow gold, and cries out after experience of its destructive social effects:

Thus much of this will make black white, foul fair,
Wrong right, base noble, old young, coward valiant.
Ha, you gods! Why this? What this, you gods? Why, this
Will lug your priests and servants from your sides,
Pluck stout men's pillows from below their heads:
This yellow slave
Will knit and break religions, bless the accursed,
Make the hoar leprosy adored, place thieves
And give them title, knee and approbation
With senators on the bench... damned earth...

Such frightful lamentations were always heard every time a society, that of Greece in this case, went over to a comprehensive money economy, and began to evolve a trading culture out of a pluralistic warrior culture. The expression of power and the increase of power are its primary purpose. In money humans have created for themselves the means suited to the drive to accumulate power through economic exploitation. Interest and credit are therefore its altogether normal consequences. This being so, we must attack this *normality*, and acknowledge the altogether functional role of interest or credit in the machinery of economic evolution.

The various ideologies aimed at 'breaking the servility to interest' grew up to serve purposes altogether different from that of stopping material expansion. Since, long ago, the original order with its 'moral economy' proved unable to resist the logic of capital, it cannot now be sufficient just to turn back to this pattern. It is not a source leading the modern world to make any further changes. Society as Megamachine has money arranged to its liking. To want to remove isolated deficiencies from it is illusionary and more conformist than might appear, since all that is being attempted is to heal a special symptom of the Megamachine.

It is true that specific attempts – as in the case of Solon in Athens – had a temporarily liberating effect. But this is because the previous order was still powerful enough in people's hearts to bind the beneficiaries of the new money economy as well. They were not inaccessible, as they are in the space-ship New York City, and they were completely different from those who set the switches in the banks, not only being responsible for correctly operating with money according to its laws, but being responsible above all for the consequences of its use.

Solon, who by his reforms first made the money economy popular, is unthinkable without the mobilisation of traditional reserves which were used up and perverted. That which was beautiful in the *polis* was made possible by these reserves and by the fact that the unleashing of money was still only partially complete. Plato and Aristotle, in consensus with their contemporaries, *still* had that 'correct concept of money' which the reformers repeatedly uphold. And the war on usury waged by intact religious cultures naturally rested on their *total world-view* and always presupposed that the production of goods and the money economy had not yet atomised the whole social body. In our case, any force capable of establishing a moral economy must completely constitute itself anew. And without such a deep-level transformation, reform projects are nothing but substitute-satisfaction.

On the intellectual level there is in fact no better protection for finance capital than that criticism which focuses only on big money, on the 'grabbing capital', because from the beginning such criticism does not understand that *all* capital basically 'works' like bank capital. Bank interest merely mirrors the fact that invested capital yields profits obtained from the exploitation of work and nature. A money reform which 'merely' takes away interest is an impossibility for capitalism. Except in times of emergency for the limited purpose of mutual self-sufficiency there will also be no circulation-protection through continuous slight depreciation, because from the perspective of capital, circulation-protection is very much a secondary purpose.

Since there is a connection between every savings account and finance capital, there is good reason why people fear for their one-family houses as soon as there is talk of taming high finance, whenever they grow angry over the amount they must throw every month into the hungry jaws of the bank. We have allowed the world, including our inner world, to be so arranged, that we tremble *along with* our dragon about whether enough profit will be squeezed out of third world starvelings, to enable their governments to make the required money transfers to New York, Frankfurt or Zürich. Instead of wanting the monster to collapse, we *fear* for our own freedom, our own safety and comfort, should the interest fail to be fed to it. The overthrow of money- and capital-masters, and the *subordination* of money, will demand the most extreme exertion of consciousness, and the exercise of a spiritual quality. It will, in point of fact, require us to withstand many immediately-experienced fears, and to be ready to upset the whole security of life.

If we want to detach ourselves from the basic patterns of capitalistic society, it is not monopolistic big capital, always so easy to condemn, which merits our attention, but *money*, the daily small-change. For it is by this that we are bound. *Money* is the transfer-point of *power* – a new, just, money order based on small property, means primarily equalising the chance for getting an allocation of financial power. The *reason* why

Communism goes so very much against the grain for the bourgeois individual is that until now, it does not optimise independence from society, but awakens the sense of responsibility for mutual aid, the reconstitution of an obligatory, reliable social order.

This is all the more scary because the individual is mostly thrown back on the older psychology of conformist group-membership (collectivism). A subsidiary neighbourly love operating case by case would not be sufficient as a basis for a common economy or small-group economy of the 'small is beautiful' type. It would be desirable indeed, but would be unsteady, varying according to the situation. It wouldn't work without daily planned cooperation.

The great (spiritual!) question is whether this creation of independent personality by means of the distancing effect of money was or was not an epochal *substitute* solution; and whether or not at least *today* it must be regarded as such. The bourgeois individual as a free personality is an ego still too weak to stand up to the full pressure of human contact, and needs distance for its own protection if it is to maintain its own special character, and not fall back adaptively into the 'collective', the 'natural realm' of immediate power relationships.

Money (as a principle, as an institution) is a preventive character-armour of the second order. In this it is related to the private automobile which, so often occupied by only one person, covers the same problem. So I suspect that we won't get rid of the capitalistic drive as long as people fail to learn to experience contact in a way that is not primarily threatening. Without a money economy the middle class individual necessarily needs either to acquire more bodily armour or to make an extensive backwards retreat from the currently achieved position of ego-development. Neither is a solution.

Here we see once again why it is that self-discovery is a precondition for being able to get out of capitalism. If this quest for self-discovery fails, we shall be compelled to defend, in the name of freedom, a basic structure of individual existence which arose with the money economy and which can only be separated with difficulty from its consequences: capitalism, Megamachine and exterminism. If we are to limit both the number of people who use money, and the intensity with which they use it, then the rest of us, who use it as a protection for weakness, must risk living unprotected. Only when it is no longer used for purposes of self-assertion and self-protection can money function as it 'should'. When this point is reached, money reform takes place by itself. Its neutralisation, its transformation into a mere means of comparison and trade, is an act of spiritual liberation before it can be 'properly' established organisationally and institutionally.

If money is a monstrous product of the subjugated ego's need for compensation, then its dysfunctions have their origins here. In the end the responsibility lies not with money, but with *us*. If we were all really able to feel what Jesus experienced when he said that we should give as little thought to food and clothing as do the birds of the air and the lilies of the field, then abolition of the money economy would be near, and a form of human existence approaching a balance with the rest of nature would be secured.

It seems to be the case that such precursors did not so much take material existence for granted, as see it as the *result* of a higher state of consciousness, and even today minorities have to take a self-conscious chance on material insecurity of this sort[11].

Money will only be superfluous for freedom when individuals no longer have to fear sinking back into personal dependency, which means that they must have achieved that inner peace which permits them to be carried by a community without feelings of guilt and subordination. A community which, for its part, does not desire to subject them to infantile exploitation. Only the person who can be secure in respect of his-her existence, can unconditionally trust a community.[12]

Thus the real solution consists in the re-establishing of such social contexts, such *small living circles on the communal and communitarian scale*, as can grant once again to the individual such an enduring embeddedness that all individual financial security measures become superfluous, while the freedom to break out in whatever direction he or she wants to remains unaffected by considerations of the resources which would be needed. The right to be a guest and the freedom to travel would together be enough to eliminate the old threat confronting the wanderer of being excluded from some particular association.

NOTES
(1) Its Soviet accessory, which as Chernobyl has so penetratingly reminded us, is, although not *unmediatedly* driven by capital, only a copy of the Megamachine, a dependent variable. The radioactive cloud teaches us about the consequences of 'transfer', of 'proliferation' (not only of nuclear technology and know-how, but of our whole civilisatory model). How aggravating, that in other places people play with matches even more naively, if possible. Whether or not blueprints were purchased, the splitting of the atom was discovered in Germany, and the bombs were first built on account of Germany. The United States dropped them cold-bloodedly on the Japanese civilian population, in order to instruct Stalin about post-war power relationships. As a consequence of the 'eastern' industrial system Chernobyl is a real picture puzzle. Communism and the Russian revolution itself presuppose western capitalism and its mighty industrial system. That is to say, as far as the ecological crisis is concerned, the system-difference is of secondary importance and has been from the start, however much friction it may have caused. It is the impulse which we have been

sending out for centuries, as a result of which now everywhere in the world they are competing with us to consume natural capital and, in order to catch up with us, are often causing more massive damage than we are doing. The former West Germany is not so destructive in its use of soft coal as is East Germany, which is driven to it by economic competition. The smog in north Germany is to this extent a boomerang. We have just heard that the world of the atomic community is about to heal itself as a result of our safety standard. So much the worse then, for it can go further. We wouldn't dare to complain if, for example, in the near future a French nuclear reactor blows up.

(2) Lewis Mumford, *The Myth of the Machine, Technics and Human Development*, New York: Harcourt, Brace and World, Inc, 1967, p274.

(3) According to a report from Basile Ypsilantis entitled *Murdering Peoples for the Consumer Society*.

(4) For the 'monetaristic' bases of our civilisatory model I refer to the red threads which run through the works of George Thomson (*The First Philosophers*), Alfred Sohn-Rethel (*Körperliche und geistige Arbeit etc.*) and Rudolf Wolfgang Müller (*Geist und Geld*): the first section of the last-mentioned book gives a lucid reconstruction of Marx's money theory, useful to those who take issue with it and thus don't want to be so unserious as the free economy theorist Yoshito Otani (certainly not a genuine Japanese).

(5) Lutzenberger, in a lecture given to the Findhorn community in Scotland, October 1986.

(6) Lewis Mumford, *The Myth of the Machine, the Pentagon of Power*, New York: Harcourt Brace Jovanovich, 1970, p165.

(7) Mumford, *Technics and Human Development*, p276.

(8) *Ibid*, p277.

(9) *Ibid*, p21f.

(10) *Ibid*.

(11) On the contrary, in the monasteries of all high cultures this basic security was directly given or at least collectively and institutionally vouched for: monks and nuns do not starve to death, even in beggar orders; on the contrary. So here the risk that 'the Son of Man has nowhere to lay his head' is no longer part of the game.

(12) The (today) conservative motive of self-assertion and individual responsibility for one's own welfare is retrospectively justified. We must learn to stand on our own feet, and not allow ourselves to fall back into the protection of parental arms of whatever kind. But in the forward direction a concept of solidarity and subsidiarity which makes the needy into demoralised beggars who have to demonstrate their lack of means is untenable. In an adequate individualised society the offer of a basic security, of a 'citizen' or still better a 'human' income can stimulate spiritual evolution and mitigate the pressure to conform. But this remains bound to the welfare state aspect of the Megamachine and its world-scale injustice.

7. The European Cosmology

Homo Conquistador

Even liberated capital is not the ultimate cause of *exterminism*. It is an invention first made by the Ancient Greeks, and again more recently by Europeans, *not* for the sake of the continuity of production of goods, but on account of deep relationships of family predispositions. The reason why the Renaissance was able to take this up so strongly is that the West had arrived at the same threshold – not on the basis of the Roman tradition, which simply went along with things – but mainly in an autochthonous [home-grown] manner. History, by shifting its epicentre persistently to the north-western Europeans, removed from Rome, made quite clear that a very specific popular impulse lay behind the industrial breakthrough: not a special technical and scientific gifted-ness, but a special type of psychic energy with a corresponding mental approach to the world.

Conventional critical analysis of capitalism, mainly left-wing, mostly misconceives the *logic* of self-extermination. True, fully-evolved capital-ism has forced the development of asocial individualism, with which our civilisation glitters more than any other has done. But this is a secondary effect: here we will trace just one result back to its cause. The issue is to comprehend *why* it was the Europeans who developed this capitalistic mode of production, extremely expansionistic.

Marx – following Hegel – was so preoccupied with the evolutionary emergence of new forms that he did not grant enough intrinsic sub-stance to earlier stages: it seemed to him that in capitalism everything earlier was absorbed. To explain capitalism was to explain everything. Since Europe was the measure of all things, unique and special features were not noticeable. But for the purpose of making corrections the most important question is *how* and by *what means* money and wealth were able to emancipate themselves as capital and *why* it could evolve into unlimited central power.

Johan Galtung has made a structural comparison between the domi-nating civilisations of today, by assessing them along six different dimensions: space, time, knowledge, human-to-nature relations, human-to-human relations, and human-to-God relations. By *cosmology* he means the collective deep psychology as it exists at various times – an unconscious basic attitude to the world, which actualises itself as cultural behaviour-patterns. According to this the western human – *homo occidentalis* – is characterised as follows:

> *He places himself in the centre, and others on the periphery, as a result of which the initiative naturally radiates from the centre, and refers itself expansively to the farthest limits of the social and natural cosmos. Thus space is arranged sharply on a perspective determined by the self-willed subject.*
>
> *Time flows in one direction, evolution is progress from the lower to the higher, and the course of events is dramatic (from Paradise via the fall of man to Salvation or Damnation).*
>
> *Knowledge embraces the world in that it attempts, by using a few very powerful parameters, to reduce everything as far as possible to a single axiom such as a 'unified field theory'. We construct things in a binary fashion and deductively. We love the theoretical building of pyramids from a single point, like using commodities as exchange values in the political economy. Galtung is of the opinion that the latter is particularly teutonic.*
>
> *Man stands as master over nature. The social structure is vertical and individualistic, so that 'dog eat dog' competition for rank is the norm.*
>
> *In transpersonal matters God is autocratically, jealously and dualistically superior to the world and people – like the super-ego, our great mirror, in front of which we alternate between feelings of omnipotence and impotence.*

Homo occidentalis is *homo conquistador*, world-conqueror *par excellence*. This is European popular psychology. In Spain, for example, families have acted for centuries on the assumption that sons will go out into the world. The world outside Europe was regarded as empty and in need of our civilising influence. Our Gothic cathedrals and our music have the same heaven-assaulting and gripping impetus. Romain Rolland says of the Beethoven of the first eight symphonies:

> *He comes from the period in which one Christopher Columbus after another strives out in the night and discovers his ego on the turbulent seas of revolution, and immediately struggles with fiery eagerness to conquer. Conquerors over-strain the bow. Eagerly they want to grab the whole world for themselves. Every single ego which has achieved freedom wants to be a leader. Whoever does not achieve this in life tries to achieve it in art. The universe is his battle-field, and he boldly unfolds his inner powers for struggle, his longing, grief, anger and Weltschmerz. The people must*

be still before him, after the revolution comes the reign of the caesar[1].

Where does this psycho-energetic foundation come from, which achieves such an explosive expression in our use of science-technology-capital? Greeks, Romans, Hittites, people in Asia Minor, the Kurgan-Aryans who moved into India, and last but not least the Germanics, derived their hereditary character from the nomadic life of the Eurasian steppes. The Jews, and later the Arabs, also originally had this same psychological disposition, of peoples who wandered in the deserts or the steppes. Our cosmology is Jewish-Greek-Roman-Christian, and occasionally it has absorbed influences from Arabian opponents and partners.

In all cases we are dealing with assimilations, transformations resulting from contact with what were initially alien traditions, particularly in the case of western Christianity, which reached us through Paul, the Greek cities, and Rome. But seen from north of the Alps, all this mixing and transforming mass is *one autochthonous basis* which the Germanic tribes brought with them from their own formative period. Indeed, Rome was in decay, so that it was not simply a continuation, but in truth a new start, in which the Germanic peoples and the Slavs played the role of 'vigorous barbarians'.

The original Germanic cosmology was much more militant than that of the Slavs. The Slavs were already settled farmers, something which the Germanics were *about to become.* For the aristocracy of the Germanic tribes, war and conquest were an essential component of the 'method of production', as is to be seen in the ideals of the robber-founders of states such as the Vandals, and then the Norman followers in the period leading up to the high Middle Ages. If life is an adventurous and militant expedition, what has become the home territory becomes a sort of 'base camp'. And then, when the spatial expansion comes to a stop, the driving energies have to seek another form of expression. The readiness to strike camp, the restlessness, the pioneering and founding spirit; these await new opportunities, be they crusades, discoveries, colonisation, industry, research or space exploration.

Such initiatives, while a part of being human, do not have to take that aggressive and lordly form which dominates all else – a form which over-values itself and is unscrupulous in execution, focusing fanatically on *one* principle. It is an extroverted cosmology: the initiative justifies itself one-sidedly in altering the *external* world. This is the result of its basic materialism.

Even our mystics are activists: Meister Eckhart's contemplative life ends in ecstatic preaching. What is implied is that the Kingdom of God must be made to embrace the whole earth: it never occurs to us that it always *did* embrace it, and that it is precisely our unceasing exertions which called into existence the storm which drove us from Paradise.

Our spiritual inheritance carries the wanderer-Wotan [Odin] within itself, and for this reason I believe in the following proposition: as Rome in its decaying days needed many alien, especially near-Asian, *impulses* in order to transform itself, so today we need those of the far-Asian. The Benedictine monastic culture, which symbolises the rebirth of Italy and the birth of the West, was Roman and non-Roman Christian, at the same time!

So what had happened? In the same way that Reagan in the 1980s stood for the USA, so Cato, who concluded every speech in the Senate with the phrase "Carthage must be destroyed!", stood for the Romans of the Republican period. That was the dominant spirit in Rome, transcending all class differences. It was the main theme of the general consciousness. Seven hundred years later the main theme of the general consciousness was the rule of Benedict: 'work and pray'.

Work, formerly for slaves and hardly worthy of the free Roman, is now the watchword of a new culturally-creative elite. But it was granted second priority, after prayer: we should not 'store up treasure on earth', but create for ourselves that subsistence necessary to live with human dignity. And living with human dignity meant accepting the raising of one's spirit to the divine level, the achieving of eternal salvation as the goal of existence. Thus prayer was accorded first priority – and by prayer was meant not the repetition of formulas, but verbal meditation.

They prayed for freedom and to rediscover the shape and perspective of civilisation. The Benedictine tradition was the first *fruit* of this. In the intervening centuries, from generation to generation, people have increasingly asked the question *'quo vadis?'*, ('where are you going?'), because the old path, taken for granted in the Roman Cato period, had ended and perished. In this way the subjective life of a whole society changed itself.

The Italy of that time offers a most hopeful example that a deep transformation, a structural revolution in the soul of a people, is possible. The significant lesson for us is this: the monastery culture spread itself according to the rule of Benedict, but the model remained contractive. Lewis Mumford has emphasised the contribution of the Benedictine order to our modern work culture and work discipline. But this contribution has been modified by being taken up later into a *different* structural pattern. The parallel monastic culture in Eastern Rome remained contractive, and did not bring about any work or economic society. The storm of the Germanic peoples contributed an exterior stimulus only. Benedict as a crusader is unthinkable.

The Unrestrained Ego of the White Man

We in the north come from quite a different cultural pattern – from that of the Burgundian ecclesiastic knight Bernard of Clairvaux, who 600 years later achieved an expansionistic renewal of the monastic culture, economically, politically and militarily, and in so doing created the basis for the Christianising of the Germanic peoples. This was a different kind of subjectivity, yet one which took Italy with it. It utilised the Crusades as its take-off point, not its home. Bernard was a mystic of great charisma, a monastery-reformer and Crusade-organiser at the same time. In Germany the Cistercian movement, which he initiated, became the vanguard of the colonisation of east Europe, with cross and sword.

The affinity for capitalism incarnated itself in the course of the Crusades in the order of the Templars, who integrated into their spiritual concept merchandising, banking and the money economy. At first capital was formally a subordinate thing in their spiritual attitude, but 'war, trade and piracy' as daily-life routine were bound to pervert the cross, and in the end they overcame it completely. It was certainly no coincidence that satanic and magical traits came to be prominent in Templar spirituality, traits which Rome then used as grounds for annihilating this order – which had broken out of the world-view of the Middle Ages at too early a date.

Like the Greeks and Romans before them, the Germanic peoples also brought with them, out of their nomadic period, a specific 'cosmological' disposition which then benefited capitalism and indeed, had to lead to it. The *pluralistic* power structure of these lineages and peoples, and its sharp contrast to oriental despotism, has often been emphasised. Right down to the lowest ranks of the people there were rights, and a latitude which permitted articulation and initiative. The lifestyle had not encouraged collectivistic theocracies, but warlike kingdoms. Minor kings made one of their rank into a *primus inter pares* (first among equals), as did the Achaeans to Agamemnon in the *Iliad*.

Galtung characterised the corresponding social psychology as vertical *and* individualistic. 'Enterprising initiative' could potentially be taken in by people of any social rank long before this pattern achieved its modern significance. Competition for rank within the same class is typical of all such war-cultures. If it conquers a foreign land and people, in the extreme case the whole community can transform itself into a feudal aristocracy. But in the area where Germany is today there were no subject peoples, so there was a pure feudal differentiation within the Germanic tribes, yet with popular freedoms, which still stood on the flags of the German Peasants' War.

Thus this individualistic possibility had very distant roots. The cosmology appealed subliminally within each individual to the desire to become his own master, and to refuse to grant absolute validity to the boundaries of birth and class. Money economy and capitalism were suited to equalising opportunity. With money in his pocket every ego could become noble and irresistible, conquer a world or at least a market, and organise a kingdom such as shines as an upper middle class ideal.

This can be followed back to the Olympic competition of the Greeks, and still further to the motto handed down through Homer, "always to be first and strive to be ahead of the others", whatever the area or object of the competition.

In capitalism this principle becomes completely degenerate, because the concrete objective retreats further and further, so that competition shows itself only in the annual dollar income. As a so-and-so-many-dollar-man the individual can never have enough, never *arrive* existentially. Personal growth takes second place in psychological householding to the addictive and usurious patterns at home there.

But this degeneration is fore-ordained in a competitively-oriented individualism. It is the point of departure from which we created the economic form which revolves around money. Nevertheless, as it thrusts itself so strongly forward, capitalism conceals the fact that we have little prospect of ridding ourselves of this objective structure, so long as we regard its subjective disposition merely as a *consequence*. The western *ego* has a more fundamental place-value in the logic of self-extermination as the capitalistic tool.

Individualistically, however, ego remains essentially lost to people. The old, traditional ego of group-belongingness had placed before itself norms in the form of visible objective powers (gods), norms which the individual would not otherwise have allowed to arise, and would have given very little rein to. The more this ego came forward within a church, the more it would have had to replace stabilising institutions with a responsible inner authority.

Protestantism also proclaimed this as a principle. Kant perfected the idea in the form of the categorical imperative and Fichte pointed it up for the public:

> *And you shall act in such a way, as if*
> *Through you and your deeds alone*
> *Fate would hang upon German things*
> *And the responsibility would be yours.*

Money and capital would have needed to be employed only by a personal intelligence acting entirely at the level of general legislation.

To this level free individuality ought to have been raised up and perfected. If all people *in such a case* were equal and free, and also brotherly, they would pursue only their 'prejudice-free love'. In this way even the famous unseen hand, which regulates everything in the market, will hardly need to have attention called to itself – and if it does, this would only be because of the absence of its services!

Everybody agrees that 'prejudice-free love' must remain a pious hope, a 'Sunday speech', in a society which no longer knows what Sunday means. And yet 'prejudice-free love' is all we have to rescue our individuality and not come to grief because of it. What we cannot achieve by our own strength will have to be supplemented by eco-dictatorial measures – whether or not they do any good.

Bernard of Clairvaux once appeared to me in a sort of rational vision: if only we could mobilise those energies he mobilised for western *expansion*, which ultimately turn into money and kilowatts, for the *withdrawal* out of the dead-end of material progress, for the Turn-around! Because we do have these strengths in us, it will even be an *enterprise* to leave the dead-end, to disarm the monster, and to build up a culture with a comprehensible life-cycle. Bernard himself began, with heart and spirit, the encouraging build-up of a monastery – as a germ-cell for the Kingdom of God – but then the demon of the will-to-power and the conquest of the external world ran away with him. Spiritual strength became the vehicle of these more elemental driving forces. It was the same with the Templars, and even up to Adolf Hitler.

Now, at a time when the empire of the white man threatens to collapse under its own weight, when it no longer offers enticements to go anywhere at all, Europe must attempt, under different circumstances, what at an earlier time Italy from Cato to Benedict succeeded in doing. But global degradation leaves us even less time. Yet the irresistible ego of the white man is in our hands here and now, each one his own. With this theme we are closer to the power that is killing us than we are to capital dynamics, the industrial system or the environmental catastrophe.

In Friedrich Heer's book *The Venture of Creative Reason*[2], in the chapter on "The Insanity of Pure Reason and Pure Science" Heer gives a portrait of Rene Descartes, the founder of modern scientific method. The example of this man speaks volumes about the great self-transformation we must allow to happen to us, if a nature-compatible science shall emerge. Starting from the dream of Ulm, in which Descartes defended himself against the demands of his 'underworld', Heer writes:

For the new monks, the pure scientists, science becomes, for 'impure spirits', for 'unscientific' freebooters, an untouchable goddess, which must be defended from the 'obscene', from 'untrained' people who are not obedient to the 'discipline'. Also through burnings at the stake, and in any case by means of excommunication by that 'new church' of Protestantism, the university (Hegel: "our church is the university").

Providing an 'example' for the schizophrenic life of the 20th Century 'pure scientist', who with 'peace of mind' experiments with humans and atoms, Descartes led a double life. He had typically two rooms: a salon de reception *and behind it an inaccessible laboratory, in which he dissected animals, polished the lenses of telescopes, and carried out other scientific work.*

The highest price which had to be paid for 'harnessing' nature, the 'animal drives', the 'lies' (of poets and literati, not in service of the 'pure truth' of 'pure science'), the subjugation of sex, of the female, and of people's childlike qualities, is the new fear. *This price is still being paid in the civilisation of the white man.*

This new fear taints the entire subterranean body/mind region of the person, and of world history, and is then discounted as 'chaos', a 'work of the Devil', 'gremlins', 'stupidity', 'insanity' or 'crime'.

While the unearthly wind swirls about Descartes in his dreams, he is continually troubled by the fear of falling – of touching the earth, reality, the female-motherly (the lap of all poetry, all-unifying of human creative forces).

Descartes builds his myth of science out of the evil spirits in his depths... in the act of overcoming this 'temptation', which is experienced as devilish. He has, still dreaming, his Whitsuntide experience: his being taken over by the holy spirit of science. 'Universal science raises our nature to its highest degree of perfection'. In this, his Whitsuntide of reason, he experiences, in a state of holy emotion, that this pure science is the science of God and the Angels.

Descartes: "I shall assume that Heaven, air, earth, colours, shapes, sounds and the totality of everything external, are nothing but a deception produced by dreams, through which he craftily places traps for my credulity; I will regard myself as if I were to have no hands, no eyes, no flesh, no blood, no senses of any sort, but simply falsely assumed that I had them."

This is quite exactly that ego-fortress out of which we men, in our capacity as scientists, put on our cloak and dagger. This Cartesian ego, born of the brain – which spoke the words *cogito ergo sum*, according to which we are assured of our existence only by the self-certainty of our *thought*, around which we have built our whole existence – is something which we must deliberately let go of, if we are to be able to live and let live. It is *the* problem of those hitherto tone-setting western elites who made the Megamachine. Bioenergetic methods, the therapies of humanistic psychology, the practices of meditation, wherever they may come from – they are for nobody more important than for *homo occidentalis scientificus*.

NOTES
(1) Romain Rolland, *Beethoven: les grandes epoques cr[ac]eatrices* (Paris: 1966).
(2) *Das Wagnis der schöpferischen Vernunft* (Stuttgart: 1977).

8. Masculine Logic Steers Toward Death

The Lost Balance between man and woman

I wrote the last chapter in an altogether patriarchal manner, as if history were made only by men, by the white male ego. This is indeed the case for a history placed in the logic of self-extermination. The *entire* material in Part II consists of patriarchal structures into which the feminine has not entered in an autonomous and proportionate manner. The entire feminine contribution, once much stronger and more fundamental – even to the structures of science derived from contact with plants or lunar astronomy – has been integrated in a masculine way. *The civilisation is masculine. Patriarchy and this kind of civilisation are identical.*

In an article in a daily paper of May 5th 1986, on the subject of Chernobyl, a Moscow woman was quoted as saying: "If a woman who understands life were to sit up there in the Politburo, at least we would be helped in the availability of food". And then comes a further sentence going far beyond this: "Men don't think about life at all, they only want to conquer nature and the enemy. Whatever the cost." It would be impossible to sum up warrior-psychology more simply and concisely. The ultimate secret of the environmental crisis is that people pursue other priorities than that of *life* – even if the life is one's own.

It is clear that, excluding mere exchange, 'war, commerce, and piracy', money and capital, state and church, rationalistic science and technology are wholly masculine inventions and institutions. The existence of Amazons, female hustlers, queens, female saints, or women like Marie Curie, cannot refute this. The roles are written out and distributed in advance, and women are allowed to play along. But the spirit and the methods are essentially masculine, and women modulate things only a little.

Today all our social arrangements and techno-structures are the result of a few thousand years of development, during which, in the shaping of culture, balance between feminine and masculine attitudes to the world was lacking. With male and female the world of *Logos* and the Gods stood here, and that of *Bios* and *Eros* there, divided and opposite to each other. Walter Schubart speaks of the self-destruction of culture

– the puzzle of all puzzles and the disaster of all disasters[1].

It would be something of a masquerade to use theatrical tricks to soften up the logic, the *Logos*, of self-extermination. I know that this whole intellectual mode still repels the majority of women, and perhaps even the majority of humanity. It is the spirit of a dominating minority of men and but a few women, which nevertheless puts its imprint on the entire modern social body.

It is 'right' and 'wrong' at the same time to withdraw oneself from this spirit. 'Right' – because the masculine *Logos* means that abstract concepts, geometric and mathematical structures (most recently the binary code of computer languages!) have advanced into the power-centres of the evolution of the species. It is from here that the whole gets its anti-natural, anti-biotic, anti-erotic, anti-feminine perspective. 'Wrong' – because to withdraw means becoming unaware of the logic of self-extermination and to accept its results as fate. New age people for example, who are usually in this only part-time, meditate on the moving train. Chernobyl spares no Findhorn community. The rituals of witch-craft have not stopped the emergence of modern technocratic man. Why should they be able to stop the finale?

Giving up the spirit rather than cleaning it up, fighting off the concepts instead of correcting them, these things result in a regression to stages which, today more than ever, must be regarded as failure. There is such a thing as a feminine rejection of reason – not just *Logos*. I mean *the lack of a feminine alternative* to reason – something which did indeed appear in history under the name of *Sophia* (wisdom), but which didn't significantly influence its structure. Human history is up to now a *tragic* ascent to consciousness.

The tragedy is linked to the male constitution *and* his spiritual loneliness, with the lack of the female companion. Of course, this is an area which has been thoroughly mined, because He pushes Her away preventatively. Meanwhile the causes of patriarchy have been extensively explained, and it has become accepted as a necessary, unavoidable mode of consciousness[2]. The rationalistic demon rests on the compensatory power-politics of the anxious male ego.

What Walter Schubart wrote fifty years ago about this and about the mental relation of the sexes to each other still seems to me to be significant today:

> *Woman reposes more closely on the central source of life, while man hunts it in the boundaries of existence, always concerned to overcome, and in the last analysis, to kill. Woman has a secret alliance with eternal life, and man with the principle of death. Woman wants to embrace the contradictions of life and to reconcile them in the act of doing so. Man on the other*

hand releases the tension between opposites by annihilating one of the sides, the one he finds unpleasant. He seeks the solution not in love and reconciliation, but in overcoming and annihilation. He has a militant, and not an erotic manner.

The male principle, born of isolation, makes solitude eternal, seeks being-in-itself, and disturbs life as a whole. His being is battle and self-service, his will-to-life is concerned with asserting his own person or overthrowing that of the stranger, until the motive of salvation kindles within him... Woman, with her sustaining constitution, is at one and in harmony with the basis of the world. But man wants to change the world, to bring it forward, to overcome it...[3]

Hypothetically culture could have turned out quite differently, less repulsive and less exterministic; perhaps it would possess a desired utopian character, if women were to have gone along with it from the initial steps taken 10,000 years ago. The whole epoch of the *young* goddess and 'her' hero, which is now being idealised by women researchers into matriarchy, was already the transition period: the dice had been thrown long before, and the solution lies on a different level from the one to which admittedly justified complaints and accusations point.

Originally man did not rob and dispossess woman of that which was hers. He built up his power in areas of activity, and with forces, with which woman did not concern herself. He gave society, step by step, different centres of gravity and a different focus from that of the reproduction of life and the controlling of the immediate living space in which the matriarchal family moved about. But all new upcoming branches of culture were of the form of abstract calculations and strategic deliberations more suited to the male mentality, which unfolds itself in this way. The 'higher' and 'later' made the 'lower' and 'earlier' peripheral. In this way woman becomes the first periphery of civilisation.

It is not at all necessary that her realm as such be suppressed, hemmed in, or more strongly exploited. Exploitation begins at the point where, in a process of exchange[4] the balance of the partners, the equal valuing of them, the equal significance, ceases to exist. It is already sufficient that the realm of the male no longer stands alongside that of the female, complementary, polar, and on the same level, as was the case in the family order of the hunter-gatherers. The more complex a culture becomes in its internal structure and external relations, the more that male mediation functions come into existence at levels above that of the family group and the locality, the greater is the power-advantage which accrues to the male mode of behaviour. "Whoever has mediating functions has the power," said Hegel. It was the new areas, the hallmarks of culture, the areas in which their evolution was taking place, out of which patriarchy grew.

Peoples such as the Greeks, Romans and Germanics were just as extremely patriarchal as they were expansionistic. Elsewhere the older, mother-right principles were not so completely pushed aside. The six characteristics of *homo occidentalis*, which I recapitulated earlier, are point for point the hallmarks of a culture fully dominated by the male principle.

All female culture, as far back as we can see, is contained within this frame. The revival of witchcraft today may be a form of reasserting the original strengths of women, but it rests on a tradition of rebellion. The witch could hardly be an ideal of emancipation. As they once belonged to the monk, being his obverse side, and their form being his projective creation, so they belong today as counterpart to the descendant of the monk – the rationalistic monomaniac in science, technology, capital and politics.

Western emancipation of woman could open the way for a turn-about of civilisation, but at the moment it is operating *within* the European progress model. The white queen says 'check' to the white king and competes with him for the first place. The black and white chequerboard with its rules and logic represent her too. The achievement of equal rights within this structure, the entry into the world of work, school, science, technology, medicine, and even the state – all this hardly touches the patriarchal structure and its lethal consequences, and this is not just a result of resistance of patriarchal ideas and authorities within and outside us. The invasion of the old positions by women does not add to the evil significantly, but legitimates it again for one last time.

I fear that we could fill all positions proportionately and formally eliminate the last remains of discrimination against women by means of planned over-compensation – and all this would not signify more than a change in the atmosphere of the *status quo*. Even an all-female list of legislators can only have a subversive effect to the extent that they do *not* comply with ordinary parliamentary norms of behaviour – that is, they refuse to give priority to political efficiency and permit life-interests to break in.

Perhaps these things are all transitions to an independence which is much less endangered by some inquisition from the outside. "The Self" from Mary Daly's *Gyn/Ecology* is, in a sense, *"the* only one in her property" – that is, the perfection of our bourgeois individualism for the female intellectual. Naturally 'spinning' and 'weaving' adds dimensions to the female spirit, and uncovering the patriarchal cruelties and subjection-mechanisms directed against women underlines the dilemma of our civilisation.

But this dilemma cannot be solved in Daly's spirit of 'whoever is not for us is against us'. The 'class struggle' approach to the question of the sexes is not only disposed to tighten up the old pattern and re-charge it with energy. It is also a brake on the reaching of new understanding[5]. The *good* female and the *evil* male, are connected not only in the victim-perpetrator circle, but also woman must have been the female accomplice of the patriarchate, just emerging.

In other words the roles must have moved in that direction *correlatively* or in a co-evolutionary fashion. No patriarchal will-to-mastery would have had a chance without a *necessary opportunity*. The human being has up to now found no non-patriarchal form for controlling social complexity. In their polarity the sexes are complementary halves of one bipolar system of human society. Neither from the one nor from the other 'half of Heaven' alone can destruction or healing proceed.

As I understand it, patriarchy was most of all a new structure of consciousness, a new ego-structure. It made its appearance with the heroic, self-conscious, mythical ego, which released itself from the motherly realm, from the role of the son-lover of the Great Mother. If this hero has now 'reached the end', so has woman too, because the culture as a whole is sick and because its civilising structures weigh much more heavily than the bio-psychic difference between the sexes, however important that difference may now be. We have truly reached the end with male dominance, as a culturally-conditioned phase in the evolution of the human spirit.

The male principle is not only present in every woman, it is in the whole, which is us all. Resentments and allocations of blame are useless here, much less than in private conflicts, where they sometimes give rise to something fruitful. Sometimes women say: 'men have driven the cart into the ditch, and they must now pull it out again'. And sometimes women say – and not always different women – that they want to take over the leadership. There is some truth in both. How does it fit together?

In my opinion the patriarchy cannot be criticised *to the limit* from the special standpoint of women alone. It cannot be seen as a *whole*, if SHE takes herself out of it or figures herself into it merely as a sacrifice or as supplementary co-player, if SHE is ultimately concerned only about the responsible man and not about human beings, about the species-problem of the 'right' relations between the two poles *now*.

Kings and Queens

The closer we come to the origin of human existence, the more labyrinth-like become the fields of identification with which we conceal reality. The primal fact, that humanity is man and woman, is today being loaded up with a mass of ideology suggesting that we are in reality unisex, just a combination of male and female principles, capable of being integrated to any degree we want, as if the real difference were merely imaginary. What nonsense!

As far as I can see, conceptions of androgyny and trans-sexuality have been for the most part male attempts to supplement themselves by 'becoming feminine', in order to perfect priestly and medical power. They are conceptions which are *against* the original architecture of life. If there was and is a basic unity, this was and is feminine. The original foundation is *feminine* and not androgynous. In the history of life the Great Mother precedes the male, paternal principle, which later differentiated out of her. This is not just a psychological reality, it is a physical and also a spiritual one, and furthermore recorded in countless inheritances from the past.

Patriarchy has been a turning upside-down of the order of life, and it only made sense as long as its secondary character was upheld – its character as a paradoxical superstructure on the supporting foundation. Why have the matriarchal social constitutions – generally in force until deep into patriarchal times – fixed the roles of the sexes so rigidly?! It was always the *male* role which was *specialised* out, because it came later. The least deviation from whatever the stereotype was for masculine behaviour, for the warrior, sufficed to force the male to change his social position and move over into that of the other sex, frequently into a spiritual function.

What we today call *individuation*, meaning, amongst other things, the adopting and integration of characteristics of the other sex, qualified early for leadership and pointed out the direction of mental ascent. But at the same time all these early-period initiations were lop-sided and coercive. They meant a breaking with natural sexual facts and a neuroticising of the whole culture. Today, it is not a question of tightening the rigid sexual polarity. The factual gradation of the sexual characteristics, which reaches back into the biological realm, wants to be expressed in life, but in its normal distribution. It is an illusion to believe that patterns of *Eros*, which until recently were discriminated against as deviant, could now become dominant. What is evolving here is subcultures, often with pioneer functions for a new general ordering. People with less fully-developed sexual polarity have always played an important role in new adaptations when the human spirit makes a jump.

But, as long ago in the tribe, these minorities are today only a ferment within the whole. They will bequeath to it a more flexible psycho-sexual order to which natural bipolar distribution will yield. For the first time in its history humanity is attempting to control the *strong* tension between man and woman. Man and woman, in the process of fully individualising and integrating their partial strengths, will be able to live more easily in a network of loving relationships, without anxiety, and free enough to give themselves to each other instead of feeling partly guilty and partly robbed, when more than one love goes out from or tries to reach into their hearts.

It appears to me to be as clear as day that – without any discrimination against other need-preferences – the heterosexual pair as a pattern will occupy the nodes of the network and will thus constitute the basis of the social structure. They will complement, perfect and make beautiful the bisexual, homosexual and transsexual attitudes of all individuals. But the time of love between man and woman is only now approaching. The image of sacred marriage, which was once an unindividual, collective metaphor, will belong to the collective mythos of every successful individuation. Unification in love will prove to be the royal road to the million-fold ascent to a higher state of consciousness.

Because there is nothing more painful than hatred between egos which have been intimate with each other, man and woman will *mutually* learn the crossing of the boundary from the power-fighting ego to the loving self. Love, with erotic love at the centre, is the way.

On the other hand, where a 'platonic' love is turned against the sexual drive of the real *Eros*, we have to deal only with the last twitches of a love-hostile patriarchal tradition in spirituality and morality. The creative energy of the human being is fundamentally erotic, and this potential will express itself fully when its mis-direction into pure *productivism* falls away again. If the task of creating a loving culture which realises itself sensually is avoided, it will then be impossible to resolve the ecological crisis, because the fighters (within both sexes) will continue their various substitute projects, by means of which they never satisfy themselves.

One thing is certain: the continued climb to consciousness must have a fatal outcome if the male *Logos* remains dominant. Leadership must change, but certainly not arbitrarily to 'matriarchy'. In both sexes *Sophia* must unfold. If up to now *Sophia* [wisdom] was subordinated to *Logos* [divine reason], exploited by him and obstructed in her development, now *Sophia* must *incorporate Logos*, making her own *that part* of *Logos* which is efficient from the standpoint of *Bios* or *Eros* – in an arrangement of things which is right from the point of view of *life*, no longer contradicting nature.

Logos and *Sophia*, from the viewpoint of the poles of the sexes, embrace the entire world accessible to us. Their structures must penetrate each other. The *opposite* is catastrophic, but to live out the *polarity* would bring us once again into harmony with the natural order of things. Lao Tzu has given us the motto "The male to know, the female to preserve". If we accept this, then 'change of leadership' is in fact inexact, and misleading to the extent that the word 'leadership' is associated for us with the idea of an expedition.

Woman shall, and now must, begin to exert her powers of *Logos*, but on the basis of 'to preserve'. And also, for his part, man needs her help. Because unaccompanied – and also driven out – he has torn himself loose one-sidedly and logocentrically from the original basis and sought his homeland in moving forward – in Bloch's famous formulation, as *something that appears to all of us in childhood, yet a place where nobody ever was*. And the search has increasingly externalised itself.

The home-country has something to do with the womb – yet from the phallus on Buddha's head to the space rockets of our super-materialistic *Logos* we take flight into the galactic anti-womb. The male now needs the goddess: *the modern one*.

Man and woman have separated from each other in nature. Now they can only find each other again led by their different spirits. That will occur in the meeting of all their senses, but body and soul alone do not guarantee it, because in the evolution of the human species spirit is the leading edge of the process. 'Leadership', feminine leadership, means here a new structure of consciousness as path, means the overcoming of that split, that schism between logical (mainly masculine) ego and body, between history and nature, spirit and earth, *Logos* and *Bios*, man and woman – all these being aspects of one and the same problem.

In opposition to this, radical feminism manifests itself, in that by involving itself in criticism of the rationalistic Megamachine structure, it becomes repeatedly caught up in antagonism – precisely the basic problem. This is the feminine catching up with the fight against the dragon: Saint George as Amazon, conquering the *achievements* of the patriarchy. Nevertheless, beneath the shimmering armour, the female violates herself in a manner quite different from the male, and scares him not by her belligerent competing role, but by the figure of the Great Mother contained in it, who does *not* compete with him, so much as regard his whole compensatory effort to be of no consequence.

Feminists love to unmask patriarchs (like for example Carl Jung and his pupil Erich Neumann), before assimilating their breakthroughs. Stricken by the patent injustice of patriarchy and its undoubted exterministic capacity, they often focus the dispute on the slag instead of the ore. It might indeed be frightful, how once upon a time the mythical god Marduk struck down, split and tore up the mythical goddess Tiamat (mother, *mater*, matter), and scattered her pieces around. How did he come to do this? Isn't a role of goddess presupposed here? And hadn't she also cut her partner into pieces?

The male-patriarchal ego, which cannot have come into existence independently of the opposing feminine pole, has now also conjured into existence a female version no less problematic than itself, and stands strongly by its side in continuing the splitting-off from the origin. The social difference between the sexes could well have been the most basic formative mechanism in the growth of private property and the state. For this reason accusatory feminism seems to me to shed little light by its selection of historical facts. The material produced is mainly a weapon of contemporary self-assertion, but not necessarily of the self-liberation which is still to be accomplished.

Patriarchy *is* indeed the most all-embracing name for the structure of consciousness which has to be replaced. Yet both man and woman are caught up in it to the same extent – both are *responsible*. The ego-entrapment, ego-cramp, is the source of the harassing and exhausting battles in our love-ties. In order that the whole 'other sex' could be suppressed, this unsolved problem of individuality – the power-claim of the ego worried about its precarious identity – already had to exist. Nowhere is this power-question more clearly recognisable as the basic problem than in the failure of *Eros*, even though the love battle is only one of its facets.

While it is relatively easy to say what must happen at the material level to stop and dissolve the Megamachine, it is still unclear in what shape the human being as body-soul-spirit will respond to the crisis of the modern rationalistic ego, the personality; and in what way the sexes will relate to each other. At first the contradictions sharpen up. No thought-through solution exists here. All that can help is the readiness to be open at a deep level for the primal potential and theme which is breaking through, and which we must meet anew as beginners. Will we succeed in differentiating between those areas where *Eros* is speaking out of its natural right, and those where is it only being used as reinforcement for some newest fashion or some older convention of self-assertion and role-playing?

The point of the contradiction between the sexes lies in the fact that the self-conscious spirit has only now achieved its full patriarchal un-folding, so that the whole of our culture and science not only cannot 'preserve' the feminine, but also must treat it as something inimical and destructive. This spirit has not integrated the female mode of knowing. On the contrary it has pushed itself away from it and, in the extreme cases in our civilisation, burnt it with the witches.

Here we meet up with the following dilemma. Not only the arising of the patriarchal ego, but also the spiritual reaction to the concomitant 'horrors of history' represented an already-lost balance, and the war between the sexes. The message of overcoming the ego can direct itself against the ascent of women, and can hold women back from achieving equal rights *within* patriarchy, from participation in the regulatory functions of rationalistic societies.

Above all it can reinforce ascetic, salvation-seeking types of spirituality which deny what Lao Tzu knew: that the difference between the sexes is one of the cosmogenic original principles. Such a bisexual androgyny cannot possibly be in agreement with the original basis of life. Patriarchal spirituality is basically *Eros*-repressing and outrightly anti-erotic. In such a climate men and women can come together only spiritually, disregarding the sexual polarity of life and pushing themselves away from it.

As a rule the Buddhas have been more patriarchal than anyone else. Buddha himself didn't want to initiate any woman, and this was not a mistake, being consistent with his sense of his place in the world. To this extent his path as a whole was not the true one, because he disavows 'half of Heaven'.

Since I got to know the *Tao Teh Ching* fifteen years ago I have always been fascinated by the special feature which distinguishes Lao Tzu from Buddha. Lao Tzu is not fleeing from the feminine and from the time of women. In substance his mysticism matches the others, whether that of the Buddha or of Meister Eckhart. In essence the *Tao* and *Logos* (the Christian spirit of Eckhart and the logic of Hegel) describe the same basic configuration of being, and seek the same ultimate background, 'higher than God and the Trinity'.

In the case of Lao Tzu we have it without monotheistic or trinitarian patriarchal accoutrement. In addition the patriarchal spirit from Plato and Plotinus to Hegel is homo-erotic. Thus this basic ground in their case is neuter, a little inclined to the masculine. For Lao Tzu it is motherly and creation is, as in all original cosmologies, a history of a world-parental pair. *Yin* and *Yang*, the two sexual poles, preceding the many thousand particular things which come into existence.

If it is true that *Eros* and *Logos* – bound up with each other along the spinal cord – nourish themselves from the same energy, there can be no peace with nature without 'the turning home of *Eros* to the gods', without the gain of balance between two poles, which penetrate each other without extinguishing each other. Ultimately there is no danger that *Eros* will kill *Logos* – the female spirit is rising as well, now more than ever. But *Logos* kills *Eros* all too frequently. A spirituality which can lead us to saving the earth must be grounded in *Eros*.

But here a great deal depends on woman. Even though she may describe the behaviour of the male as being to her disadvantage, there remains an elemental common fate, an unsolved original problem for *both* sexes. The female is not fixed at the rational, male, mental-ego stage, but since prehistory she has been just as egocentric as males in her demands (in an anthropological, not moralistic sense). Her interest just has a different centre of gravity. The more it is unfalsified by the patriarchal stage, the more her identity is rooted in vital deep layers, and the nearer she stands to the original matriarchal period of culture, the clearer this is.

Over time the difference between the sexes may have become over-ideologised. Even so it nevertheless corresponds to a degree with the Chinese *Yin-Yang* pattern. In the present situation the return of this difference could have a repressive tendency against the female. So the issue then is whether the egocentric tendency in the male crystallises more around *Logos*, and in the female around *Eros* – with the military campaign and expedition, and with the encampment and the bed.

There is already a manifest hostility between the sexes, and we could hardly solve this by looking backwards, by uncovering some earlier paradise-like natural state or idealised matriarchal conditions – as if these ancient times had not been pregnant with conflict. It is more likely that the only chance of overcoming egocentricity lies in the forward direction. The primary key lies in the liberation of one's own self, which requires the overcoming of indigence. In the words of Hölderlin: "Kings [and queens] of finiteness, wake up!"

The spiritual-erotic pair is possible, in the ascent to awareness, and ego-transcendence is the next step. The pair is only possible, love is only possible, when we stop *expecting* satisfaction, happiness and salvation from the other, or from Godhead – while we may indeed need cooperative help. Two people who have really achieved their inner autonomy and freedom and are no longer *imprisoned* by their wishes, who have half-way succeeded in putting arrogance and jealousy behind them and do not mainly make demands on their neighbours, are capable of bonding as a pair. Before this, love is a substitute project, favoured by the woman. Other logocentric projects of the man are also substitute projects, and on the threshold of psychic intimacy the old game, the power struggle, begins again: *if you give to me, I will give to you.*

If it is true that in the individuality of both sexes sexuality and spirit are polar, but inseparably interdependent, then the love encounter – where both sexes eat from the tree of knowledge – cannot succeed without reflection, without the will to transcend the power game. Both sides need to agree to unilateral disarmament. For this reason self-discovery, the acceptance of solitude which is bound up with individuation, the unlearning of expectations projected on the other – all these things *precede* their communion.

In *this* matter the woman has a longer road to travel, because as a rule she attaches herself to an earlier stage in history – and yet at the same time she has perhaps the shorter road. Because beyond *Eros* there is no longer any substitute project of equal value, while the male can always flee from one logocentric project to the next. In other words: *against* HIM, *against* his projects, *against* his failure in love, SHE will only drive him further away, as hitherto, and at the same time make longer the journey to her inner self. And he too will make his road longer if he seeks liberation by *fleeing* from woman, from the Great Mother, from the young goddess. The judgement will then be handed down against him that he has failed the Great Goddess, that he has failed *Sophia*. The flight from woman leads away from love and life, away from the living spirit to the dead spirit.

Thus the passionate question remains: whether and how man and woman can work together in a new spiritual practice.

NOTES
(1) Walter Schubart, *Religion und Eros* (München: 1978), pp205 & 269.
(2) Here is not the place to go into this comprehensively, but I will at least mention the authors whose work has – collectively – explained the roots of patriarchy to me, for while they were not concentrating solely on this theme, they also did more than just mention it in passing. In this sense I refer to the works of Erich Neumann (whose *Origin and History of Consciousness* first showed me the light), Jean Gebser, Julian Jaynes, William Irwin Thompson (he demonstrated, by means of the Gilga- mesh epic, the heroic psychology which emerged after entry into urban civilisation, and its conflict with feminine cosmology), Ken Wilber (*Up From Eden*), and once again Friedrich Heer, whose book I have already quoted. But the most extraordinary work that I found was Walter Schubart's *Religion und Eros*, written back in the thirties. Schubart got to the bottom of the difference between male and female cosmologies and showed their relationship to the poles of life and death. For him woman and man must, in view of the difference between them, find themselves on their own, but their saving utopia is unification, ultimately the loving pair, and I think that whatever may be understood by 'androgynous' or 'trans-sexual' will turn out to be illusory as long as the original problem of the sexes is not returned to and solved afresh. Even though Schubart's book in many details, and even as a whole, is a little old-fashioned, it made clear to me as no other has done, how much *flight* from woman and therefore how much non-mastery of that original problem is to be found in all male cultural achievements and, by no means last, in all patriarchal high religions; and that there is something basically false in all spirituality which does not just want to sublimate Eros partially, but ultimately wants to overcome it. Those to whom I refer here are all men. Yet the feminist literature which I read concentrated itself much more on the uncovering of scandal than on explaining patriarchy. Only recently did I discover a book – without prejudice to the open question of whether Christianity can be rescued in a feminist manner – with which I very much agree both emotionally and as to content; Elga Sorge's *Religion und Frau* (Stuttgart: 1985).

(3) Schubart, *op cit*, p111f.

(4) All round the world, first men are attracted by the production of the industrial society and corrupted, whether by fire-water and weapons as in the case of the North American Indians, or by transistor radios and motor-cycles anywhere in Latin America, Asia, or Africa. 'Development Aid' everywhere destroys the traditional living domain upheld by the women, instead of supporting it. What is the meaning here of 'appropriate technology'?! The civilisation shaped by the white man passes on its values and priorities further and makes the non-white man its accomplice. He widens its radius of action and becomes cosmopolitan. Naturally he does not get enough, but merely becomes fattened up. Earth, life, women, children get pushed more toward the margin. Even Richard von Weizsäcker saw this after his Asian tour, but didn't want to draw the conclusion that everything must change *here*, otherwise there can be no checking things *there*, and finally the boomerang which we threw out will all the more surely strike back.

(5) Schubart's assessment of the 'modern emancipation of women' is in tune with this: "This means a subjection of woman beneath the male world-evaluation. The emancipated woman does not seek to enforce the appropriately female way in opposition to that of the male (humility against pride, creativeness against criticism, the drive for wholeness against the mania for subdivision, organic mode of experiencing against the mechanical mode). She proceeds from the (allegedly) superior rank of male values and only wants to secure for woman the full enjoyment of these values and participation in their actualisation. This shaping is not a struggle for the equal ranking of the sexes and of the male and female typology, but only a struggle to achieve external equal rights for women in a male world. Woman's emancipation struggles for something non-female, and struggles furthermore with male weapons. In both respects it resembles the Amazon culture of antiquity, the earliest betrayal of the matriarchal idea, wanting that women become like men, desiring to be treated as men, and expressing contempt for the authentically feminine. To this extent the latter-day emancipated woman shares the basic outlook of – the Christian ascetic." (*op cit*, p260f)

9. Conditio humana

It is not Feeling, but Intellect, which gets out of Control

Patriarchy is a fundamental mode of consciousness, but still not the deepest level in the 'geology' of exterminism. Indeed, as far as the polarity of the sexes is concerned, it reaches back directly to the origin of species. It then shows itself as an apparently pre-formed tendency of the human spirit, at an early stage of cultural development in *all* ethnic groups. So we must assume that it has its roots in the human genotype, in the species-character of the 'brain-animal'. The masculine has a transient function as a privileged organ of species evolution.

With the coming of patriarchy humanity breaks out of the cyclical rhythm of its prehistory, in which social evolution proceeded slowly enough to be compatible with a myth of eternal return. In patriarchy, history and anthropology, progressive *civitas humana* and the enduring *conditio humana*, coincide. It is from the latter that the arrow of evolution takes off.

The seam joining the patriarchal level of self-extermination logic and the anthropological disposition which made exterministic excess possible is characterised by Walter Schubart's remark: "The physically weaker being is victorious because it put its energy into the mental side... In the same way that humans triumph over animals, men triumph over women"[1].

This second victory is one with enormous consequences, one which penetrates into all exterministic structures. But more fundamental is the first victory, the *conditio humana* itself: humans, men *and* women, are victorious over animals, and subdue the earth by means of investing in mental development.

There is a dire fate lying in human nature itself, in the entire manner in which humans function – how they relate their capabilities to their context. It does not lie only in specifically evil ways of behaving. This is the primary reason why we ran up against the question of *why God has permitted evil*. God, conceived as a personal and responsible Creator, doesn't exist. In this form he is only the projection of our problems with ourselves and with life – we extrapolate from our personal responsibility, seeing an analogous structure in the cosmos.

The truth is that from our point of view, many things which go on outside the human realm are 'evil'. It begins in the animal kingdom, in the business of eating and being eaten. Voltaire even protested against the earthquake in Lisbon. The Creator thus conceived is already 'to blame' for having set the clockwork in motion, and also for setting up biological food-chains in which sentient beings mutually devour each other.

If we, having become vegetarians, get around to thinking that we ought to train the cat to stop mousing – in order to be ideologically 'consistent' – all we are doing is projecting our peculiarly *human* situation. It's only for *us* that there are *problems* here. The yogi who is at pains not to tread on ants is in no way behaving naturally. If we had not eaten from the tree of knowledge, we wouldn't *deliberately* kill animals, and it wouldn't have occurred to us to avoid unintentional killing – or still further, to push awareness so far that unintentional killing begins to seem intentional. "We have knowingly not developed the level of attention necessary to avoid bringing unhappiness to other creatures."

Non-violence is the extremest cultural performance imposed on us by our specific natural equipment, by our overkill-capacity as brain-animal. At the same time non-violence is the extremest example of deliberateness. Only s/he who sleeps does not sin. The moment we are awake we must be aware. If the oldest sages have reached the conclusion that we should do as little as possible, this is also a way of escaping the *curse* of continuous vigilance.

And yet our history has brought us to a point where non-violence in this extreme sense appears to be demanded if we are to survive. This means either that we must all become *yogis*, ready to be fully aware the moment we are awake. Naturally, for a number of reasons this will not happen. Or we must create for ourselves institutions, a *culture*, which relieves us of the burden of sustained vigilance, so that we could disengage ourselves and live uninhibitedly.

Arthur Koestler has introduced some confusion in his – in my opinion – only half thought-through book about humans as 'mistakes of evolution'. He considers that all world-improvers, the 'gifted reformers' of whom there was never a shortage, could have been mistaken as to the causes "...which compelled humans to make such a valley of misery out of their history". Their basic mistake is said to have been "...that the entire blame was ascribed to egoism, greed and the alleged destructiveness of humans, in other words, to the *self-assertive tendency* of the individual"[2]. According to Koestler the tragedy of humankind is rooted not in its aggression but in his "devotion to super-personal ideals... in a functional disturbance of integrative tendencies", that is, in the con-

formist spirit of group-membership. This reflection is completely misleading, because ideals are often not at all transpersonal or beyond the
ego.

And is the tragedy really rooted in the fact that people participate in
everything? Indeed most of the time they *live* in this group spirit, but
this says nothing about how good or bad the matter is, in which they
conform. Self-assertive and integrative tendencies are not opposed to
each other in the same way that ego and group are, but rather are
tendencies *within* the ego, which belongs more to the collectivity than to
the individual self. The group spirit is the first large-scale manifestation
of the human spirit – which rests on symbols and language. From this
sphere gradually emerges the historical reflexive, self-conscious ego, in
patriarchal form.

But we need *more* than merely conformist dependency of the not-yet-
liberated individual, to explain *excesses* of hate against strangers and
others, or *excesses* of cruelty and destructiveness. Such 'super-personal
ideals' have first of all to be set charismatically before they can possibly
function as 'permission' for the release of atavistic emotions! Wilber[3]
points to discoveries according to which hate-leading-to-violence is
almost entirely a *cognitive* and *conceptual* product, going far beyond
mere biological aggression. Ideals are ego-authorities which compensate
for individual fragmentariness and limitation. It remains a question for
the capacities, personal strengths, and powers assembled around the
individual, to decide who will lead and who will be a follower.

Even when the ego is not fully conscious of itself, states of
consciousness-conditioned power-unbalance already appear. Ideals have
powerful representatives. There is no sense in setting 'self-assertive' and
'integrative' tendencies in opposition to each other in a dualistic fashion, and then dragging this scheme through completely different historical stages. They are correlative sides of the *one* process of getting
control of the world, for which the human constitution as a *whole* is
equipped, and which it is going through. Egoism, greed and other ills
are excellently equipped to tolerate ideals. They can slip into ideals and
hide themselves there.

The whole distinction between ego and group makes the tacit assumption that competition for security, satisfaction, comfort, power
and significance is the decisive drive behind evolution. The more
individuality there is, the more power-determined is the whole of
history. The extent to which people let themselves be irrationally carried along with this, and the extent to which the psychic underworld,
rendered evil by suppression, manages to express itself, is of secondary
importance.

This volcano has erupted only at times when the total social structure had become inefficient and destructive, obstructing the satisfactions which it originally guaranteed, and inhibiting an individuality grown stronger with time. In all these cases we are dealing with catastrophes which were not caused by the beast in us, but which were connected with the dynamics of large-brain processes and their increasing objectification in language, social structure, state, and so on.

The very first western work of political science, Thucydides' *History of the Peloponnesian War*, argued anthropologically: in human historical struggles we are dealing with the two original drives for mastery and freedom, which have common roots in the demands of self-assertion. He took the view that these things, as exemplified in the barbarian 'world war' of the Greeks, would continually recur *so long as human nature remains the same* – caught up in this dilemma of mastery and freedom. Thus the direction of salvation lies in the overcoming of this.

In reality however, the 'human nature' of Thucydides is characterised by only *one* distinct stage in the evolution of the 'brain-animal'. This evolution still has further to go before it reaches its culmination – provided our species survives its current crisis, as *top-parasite in an untenable position*.

Naturally, the problem lies in the *total* constitution of our species, not in the large brain alone. But it *is* human nature to possess this over-heavy organ. In this sense human nature is 'to blame', even though it can itself be frustrated and coerced by this organ. *Right from the beginning* the mind was a *compensatory power instrument*, and we *had* to make the flight forward into culture. We are subject to a compulsion to act, and thus culture and civilisation have become a process of increasingly taking up arms against all the risks of life. We still think that we don't work enough, that we don't make enough changes in the external world; we are never finished with the business of storing up supplies, not even spiritually – early on we stored God in our temples and churches. We have remained anxious hunters, and never have *enough*. All this is turning against us now. Our striving for security and for the elimination of every risk to life is bringing us death.

We could put it this way: our *oldest* strata interfere, because we can react to their perceptions and urgings with our *new large brain*, and we often do it inadequately because we are anxiety-ridden or too self-interested. Our superstructure is a 'security-politician' who does not permit the flow of energies thrusting up 'from below', blocks them and deflects them from their course – and in doing so limits itself. But if we could get to the point where reason has faith in the superstructure's capacity, so that it could permit things without fearing to be flooded – then perhaps we would have opened the door to the next phase of evolution.

Empirically our mind is not free, being conditioned by phylogenesis (racial history) and history, ontogenesis (individual history) and socialisation. And it certainly cannot become free by suppressing what conditioning has made it. Everything points to the fact that up to now our mind has not been able to handle those traumas which cause the universe to appear to be dangerous to the point of hostility. Those traumas, particularly associated with being born, have grown stronger with the progress of civilisation – probably because they have become more conscious, but not yet fully conscious. Here redemption is both necessary and possible.

Unavoidably our path begins under the auspices of absolute matriarchal power. And to the long period of dependent childhood is added the modern fact that practitioners of childrearing become ever colder, until the hospital-delivered child must do without decisive contact with the mother immediately after birth[4].

What has been spoiled in early childhood looks even more serious against the background of research into the birth-process carried out in recent decades. For example, Stanislav and Christina Grof have shown how experiences during pregnancy and birth determine character far more basically than the subsequently-added socialisation influences.[5]

The Grofs' material reveals the extent to which our dark, cruel and perverted tendencies are predetermined. But the result is not incapable of correction. Grof's general position[6], a synthesis of humanistic and transpersonal psychology, shows how the act of liberation from unique individual 'peri-natal matrices', through 'rebirthing' (a psychological experience of death and rebirth) opens up the spiritual dimension. And this opening up is totally without patriarchal asceticism. True, this is not the only solution[7]. Even so, we have here one of the most hopeful and promising approaches to overcoming the ecological crisis and to giving people a better relationship with the world. Apparently it is possible to change the inner relationship of forces between aggressive and antagonistic impulses, and motives of love and solidarity. The adaptation of tantric traditions to our western conditions points in the same direction.

All those weaknesses of contact pointed out by bioenergetic theorists (who take their departure from Wilhelm Reich – Lowens, for example) bring about a widespread unhappy consciousness, which in its turn results in an ever more unbearable state of the world. When there are no positive, happiness-promising prospects in the offing, limitations and renunciations resulting from the ecological crisis only intensify the psychological pestilence.

In our cognition, feeling and action we are steered by our subjective minds, from our self-concerned egos, whose specific expression is the rational demon. We cannot act in a manner which is true and genuine to life. The objective observer remains a partial person, separate from the human being. For this reason science has never achieved the rank of another theology. The experimenter is not hunting for truth, for a reconstruction of the whole, of God, but merely for fragmentary knowledge. Thus modern science has at the same time both inherited the church and remained a long way behind it, because it remained stuck in the ego-trips of its adepts.

If all we are concerned with is partial victories, then the rationalistic demon has ideally equipped itself for this task. But if we regard the mind as an organ of the whole, it is hardly possible to imagine a more disadvantageous position than that of the specialised intellect, which the mind has so conspicuously adopted. It resembles an extended antenna fastened on the outermost twig of human undertaking. In this location it makes our over-developed peculiarity absolute. The antenna, directed to the furthest galaxy, will hardly notice that the 'ground station' has collapsed. Without moralising: we are *de facto* parasites located at the top of a whole hierarchy of parasites.

In a sense it is possible to see all life as 'parasite-like', exploitative and entropy-increasing for the mineral world. Right from the start there has never been a perfectly-circulating economy. In an analogous manner animal life relates to plant life and to the inorganic realm. Above all this rises the human, and above this the man. True, the ever 'higher' parasite always gives something back, but on the basis of exploitation.

Up to now this has not been seen as a problem, because up to archaic times the balance seemed to be secure, the species disturbed only small things and, in cases of its taking a step too far, it was merely self-destructive. But the human being, and the human male, has understood from the beginning how to protect himself against setbacks.

Culture means that we withdraw behind walls and build protective layer upon layer. Thus the city stands above the land, and one or more elevated ruling classes stand over both. Today we recognise 'primary', 'secondary', 'tertiary', and 'quaternary' sectors. Above all this stand the governing centres: banks, laboratories and states. Laboratories of natural science now regard the whole as something to be split up and dissected; and in doing this they pay no attention to the relation of the top parasite to its distant basis of support, from which it is separated by a series of subjective, self-interested regulators.

So far we are not concerned with perception of nature or with the conditions of balance between mind, society and nature, but with a single pandemonium of derivative interests which have torn themselves loose from the supporting base, so that the entire structure of culture refers to its host in a lordly fashion from above. Natural science is guided by exploitative interests rather than those of inquiry, and everything else – social sciences, monetary theory, the political sphere, the arts insofar as they are concerned with making a living – is exclusively oriented to what is *within* the cultural system.

In social hierarchies the feedback from below to above is slow and inadequate, so that *those at the top always learn things too late*. Humanity as a whole has organised itself in a similar way: the male, the white empire, capital and the Megamachine constitute a pyramid of the stages of self-extermination. And at the base of all this is the *conditio humana* itself.

We can get this parasitic trait of human existence under control *via* the Origin – or not at all. But in origin the brain is the organ of the feeling body. At the same time mind is located in it, *able* to make itself independent, to become the elite, from which it acts from secondary interests and violates and exploits the primary ones.

Danger lies in the vertical division of labour and the very narrow specialisation of leading offices – so that in these places we have scientists but not humans, managers but not humans, politicians but not humans – and because of this it is not basic principles, but the prestige of these functionaries which rule – and this destroys our communication about reality, which gets trapped in a network of special arrangements needing no external sanction. *Positional* interests have automatic priority. Where the boat as a whole is going is systematically rendered imperceptible.

But in general, the functions serving social synthesis are all-too-human: maxims of the principle of self-assertion such as 'a bird in hand is worth two in the bush' are the purest philosophy of suicide. They were not permissible in any other high culture, and signalled, *if* they turned up there, the climax of decay. In our decayed modern society there is no instance of successful institutionalising of the ethics of responsibility.

Three connected factors are bound up with our natural constitution as brain-animal, and together they lead blindly into the dead end of parasitism and become ever more dangerous to our success as a species.

Projection

The *first* evolutionary ground-laying factor, which reaches back deep into the pre-human history of cognitive reflection, is the *projective* character of consciousness.

In its property as an outward-directed mirror, consciousness normally makes for itself representations of the outside world. It is an enormous step forward in cognitive ability, leading to the separated ego, one which even distinguishes between its own memory and itself. In the beginning the archaic ego is not independent and does not see the world as *subject* opposed to *object* and does not yet project – it does not yet say 'those things are not me, they are nature separate from me'.

Then consciousness makes for itself magical powers as 'partners' pulled out of nature – firstly objects and associated concepts – and also powers over human society. Later its own body becomes its object, and finally its own psyche – for example the so-called *shadow*, the sum of the properties it does not like and has repressed, which sometimes move over into other persons, 'as if it wasn't a part of me'.

This is the enormous concept of projection: we have fenced it all off from ourselves and *identify* ourselves *secondarily* with it, while all the time we *are* it ourselves. Ken Wilber has outlined this in a specially striking manner[8]. But he exaggerates the word 'only' when he defines: "But all these 'objects out there' are only *projections* of the personal being of a human, and they can all be re-discovered as aspects of one's own self". And yet, as the poet Brentano writes:

> *O star and flower, spirit and garment,*
> *Love, grief, time and eternity...*

He meant this as well: *I myself am everything.* The modern ego was called upon at the moment of its emergence in the first millennium BC, to reverse the distribution of its urges towards facts of the world[9]. *Know Thyself* – in everything! You yourself are everything. And it reaches further than *object*-recognition[10]. It is not us westerners, but orientals who have taken the path of self-knowledge, of inwardness. The Occident has created a praxis which is outward-directed and obliterates even social communication, because it directs itself wholly to the task of altering the external world – excepting the esoteric branch of our monastery culture, and single individuals who intuitively understand how to pray[11].

Modern psychoanalysis (a western path to systematic self-knowledge), in its capacity as the *Fury* of Cartesian science, and as a painstaking questioning of the insecure ego, demands that the human being reverse the outward-orientation of his organs of perception and become the objective observer *of one's self.*

Still, as a rule, a controlingly-rationalistic subject, a human being, makes for him/herself another less conscious subject-as-object. There is hardly a discipline in which oppression and emancipation are more inextricably fused together than in psychoanalysis. And yet nothing is more important than this inward self-enlightenment.

Politically and psychologically the concept of projection calls attention to how we are accustomed to look outward from ourselves *as cause.*

This is because of the external orientation of the sense-organs, which makes inner nature like an unconscious interruption – we have not created it in a Cartesian-schizoid manner. Above all, it is our habit to regard the work of our heads and hands as being just as 'objective' as actual nature. We do not like to see ourselves as *perpetrators*, but rather as *victims* of our own powerful praxis. And if we are in fact victims, this praxis is the very reason! We need to learn to see world-changing and self-changing as a unity. Yet in this unity the changing of oneself comes first. The logic of self-extermination resides in our own structure of consciousness. We must demand this insight and experience of ourselves, if we are to get into the forecourt of a Turn-around initiation.

What we *do* depends upon how we define the challenge. *If we had not merely perceived the atom bomb, but understood it, we would not now permit gene manipulation.* Yet our psycho-social constitution is organised for tampering with the handiwork of the Old Master, in order to *save labour*. Faust had at least an inkling of this: "If I could ban magic from my path, I would stand before you, Nature, as merely a man..." But even so, what we are dealing with is the *power-magic of institutions*, the admixture of a drop of tar in all the honey of genuine regulative requirements, on account of which more darkness than light flows through institutional arteries.

Who is a servant? Who is really *ministering* instead of wanting to rule? Clearly we are not at a stage of maturity in which true knowledge could function in a divine fashion, rather than in a satanic one. Even the will-to-truth and the neighbourly love of an Einstein could not guarantee anything. The motives of genetic researchers and others are simply not an adequate argument – and if they cannot see this for themselves, this alone is sufficient to disqualify them.

We let ourselves be persuaded by would-be Nobel Prize-winners about 'assessment of the results of research', in order to generate a legitimising 'positive list' of 'humanly desirable' research, which shall then be permitted. Gradually this turns into fully-conscious lies. Proofs can be made available for whatever we want. The advance decision to proceed further has already been made, so that it is only necessary to court favours for the licence to proceed, which will calm all bad conscience and appease people – and to secure priority in the distribution of resources for one's own research programme.

But the psychology of the scientist, who wants to be successful – even if as a result the world is brought to an end – is only a special case, though significant. Up to now we have treated the ecological crisis *in general* in this sort of way: if something goes wrong, the cause lies in something *external* to science. We talk about undesired *side*-effects as if they could in no way be traced back to the perpetrator, and as if they could have been avoided if we had been a little more careful and if we had caught a few unscrupulous sinners by the hair. Meanwhile we have located 'human error' as the most prominent among these 'objective causes' of failure. As if the human being could afford to fail any more! According to the mechanical method of trial-and-error we see consistently from the natural environment that our actions are defective, and we modify our methods using this feedback – in such a way that we stumble along still further in the same exterministic direction.

Thus radiation leads us to develop safety measures for the atomic state, and our sicknesses and our incalculable chemical production lead us to still more experimentation with animals and genetic human tampering... just so that we don't evaluate *methods* by the *effects*! Just so that we don't evaluate civilisation by the methods and principles it uses. Just so that we don't evaluate the human beings by the civilisation they support! Just so that we don't follow the feedback right through to the *subject* of exterminism!

Anthropocentricity

Our brain makes us suffer from the fact that each microcosmic individual grasps the Whole only potentially and intuitively, and never completely, and that we are very restricted: "Suffering is limited action" (Spinoza). A consciousness of this power had to get to the point of placing itself, as an isolated monad, in opposition to the universe in general – this unmistakable subject facing *everything else* as object, this 'I' facing everything 'not-I'.

By nature the human brain could not help but create an anthropocentric world-picture, and see everything in a short-term and short-circuited manner from the point of view of self-interest and self-utility. In this way we are not reasonable, but idiotically self-identified, like a drop of water which would like to make itself eternal without thinking about the sea.

The divine omniscience which we would so much like to have we take indirectly as given, and we falsely perceive the disturbing effect resulting from our ignorance as a 'residual risk'. We find out how great this is with all the more difficulty, and we automatically cut out the warning signals from the brain, withdrawing our energies from the senses and limiting them to 'rational' functioning.

Indeed, intellect claims the central position in human existence, in opposition to body and soul. Even this view of our special interest, out of which we react to everything that exists, knows itself as bound up with death. If the subjective mind were not so obviously sawing off the branch on which it is biologically sitting, it could easily get itself beyond the 'silent spring'. It *can* live on letters and signals in the artificial space-capsule it has created – the deprivation reaches it only indirectly, *via* the body, which can be forgotten as long as it receives the necessary minimum, so that it does not disturb things by failing to function.

Interest concentrated on abstract knowledge can arrogate to itself the energies it needs – because human energies are generally available. The head-human is a possibility, as we have seen in Descartes. 'Divine curiosity' nourishes itself and has secured for itself a corresponding social position. As *homo scientificus* we reduce our cognitive apparatus to our dead artificial world, instead of using and qualifying our entire organ of cognition, which in reality is equipped to know everything, as illuminati have always taught.

Egocentricity

This anthropocentric position is in the widest sense also *egocentric*. This does not mean that we are all equally 'egoistic', nor does it signify the predominantly ego-oriented, narcissistic character that we sometimes mean by this expression. It is rather that *conditio humana* as such entails ego-development, in which individuality is elaborated and culturally steered toward the self-conscious, reflective ego, that is unable to do anything else except experience the world in reference to itself and draw a dividing line between 'I' and the 'not-I'.

It is possible rationally to renounce the anthropocentric manner of thinking. But then it still remains anchored in our much more basic egocentricity. It is not just the human being who stands in the centre of things, but the human ego 'alone in its property'. It is precisely here that Europe in its individualism has pushed furthest. Again, each man or woman is his or her nearest and most important person, yet as such can be nonetheless altruistically motivated. We are inclined to make even the most essential general interests into psychological sinecures, even ecological exigencies, and exploit them in the struggle to assert oneself against others.

As a rule human beings don't just want to *survive*, and they don't want *only* to live. Our behaviour is determined less by fear of physical death than by fear of the insignificance and meaninglessness of our individual existence. Meaninglessness is the real death-fear of a person who has a lowered experience of his-her natural productivity. It is here that individual and social suicidal tendencies touch each other. And have we not wished as children, on account of some narcissistic insult done to us by adults, that the world would come to an end? Later it might indeed be acceptable to give up the project of living *after* one has 'made a name' for oneself, but those billions of egos who need more material for this task will certainly not give up, as long as the more advanced pyramid-builders keep on.

With a little exaggeration one could say that each human being needs the whole earth for her/himself alone, in order to display it as his own to his neighbour – and what the richest have is so little that they have to be preoccupied with fears of loss and surround themselves with fortifications. The concrete object of our selfishness is a substitute with which we attempt to cover up our existential nakedness. We would like first of all to assemble a small world around ourselves, in which we can see ourselves as complete.

But then the earth turns out to be too small: moon and stars must also be ours. So we move away from the place where we could meet *within ourselves*, and with the Godhead, the One, and All. I first sensed this some years ago when, in my *Alternative* I spoke about the 'journey within', and added that our civilisation has reached a limit of expansion at which *the inner freedom of the individual* appears as a condition of *survival*. It is simply the precondition for the insightful collective renunciation of our disastrous and subjectively purposeless material expansion[12].

Because of the lack of *this* inner sovereignty people competitively accumulate power, security, comfort and armament – and the dynamics of expansion are the unavoidable result. I refer to the most recent systematic overview of the ego problem in the works of Ken Wilber. They are helpful for orienting us in the contemporary psychological jungle[13]. Before I allow Wilber to have the last word, I would like to indicate how the same subject-matter is dealt with by Meister Eckhart and by the ancient Chinese Lao Tzu. We are dealing with a theme which is effective over a very long term, but which is now approaching the point at which its matrix bursts open.

What brought the older teachers of humanity to despair was the question: *Why* is it so hard for us to give up the wilfulness and private selfishness which make us like embattled billiard-balls in the social machine? Meister Eckhart taught that we must make certain our original identity with the One, *since we need this so much*, because in our socialised condition everything we do not have and are not is lacking to us. Thus he said: "Here God's ground is my ground, and my ground is God's ground. Here I live outside my own, as God lives outside his own"[14]. Here whole and self overlap into each other. He who experiences this intersection of the Whole and finite being in this 'city of the soul', this 'inner Jerusalem', would be what a human being should be, that is, "like a morning star, continually in the presence of God". If we had proceeded from this place, we would have created a different everyday world, since:

To the person who has glanced into this Ground for only a second, a thousand pounds of yellow minted gold is worth no more than a false penny[15].

The antagonistic 'human nature' of Thucydides, struggling for power and freedom, would have been jumped over.

Like Eckhart, Lao Tzu, a thoroughly political saint, regards the human being of Thucydides as something fallen from natural order and grace. He calls their behaviour the "pitiful boasting of robbers", and makes powerful people more responsible for damage to world harmony. Above all he teaches that those responsible for the polity should empty their hearts of selfishness. The heart would then find peace. It would no longer have to reach for material things, but would be able to see its way back to its correct place in the Great Order. Only then, as is written in the sixteenth saying of *Tao Teh Ching*:

> *Of all things in their manifold variety*
> *each one finds its way back to its root;*
> *the finding again of roots means stillness –*
> *what one could call 'turning back to being'.*
> *Turning back to being means to last for ever;*
> *to know everlasting things means clarity;*
> *he who doesn't know eternal things*
> *blindly brings about calamity.*

He who 'knows everlasting things' is not continually *in need*, must not *have* so much as a precaution, will not embark on the flight forward into pseudo-immortality, because he 'embraces everything' and:

> *He who embraces everything, belongs to all things;*
> *he who belongs to all things is kingly;*
> *kingliness is like heaven;*
> *heaven is like the Tao;*
> *the Tao is like eternity;*
> *he who resides in the Tao*
> *plunges without danger into the depths.*

What a definition of kingliness – formulated as a condition for survival! Quite differently situated in the world is the person trapped in ego-centricity. Wilber thinks:

> *Mankind will never, but never, give up this type of murderous aggression,*
> *war, oppression and repression, attachment and exploitation, until men*
> *and women give up that property called personality. Until, that is, they*
> *awaken to the trans-personal. Until that time, guilt, murder, property*

and persons will always remain synonymous[16].

The species-dilemma is thus as follows: the brain as a distance-organ makes us into the *most powerful cause* in the whole earth and its atmosphere. Yet *this power is not guided by the general interests of earthly evolution and the preservation of the things it produces, but by our immediate short-term interests and volitions.*

This anthropocentric, egocentric orientation is normal, to serve us as an instrument of self-assertion. But in *this* position of power things cannot go well if they are directed from the parallelogram of ego-forces. The ego then turns out to be not only spiritually a prison, but to be material armour which drags the hero into the depths.

NOTES

(1) Schubart, *op cit*, p114.

(2) Arthur Koestler, *Der Mensch – Irrläufer der Evolution* (München, 1981), p93.

(3) Ken Wilber, *Up From Eden*, p182.

(4) Morris Berman in his *The Re-enchantment of the World* (Ithaca: Cornell University Press, 1981) describes what has happened in Europe since the 13th century. He reminds us that J.B. Watson, the founder of Behaviourism, made an ideal out of rigid cleanliness-training and out of distance between mother and child, because these things enable the child to conquer the world. To this end they must be "as free as possible of sensitivities to people" (Watson). Berman (pp169-170) continues: we have allowed a character structure to become typical which "evolved to obtain love by way of mastery in an unloving world," even though physiologically love and mastery are incompatible goals.

(5) This is true both for the positive effects (for the oceanic feeling, resting on the feeling of protectedness in the mother's body during pregnancy, and for the Promethean feeling, resting on the ultimate liberation through the birth canal) and for the negative effects (for the depressive experiences which result when the biochemical changes and the first contractions herald the birth process while the exit is still fully closed off: a hostile and threatening world; and for the mixture of pain, desire, and struggle which the foetus, now an active participant, experiences during the actual birth phase through the vagina).

(6) Stanislav Grof, *Beyond the Brain: Birth, Death, and Transcendence in Psychotherapy* (Albany: State University of New York Press, 1985).

(7) Among other things Grof mentions character structures for which the method is inapplicable or works badly (*Beyond the Brain*, chap 5) because they can only be experienced as an 'invitation to a journey through Hell', as a consequence of the after-effects of the original splitting, the introductory phase of the birth process.

(8) Ken Wilber, *No Boundary, Eastern and Western Approaches to Personal Growth* (Boulder: Shambhala, 1981); see p146, to the end. In this he concentrates upon that aspect of the phenomenon which manifests itself in the individual psyche, whereas at this point it is the species aspect which interests me. Not only individually, but also collectively, projection functions as a

powerful defence mechanism against that inner look which would show us as participating in all the sickness of the social world and as ourselves sick.

(9) Arnold Gehlen, *Der Mensch; seine Natur und seine Stellung in der Welt*, (Wiesbaden: 1986), p336.

(10) *ibid*, p303.

(11) Yoga on the other hand is a path of inner activity (in India just as one-sidedly followed on the inner side as in our case on the outer – Reinhard Taube has developed this theme,in a way which we could apply to ourselves, in an excellent dissertation on 'Inner Experience and Society'), a praxis of self-transformation and – we could almost say – of 'psycho-synthesis', of self-determined integration – if this is the wish of the adept.

(12) Rudolf Bahro, *Ich werde meinen Weg fortsetzen: eine Dokumentation*, 2. erw. Auflage (Köln, Frankfurt: 1977), p16.

(13) In *Up From Eden* Wilber starts from the assumption that there are two ways of approaching the fact that our social existence is finite, partial, and separated from the One. Either we can orient ourselves toward reunification with 'Atman' (the Indian term by which he means the One, Lao Tzu calls it the Tao), that is, to attempt to experience the fact that in the basic ground we are ourselves one with it. Or we concentrate on the '*Atman-project*' as a *substitute* for it, on the compensatory hunt for meaning and crutches. In the latter case we are for the most part trapped even up to the egocentric, greedy, pleasure-seeking spirituality of the *New Age* style (which he pointedly criticises in *Up From Eden*, pp. 323-28).

(14) Eckhart, *Meister Eckharts mystische Schriften*, published by Gustav Landauer, p43.

(15) *Ibid*.

(16) Wilber, *Up From Eden*, p286.

Part Three:

SALVATION'S ORIENTATION

10. The logic of salvation

What can that Mean?

I have said what I mean by *salvation* at the conclusion of Part I. And I tried to make a convincing case in Part II that there is a *logic* of self-extermination. But *logic* of salvation? When it is precisely the intellect which runs amok with us? When it is precisely the abstractionistic character of our culture which is a central exterministic factor?

How precise is it to say that the intellect runs amok *with* us? Indeed, in the case of its externalisation in the form of the Megamachine, the dead spirit runs amok taking the living spirit with it; yet something precedes it, the fact that *the human runs amok with the intellect*, where earlier he was accustomed to run amok with feeling. In the end intellect and feeling are not real entities, but aspects of human behaviour, human activity, and it is the intellectual form in which *we* have so over-poweringly materialised our forces, in whatever emotional way they are motivated.

Among all those who hope to manage the new age as cheaply and comfortably as possible it is the fashion to complain about intellectual top-heaviness the moment energetic thinking is demanded. However, in today's period of transformation, what is at issue is a *qualification* of thought, indeed, a *higher* qualification of thought, especially a higher degree of freedom in thought, a de-automating of it. What is needed is an *integration* of the instrumental intellect (as *one* faculty of thought) in a manner which is *consistent with the principles of life*, in the psychological as well as into the social *whole*.

On the one hand 'non-logical' bewilderment comes to grief on the complexity of the alienated social whole, whose landscape has to be very well-mapped if we are to locate ourselves in it. On the other hand we are bound by mere logical analysis, which claims to be controlling, all the more because of the complexity it describes. A whole futurology depends on accepting the existing state of affairs as reasonable, just because it is logically deducible as long as the old premises are valid. The scientific intellect governs the technocratic world. From right and left adepts are on hand to create from this the ideal of a scientific, information society.

Naturally neither intellect, logic nor knowledge are to blame for anything – no more than the knife is to blame for being an instrument of murder. The problem with the rationalistic demon lies with the *demon*, not with the reason in which it likes to express itself – often all too irrationally! As we saw, it is a quite definite, historically-determined subjectivity which, over the last 3,000 years, has ever more addictively inserted itself into the instrumental intellect, transforming this into its own life-damaging power instrument. A logic of salvation begins just at this point, first putting the question about the *subject* of exterminism and then wanting to pursue it to its ultimate roots.

To call a theoretical book top heavy can only indicate a desire to abandon *theory*. Creative thinking can just be a pleasure of life as much as love-making, and does not need to be placed in opposition to it – life has many hours. Admittedly a logocentric *culture*, in which the whole is subjected one-sidedly to the domination of intellect, deforms its members right from the beginning. But why should we, because of this, forget that originally the human excelled because of his ability to think, and to think abstractly?!

'Logic', an approach to things which is *not just* intuitive, most certainly has a place in the task of finding a direction of rescue and in drafting a politics of salvation. Only when we know the coordinates of the situation, and have achieved insight into layer after layer of the challenge, is it possible to analyse where and how a change could make its appearance: up to the point of a synthesis of a path of salvation. It is also helpful to use such evidence as is available to exclude false trails and block dead-ends in the labyrinth. I think that we should counter the *spontaneous direction* of civilisation, which does *not reveal itself* as guided for the good by an Unseen Hand, with a new *idea*, correcting the old idea which contains this tendency to exterminism.

In both cases we are concerned with *active* human subjectivity. It is absurd to regard this active mode as inadmissible just because some people act exterministically. 'Non-action', which old masters have long recommended, means acting without an ego-obsessed, addictive drive to action. It calls for self-criticism, noticing where we work compulsively, where we don't wait and are unable to allow anything to ripen, and where we go against the stream instead of going with it.

The fact that earlier idealistic investments in the course of history often led to nothing doesn't mean that for us, in face of our dilemma, reverse gear remains the only possibility. Newly-ripened subjective forces have the right to form new social structures, to give new necessities radical expression. To allow disturbed conditions to continue without intervention, instead of re-structuring the whole, indirectly assumes that one ascribes to the bad *status quo* the dignity of an original harmonious state of affairs, which may not be disturbed by arbitrary intervention.

If Fichte's "Act, act, act, that's what it's all about" was ever valid, then it is valid now, in face of the ever more rapid turning of the spiral of death. *How* we should act, on the basis of which inner constitution, which attitude to nature and human nature – that indeed is the question. Altogether the most important action of all *could* be to create the subjective preconditions for adequate intervention. At the present time the subjective factor is altogether decisive, because nothing more is to be had from old basic attitudes which react to the repeated new occasions for action which our pathogenic civilisation presents us.

For these reasons our logical exertion must direct itself much more to ourselves, rather than to the world we have created – the objective mirroring of our own disturbed condition. Subject and object correspond naturally to each other, and comprise *one* system, which can only be split apart by secondary analysis. But first of all the shift of emphasis is important. There is, incidentally, hardly anything which is logically shrewder than Buddha's subject-centred epistemology, as can be seen in *Space, Time and Cognition* by Tarthang Tulku. Writings by the Dalai Lama are even published under the title *Logic of Love*. In short, logic remains the most universally valid tool of our powers of thought, and further progress will not invalidate its ever more refined calculations.

On the other side there are a-logical (not anti-logical), a-rational (not anti-rational) practices whose use today is logical and can be justified (as in the case of bioenergetics, transpersonal psychology, tantra or meditation) because they are so important for loosening up this imprisonment and confusion, for dissolving or relativising the fixed and automatic connections in our psychobiocomputers, which connect us with the lethal automatism of the Megamachine. They are suited to creating some free space for our natural bodily potential. The automated part of our will cripples and blocks the true purpose of our existence with its prejudice-filled purposes, and makes us into robots of the exterministic culture instead of creators of a new biophile culture which we could be.

In this perspective the logic of salvation shows us the way to reconciliation with the *Logos* as the natural, divine consciousness, given with the human *Bios*. *In itself* the *Logos* is *Bios*, its intelligible side. In moments of illumination our thought is not filled with thought-out purposes, but with the *Logos* of life. "And in the face of Will arbitrariness is silent," as Goethe says in *Urworten orphisch*. So a logic of salvation would require that we consciously bring about such moments, moments in which we are open to the message of Beingness deep in our thought-apparatus. And again from this it follows logically that we should find a social constitution in whose framework experiences of this sort spontaneously occur for all people, as a part of general education and the removal of socialisation-conditioned fixation, ushering in a form of socialisation unfinished right to the end of life.

In truth almost the entire spiritual tradition is naively individualistic. In that it gladly explains social reality as illusory, or ignores it, it reveals itself incapable of *organising* social consciousness. Very many masters have on principle overestimated their subjective free spirit. Thus Buddhism in its noblest figure, Avalokiteshvara, the Bodhisattva of compassion, "who hears the cry of the world", leads to the paradox that he can *never* enter into the so-much-desired Nirvana, because service in bringing about the salvation of all sentient beings is a work which can never end.

All too many individuals find no runway for the take-off to God. Lewis Mumford is all too correct when he calls the 'axial' religions *whole world beliefs*, "that the salvation of the individual can be secured independently of the welfare of society, or at least under conditions of exclusion of the public; here *human* is falsely identified with *private.*"[1]

What are these unpolitical people saying (for the human being *is* a political animal since he lives in a society), when they reiterate the esoteric maxim, "as the outside is, so is the inside; as the inside is, so is the outside"? Can one assert this correspondence, only to ignore it as soon as it concerns the social world? Here we are dealing with a short-circuiting process of simplifying reality. All that will emerge from this in the modern world is a bit of private·magic.

Spiritual individualism is the weakest point of almost all the Far Eastern traditions – they differ from the Christ-impulse, and correspond with the anomie of late-bourgeois society. From the beginning this attitude has meant capitulation in face of unconsciousness of the collective process of history. Meanwhile the important task is to spiritualise the social framework transparently such that individual consciousness can see and experience itself as its microcosm, without succumbing to collectivism. It is the most spiritually aware people who have the *responsibility* to organise themselves politically.

In all pre-modern high civilisations this was taken for granted. Even the teaching of Buddha inspired a great emperor. Until far into the collapse of its order, the European Middle Ages stood under the idea of theocracy. Religious matters were to the deepest extent political, and everything political was subject to religious justification. As also was the case in the former Soviet bloc.

If Hegel and Marx were right in one thing, it was in their conviction that humanity must come to the point of carrying on the total historical process with *conscious awareness*. In short, the *spontaneous course of history*, the blind result of the action of human beings, destroys us. Automatic mechanisms regulate the market which controls us, except that the sum total of its actions is suicidal. So we must free ourselves to make a new collective decision, and to *want* to do this.

The object of the newly-arising spirituality is not individual sanctity, but personal contribution to establishment of a good social order, once again holy – a reconstruction of institutions such that the life of the human species can continue. And the point of entry through which the new age movement has begun to do this is the *Gaia* concept. This means that the human being must identify with the whole animated Earth instead of his own ego, and think from *that* point of view. But since the ego proceeds in a manner separated from the rest of the world, the human being needs a non-egocentric self-concept which corresponds to the *Gaia* concept – 'as the inside is, so is the outside'.

One Earth means primarily *one* humanity, for only through its planet-wide technical activities can the problem of *Gaia* be revealed at all. The point at which humanity must start to create unity is the highest lotus of the logic of salvation: if we create a world-regimen of divine light, would the light of divine justice drop down from above, like the tones of a Bach toccata down pillars from the cross-vaulting?

The Holy of Holies around which humanity assembles – like the Grail of knighthood mysticism – can only be a symbol for the dignity of a comprehensive awareness in which human beings are potentially all one, an incarnation of their own body-soul-spirit potential, that on its own initiative leads to enlightenment – the overcoming of all imprisonment to ego-concerns. The dissemination of such an awareness is the precondition for a rescuing process of institutional renewal. A *Gaia*-type ethic, pledged to life on Earth, can only be grounded on a mythos of humanity of this sort, an ethic with political consequences – namely the creating of a world government *without* any power calculations except that of the necessary self-limitation of the behaviour of our species on a finite planet.[2]

The human self is and remains *individual*, because each of us is genotypically unique. But it identifies itself with the whole in that it understands and experiences itself as a microcosm. The self is not *individualistic*. But this identification with the whole, with *Gaia* as representative of the cosmos, must be complete at *all* levels of human activity. Nirvana is only *one* level, that of the *ultimate* archaic unity which is to be achieved again in a new, higher quality.

Since we have left certain stages of development behind us *without* integrating their riches, regressions are indeed necessary. But they should be understood and practised as *partial*, and to the accompaniment of progressive enlightenment. Shelley's 'republic of kings', an ideal picture of western social constitution, must today be consistently spiritualised. Because a few hundred million or even five billion pluralistically competing kings and queens could not establish a good society. This would only work if they learn to comprehend and experience themselves as flowing out from *one* evolutionary vessel, *one* Grail, *one* idea of humanity.

Are politics political enough yet?
The logic of self-extermination principally makes clear all those things which won't work, or would be insufficient. A major Turn-around presupposes nothing less than a transformation of the human self. All interventions necessary at levels higher than the *conditio humana* must be seen from this perspective. And a new politics begins with the new human being. This new human being is not another genotype, but another consciousness-structure. For this reason, in times of epochal change a praxis of human self-transformation is *the* basic political issue.

The business of politics is concerned with the insignificant modulation of given power relations, which change according to non-rational criteria, and are also today increased by running up against the boundaries of the Earth. The more 'representative' democracy is, the more strongly politics remains prisoner of immediate and short-term interests, while essential processes and decisions take place outside the political sphere. We leave our fate to the blind play of extensively anonymous forces which follow no other laws than the partial logic of their own extended reproduction. Should there be a last cunning remnant of reason, it appears precisely in exterministic output, which teaches us empirically that the whole thing is running in the wrong direction.

The established business of politics has no other mechanism than reaction to those *symptoms* of crisis which pose a 'need for action'. The resulting *realpolitik* never gets to the causes which are giving rise to the ulcers. Up to now the ecological crisis has not been able to bring even *one* political factor of our society to the point of wanting to intervene even at the first level of cause, that of the industrial system, of the complex of science-technology-capital. All the studies about 'research and technology assessment' which will be necessary from now on are culpably routine-blinded appendages.[3]

Socialist and communist intellectuals came early upon the second level of cause, that of capital-dynamics, although admittedly not that of ecological crisis. But their strategy fails from a variety of causes. In particular, that proletarian-revolutionary person whom they wanted under their command doesn't exist. Even if such a tectonic of exterministic tendencies were to exist only in principle, the access to reality via capital analysis would still be neither wide enough nor deep enough.

It is clear that the processes on the first two levels of cause (industrial system and the dynamics of capital) in no way exhaustively explain exterministic symptoms. And even on these three levels together, where at first glance it appears we are dealing with material factors, where the material side is in the foreground, it is in truth a structural, informational, mental context which determines the process. The Megamachine together with banks and bureaucracy is mainly dead spirit.

It is not at all the case that a logic of salvation follows in the track of exterministic extremes. For the most part far too much energy is expended on the level of symptoms, and far too little on the level from which the thrust comes. A Green politics based on symptoms has been effective in the beginning for changing consciousness, because it first had to direct general attention to the harmful effects of the industrial system. But now the job is to direct perception to the context of all these phenomena, so that the readiness grows to sum it all up and think about a total social change. For the moment the task is to loosen up the psychological anchoring in the *status quo*. The main problem is no longer an inadequate knowledge of the dangers, but the threshold-anxiety in the face of changes which will cut deeply into private and public habits.

Probably all these burning questions will only be solvable on the far side of the confrontation between those who in one way or another are 'affected', in which scandals, when uncovered, can rarely be removed, because everything is overshadowed by the problems of their injured or threatened self-interests. Interests which, reversed, do not speak for the 'objectivity' of experts. They have it easy now, protected by officially valid scientific and bureaucratic code, to be egocentric in a self-controlled manner. Even questions of life and death are subordinated to the reciprocal game of egocentric confrontation. Nobody dare lose a debate, nobody dare *lose face*. Problems typical for the ecological crisis turn out to be very difficult to handle within our customary ways of doing things. Sufficient positive energy for their solution would then only come together if people were capable of jumping over the shadows of their immediate interests and allowing their neurotic masking to be offended.

As long as it is only concerned with defence against immediate dangers and the winning of time for a spiritual Turn-around, ecological politics revolves around the question of bringing the Megamachine to a stop. But on the axis of the path to salvation stands the task of stopping the patriarchal ego. Stopping the Megamachine is politics of emergency.[4]

From bottom to top, the logic of self-extermination demands an answer, which can only go in the direction of consciousness-change and self-change. Stated more precisely, this is a politics of consciousness *revolution* to which we must trust ourselves, and *awareness*. The way forward is a continuous and aware observation of what we actually do and live every day. Sinking oneself in mysticism is an *element* of the way, not the way itself.

The thousand year long striving for enlightenment is a ferment that plays a part in all high cultures, but is not directed toward the solving of acute problems – being able only to contribute to this indirectly, in that the experience of 'oneness' facilitates the building of innovating groups. More unbiased mixing is favourable to freedom, and to the furthering of creative design of new social conditions. Not all mystics are candidates for this sort of thing.

The awareness of which I spoke means first of all concrete knowledge about our imprisonment at all levels of the logic of self-extermination, and commitment to concrete steps toward mental and practical freeing from it: an ecological politics of salvation. Clearly an ecological politics of salvation cannot begin either with exterministic symptoms only, or with individual structures only. It will direct itself against patriarchy, and for a new balance in sexual relations; against the colonialism and imperialism of white civilisation, and for the withdrawal out of all conquests; against capitalism and for a domestic, household economy in one's own land and for the world; against the industrial Megamachine and for a social rebirth on a communal-communitarian basis.

The concrete alternatives at all these levels will not unfold as isolated single projects, but as integrated parts of a composite answer, a new cultural design. This design will proceed from the association of people to form a community, guided by a spiritual vision. Naturally it will actually be many separate attempts, many of which may come to grief. But only where there is a vision at the centre of things can we climb out of the multilateral power-play of the individual man or woman which, all too similar to sovereign states, is typical of the average suburban household community.

The next goal is to achieve a variegated archipelago of such commu-nitarian projects, in which we can unify transformation of the world and transformation of the self in a new form of every day life, while at the same time radiating outwards actively to the general consciousness and feeling for life and hold ourselves ready with proposals for a new general politics. To create for ourselves a social context different from that of bourgeois society is of the same importance as the techniques of self-discovery in therapeutic and spiritual groups.

The social whole can most easily be healed from the roots upwards, from the *conditio humana*, from the transformation of the subject, from the changing of its self-concept and situation, from its ascent into a different structure of consciousness. To create conditions which make this possible on a larger scale will be the most effective intervention, and would also benefit all the special activities and projects which the ecological crisis demands.[5]

The secret of an initiative which really produces a change of direction is always a change of direction within the human being. The Megamachine and the Empire of the white man are now driving ever more singled-out individuals to the point of wanting to transcend their customary existence. Finding themselves together in a new 'place' will be the natural consequence.

In no way does this mean political abstinence, through which, tearing the inside and the outside apart, we would just be denying that we have built a world of real structures too powerful in their autonomy and which, paying no attention to us as their creators, could roll over us, however subjectively purified we may feel. What the independent powers of capital, the patriarchate and its science, the white empire and the Megamachine bring about in their sluggish forward movement, no navel-contemplation by the ego can undo.

We would like to take the standpoint that even the ego is an illusion which we ought to drop. But the ego is by no means still absolutely available to us, since it is present in all those objects and structures which we have externalised. Ego is made real for a second time. This self-alienation is not merely an illusion. Even the habit of placing subject and object opposite to each other is more than a false perception. No imagined or actual state of illumination could change anything about the cloud from Chernobyl. No 'chosen' ones will remain protected. And whatever facts may support our belief or our knowledge that there is something more than this life, it is still the case that the most wonderful esoteric phenomena rest upon the assumption of the existence of humanity. They are a luxury a human being can grant himself – as long as he exists!

At the same time we find that the deeper we climb down the series of steps of exterministic causes, the more the visible apocalypse separates itself from the invisible one, which has so much head start. It is in these inward places that things have already been decided, which we now seek to stop in the outside. Thus it is that those of us who saw the symptoms of this early on and took action, accomplished very little in a material sense. The spiral of death continues to turn.

With mass democracy, which works like a security organisation for smaller injuries, we have created for ourselves the ideal device for avoiding all interventions, and for allowing the main activities on the diagonal of destruction. A logic of salvation by-passes this useless device by orienting us to the task of stopping the *invisible* apocalyptic thrust, the task of dissolving the complex of habits comprising the logic of self-extermination, and moving towards spiritual readiness for a new general constitution, a re-institutionalising of the culture.

The main thrust of a logic of salvation is to spread the idea of a 'catalyst of the ecological transformation', that is, a programme of a reconstruction. This 'catalyst', part of a new identity of us all, would be a political structure which reacts to exterministic symptoms, mechanisms and drives with very definite interventions. It would, however, 'knowingly' correspond with the true subjective causes and in this way reach a genuine consensus, to which we will want to subject ourselves. Then ecological politics would add no special interests to give their weight to numerical results, but would form its roots in fundamental interests which human beings have shared for ages – until recently without knowing it. Prioritising these fundamental life-interests – if we could manage it – would lead to a different world, contrasting completely with the business of antagonistic struggle over single issues, which are firmly programmed into our given political structures.

In the foreground of things an ecological politics of salvation would approach the 'geology' of self-extermination from the opposite direction to the spiritual path of salvation, working 'from top downwards' against the symptoms of destruction, ranging from changes in material foundations and socio-economic structures to the securing of the space needed for the practice of self-experience and for communitarian experiments.

Even if the aim of such political interventions is only to defer the catastrophe, they can at the same time be helping instruments of the unfolding of a new structure of consciousness. The necessary self-transformation, which will stop the material self-destruction processes, can be hindered or benefited through politics, and in this the mass media could play an important role – if properly used.[6]

There is no path to salvation which avoids individual transformation. At the present moment the most important social process is the growth of this movement, the stimulus and the encouragement to more and more people to pursue a path of intensive self-knowledge.[7] Only by these means is there a qualitative change in perception not only of dangers, but also of the chances of meeting them from 'below' and 'within'. Only if in the struggles of bourgeois society there is a backing-off from continually reproducing unfree patterns of behaviour, can we agree on a politics which stops exterminism and create for ourselves the appropriate equipment for renewal.

NOTES

(1) Lewis Mumford, *The Transformations of Man* (London: George Allen and Unwin, 1957), ch 4.

(2) I also once regarded this in a super-bureaucratic perspective, as an empowerment of the nation-state monster, but in doing so forgot that power competition and the external enemy are *conditions* of internal despotism. In the case of a world domestic policy this precondition falls away. Humanity needs an instrument for its common affairs, and as a means to achieving it needs not least of all a decisive subordination of national sovereignties. Because the equalising of interests between national states, when this is the highest mechanism, can only result in a zero sum game, which carries the name United Nations and ridicules the idea of united nations. This idea can only come to rights when the fact that the whole is more than the sum of its parts is institutionally portrayed and realised. As a first thing the national delegates must precisely *not* be representatives of national *states*, but representatives of the *people* of a district or race, region or ethnic grouping.

(3) The experts who get into competitive struggle with each other on these issues know nothing at all, or know still less than the politicians about the general cultural situation in which they must 'assess'. Their professional competence does not furnish any basic social position, not to speak of one which is legitimate in view of the natural order; but rather inclines to just the opposite position. A single glance back to the history of physics in this century should teach that its basic discoveries never ought to have been made if there had really been any concern about excluding the possibility of their 'misuse' (a totally dishonest and apologetic term because the atom bomb and the nuclear power station are conceivably legitimate children of this science). Science is an *institutionalisation* of our modes of cognition, conditioned by our exterministic total culture, and thus cannot help but continually create more and greater problems than it solves. The human being as scientist (not the same thing as a person of knowledge) wants to heal the wounds he caused, but without giving up his position as top parasite. The scientist as human being could admittedly move over to assessing the consequences of technology not in detail, but as a whole. He would then recognise that the human being has overextended himself to replace steering according to the laws of evolution by control according to the subjective and *interest-captured* mind, but has also increased technically and materially by ten-fold the destructive capacity unavoidably given with it.

(4) If – as an example – the supervisory officers, committees, top managers, and work council members of the chemical concerns are neither willing nor able to place the general interests of life above the profit interests of their economic units, in that they drop merely on the basis of suspicion whatever has danger potential, even if this costs mass-production as such, then they must be rigorously dictated to. And society must create for itself the requisite institutional tools, in spite of whoever may want to lament about eco-dictatorship. the economy *must* be tamed, *must* be subordinated, and the alternative softies, who wish to adopt a 'hard' language style which still recognises the little word 'must', would better ask themselves what necessities they would wriggle out of, and what they would like to be defended against. Their true tenor or even soprano voice would frequently and once more sing: "Don't prevent *us* from living as we have been accustomed". It is a wholly different and justified question, how, on the basis of individual ethics and in

accordance with the constitution, we can ensure that the demand for these interventions does not come to benefit private lusts for power. The 'inner enlightenment' which is current in the psycho-spiritual scene and already radiates into large parts of the active elites, finds here its test case. It is therefore very important within these circles that enough control and self-control, criticism and selfcriticism be maintained intact, so that the allure of animal training and spiritual manipulation do not become widespread.

(5) Take, for example, the death of forests. Those causes which, without specially mentioning death of forests, I dealt with in a general way in Part II, are far more basic than those which can be discovered by natural science, where the researches much too slowly progress to the simple conclusion that the forests just cannot survive an industrial system of the size it is today. And in the meantime we can help trees much more readily with methods intuitively arrived at on the basis of a different world-view and world-experience, as is illustrated and examined and applied by the initiative of Maria Felsenreich in Austria in healing root damage with powdered stone and grape-mash.

(6) On this, consult Gunther Anders in his then, as now, contemporary book, *Die Antiquiertheit des Menschen, über die Seele im Zeitalter der zweiten industriellen Revolution*, 2nd ed., München, 1956.

(7) Since here we have to do with a process of liberation, it must not be pushed forward in a state of panic. For then the temptation to force individual transformation by psycho-terroristic means is all too close. There must be an ethical code obliging us to avoid any attempt, however friendly in intention, to 'force people to be happy', to compel 'outsiders' to come in etc. We do not have to survive at any price. Whoever thinks otherwise and is egoistically impatient is unsuited to be a therapeutic or spiritual teacher. With good reason Canetti sees those who must survive at all costs as being the most dangerous type for the future of the species. Survival governs only the lowest mechanisms of human existence (Robert Anton Wilson, *The New Prometheus*, linking into insights of Timothy Leary), and fixation on these is just what has driven us into this exterministic pattern of security-obsessed accumulation. Survival as the dominant maxim means civil war about places in a bunker and about reserves of life-essential supplies, elimination of the weak and sick, etc. It is this sort of answer to the ecological crisis which is fully in conformity with the logic of self-extermination.

11. What won't stop the Apocalypse

It cannot be done by stopping the avalanche. Naturally, it remains an elemental necessity to protect ourselves against the direct symptoms of exterminism. Yet disaster is marching rapidly, because the annihilating functions all have an exponential rate of increase taking them beyond all limits – and in addition they overlap and reinforce each other in ways which cannot be calculated in advance. It sits too deep in our cells, or more precisely in the programming and switching of our externalised symbolic brain-cell contents, in the *order of the elements of our culture*. To make changes in this demands something quite different from what political activity in the framework of state- and citizen-initiatives born of dismay can ever accomplish.

Political activity in the Framework of the state

Whoever accepts responsibility in old institutions *can* only achieve responsibility for the functioning of the Megamachine, for the computer-supported steering along the edge of the abyss. *And if an opposition does this, it has the additional task of re-harnessing already-disturbed people and their energies.* Green ministers on the command bridge of this undertaking – this is perverse. In Germany, the Greens have opposed the dragon with second deputy mayors, who eventually become reliably harnessed, absorbed by current events.

The direction symbolising fundamental opposition and attracting sympathisers from social consciousness must be not *inwards* but *outwards*. If the opposition exhausts itself in the administration of cosmetic measures and the making of plans as to how the Metropolis can better solve its problems, it changes sides and gives credence to the competence of the Apparatus. It creates illusions that small results permit one to conclude that the whole has indeed changed. Thereby the real new purposes perish, on whose behalf a degree of intervention could otherwise have been made.

Parliament, the bait which the German Green movement once went for, in order to carry out things which were inaccessible to juristic or extra-parliamentary methods, has its place in the institutional realm, as a political regulator of the Megamachine. In that place it is not people who are represented, but government which is legitimised. Parliament is an anachronistic residue of a bourgeois class society which long ago arrived at corporatism (a quasi-Caesarism). To speak of democracy as if the citizens of industrial society had even the smallest chance of influencing the *course* of the Titanic is a flat lie. Parliament is an appendix of the Megamachine, one of its lesser regulatory peaceful mechanisms, in order to keep the procession of the lemmings.

True, at the community level the possibility of influence is greater, but competence is small. In administration from the town hall up to the ministry nothing at all can happen that can seriously put a check on the reproductive purpose of the Megamachine. The message which goes out from Green officials can only be that a politics of salvation cannot be carried out. They already call upon the voter in exactly the routine manner that any other delegate of state power does. For everything else which they might say their teeth have been pulled.

Environmental protection as carried out from the institutional perspective does not aim in the direction of salvation, but is in reality an indulgence to protect the exterministic structure. Furthermore there are always special system components whose function is to take the load off all other components. To the extent that the others, which otherwise would *have* to concern themselves with environmental matters, have the responsibility taken away from them, the processes of learning are slowed down.

Most of what is resolved in parliaments gets at least the passive toleration of the population. This toleration consensus is firstly supported by the privileged status of the whole Metropolitan social body, secondly made secure by identification with the money economy, and thirdly guaranteed by the mental-cultural hegemony of exterministic elites, the whole complex of science, technology, capital and state. It is not so much a relationship of forces between heads, as *inside* heads.

So what sense is there if a party with radical intentions forms itself around the *general will* of its voters, most of whom remain in the old consensus in most of their attitudes? Originally the Greens were not greeted at all by these conventional sectors: they stood much more for non-conforming elements. But then they offered themselves more and more to conventional voters, who only want a goad to rouse the main parties or bureaucracy a little. The Greens have never really been candidates for ecological politics, except on their programme pamphlets. The one service which the Greens really perform in their march through public institutions is the integration of a thematically fundamental opposition within the old structures.

In its essence eco-politics is neither *Left*-radical nor radical-*liberal*. It cuts across *all* the traditional 'isms' of bourgeois society, from Left to Right. Even if it would fit a radical conservatism best, here state positivism puts the brake on internally and externally – this is the bedrock of the imperial consensus. *If the power syndrome from the patriarchal ego up to modern scientific-industrial excesses is the hard inner core of the ecological crisis, it is impossible to climb off the diagonal of destruction just by making a bow before the power-monopoly of the established state.*

I am convinced that it would have worked if we had used the parliamentary terrain just for the purpose of getting the message of pulling out of industrialism into the mass media – to publicly interpret the real meaning of exterministic symptoms. If the Greens had appealed to the people simply for a mandate for this radical enlightenment, instead of promising environmental cosmetics via public authorities, a basic constituency of support would *also* have been permanently achieved. The 'responsibility' talk of politicians and press were effective only because the Greens were absolutely unclear *what* that they actually wanted to be responsible for.

It came to look as if Greens wanted to heal scratches on a patient who is suffering from cancer. With few exceptions they were not oriented towards the true therapy, the mastering of conflicts and stresses in consciousness which lead to self-destruction. We all came to grief in our Green activities because we didn't get to the bottom of things – above all, ourselves – in our civilisation. We operated out of identities which were alternatives to the one which must be overcome. The thoroughly widespread presentiment that we should be less concerned with our 'environment' than with our psyche, less with the limiting of external damage than with an internal psychological revolution, remained private.

Today the Greens are simply one more stall in the political market of the Metropolis. They have fixed the party name which promised an alternative onto the bridge-housing of the Titanic. A pity about the sunflower symbol. The politics of German Greens was primarily to secure roles on the stage of the state theatre, so that they did not become unemployed actors. If today we ask why people with fundamentalist views still continue to participate and to defend their sterile districts, we discover that they stick with it because they don't know any other way. When I later speak of a politics of salvation, I shall be wanting to work methodically toward something quite different, and certainly not just making one last attempt to re-phrase parliamentary speeches in a more fundamentalist way.

As long as deep identification with the logic of self-extermination is not socially undermined (the decline of the 'expert' image after Chernobyl, and the crises of political leadership in 1993 are foretastes), nothing in the institutional superstructure can seriously turn against it. Under the new auspices of ecological crisis, whoever attempts to go in this new direction needs to be spiritually-rooted – not in a lost old view, but in a new kingdom 'not of this world' which is just rising up – just to be able to defend his or her identity.

The entire political reality disconnects us from the essential things of life, from contact, from love and from hate. It is unreal because it is not rooted in people and society, but in false social structures based on Megamachine mechanics. Politics which once again belong to people must be anchored in a different 'place', to whatever extent it may at first appear to be without influence or echo.

How has the ecology movement been politically active up to now? How has it understood politics? Certainly from the beginning there were impulses mobilised from the deep region of our genotype. Their mobilisation was caused by the industrial Megamachine. The power-complex exasperated us with new rockets, nuclear power stations, chemical poisons, dying forests, collapsing watersheds, and all the rest.

Isn't it evident that from political positions located 'behind' or 'above' the economic realm or techno-structure of the Megamachine, *nothing else is possible* than reformistic maintenance service? Clearly the 'march through the institutions' is a false orientation. Ideas of partisanship or of Trojan-horse tactics mistake the nature of business. The Church has so far tolerated any monk so long as he was rebelling against her on *her* terrain and not from any *outside* point. And now the Great Church of science-technics-capital-and-state with its 'objective' administrative and communication apparatus does just the same! And naturally it *needs* a reformistic impulse from case to case – for its own stabilising! A party which can get by in this situation can never be the tool of an ecological transformation.

It *is* possible within the dominant structure, in order to rescue it, to 'soften' technologies. But this project presupposes the existence of alternative *fans* of the Megamachine and its science and technology. It is also possible in the *interest* of the Megamachine – slowly enough, so that the return from invested capital remains secure – to get out of the nuclear option, even if this has been difficult on account of the ambitions of military strategists. Single fractions of industry can be sacrificed so long as there is enough time for capital to modify its technical identity. In fact it is even necessary to adapt to a cost-estimate of the *relative* ecological stabilising of the Megamachine. The resistance of single units of capital against the internalising of repair costs caused by them can be broken, and over a shorter or longer period will be broken.

Also social innovations are urgently needed, even though they are not immediately desired. Even the rulers now and again want to be coerced in the direction of their own happiness. The 'reconstruction of industrial society' which Greens are quite consciously delivering, is already a fairly developed restorative project. Whatever is useful here we shall find taken up again into the strategies of the two main parties. Even a great deal which is 'ecologically radical' can be expected in this way to become a current issue – never fear!

In the meantime there is nothing more ridiculous than the expression 'city-hall fundamentalism'. In the current situation of the Greens, a man or woman must be extremely eager to run for office, in spite of the fundamentalist or radical-ecological party position. Yet to want to be a 'watchdog' for Green principles is nothing but an evasive defence.

Altogether, my experience with the Greens convinced me of the absence of prospects for a purely political fundamentalism and radicalism – even, indeed precisely, in view of the much more auspicious resonance of the ecological crisis. Politically things are organised and added up according to heads, while the fundamental opposition grows up in those same heads and hearts which in other contexts still stand in the imperial consensus. And the Greens became involved in almost the same way. Whoever has respect for his or her mental integrity must stop playing this game.

Citizen Initiatives arising from Perplexity

The political activity of the Greens no longer has any existential relationship to the exterministic *symptoms*. The contents are means to improving the image. Citizen initiatives, with which the *ecopax* movement began, have a serious character. Concrete local protests and small changes in attitude, which affect daily life, point mentally in the right direction – even though technically they have drawbacks – and although for the most part they don't touch the real dimensions of the problem.

Even when these things are transient, or for many people lead to total resignation, there is pay-off in the process of learning about what either won't work or is inadequate because it doesn't reach to the roots of the catastrophe. Only a minority among minorities had, by the middle 1970s, come to recognise that what was needed was not the sum effect of a lot of small changes, but the introduction of a different life-style – far deeper in the *ecopax* movement than in the socialist movement, who as a group had never won through to the perspective of a *general* emancipation ascribed to them. And even less visible was how *much* change this means and how *deep* is the resistance to it, even in people whose spirits are open for new things.

Now, partial motives to defend against dangers must fuse together with a general perspective of salvation, and the concrete despair arising from the increasing prominence of exterministic symptoms must be met by techniques of encouragement coming from the depths of our being. Let us quickly recapitulate the experience of the 1970s and 80s.

What happens to a normal sensitive human being if he or she notices serious dysfunctions in the general style of life, which can no longer be kept out of his or her own house and garden? He/she at first experiences *perplexity*. This may be extremely unpolitical and, depending on the beliefs of the perplexed person, may be nearer to the principle of St Florian. But the emphasis has remained on the ego-oriented defence against immediate dangers, and only a few people are ready to question individualism, which is the entire style of life we have learnt, into which we are 'socialised'.

Even dedicated protectors of the environment still believe that by taking the correct rehabilitative action, ecologically and socially, we could get back to an imagined 'normalcy', and that we could keep the industrial system while getting rid of its dysfunctions. It is only different in the case of those few who either have so much sympathy for everything living, or who are analytically so penetrating, that most of the time they cannot repress the apocalyptic character of all that is happening; and even these people allow themselves to be deceived again. Normally the disappearing lifestyle as a whole is all the more intensively affirmed, and shines all the more beautiful in memory. In truth the world in the period reachable by today's memories was never so 'in order' as the nostalgia of the heart makes it appear.

The idea is that the setback didn't have to happen, that it would have been avoidable with a little reason and moderation on the part of all participants. Outrage arises because many people, especially those with influence in industry and administration, for the sake of their own advantage, do not stop what is obviously false and harmful to life. That the 'forces of coercion' have to do with the *substance* of civilisation endorsed by overwhelming consensus, is now being slowly learnt, to the discouragement of the first naive attempt, and painful for the individual consciousness. It turns out that the *contents* of what was intended – 'things to be abolished' as well as 'things to be added' – cannot be carried out in such a form.

Gramsci once attached great value to distinguishing between the official 'bourgeois society' and 'civil society': the latter being the power which, in conflict, had to articulate itself outside parliament and achieve enough cultural superiority to give a new institutional constitution to the industrial civilisation. But it is the industrial *'civil* society' which is itself the problem! And from this point of view it can in no way be called in question by its perplexed citizens, with all their demands for partial interventions to uphold the quality of life.

The citizen initiatives which were based on perplexity signalised by name that they did not see themselves outside the political consensus, and certainly not outside the general consensus of civilisation. We shall not overdo our civilisation, nor shall we destroy it: the whole thing shall be cared for and improved, and the full potential for life-quality shall be realised in it. This attitude has exhausted itself, and now to the perplexity comes the fact of being sacrificed, of being handed over to the spiral of death and to the forces which are driving it further.

What can we do now? Especially in moments of acute threat such as after the catastrophe of Chernobyl, the Gulf War or Bosnia, the need is always expressed to get something helpful and comforting done *by the state*, which at the same time is less trusted. If the situation really turns into a state of emergency, then at once we would have the atomic state, with army, police and security forces practising it for the benefit of the population. *The more efficiency we expect from the organs of the Megamachine in cases of acute crisis, the more totalitarian will be its manner of functioning.* The alarm after Chernobyl only helped to tighten up the powers of information.

The total effect, up to now, of the *ecopax* movement appears to be to train the dragon which it is fighting. The most visible result of the anti-nuclear power movement is technically and ideologically exportable reactor 'safety', which at the same time is the finest argument for not shutting them down. The effect of the peace movement was very similar. If nuclear deterrence gives you an uneasy feeling, we can put rocket-catching Star Wars nets above you (at least first of all above our headquarters), says the Pentagon. And after the end of the Cold War, the proliferation of nuclear and chemical weapons, officially lamented, is still supported by a voluble weapons industry, justified in its existence by the need to maintain employment. And 'protection by non-nuclear defensive weapons' is an argument for more conventional weaponry, while 'social defence' is an absolute flop.

None of this is coincidence, but the normal consequence of short-circuiting 'correct' behaviour in an exterministically-functioning whole. The entire Green uprising has remained a prisoner to the foundations of western civilisation, even though it began to cause crumblings on the edges of personalities. But within ourselves we are now much more identified with the pleasant successes of the western way, with our cities and boulevards – than we are with cultural overload and with our own origin, out of which we could build a new overall structure if only we weren't so full of fears of loss, and if only we didn't attach so much value to the comforts and pleasures of the parasitical Metropolis.

This is a mechanism by which resistance is *consumed*. At the end it helps, via 'get out' scenarios, to finance the accelerated closing of nuclear power stations, already obsolete, so that the park is cleaned up and capital continues to flow. In the process of 'reconstruction of industrial society' no grain of comfort must suffer, and there are many people who lack a great deal of the standard comfort of the white Empire: it is this which constitutes the Megamachine's ideological share.

Last but not least, expectations are directed toward the state, being as it is the executive organ of the Megamachine. Ecological modernising demands the extended reproduction of the *whole* monster, and not least a strengthening of administration and the quota of the state, so that it does not come to grief financially.

But the total logic of this policy is false, something which is a consequence of its industrial society perspective, and which is still shared by the largest proportion of disturbed citizens.

Apart from this the movements are still subject to the patriarchal mode of procedure. William Irwin Thompson[1] has compared the cultural projects of the male mind, with their dramatic cycle of rising up, climax and decay, with the progression of the male erection. In this way social movements are progressing against single exterministic factors: like brief erections. The insistent continuity said to characterise 'female' forces (not just those of women) is the movement behind or under the movements.

At this point of departure we cannot be dealing with one more *action proposal*. It is much more likely that we are dealing with a spiritually-based *design* of a political *project*, that has a long way to go – not necessarily measurable in time units. After Chernobyl the indefatigable Gunther Anders demanded a resistance which would *really* cripple, *really* tie the hands of those who are responsible for the crime of continuing to develop nuclear energy. But we can't really get at them through their 'hardware'! In this our strategy is exhausted.

We must concede that in this perspective we are powerless and drive ourselves uncreatively into a self-destructive escalation. The protest, the act of resistance as a *concept* turns out to be a dead-end. The question is no longer whether we carry flowers and hold hands or prefer some tougher proceeding. Nothing is achieved either way.

Incidentally we are dealing in *both* cases only with strategies to appease our *own* consciences. "But surely one can't just do nothing against the accepted, *de facto* planned nuclear destruction?" Yes, one can! One can stop going once more for the most obvious symptom and getting involved in notoriously dubious accounting about partial majorities, ninety percent of whom in any case do not want the *general* changes with which individual horrors are to be avoided!

A society is a whole. Ours would not be the same without nuclear power stations – because they mean more than a supply of electric power. It is exactly this that people mean when they want *gradual* change: a change which is no change at all, which doesn't even remotely challenge deep structures. There is no point in wanting to represent interests *for them*, which they do not (yet) have.

The only places where it would have a transient meaning are where 'new' and still untouched populations are being politicised by the initiative of the technocracy. The only point of the various anti-actions and demonstrations is the general concern that knowledge about the implacability of society, about the untenability of social peace on the basis of terroristic large technologies, does not fall asleep. Then we shouldn't deceive ourselves about 'active obstruction', about direct defence against dangers. Gunther Anders is altogether right: *these* goals are not to be achieved by 'fasting for peace'. Nor in any other way. And people fast mainly for themselves and not from masochism. It elevates the soul.

Abstract Analysis

Action based on perplexity, in a society so objective and alienated as ours, is continually and unavoidably disappointed. It is *impossible* that any single special perplexity should achieve its special correction. From this those energetic characters who engage themselves at all learn fairly early to think whole-system critically – placing in the centre of their attention the general conditions for the solution of the problems they personally favour.

It is in any case hard work, from two points of view. On the one hand the ego-structure is in the way – that system of defence-mechanisms and self-deceptions, projections and prejudices, that fixes and limits the perception of the world. On the other hand the objective structure is more complex than it has ever been.

Although even in the simplest tribal formation the clarity of things is deceptive and the medicine man and chieftain possibly have quite a different understanding of the world than other tribal members, it still remains possible for most people to see through the whole. Alien stereotypes help in relations with the outside, and if the tribe is defeated in a confrontation, it was 'fate'. Today, by comparison, every household, every community, every region, every country is predominantly dependent upon the ever larger unity, and in the more distant circles which are erected round our existence there are continually so many thwarting forces that it is altogether impossible to know everything that is relevant.

Higher powers of abstraction are required, in spite of this extensive ignorance about important details, more or less to understand the whole business. Only he who has built up an inner model of the implicit order of the natural and social cosmos, and of himself as microcosm, partly rationally and partly by intuition, can operate in a conscious manner on the whole, and then concentrate on a special object without losing his overall view.

However, the ego which is embarked on this path tends to sacrifice its sensibility and its ability to approach concrete needs and sufferings with sufficient energy. It undergoes in a quasi-voluntary fashion a kind of sensory deprivation, withdraws that contact which is to a great extent identical with the capacity for sensual love. This theoretical practice can, even without a neurotic impulse, make one more or less schizoid.

These two paths of abstraction and perplexity are two sides of the same coin. For this reason apparently more is needed than the necessary re-sensualising of the intellect and the intellectualising of the emotionally-perplexed. We must find a new way. It is naturally not the intention of the critic to deprive those impulses of their driving force, with the spreading of the ecological crisis time and again, here of perplexity, there of the abstract understanding.

There are no short cuts with which, with the failure of immediate reactions, personal experience could be replaced. Apart from this a transformation as deep as the one which is getting under way will certainly find unexpected breakthroughs. For indeed in every impulse the entire situation is present. Nobody can know exactly how things function in the basement of social consciousness. Without conscious intent even this or that act of Green *realpolitik* could have an effect in a different matrix from what the newspaper report would lead us to expect. *"L'homme propose, Dieu dispose"*, as people used to say in earlier times. But I am primarily interested in those who are not content with such small comfort, and for this reason want to endure a relentless review of hitherto existing practice.

NOTES
(1) William Irwin Thompson, *The Time Falling Bodies Take To Light, Mythology, Sexuality, and the Origins of Culture* (New York: St. Martin's Press, 1981), p167ff.

12. The subjectivity of salvation

The Logical Place for a Politics of Salvation

What could stop the apocalypse? The basis of a politics of salvation is the withdrawal of the living spirit from the infrastructures of the Megamachine. The following sketch clarifies the necessary shift, the new focus of the social network. At first glance it has something mechanical about it, as do all such schemes, which makes the message seem alien. So I will give the gist of it in advance: *only by re-unification of our living spirit with its natural roots, with the wellsprings of culture, can we create for ourselves a chance against dead and alienated work, dead and alienated spirit.* We need to distance ourselves from the Megamachine, the artificial heaven of the dead spirit, instead of distancing ourselves from nature, if we are to correct the orientation of our psychic energy and the colossal disproportion in the way we invest it.

This distancing, this de-identification, begins not with the *material* of the Megamachine (concrete, money, or the organs of state), but with the *inner hang-ups and motivations* from which the Megamachine has proceeded. The building-site of the new culture lies primarily *in us* – as did the building-site of the old one. I speak of the inner model that we ourselves have and *are*, according to which we observe and deal with our world. The five factors N-U-C-E-I (*see next page*) represent not only the 'assemblage of social relationships' which comprise the human being, but also represent the individual, our empirical ego, which participates with its energy in all these five factors, levels or activities.

There is a proportion, or rather a disproportion, in our timetable, in how much we are involved productively and consumptively in the Megamachine, and how much in the world of our own life. In the absence of awareness of the real-time economy and the fact that it is *only relatively* imposed upon us, our energy-flow remains fixed as it is: in the inward direction, in order to feed the monster.

The ellipse expresses the fact that the largest part of the powers of the human being go in the horizontal direction of material development, thus increasing our bondage, our self-blocking of every possible way out. So we must now find a technique by means of which we can free

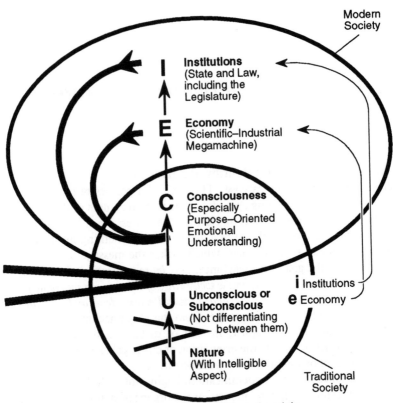

Diagram of our splitting off from the origin

The splitting off from the origin, from the nature from which our spirit comes, begins already at the point where what we today call the unconscious "U" comes into existence, and what was originally the growing point of the evolution of consciousness pushing beyond the archaic experience of oneness: with magic and myth. The lower small split indicates that tribal people were already impressed and shuddered in the play and counterplay of natural and human powers. But "C" for consciousness, that is, rational understanding, had from the beginning introduced a new deeper split and thus treated its own preceding stages, along with nature, with hostility and violence. Even so, this second split only achieved its strength, width, and depth, its ultimate chasm character in our modern societies. Here the spirit of the social collective (the small lower circle) extended upward out of itself the institutions "i" and the economy "e", which were originally subordinated to it (for example in the tribe and even still in the theocratic state): into an independent production apparatus ("E"), and further up and still dependent on it into the modern bureaucratic state ("I"). Now the living rational spirit gets captured from "above" and turned into a subordinated helping force, becoming a functionary of the "society as megamachine" (the large upper ellipse), as symbolized by the large arrows which embrace "C" from above.

ourselves from this having-our-centre-outside-ourselves, this state of distraction in a controlling material world. This means calling our powers back from the horizontal direction of the world of material goods, and concentrating them upon the vertical one. In social practices there must be no more automatism: everything needs to be consciously reflected upon, determined, and regulated by us. Otherwise the spontaneous evolution of species will push us over the edge. At this point all liberal and anarchistic world-pictures fail. Even a giant cluster of communes having only horizontal connections, and dedicating themselves only to the simple life, could be too much for the earth. And from the point of view of a decentralised, communitarian future society, certain planetary life-relationships are simply imperceptible. It is the vertical dimension which includes a world government.

If we are to escape the logic of self-extermination, the first step is to *think* of ourselves as independent of the work of our hands, to put to one side all those memorised concepts which stand for the cultural context which we have created for ourselves. The spirit, human energy, must relinquish its cooperation with the Megamachine and concentrate on re-making its broken-off connections in the other direction.

Naturally we must also get busy with the job of creating another world, not alongside the death machine and remaining dependent on it, but replacing it. The worst temptation is to want to rescue the Megamachine, under-girded by a 'dual economy', and make it into a Metropolitan play-province, while outside, the service-information-scientific society ticks away.

Behind this label is concealed the fact that living consciousness has disastrously changed its position. Formerly it was an organ of the *whole* of human nature and the social collective. Today it has become a functionary of the Megamachine and the institutional sphere which this machine has thoroughly penetrated. How can a mind be reasonable when it is torn from its roots, and forced into a dependent collaboration with its steel-concrete-silicon inorganic body, which came into existence in the absence of its awareness?

In institutions the living mind is subordinated to the dead mind, delivered up to the entire regulatory structure which the Megamachine has brought into existence in financial, legal and techno-normative fields. The ego, which the Machine has co-opted for these things, discovers that the framework within which it can meet its needs is completely determined in advance. Powers of perception exist essentially to connect us with life at a higher level. But now they serve to re-adapt the Megamachine to an 'environment' which is already its ruined product. And we are pleased to call this 'ecological modernisation'.

Only a complete turn-around can be of any help here. But where do we constitute the powers of initiative for a new structure and form? Or more modestly: where do we meet together in order to make ourselves 'empty' and receptive enough for this task? What the solution must look like can only be determined by making every decision consciously, as a provisional and experimental step.

But where shall we go with that surplus and open consciousness which is the kernel of the new institutions? *To that place where the split is now!* To that place where the human being has torn itself apart by means of its own culture! To that place where *Logos* and *Bios* have separated from each other, the place where *Logos* went in order to change from being an organ of *Bios* to being an agent of the Great Machine.

Precisely at that place, where the split has torn open, lies the lost wholeness of the human being, from which s/he could with moderation hold social life and nature-related practices together. This is the place at which the logic of salvation can make its start. Splitting off from the Megamachine instead of from nature (in order to correct the colossal disproportion of our rate of energy use and our time-planning, and thus also our structure of consciousness) would mean in a mental-political sense the 'splitting of the elites', the splitting off of today's scientific-managerial priesthood as an essential co-condition of an ecological reformation of the people.

This must not be conceived of as just an individual and spiritual change, but also as an institutional and political one. A connection must be made where the great split is: the gap must be closed. This split must be removed. And conversely, where great connections spring from vast institutions and the techno-structure, claiming consciousness as their functionaries, we must initially insert a *clutch*, which we can disengage whenever living interests prevent information-structures of the Mega-machine to turn with the rest[1].

Naturally such a clutch would only be makeshift, for defence against danger, for gaining time to accomplish the Turn-around. Ultimately the whole large ellipse must become empty and fall away, and economic and political activity there must be drawn out and renewed below, and find a relatively autonomous, but *integrated* role, such that it can no longer run amok, taking everything with it. Things never went to hell so fruitlessly and finally as they do in modern society. In comparison with the dominance of market automatism and vote-counting democracy, an archaic theocracy is a high cultural achievement, in which state and law still stand *above* the economic realm and both spheres are subordinated to the spiritual realm.

In the present state of affairs the small overlap between circle and ellipse is almost deceptive. Whatever still remains from the old order of justice has residual character, and as such serves only as supplementary legitimation of the false whole.

There is no simple way to re-establish a traditional society which does not inadvertently pass over into modernity. After being released from the custody of the Church, the modern ego has not been able to integrate social responsibilities without metaphysical support: pluralism is nothing but a cover-up for individual irresponsibility. This leads to the idea that a reconstituting of the human self is the pre-condition for a re-institutionalising of society. If individualism remains dominant, it can only bring about a totalitarian 'solution'.

In this the 'damage-limiting' version of the ORDO idea is correct in requiring that the economy, state and justice must be pulled back. In a 'correct' society the structures of justice comprise the first circle around spiritual life. Also originally they emanated directly from the social traffic. They are nearer to consciousness than production, which lies in a wider circle, nearer to the outer world. Historical materialism, which sees this the other way around, correctly describes something which, in the short history of humanity, has become increasingly false: this shifting of power over to objects, on which we make ourselves ever more dependent, for the sake of 'progress to freedom'.

By nature humans have the freedom to draw back from a cultural dead-end and to establish a new pattern. But in the big ellipse, the energy of consciousness, once invested in state and law, becomes firmly programmed and exerts ever-renewed control over the living. Here we are not dealing with the existence of a judicial sphere as such, but with the concrete shape of justice and the state. Today every student of law automatically becomes a prisoner of exterminism, his brain being made a captive of the tradition and needs of the Megamachine, and thus claimed for the wrong overall social spirit. Only s/he who has internalised the whole codex is entitled to be creative, and may alter matters of detail. This may be fine in times of an arising culture which has a positive attitude to life. But in this time of crisis in civilisation it is unbearable. Society must stop reproducing this whole structure, this law and this state.

Communities of only a few thousand people can become an enormous force, and can concentrate in themselves the power to disrupt. At this order of magnitude, where people remain in immediate contact with each other and with their local community, it is still possible to exercise self-limitation. Everything which is a necessity of life can be brought together in this place, with the exception of things which can be had by exchange. Only such an alternative society could approximate a cyclical economy and a science-technology which is responsible to society and to life, instead of being dominated by the demons of greed and prestige.

The contraction of the large ellipse down to the small circle – to a world-circle and to many organismically-coordinated small circles – is anthropologically and ecologically necessary. What is needed is to cultivate this design, to build it out within ourselves, and to re-learn a more compact form of life as it used to be in old societies – but now on the basis of a different awareness. Nobody knows exactly what it will be like, but we can know that, on a higher level of the spiral, there will be a different solution for basic human problems of exterminism. We are in the expansive phase, fleeing ever faster in the face of these basic problems. Precisely here we must push through. To this end we must *regain* those powers and forms which we lost on the other side of the split, because we couldn't yet integrate them. We are now assigned this task – and the task itself determines the place of action.

The question of the social instrumentalities of the Turn-around, indeed of the homeward path of humanity, now arises more urgently. The temptation to jump straight back into politics is great, especially since we are undeniably in a race with the forces of inertia of the spiral of death.

There has already been much meta-political abstract talk about a paradigm shift to the 'new age', and much of it is twaddle. 'New thought' becomes practical if political forces constitute themselves to develop a politics of Turn-around. The 'new thought', the new subjectivity, must first of all get itself together. But it is important that this occurs with a political intention, right from the beginning. Otherwise the spiritualisation adapts itself once again to the *status quo*. To avoid this, I turn first to the question of the *elaboration* of subjectivity, because it is this subjectivity which determines the *quality* of the new social power that we need. The fate of a new order will be determined by the human image of the movement it brings with it.

The Rise of Kundalini – Politics of Love

We could ask ourselves why the human spirit, with some exceptions, has not progressed beyond externalising itself in smart material accumulations and power-structures – even though it has frequently wanted to rise up beyond love, art and philosophy, into the worship of the absolute. Sometimes it reaches these higher levels, but it has not yet stabilised itself there. Even individually we cannot live from that level, and we certainly cannot do so in social groupings.

A good outcome cannot depend primarily upon our already *being free*. It will suffice that we *intend* this. We *do* participate in the highest intelligence – let us be led by it to the point of entry which, if we follow the insight of Jesus and so many other masters, is called *love*.

We may hear it said that *this* appeal has accomplished nothing over a period of two thousand years and more. Yet what does this prove? The evangelists may have been precursors. Their very existence shows the human possibility of a politics of the open heart. Evolution may now have led many to this step. This time it is more than an appeal for love. There is now a set of techniques and practices, in line with our true vital interests, for a social and political transformation.

The general mood which establishes itself in a critical phase of social evolution, when society is looking for a new solution, is decisive in determining what it holds to be true, or how close society gets to what is objectively right and necessary, true and beautiful. In the final analysis the true, which is the whole and acknowledges the whole, which precedes and overarches love of the heart, does not oppose this love of the heart, but cooperates with the basic ground we have within us. And from the heart, from contact with other beings, we also see more clearly into things absolute.

I find it remarkable that Lewis Mumford, in his *Transformations of Man* of 1956, has the same perspective: to take a gradually-emerging *politics of love as the centre-piece for creating a new self*. Mumford, who on occasions has waded through the entire substance of world history, and who developed a concept of salvation which is anything but esoteric, came to the conclusion:[2]

> *Love, like mind itself, has been slowly gathering momentum through the organic world: by reason of its late introduction into the drama conceived and enacted by man, it has absorbed only a small share of man's working and learning activities. But in the development of the person, love is actually the central element of integration: love as erotic desire and procreativity, love as passion and aesthetic delight, lingering over images of beauty and shaping them anew, love as fellow-feeling and neighbourly helpfulness, bestowing its gifts on those who need them, love as parental solicitude and sacrifice, and finally, love with its miraculous capacity for over-valuing its own object, thereby glorifying it and transfiguring it, releasing something which only the lover at first can see. Without a positive concentration upon love in all its phases, we can hardly hope to rescue the earth and all the creatures that inhabit it from the insensate forces of hate, violence, and destruction that now threaten it. And without a philosophy of the person, who dares talk of love?*

Doubtless Mumford here means the human being as one who suffers and enjoys him/herself, not as a switch-circuit representative. But everything hinges on priorities, for otherwise the consequences will be technocratic or ultimately neurocratic, and psycho-pharmacological-trainers will obstruct liberation while claiming that they are furthering it. Mumford continues:

> *What is ideally desirable, at this stage of man's development, does not exist in any past form of man, either biological or social: not cerebral man, muscular man or visceral man: not the pure Hindu, the pure Muslim, the pure Christian, nor yet the pure Marxist or the pure Mechanist: not Old World man or New World man. The unity we seek must do justice to all these fragments, and lovingly include them in a self that shall be capable of transcending them. Any doctrine of wholeness that does not begin with love itself as the symbol and agent of this organic wholeness can hardly hope to produce either a unified self or a united world; for it is not in the detached intellect alone that this transformation must be effected.*

While no Marxist, Mumford is in a sense a more consistent materialist than Marx. At least he is truer to the monistic conception of the world than were Marx and Engels themselves. He raises Marx and historical materialism to the level of a 'unitary' world-picture. Thus he could show the materialistic Left the path not only to an ecological perspective, but even the path to the threshold of this comprehensive capacity for love; the capacity on whose intensification everything depends.

I shall elucidate this possibility of entering the spiritual realm by means of a concept defined by the Indian concepts of *Kundalini-Yoga*, *Chakra*, and *Tantra*[3]. Tantra is, in the narrower sense, the name for the art of spiritual love of ancient India. The concept has the great advantage of emphasising the *connective tissue* between the 'average' and the 'superconscious', the 'profane' and 'spiritual' regions, and even of locating it in the middle, the heart chakra. This connecting tissue *is* love and the important thing is the feeling-*quality* of awareness, as a *precondition* for our abandonment of our mass-production and power-structures.

Kundalini is the Indian name for *serpent-power*, lying tightly coiled at the lower end of the spinal cord, and from there experienced as erotic *life-energy*, climbing up the spine to a greater or lesser distance and intensity. Fully extended, the Kundalini snake stands with its head in the *Logos*, so that this idea assumes the dialectical polarity of *Eros* and *Logos*, sexuality and spirit.

Kundalini, our life-energy, has the tendency to climb up through a sequence of *chakras* to the top of the head – the chakras are *nodal points of psycho-physiological energy-transformation* in our central nervous system. In the spiritual culture of India this has been especially cultivated, but all old high cultures have worked with it.

Embedded in all-embracing philosophy and ethics, many practices developed in order to stimulate and train *kundalini* to rise up more quickly, more intensely, and more completely than usual. The phenomenon itself is a bio-electric or bio-psychic given, and almost everybody has a vital experience of this upward movement through the spinal cord up to the cerebral cortex[4].

The chakras are arranged along the spinal cord and up into the brain, as shown in the accompanying diagram. According to the level on this

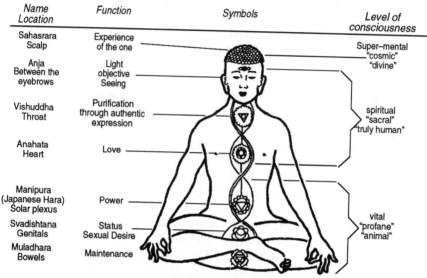

Name Location	Function	Symbols	Level of consciousness
Sahasrara Scalp	Experience of the one		Super–mental "cosmic" "divine"
Anja Between the eyebrows	Light objective Seeing		
Vishuddha Throat	Purification through authentic expression		spiritual "sacral" "truly human"
Anahata Heart	Love		
Manipura (Japanese Hara) Solar plexus	Power		vital "profane" "animal"
Svadishtana Genitals	Status Sexual Desire		
Muladhara Bowels	Maintenance		

The Kundalini Scheme

The two curved lines which rise up with the spinal column correspond to sympathetic and parasympathetic nervous systems and respectively left and right cerebral hemispheres. Wilber explains that the localization of the chakras is a reality and not to be understood just symbolically. In that he is concentrating less on the function than on the represented forces or energies, he assigns them as follows; the first (i.e. anal) chakra represents matter (as in faecal matter), the second, sex (genitals), the third, gut reactions (emotions, power, vitality), the fourth, love and belongingness (heart), the fifth, discursive intellect (voice box), the sixth, higher mental-psychic powers (neocortex), the seventh, at and beyond the brain itself, transcendence. (Apart from this his book comes close to making another distinction within the seventh chakra, which can perhaps be externally located in the difference between the top of the head in the narrower sense and the sketched in kalotte. Thus there would be eight chakras, which would repeat the "tonic" in the intergral "octave."

step-ladder at which we mainly live, and to the point to which we have integrated our powers from below to above with the help of glimpses of light from above, we can, with their help, identify our philosophy of life and our manner of existence in the world.

It is according to this that we can distinguish not only between individuals and biographical stages of the same individual, but also between cultures (civilisations) and their epochs. According to the anthropology and epistemology of the Buddha, preserved in his teaching, we have reached in the social average which has precipitated itself in the dominant customs, laws, and institutions, a use of our forces which is little above the third chakra. Even at this level we don't seem to have our powers at all well under control, so that self-actualisation expresses itself mainly as a compensatory wielding of power.

We are not dealing here with nuances, but with the principle of rising to a more comprehensive, *truly human* consciousness, which is now involved with real history – and less with transcendence at the highest point. This focus comes through very beautifully in an intense concentration on the opening of 'gates' offered by Margo Naslednikov,[5] where she concentrates on the third, fourth and sixth chakras, which need to be opened.

In the third chakra (*Hara*), to the extent that we have mastered the life-problems of the first two chakra-levels, the problems of all three vital-energy centres come together. The theme in *Hara*, the centre of gravity of the body, is preservation of life and the body. To have everything open and harmonised here, without ascetic violence or greedy excess, is a precondition for all further ascent. This centre focuses the instinct for self-preservation, and since our subsistence, status and self-realisation depend initially upon the mother, with whom we initially comprise *one* world, we remain up to this point autistic and narcissistic according to the motto 'each person is his own neighbour'.

The heart concerns itself with social things, relations to others. If *Hara* asks "*who am I?*" the heart asks "*who am I with?*", and since the first other person in this sense is usually the father, our problem retrospectively is often with him or the symbolic world of the father.

For agreement with our wider environment we have the brain as the seat of logical thought (left hemisphere), of intuition (right hemisphere) and memory. It asks "*where am I, what happened?*", and its achievement, admittedly bound up with the fifth, the chakra of speech, is objectivity, for which stands the sixth chakra, the 'third eye'.

For the three 'gates' Margo Naslednikov uses[6] the adjacent triple symbol and explains: the moon represents the brow chakra, the receptive pole for information coming from outside; the sun represents the heart, which harmonises and unifies the higher with the lower; and the cross represents the solar plexus, in which horizontal and vertical equalise themselves. The next step could be the opening of the heart together with a full 'alchemical' marriage of heart and solar plexus, if we want to follow this entire model demonstration. For *how* we use our instrumental understanding, how we use our reason as a whole, follows from it.

The 'vital', 'profane' position which we have taken, which arises from below and comes together in the solar plexus, is not 'earthly' (as Leary calls it[7]), but still 'bestial'. Anthropocentrism-egocentrism is the natural-earthly attitude of the human brain-animal. And the 'superconscious' or spiritual-divine level is not 'post-worldly' but in fact truly human.

Enlightenment writers like Chernychevski called the first form of this human position 'reasonable egoism' – a correct idea, though with an accent of rationalistic abstraction. And without doubt psychosomatic and neuro-electric euphorising can improve one's state of wellbeing to prepare us for a higher strategy – when a loving social context carries us along, we can loosen our defences and stop holding limited, shortsighted and anxiety-determined patterns of behaviour, and take back our mistrust of the human environment.

No miracles are demanded of us concerning thought-*content*. Clearly, however, the same is true of 'reasonable egoism' as of communism: it is a simple thing which is hard to do. On account of anxieties that stand in the way, therapeutic and meditative techniques are the path to pursue – especially the body-oriented tantric ones with their purpose of uniting *Eros* and *Logos* above the heart. Leary has shown that precisely this bodily, somatic sphere is the natural entry-point into the spiritual realm. To secure the space needed for relevant practices and to stabilise the results, deeper social association and more spiritual communes are required in order to satisfy people's need for security at a new level.

We are still governed by solar plexus energies, not completely integrated, and not integrated with higher levels. More precisely: only our civilisation-determining elites have got there – if we measure elites according to their capacity for powerful use of the intellect, as with scientists, politicians, managers, engineers, sociologists, priests and therapists. The majority still lets its energies run mainly through the first two chakras. It has been sufficient to go just one step further to become patriarchal and aristocratic, to exploit the disposable need for food and sexuality, in order to *rule* everything.

At the level of the third chakra, character builds itself up in youthful dis-identification with paternal authority, and with other people as competitors for possessions, status, and self-assertion. In individual life it is the third seven years, years in which we want to prove ourselves to the world, and move away from our parents. At the planetary level we prove ourselves to God the Father and to Mother Goddess Earth. This immaturity is behind many observations that we are psychologically, morally, socially and institutionally retarded in relation to the reality of our power. Every social constitution has to take into account this state of development – but must it also be *based* on it? Yet ours is.

The main issue is to climb out of this state of affairs, so that higher human energies are channelled. The result would be to reverse the power-relationship between heart and solar plexus, and to direct the solar plexus forces from the heart. We are born to loving knowledge. We are born for the purpose of using our energies across the entire range of energy-centres. *To this end* we need *schools*, schools of love and of knowledge – all else would then order itself in its proper place.

We now let ourselves be directed by the lower chakras because we do not use our whole being, our whole body of awareness, as our organ of communication. Our new acquisition, the forebrain, is our large data-storage and processing unit, because we are quite unenlightened in this area, so that it must slavishly obey a will-to-power concentrated at a much lower level. If it were to obey the heart, then everything would already be different, even if we did not yet have immediate access there to neuro-electrical, genetic, and quantum-mechanical levels of reality.

When governed by the will-to-power, the intellect knows only what we allow into it from outside, or what we intrusively investigate in the world. For this reason Godhead speaks to us merely in charades, and we jump out of our skins if we run into one of its smallest tricks. But from the heart we can recognise that 'divine curiosity' (our most noble excuse) is a self-deception, a contradiction in itself – the Godhead by nature can be neither greedy nor curious.

From the level of heart we can bring brain and solar plexus into far better relationship, and remove the demonic elements from our existence. For we have, in the *unreflected* force of nature for which the solar plexus stands, and whose blade is our brain, the demon driving us to the Megamachine. There is no other force in us not also present in every animal: what is evil comes as something added, as an accelerator and strengthener. It is seen throughout history that power cannot control itself, and that in making the attempt to do so it is much more likely to pull one more trigger.

However, to control our forces and powers from the heart is something which up to now has never succeeded institutionally. Hitherto it was opposed by the hostility of the spirit of patriarchal asceticism, in which love is only an additional power-instrument, because the alchemical marriage between heart and solar plexus takes place from the lower pole, and then becomes the extremest of perversions.

Recently in the new age 'Magazin 2000' someone quoted an angry text by his guru Narayanananda against Margo Naslednikov, the thrust of which was that she deceives credulous adepts in promising them freedom by passing through *Eros*. The guru and his pupil snarled frightfully! But have there not been, through the thousands of years, legions of such saints in India, while at the same time the ascent of humanity stagnated there? This is quite obviously an inadequacy, even in the case of the Buddha who, in his flight from women, strongly differentiates himself from the Chinese Lao Tzu. In the following two lines, which I got to know in a *puja* to his reverence, is perhaps expressed the ultimate secret of the Buddha's holiness:

> *He has overcome the greed for pleasures*
> *And no longer goes into the mother's lap.*

In Rainer Langhans' *Theoria diffusa aus Gesprächen mit drei Frauen*, which is defending the same theme, I am alienated precisely by this posture of flight, this perspective of progress away from the 'external' to the 'internal' opposite sex. It is something completely different which is written in a prospectus of Margo Naslednikov: "You will discover that you can feel ecstatic with a partner, but that nevertheless you do not need him for this purpose." It is one thing to overcome *obsession* with the other body, but something else to overcome it with sex. With Langhans we impose a blockade on woman, basically a violent interruption of the natural expression of *Eros*. Why, really? Are men so afraid that we might be physically overpowered and brought back? Here something is rotten on the ascent – it is a new version of the ascent into the spiritual patriarchate.

I think that in this matter Europe has a better solution than the ascetic Indian Yoga, a solution which has been subliminally preserved from pre-Christian Celtic, Germanic, and Slavic times. Our epics from the age of chivalry regard the pair, even in bed, as cooperating toward the Godhead. Our romanticism was close to the tantra of love. In Novalis we find this only superficially naive fairy tale of *Hyacinth and the Little Rose Flower*, the dear boy and the dear girl. Then comes from afar off a gloomy ascetic and makes the boy estranged and sinister to the girl. But an eccentric old lady in the forest throws the guru's book in the fire. She sends Hyacinth to the place where the Mother of All Things lives, the veiled virgin Isis, and he finds the loved one again on the long journey under the veil of the goddess. A distich of Novalis, aside from the fairy tale, adds:

One person succeeded – he lifted the veil of the Goddess of Sais,
But what did he see? He saw – miracle of miracles – himself.

And one last thing: "Love is the final purpose of world history, the Amen of the Universe". Little Rose Flower needs Hyacinth. But still more the man needs the goddess who initiates him. Man and woman must learn this freedom, to refrain from mutual sexual exploitation.

On the whole everything points to a shift of emphasis toward the feminine. If both sexes proceed along their path of individuation, of integration, they will meet each other more often than ever, and perhaps find themselves for the first time. There is a zone here where that which human beings have in common begins to count for something – the mutual projecting and blaming gives way, and the spirits can complement each other. The return home of *Eros* to the gods, which Walter Schubart desired, might have a chance.

Novalis described exactly the point at which modern man gets taken in by machines, science, and technology, and how he should respond to this circumstance in a manner very different from the mentally homo-erotic. In a letter written in 1797 he expresses the opinion:

I do not deny that I fear this terrible ossification of the heart – this tuberculosis of the soul! Its tendency is beneath the tendencies of my nature. Tender at birth, my intellect has little by little extended itself and unobserved excluded the heart from its possessions. Sophie restored to the heart its lost throne. How easily her death could restore control to the usurper, who then would certainly annihilate the heart in revenge! I have very much felt its indifferent coldness – but perhaps the invisible world, which hitherto has slumbered in me, will yet rescue me.[8]

The path of initiation of Wolfram's Parsifal also does not exclude *Eros*. In his *Book of the Grail* Trevor Ravenscroft has already made clear that the expeditions in our epics are arranged on a circle which leads back to her. In our region there has been from early on a strong womanly *individuality*, a strong womanly *spirit*.

Here the pure patriarchal spirituality of the ascetic Yoga path, on which the man seeks a supplementary feminising in order to complete his dominion, is not yet proclaimed. Apart from this it is, under our conditions, a strengthener of rationalism, rather than a medicine to cure it. From the social and historical point of view, it is not pure illumination which we are now lacking, but the power of love, and its social emergence does not depend upon gaining access to the divine centre, but to the *human* one, the centre of the heart. We shouldn't just take the body with us, but use it as a transport vehicle for our journey within, without losing ourselves in doing this and making a drug trip out of bodily sensations. There are really good reasons for this.

It is a characteristic of the human condition to have a depressive element. From Buddha to Hegel the counterpoint of thought has been the relationship of mind to suffering, a focus on the unhappy consciousness. Hence the 'revolutionary role of evil in history', which is 'not the place of pleasure' – the entire Satanism of progress. And since Hegel thus spoke, this situation has turned somersault once more. Look at the extent to which our whole civilisation is a 'guide to unhappiness'! *Joy through suffering.* More than any other species, we stand under the weight of inadequacy, and we shrivel defensively. But if we remain unhappy animals we will hardly escape the apocalypse, and the measures we use to postpone it will make the world more ugly. The building of bunkers, the hoarding of food supplies and defence weapons, in order to save – what? It is the grasping life-style which brings scarcity!

Contemporary changes in the sciences, in the direction of systemic, holistic, non-dualistic thought, are certainly important. But physics did not create the Western world-view: it only multiplied it mightily in an increasing *secondary* autonomy. The paradigm-change in physics today is hopeful mainly because it shows how the motivational foundation, on which the scientific priesthood of the Megamachine is still resting *en masse*, is breaking up.

The turn-about from necrophile science to biophile knowledge will need a different avenue of approach from the *Tao*-analogue mathematical model used up to now, which, if we are not ourselves mathematicians and physicists, we hardly need in order to re-equip the inner and social worlds for us. Apart from this biophile knowledge is almost unquestioningly offered on existential grounds, but only conditionally on those of the scientific tradition. Up to a point it is almost identical with the re-visioning of politics. Physicist or politician – we are attempting to convince ourselves on rational grounds that we must bid farewell to rationalism (abstractionism), but not at the same time to physics, nor to politics.

Well and good, but the real question is whether we humans can improve our sense of wellbeing, our feeling for existence in the world, and the atmosphere of our communication with it; whether we can free our lives of domination by negativity, and whether we can raise our capacity for happiness. If, in what follows, I take up Jean Gebser's idea of *homo integralis*, it is because it interests me not for its philosophical qualities, but for its impact on the quality of life, on our ability to cut a happier figure. We are the ones who decide how joyful the message is, and how friendly the universe is.

What we must reach as the next stage is not the highest enlightenment, but love – a discerning love which includes the social whole. This
is the 'small' leap from the third chakra to the fourth, to relating to the
world through the heart centre of the brain animal that we are – and up
to now even the powers of our heart go mostly through the will-to-
power. We would have to re-equip our world to the standards of heart –
not so needful, not so arrogant, not so jealous, not so greedy, not so
curious. And then, with growing peace and happiness, we must proceed
further. This could be the key to the impending reintegration of social
consciousness.

Connecting Back to the Origin

Every human cultural revolution has included a partial regression, a
renewed passage through the original problems of human existence,
and thus also through its original anxieties. We are dealing with Faust's
journey to the mothers, to the sources of our vitality. The spirit with
which we must set out on the road to the mothers has not been better
characterised than by, once again, Lewis Mumford, in perhaps his most
visionary book, *The Transformations of Man*. Looking at the dead-end of
'post-modern man' – as of a thinking ant which leaves itself to the
spontaneous course of its alienated native powers and "applies to itself
the same principles according to which it deals with the physical
world"[9] – he comes to the conclusion:

> To overcome the blind drift to automatism mankind as a whole must
> deliberately resume the long effort that originally turned hominids into
> men[10]. Man's principal task today is to create a new self, adequate to
> command the forces that now operate so aimlessly and yet so compulsively.
> This self will necessarily take the entire world, known and knowable, as
> its province, and will seek not to impose a mechanical uniformity, but to
> bring about an organic unity...
>
> Many social agents that now work to the undoing of man, like science
> itself, will actually contribute powerfully to this transformation, once the
> seminal ideas, with their unifying images and designs, have become
> clarified.[11]

Here Mumford reminds us of prophetic minds like Isaiah, Mo Ti and
Joachim of Floris. Naturally Mumford regards science as a human
function, not as the work of specialists who seek to secure a social
identity against that of others. His eyes are directed toward wholeness
and balance in human subjectivity:

> Now this change toward world culture parallels a change that seems also

*it] on the point of taking place within the human personality: a change in the
direction of wholeness and balance. In the new constellation of the person,
parts of the human organism long buried or removed from conscious control
will be brought to light, recognised, accepted, re-evaluated and redirected.
The ability to face one's whole self, and to direct every part of it toward a
more unified development, is one of the promises held forth by the advance
both of objective science and subjective understanding.*

Here Mumford's perspective coincides precisely with that of Gebser's
homo integralis; he continues:

*Wholeness is impossible to achieve without giving primacy to the integra-
tive elements within the personality: love, reason, the impulse to perfection
and transcendence*[12].

So it is not just choiceless and purposeless 'liberation of impulses
repressed into the unconscious'.

*Perhaps the greatest difficulty today, as a result of the general hostility to
values brought in by seventeenth century science, is the failure to recognise
that wholeness demands imperatively that the highest elements in the
human personality should be singled out, accepted and trusted, fortified
and rewarded. The integration of the person begins at the top, with an
idea, and works downward till it reaches the sympathetic nervous system,
where organic integration in turn begins and works upward, till it emerges
as an impulse of love or a vital image... Unified man must accept the id
(the unconscious) without giving it primacy: he must foster the superego,
without making it depress the energies it needs for its own fuller expression*[13].

Even though Mumford is here still terminologically tied to Freud he
certainly doesn't mean the repressive superego, rooted in alienated
social forces and moralising within us, but much more that authority
which today we would prefer to call our *true self*. Similarly his concept
of personality, which he conceives as something internal and surpassing
egocentric expansion. He is concerned about the demands which the
human being must place on his contemporary self if he wants to resist
past activities and subordinate his behaviour:

*To be on friendly terms with every part of mankind, one must be on
equally friendly terms with every part of oneself; and to do justice to the
formative elements of world culture, which give it greater significance and
promise than any earlier stage in man's history, one must nourish the
formative elements in the human self, with even fuller energies than axial
man applied to this task. In brief, one cannot create a unified world with*

partial, fragmentary, arrested selves, which by their very nature must either produce aggressive conflict or regressive isolation. Nothing less than a concept of the whole man – and of man achieving consciousness of the whole – is capable of doing justice to every type of personality, every mode of culture, every human potential[14].

Mumford expresses the basic attitude from which I approach the political problem of building a bridge between our ego-structures and our institutions. This is because it is Mumford's basic idea that, in order to arrive at a livable world culture, we must create a new self, a new integration of the subjective forces of our being. Naturally those things which we can convert into institutional form will then exert their force to widen the stream of the new subjectivity. I only want to add one accent to Mumford's quotes: if we want to advance the true self we must not be shy of passing through *periods* of disintegration, nothingness and chaos, because the 'highest elements' would then never lose their Apollonian, repressive element. Without the courage to call upon Dionysus we won't escape; it is much more likely that Dionysus will show himself to us anew and unmistakably as Satan.

Unquestionably the integration can only be a forward and upward movement which more than annuls every partial regression. But the Apollonian anxiety in the face of deep forces will make sure that we continue the *flight* forwards and upwards, so characteristic of the male spirit, and it simply will not accept and adjust to the fact that it itself has re-created Dionysus as the Devil. We must turn back to the site of the fracture and finally cure ourselves of this anxiety. Admittedly Dionysus was a god of the *offended* Great Mother who also wanted to tear the man apart. The human being – man and woman – should now have reached the maturity to handle this original problem of sex and spirit, but in any case to *handle* it courageously instead of disregarding it and continuing to keep it repressed.

After contact with the World Spirit and the Earth Spirit (the sphere of the mother) had overtaxed him, Goethe's Faust had completely devoted himself to magic and allowed himself to be enfiefed by the Devil, with the 'riches of the world and their glories'. The substitute character of the projects Faust chased is shown in the services of Mephisto. How otherwise has contact been lost with 'what holds the world together in its most inward places'? How has it been torn off, so that we now confirm our belonging to life through knowledge of the outside world, because we no longer *know* it with organismic immediacy? For it is in this *split* – self-consciousness in the form of the European-male *Logos* fearfully defending itself *against* nature, the body, woman, and the feminine – that the root of the ecological catastrophe lies, in the drive

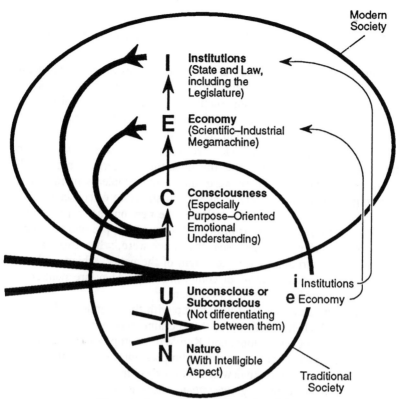

Diagram of our splitting off from the origin

The splitting off from nature begins already at the point where what we today call the unconscious "U" comes into existence. The lower small split indicates that tribal people were already impressed by the play and counterplay of natural and human powers. But "C" for consciousness, (rational understanding), had from the beginning introduced a new deeper split and thus treated its own preceding stages, along with nature, with hostility and violence. Even so, this second split only achieved its ultimate chasm character in our modern societies. Here the spirit of the social collective (the small lower circle) extended upward out of itself the institutions "i" and the economy "e", which were originally subordinated to it (eg. in the tribe and theocratic state): into an independent production apparatus ("E"), and further up and still dependent on it into the modern bureaucratic state ("I"). Now the living rational spirit gets captured from "above" and turned into a subordinated helping force, becoming a functionary of the "society as megamachine" (the large upper ellipse), as symbolized by the large arrows which embrace "C" from above.

for compensatory accumulation of insignia, things, experiences and victories.

Jean Gebser in his *Ever Present Origin* has discerned five sequential structures of consciousness in the human species, and has identified the steps tying them to our cultural evolution. I shall come to them later, in the chapter about *homo integralis*. Here I am interested in his scheme, his road map, and I am especially interested in the downward-pointing arrows which I have emphasised by using thick lines. They stand for the

downthrust or *backthrust* which always accompanies the forward thrust
to the next higher level of development. The small side-arrows symbolise the growth of criticism, inefficiency, deficiency, obsolescence,
failure of the respective structures of consciousness, that lead partly into
dead-ends, and partly push up to the next step.

Often when the next step looks threateningly overtaxing, we wish to
flee back to earlier states, and the downthrust energy directs itself
against this tendency. These were once acute problems in historical
jumping-off places, the more so as the old structure of consciousness,
anchored in rites and customs, releases the new one as willingly as a
blackberry thicket releases its princes. Today, earlier pre-mental conditions are certainly no longer what they once were, when they corresponded to the circumference and extent of the polity, which made do
with less-developed patterns of communication. They are neither so
powerful nor so efficient as they were then.

When we regress, we tend to wind up with the fragments of former
structures, which had split up as they became deficient. Even Gebser
has warned about regressions, and Ken Wilber emphasised this warning on the basis of corresponding glimpses into the contemporary
psychological scene and the new age field: except *temporarily* and for the
purpose of forward-moving *integration*, there is no sense in getting
involved with older structures of consciousness.

But there is a big problem that is not so easy to distinguish in reality
from the above-mentioned aspect. This problem is the cause of our
disposition to regress, and it is grounded in the necessity to regress: the
release from obsolescent stages in personal and tribal history does not
take place without conflict and struggle. The single psyche grows out of
conflict, relatively powerless and unsure, feeling itself held back. The
psyche then turns itself with *power magic* against the common ground,
the Origin, from which it comes. This repeats itself in the 'dragon fight'
of the mythical consciousness-hero against the psychic structure of the
Great Mother, in order to get free of the 'cave' and come into the full
light of the sun. And for the next step Julian Jaynes has described the
transition from mythic to mental as an altogether dramatic and an-
guished 'breakdown of the bicameral mind', a full-scale social catastrophe.

Every time there was a 'battle', in which the earlier structure of
consciousness was treated as the enemy. On the other hand the later
structure did not yet possess the necessary sovereignty for integration,
tending spontaneously to bolt in panic, or at least to withdraw. Only in
the case of the climb from the mental to the integral structure of
consciousness, on the way to *individuation*, which even yet has hardly
begun, is there a promise that it could be different. But for many

individuals and peoples the previous transformation has not yet gone through to its conclusion, while at the same time its goal, the *efficient* mental-structure, is blocked and discredited because the rationalistic demon is in charge, entrenched in the Western Megamachine.

As a sign that a structure of consciousness is insufficient or deficient, Gebser offers the *inflation of quantity*. This inflation was once of magical objects which cancerously multiplied through cultural exchange and tribal collapse, then later through ancient Hellenistic mythology which grew ever more obscure, decadent, and devoid of context, and today through the cult of *facts* and mass-produced articles. Even in 1953 Gebser wrote:

> *Prayer wheels (of ancient Tibet), the fragmentation of myth, and computers are expressions of man who remains confined in his familiar consciousness-frequency while the necessary tide-turning consciousness-mutation begins to superimpose itself over the exhausted consciousness-structure. Each excess of quantification leads to powerlessness, vacuity and helplessness. Wherever this is evident it is an indication that the inadequate consciousness-structure is already surpassed. In this light, the computers are a negative omen of the new consciousness-structure and its strength*[15].

This sounds optimistic, but he adds that if the task of transition is not "resolved soon, its solution will demand unthinkable sacrifices". And: "the number of people who will experience the solution depends on the temporal intensity of the emergent consciousness structure". And finally: "No new structure proceeds from an exhausted one, but a mutation can readily spring forth from the originary presence of the whole".[16]

The words in italics mean that the genotype has, here and now, those forces out of which the structures of consciousness were built, and also those dispositions which entered into the *efficient* old ones, but only imprisoned and confused in the ruling structure. Gebser has insufficiently emphasised this unparalleled *dimension* of alienation, how very much those forces are imprisoned because we shy away from the origin and have even broken off connections with sensibility and physiology. We are kept out and split off by socialisation geared for our Megamachine. And other parts of our psyche are captivated in the breaking up of older structures of consciousness. This non-simultaneity, more widespread than ever, is a monstrous problem making social solidarity more difficult.

Precisely the *efficient* mental-structure unavoidably suppresses all psychological reaction, having its roots in older world conditions.

People who still have their centre of gravity there, and thus are more frequently aware of their originary powers – children, many women and tribal minorities – suffer directly under the collective pressure of a culture which has enthroned the abstract and the anti-life. This doesn't mean that they cannot think, but they are negatively impressed by the ability of the tricky Odysseus to tell falsehoods without being caught at it – an advance in consciousness for which he is valued.

Even Socrates was an enemy of the concrete life. He belittled contact with nature, with everyday things, with the body, and with the female. There is something in this mentality which is fundamentally false to life[17]. 'Affairs of state and philosophising' were notably the only worthy occupations for the man of the *polis*. Even then this was abstract enough. How much more then in the case of today's mental sphere, sizable and complex, which is the correlative of the Megamachine! Identification with science, technology, world markets and with the state to be 'with it', will lose one his concrete life, and will spread frustration and unhappiness into the most intimate spheres of his fellows.

NOTES

(1) The immediate switching off of all the West German nuclear power stations was impossible precisely for the reason that this clutch was either missing or not used. Intrinsically, a people *is* capable of wiping off the judgement tables all juristic activities and recourse demands of the Megamachine and its partial subjects. The principle of the continuity of justice must be able to be broken through at points to avoid the whole thing going by the board in the near future.

(2) Lewis Mumford, *The Transformations of Man*, (London: George Allen and Unwin, 1957), p184.

(3) One can orient oneself in relation to this by, among others, Wilber (*Up From Eden*, pp33-35) and Anand Margo Naslednikov's *Tantra – Weg der Ekstase* (chapter seven); Sam Keen treats the theme compactly, and also with reference to the consequences for political behaviour, in the book about the seven *kingdoms of love*, which has already been mentioned.

(4) Under the title of *The Play of Life* Timothy Leary has proposed a *map of the evolution of consciousness*, the ascent through a *step sequence of modes of utilising the brain* (which is further developed and popularised by Robert Anton Wilson in *The New Prometheus*. In correspondence with ancient Yogi knowledge, Leary counts a sequence of eight neural switching circuits in groups of three, that is, twenty four steps altogether. He calls it 'neurological Tarot', in which Tarot refers to that ancient spiritual card game which now is much in use again. In Leary's work the letters of the Hebrew alphabet, the animal circle signs, and the titans of Greek mythology correspond with the Tarot cards, which mirror the evolutionary stages of consciousness (in this context he speaks also of 'castes' in the social-structure sense). Not least in importance, his eight switching circuits correspond with the Periodic Table of the elements of Mendeleef, and also with the doh-re-me-fa-so-la-ti-doh of the octave. The twenty four Tarot cards themselves (he increased by two the traditional set of cards) stand, as we have

saïd, for sequential stages of organismic information processing (see in this context also the two books by Friedhart Klix). There is also, as indicated by the parallels between the 7 ¢ 1 tones of the octave and the 7 (¢1) chakras in Kundalini-Yoga, a cross-connection to this very ancient neurological system of schooling. In this connection it is stimulating to relate to the concepts of Wilson and Leary the two books of Sam Keen, *Lust and Love* and *The Kingdom of Love, the Seven Stages of Ecstasy*, which are more theoretical than their titles sound, and also rest on sequences of stages. Further correspondences can be found with Ken Wilber's stage sequence in *Up From Eden*, and through this to Jean Gebser's earlier achievement on which Wilber's work is based. Finally Lewis Mumford's *The Transformations of Man* feeds into the structure, and the foundations of the whole problem complex are more clearly seen in Erich Neumann's *Origins and History of Consciousness* on the one hand, and Bateson's *Ecology of Mind* and Berman's *Re-enchantment of the World*, analyses or statements of theory of learning, on the other hand. All the works mentioned are convergent in view of the necessary evolutionary jump.

(5) Margo Anand (Mitsou Naslednikov), *Tantra – Weg der Ekstase, die Sexualität des neuen Menschen*, (Schloss Wolfsbrunnen 1982), p104ff.

(6) *Ibid*, p167.

(7) Leary gets to call it this from his obsession, intensified by his thrice uttered cry for Challenger hardware, for emigration into a cosmic black hole. It is with this regression that he is paying for his drug trip, which we also have to thank for his 'neurological Tarot'.

(8) Novalis, *Dokumente seines Lebens und Sterbens*, (Frankfurt: 1979), p58.

(9) Mumford says directly, also with the megamachine in mind: "The machine in fact is precisely that part of the organism which can be projected and controlled by intelligence alone. In establishing its fixed organisation and predictable behaviour, intelligence will produce a society similar to that of certain insect societies, which have remained stable for sixty million years." (p. 121).

(10) "Resume the long effort" does not mean go back to any specific beginning in time, but to go back to the contemporary genotype within us which now lies concealed under the concrete pattern of civilisation, which is now failing and was 'always there'.

(11) Mumford, *Transformations of Man*, pp. 138-139.

(12) *ibid* p167.

(13) *Ibid*, p144.

(14) *Ibid*, pp144-145.

(15) Jean Gebser, *The Ever-Present Origin* (Athens: Ohio University Press, v1984) pp. 538-39. *Ursprung und Gegenwart*, 2 v, 1949 and 1953, p685.]

(16) *ibid.*, p539 and p142.

(17) I also experience this strongly in working on this book. For months at a stretch, and then, after a pause, to live once again for months on end with the typewriter, was easier for me at an earlier time. It ultimately weakens communication with the environment and with one's own bodily and mental originary powers, and the torture which, apart from a few light moments, it in fact is, certainly contributes nothing to the maintenance of world harmony. Admittedly this is disturbed anyway, and compels us to make an extreme exertion to achieve a revolution which is perhaps nearer than ever.

13. Homo Integralis

As has been shown, the trouble resides in the separation, the splitting off from the Origin, in the antagonistic thrust itself. Initially it is apparently *a priori* unavoidable either in history or in individual life, so that we need a technique of re-unification or integration, both socially and individually – bearing in mind the saying of Goethe, "Nothing is inside, nothing is outside, for what is inside is outside". Yet our greatest successes are bound up with the personality, which is armoured against the world.

For this we were driven out of Paradise, cut off from the world outside our skin, often from our own body, yes, even from our own undesired ego-parts (perhaps the most vital?!), and each of the excluded things becomes our enemy[1]. To this comes the desensitising training of urban, industrial and organisational everyday life. As when we originally left the animal world we had to abandon our instincts for the sake of our freedom, so later for the sake of civilisation we abandoned our older structures of consciousness, with their satisfying sensual contact with the world.

The ego, character or social personality is the guarding authority behind all these separations: the personality not as a chosen pattern but as the unilluminated product of socialisation. Our European culture is distinguished by the space it offers the personality for its unfolding. Yet the wolfish absence of commitment which has emerged, this unavoidable misunderstanding of freedom, is at the same time its curse. We see this now.

We like to reproach Hegel for his misunderstood sentence "freedom is the recognition of necessity". But for this rational mystic, freedom was naturally *in us*, identical with our highest capacity, with the divine spark of Meister Eckhart. For Hegel, freedom, properly understood, means to recognise the equality of our inner being with the divine, and to identify ourselves with it as our highest necessity. In comparison with this, the anarcho-individualistic concept of freedom is a load of garbage.

The positive content of the bourgeois personality is primarily its maximal invulnerability – security of supplies, comfort and control of circumstances – an egocentric position of power, within which love cannot unfold itself. This ego-profile is inseparable from bourgeois society's ideal of freedom and independence, a human image which we must inwardly transcend. With us, turning to each other and communication are definitely subordinated to the ego-interests thus defined. Difference and competition between personalities dominate to an extent such that communication is impossible. All the strength of life is spent on differentiation, separation, the alienation of person from person, and on this self-alienation from the body and from one's own unconscious powers.

Freedom in that great Hegelian or Eckhartian sense would consist exactly in overcoming these things. Guardini once spoke of that centre-point in which the human would find both him/herself and God. That is where freedom is, and, despite our differences, that is where we are to a great extent one. Why then should it be impossible to found society and community on this? To this end differences do not have to be suppressed. Hegel, Hölderlin and Schelling noted four ideas within the European spirit: the kingdom of God, reason, freedom, and the invisible church – and at the same time these show the step beyond the European limitations[2].

They achieved this mainly in their minds, for such was the nature of the times. It was, so to say, German *Jnana-Yoga*[3]. They were Bodhisattvas like never before. They all knew ecstasy. And they did not flee from women. It is the free use of all our powers which brings joy, and for this we need communion with the full extent of the universe which can be reached by our senses, our soul and our spirit.

True, the personality wants all this for itself. It has chastised itself for the sake of such gain, for the sake of love, for the sake of deserving it, being worthy of it. But in all this the desire to be loved takes priority over loving, so that the means contradicts the end. Pertinently and in great detail, Niklas Luhmann has shown erotic love fails, not only because we present each other with our defences, but because we encounter each other as ever more differing worlds, while demanding confirmation in them. We want our empirical ego loved, we seek 'validation (positive evaluation) of its public image'[4], whereas Novalis had seen love as aiming at transcendence in 'the ego of our ego', in our higher self. Isn't it the case, as Luhmann contends, that 'individuality becomes a demand for recognition of obstinate concepts of the self and the world, and hence an imposition'[5], and that 'the situation becomes the more pregnant with conflict as the partners intensify their relationships'?[6] The personality came to be a faulty design, or it comes to be one.

The personality which I have presented is the ego of Gebser's mental stage. It is something to be overcome, and contrasts with what classical writers, including Tagore, are all aiming at: the *integral self*. Gebser offers a few strategies concerning how we could handle what is excluded and split off, so that the ascent to the integral self shall succeed.

This is now the point of departure: step upon step we have been unable – especially we white people with our hasty competition – to integrate the roots of consciousness. We have failed in this in two ways, from the point of view of the culturally-conditioned stages of consciousness, and from the *socio-biological* evolutionary stages lying even further back, which contributed to the quality of our consciousness.

Structure of Consciousness	Stage of Evol
INTEGRAL	
↑↓	Individuatic
＼↓／	
MENTAL	
↑↓	Ego Developr
＼↓／	
MYTHIC	
↑↓	Coming out the Cave
＼↓／	
MAGIC	
↑↓	Awareness Separatene
＼↓／	
ARCHAIC	

• *Archaic* corresponds with the spinal cord and the reptile brain-stem. In that state the mode of experience determined by these organs dominates (even though abstract mental operations do occur very early);
• *Magic* corresponds with the limbic system, and our 'mammalian body' which has the control (in Wilber, the *typhon*);
• *Mythic* already corresponds with the big brain, and with its objective organ-wisdom: although the human being once believed the heart to be the organ of thought, and the gods spoke from his intuitive right hemisphere into the left hemisphere, the big brain still has much more of this than we would believe;
• *Mental* corresponds only to the big brain as *our* organ. The ego attempts to be the rider of the body as horse, but it sifts and limits itself;
• *Integral* – this is the subject of this section.

At each *older* stage we are less inhibited, more ego-less in relation to elementary life-processes. Each *newer*, higher stage tends to disturb the wisdom of the 'objective' spirit, the spirit of *being-in-itself* which is contained in the code of life itself. We distance ourselves from the immanent godhead, and block the entrances thereto. We then leave them behind instead of successively developing them. Our true self, the original foundation within us, is no longer able to express its will on account of the purely self-willed directives from above.

Naturally all of us participate more or less in all five structures of consciousness, and also in the masculine and feminine spirit. But the centres of our identity are different. It is just the same with the chakras and switching circuits, whose step-ladder can be seen as a more detailed analysis of the same history.

The *deepest* social tensions and dimensions of inequality are bound up with the way individuals are indigenous to these different levels. The relations between dominant and submissive groups, *within* their class-interest, could be unified. *Caste* (a psychological approach) takes precedence over class (social roles). Opinions divide according to which structure of consciousness, which switching circuit we principally use for communication with the world.

This is what is meant when Ernst Bloch speaks of the *non-contemporaneity* of social groups. Peasants, for example, not only belong to older (feudal or pre-feudal) social formations than do industrial workers *and* capitalists, but they also live psychologically in another world – and this is far more basic than any sociologically-calculable qualities which fit into the scheme of capitalistic modernity.

The societies of *one* period and of *one* country are stratified: horde people, tribal people, city people, rationalistic modern and spiritual post-modern people all live among us. And the initiative lies *above*, in spite of all the inertia and disturbances pushing up from below, strengthened by suppression. The future will be decided by the struggle between the mental and integral elites, in which the frontline frequently goes *right through the middle of one and the same person*, and elements of older structures of consciousness always get into the act[7]. It depends decisively on integration: higher consciousness dominates because it *includes* its earlier stages and contradictions, and achieves reconciliation with whatever is split off. Hölderlin: "Reconciliation is in the middle of the struggle, and whatever has been divided finds itself again".

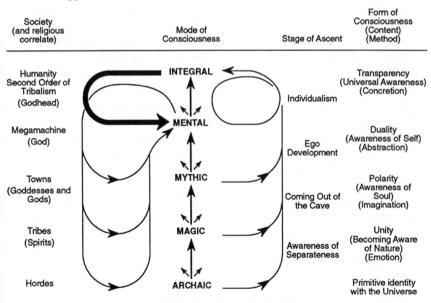

Scheme of Consciousness Mutation (free after Gebser)

The curved arrows which I have drawn into Gebser's scheme are intended to symbolise the movement on which this integration process depends. For even if I have shown the integral stage as manifest, in reality it only comes into existence naturally, by exerting a strong *pull*[8].

So what has to be integrated is not so much the widespread variety of products and knowledge, but the anthropologically-unrenounceable basic stage upon which, no matter how, modern consciousness ungratefully builds itself. The crux of the matter is not alienation from things we make, but alienation from our natural potential – including the potential for further development of our mental capacities, which we allow to be atrophied through our service to quantity. The spontaneous wisdom and vitality of the archaic, magic and mythical structures of consciousness are an irreplaceable regulator. But we already drive them out in early childhood. Thus striving for power, the desire to show to the world, become the nearest compensation for the suppressed *Eros*, for the *tonus* which is repressed in melancholy.

Thus the (simple) arrows descending from the mental level on the left side characterise a masculine necessity, and the rising arrows on the right a feminine necessity. Masculine and feminine are not necessarily the same thing as man and woman. Even so men in our civilisation very much more frequently become one-sidedly mental, cerebrally-fixated, and function in a rational and machine-like manner, whereas women more frequently have contact with consciousness-structures in which the roots of human culture are to be sought – on the other hand they will frequently react inadequately, because the forces living there are deformed and repressed, and not attached to a balanced whole[9].

We can hardly hope to climb up from the mental to the integral structure in a straight line, because precisely those who are most representative of 'mentality' and whose characteristic habitat is the Megamachine hardly experience the origin any more. On the other hand the patriarchal mind, especially in its contemporary defective form, has made the climb up to the mental ego and above it – disgusting for many people, mostly women, who have their existential centre of gravity nearer to life.

Feminine thought in the last 200 years has moved ever more in the direction of conquering this position. Every modern feminine consciousness goes through this – not without signs of intensified self-alienation. A self-conscious, self-knowing ego, the result of a self-determined internal psychoanalysis, has become a necessary condition for individuation. And yet on the whole it should not be necessary that people – from childhood up – should still have to be forced through this dysfunctional structure of consciousness. The acquisition of rationality could be made possible in a new way from the integral level. For this reason the curved arrows on the right side of the diagram above, which connect the integral level with the archaic, magical, and mythical levels, are shown passing by the mental level, which is then contacted via a loop, from above as it were.

With the descending arrows on the left side I wish to indicate the diving-back, the partial regression into the older and more foundation-laying layers, and then, climbing up again, the mental and integral inclusion in the journey through the underworld. This traverse is not only biographically of the greatest significance for individuation, but is of the greatest importance socially. It applies not only to the break-up of the herd, but also to reaching an understanding with 'non-contemporary' potentials, through which paths to integration and reconciliation are opened. The mental ego then experiences a return to life, a revitalisation of its own bio-psychic basis. The upward stream of energy grows broader.

The discipline of the rational level must in no way be given up. The Indian criticism of 'mind' directs itself against robot-like automatism of the thinking apparatus, not against precise, clear thought – for we need more of this, not less. Emotion is much more automated than intellect, being often taken into the service of, and corrupted by, social and status interests. The key to reasonable egoism is naturally reason. In other words, the process of integration must also be *understood* integrally.

What we want to exclude, in order to embark on the journey into the underworld, is *censorship*, for which intellect gives us refined means, effective obstacles against giving up egocentric positions. But it is this basic egocentric position, not its intellectual means, which is the problem. We can use intellect just as well for making clear the process of integration in making a holistic, body-soul-spirit contact with what has been severed off and repressed. And then we need critical reason in order to master the experience, and also a certain amount of old-fashioned discipline, in order not to abandon ourselves to the inflation of psychic phenomena we meet in the underworld.

Integration (individuation) is the principal way of climbing out of the old, death-dedicated cultural context. The methods all have the same goal in mind: to free us from the narrow socialisation we internalised down to our deepest levels, through which we were prepared for this exterministic civilisation. The new configuration of our inner form – which lies nearer to our inherited inner picture than does our customary armament and masking – is not determined by any psychotherapist or guru, but by the freed vital potential itself. The human being would not have climbed to this point, and would not have lifted above his self-humiliations, had not this potential been positive. We must free it from the remains of the trauma it experienced with the emergence of culture, a trauma which found its expression in the concept of original sin, hostile to life.

The whole process will be not only individually but also historically fruitful, in that we can come into possession of the forces of our being only when we already have a model of the new *objective spirit* which grows with us: a different social design circulating in the network of the turn-around movement. *Homo integralis* (which in Europe contains *homo occidentalis* and *homo conquistador*) means as much the individual as the social ensemble which steers its freed forces in the direction of salvation.

All the stages of evolution of consciousness are stages of evolution of the ego. Ego-transcendence, overcoming the egocentric position, presupposes the ego. In the higher self it is transcended, not extinguished. All the epochs of history are derived from predominant forms of personality. The new self, the superconscious *homo integralis*, is not the first integration, but a more all-embracing one. The decisive difference between 'ego' and 'self' consists of the fact that the egocentric perspective is replaced by the experienced psychic position that *the centre is everywhere* – and *the whole spreads everywhere* or *the truth is the whole* (Hegel).

To leave the disastrous position of 'top parasite' means nothing less than this transition, where we place fundamental human interests over our immediate interests, and in the same way place long-term interests over short-term interests, and social and community interests over individual interests. However these comparisons lose their meaning once the leap has succeeded, because then it becomes clear that in this way immediate, short-term and individual interests can best be protected. As the Tibetan Tarthang Tulku says: if our starting point is selfish existence, then we exclude fundamental, long-term, and general interests. Then one occupies a niche, exclusively and aggressively, a position where 'all subsistence and all contact can only be achieved to the extent that we send out to them'.[10]

If we imagine to ourselves that world totality is a sphere, then the egocentric observer, even in the centre-point, can pick up on only few of the 'ten thousand things'. Each single science, art, manual skill, or life-skill means *one* other perspective. To participate in the whole, we shouldn't regard it just from each point on the periphery of the sphere, but experience absolutely every point in the sphere at the same time. This is what is meant by the formula *the centre is everywhere*. Even if we cannot realise this individually, we can nevertheless come close to doing so as humanity. For us as individuals, finding connection with all possible perspectives depends on whether we can achieve some distance from our immediate interests, and whether we can achieve communion with others (which are the two sides of the *same* coin).

The thought is not new. The first person who demanded this release from the ego-perspective, both politically and spiritually, was Lao Tzu, and he comes very close to our understanding because, in the characteristic manner of Asian thought, he does not need to come first to God in order to reach the godhead – something which for one such as Meister Eckhart was unavoidable. Spinoza's great achievement of equating God and nature would have amazed Lao Tzu by being such a detour. Right from the beginning he says *world* when he wants to indicate the whole, to be an organ of which is the human calling, and he develops from this point his picture of a prince. Let us take a closer look at this at the end of this section, on the one hand as a piece of necessary regression, and on the other hand as a piece of forward integration, because the Old Master was at the same time ahead of us. I am interested in *homo integralis* precisely in this dimension of political responsibility, and in the kind of subjectivity capable of supporting it.

In his *Tao Teh Ching* the illuminated sage and the person who is called to be 'lord of the world', are one and the same figure, and it is at the same time identical with the subject of the whole teaching. Every person should be of such a quality as to be able to be lord of the world. Or female ruler of the world: Michael Endes' childlike empress popularises the same figure, even though she is not so politically concrete as Lao Tzu was. Wisdom and the capacity to be emperor are within every man and every woman. The trouble is that the path to this figure latent within us is cut off through self-centredness by the ego, through the self in the sense of selfishness and subjective obstinacy:

> *I am beset by great evils*
> *because I possess a self –*
> *were I free from self*
> *what evil would there be for me?*
> *But we may leave the world in the hands*
> *of him who lets the world be his self,*
> *to him who, loving the world, makes it equal to his self*
> *we may entrust the world.*[11]

And he who, in this spirit, 'takes upon himself the unhappiness of his country' is 'worthy of being lord of the world'. Such a one 'does nothing for himself and does not want to be praised'. To make the *world* into a self, instead of the little, private ego – with Lao Tzu this is the 'a-perspectivity' which Gebser singles out as the most important characteristic of *homo integralis*. Not to be identified with the ego but with the world ('godhead identification'), and then, 'to him who, loving the world, makes it equal to his self, we may entrust the world'.

Lao Tzu himself interpreted his position, which in reality was highly advanced, as a regained archaic one, and set himself *against* history. Shocked by the doings of spirits grown selfish during a period of warlordism, he didn't just want to end it, but to undo what had already happened. He did not want to integrate what had differentiated itself upwards, but reverse and erase it: names, tools (division of labour), compensatory morality and supplementary ordering institutions should be closed down or made superfluous. (The other path, of Confucius, did not promise to annul this harmony-disturbing knowledge, but merely to set limits to it – and this would make eternal the epoch of unhappy consciousness).

A consciousness such as we now need, which would be capable of reconciling cosmos and history, to permit the arrow of development to turn into the cycle of eternal return – the idea of the *spiral*, which is the circle and the rising arrow all in one – such a consciousness was at that time not yet conceivable. Lao Tzu's spirit brings to mind Grof's second matrix of birth: to the terror bound up with the beginning of the birth process comes the response of the desire for return to the earlier 'oceanic' protectedness. The Tao describes the cosmogeny in the body of the mother as *one* pole of an order which is true to nature, the pole of basic trust which supports it.

The question came to me, what could it mean if we could all experience the way back into this paradise of Lao Tzu? Not to stay where the individual conscious mind is empty and simply doesn't exist, but to unfold the other modes and later stages of our existence out of this protectedness and tranquillity, and to pull up short the demons which lurk in our unconscious, waiting to emerge in the next two birth-matrices.

We must assume that with every progress of our culture, rejecting the original ground as it does, our social conditions have confirmed and reinforced the negative experiences arising from our unconscious. The wheel has simply turned in the wrong direction. Humanistic psychology and meditation exert themselves to reverse the direction, to relocate the emphasis into the positive – and from there to integrate demons who lose much of their power when they are localised by the re-encounter and are recognised as partial forces. As a result there is practice in discriminating among the spirits which lead us, so that we do not so easily fall for the wrong ones.

Lao Tzu so thoroughly re-established his original trust that his *Tao* did not have to exclude destruction, pain, peril, and death. The contradictions, or more precisely, the polarities, are all there – the social world stays in order if one accepts the polarities, instead of creating a culture which is fleeing from them, and which becomes exterministic from an excess of security-policies.

Lao Tzu knew also that humans *have* deviated from the Tao at any period we choose to examine, thanks to the strength of their individuality and wilfulness. They therefore have to make *cultural* arrangements such that negative feedbacks check the disturbances of harmony emanating from them. For this reason they always set up a religious, ethical, moral, and legal order, above all concerned to hold specific basic phenomena of human existence within bounds – liberated sexuality, intelligence, individuality and interfering relationship with the environment. But his way was not to set these bounds restrictively from outside, but *to imitate in the mind that same self-regulation which is created in the mother's body for meeting the needs of the foetus.* This mother-child dyad doesn't need to know, because it *knows*; doesn't need to do anything, because everything happens. Lao Tzu's way is to realise the wisdom of *Bios*.

Today it is beside the point that he absolutised this regressively – we can hardly correct ourselves enough in this direction. It belongs certainly to the human being to be a warrior (the third birth matrix) and to be a victor (the fourth). It is written in *Tao Teh Ching* how the human being can be warrior and victor, *if* he or she is rooted in this original trust and does not fear even death. It is a different basic tone from the power-magic of Don Juan in the works of Castaneda, or even that of the Samurai. "Where in battle equal opponents measure each other, the one having pity is the victor", says Lao Tzu[12] and:

> To be victor is good – and that is enough –
> one should not risk being a tyrant;
> be victorious and do not boast
> be victorious and do not glorify yourself
> be victorious and do not be proud of your victory;
> one may be compelled to be a victor –
> but one is not a victor in order to compel[13]

I remember reading somewhere that, according to Carl Jung, half his patients needed religion rather than therapy, and that people over forty do not need any therapy at all, but must learn to pray. Therapy begets the self-definition of the person as *patient* and is directed to the cure of a *defect*, around which the person first gathers himself.

On the other hand meditation in its manifold forms (and rebirthing can be counted here) creates space for the natural strength of our genotype, which is waiting beyond 'sickness' and 'health', to be effective; it heals, it harmonises from the roots, and sets weakening and deforming patterns, which inhibit the natural energy-flow, out of action, or at least it damps them. A great many things then become ridiculous or insignificant, which otherwise would have eaten at one's heart.

Purification – what is Meditation otherwise about?

To achieve *homo integralis* does not just mean that we *repeat* our collective historical losses. If it is a question of the people who want to contribute something, to do something for the arising of an ORDINE NUOVO which is right for life – people who, whether they want to or not, will make a law-giving effect with their subjectivity – then the integration of their *own* history becomes a political issue of the first importance. So the necessity for a purification follows from the mere fact that we have subjectivity.

On the biological level all coordinations operate *involuntarily*, non-egocentrically. In the arrangement of the central nervous system, which functions every time we move our little finger, there is no ganglion which would pursue its own special project. The various levels in the hierarchy of biological information do not compete or discuss, any more than do the neurons which are arranged in parallel, which carry out different commissions at the same level.

In the social organism all these mediating functions are carried out by actors who mainly want to serve their own existence and subjectivity, as long as they follow their spontaneous impulses. This explains and determines the incomparably high level of disruption, the more so as we, in our singularity, finitude and fragmentariness, are essentially unknowing. Where we are dealing with matters of super-individual significance, intervention guided by our special interests or the smallest admixture of egocentric subjectivity, *can* disturb the balance of the whole assembly.

Our ego – insofar as it is a nothing fenced around by defence mechanisms confronting an alien universe – *must* create for itself an infinite artificial world. In this we are dealing only with concrete things which, case by case, have to be researched and carried out – but as soon as the whole earth has been conquered, then interplanetary space must come on line if the pioneer spirit is to have its next object to work on. As Günter Nenning once expressed it, from the ground up our practices are those of 'Promethean criminality'. Now we want to rescue ourselves in the same sort of way, with a cybernetic ecology project, which must first of all learn about and thoroughly calculate the entire complexity – our whole hopeless dependence upon the work of our heads and hands perishes once again.

It is not *that* the human being takes himself seriously, but *how* he

does it – what kind of constitution it is that is leading him into nothingness. We are running a planetary business, but with the competition of
our limited special interests as driving force and organising principle.
While we no longer recognise any divine authority, there are naturally-
real forces, or the *one* real force: the Megamachine, which makes our
individualism into an absurd grotesque.

How – now that we are using the whole earth – *does the whole earth
need us?* In what way does the intelligent context, the earthly balance,
need us? How must we be if we are not to disturb it? The effect we have
socially will be no different from the way we individually are. Transformation can only proceed from what is transformed. The person who
is the enemy of his body, who doesn't know and accept his shadow, who
is not 'reconciled with Satan', who has not experienced the other sex
within himself, who is governed by the inferiority-complex of their ego,
is unsuited to be master or mistress of the world, even in the smallest
circle.

We must travel these 'ways to the self', because we have the chance of
making decisions only to the extent that we are aware of what we are.
Biased forms of behaviour, when we are aware of them, lose their
power, and in time disappear of their own accord. Or uncleanness
spontaneously falls away from intrinsically sensible reactions. The moment we want to act in a way which changes the world, *being unaware* is
the sin. The new world begins with the new human being, this new self
that can raise itself in us above the needful ego, in that it experiences
that '*everything* is *in* us', everyone has the whole of what he or she needs
within them – whatever we get from others is over and beyond this, and
a gift.

Between the heart chakra and the third eye lies still another 'gate',
which was not brought out earlier: the fifth chakra at the top of the
windpipe, through which the connection between head and heart must
pass if it is to be complete. The heart distinguishes between hot and
cold, rejecting 'cold', and with it half a world... The fifth gate leads into
the 'kingdom of purification'. Here the theme is authenticity, the truth-
fulness of our communication. Our capacity for objective truth rests on
the assumption that we know ourselves right into the darkest corners of
our motivation. Otherwise there's no way we can know what we must
let drop, if we want truth.

After the 'marriage between heart and hara', we may not spare
ourselves that other 'alchemistical marriage of waking and sleeping
consciousness, light and shade, conscious and unconscious, rational
and emotional sides'. Yet we are indeed disposed to do this, for here the
climate changes, because the path first leads from erotic ecstasy into the
cold – the heart doesn't only have 'its reasons, which the intellect does

not know', as Pascal has told us, but also it has addictions, for example the addiction to 'eternal sky-dancing', as Tantrics call euphoria.

Novalis gives us also this small poem:

You are looking into a whirlpool
Of human fate,
And seek and ask in vain
For the meaning of this puzzle.

Sometime it will solve itself easily,
The key has been there for a long time,
For were not love and simplicity
Always close to humans?

Things in this state of simplicity cannot be made to work with love alone, for in the end we are more individualised than ever, and this will have to be recognised. It might have been possible in ancient India to leave true intimacy out of consideration. The European feat would be to meet God in man and Goddess in woman, not only in their archetypical natures, but also in their individuality.

Nobody has more deeply or boldly understood this theme than Dieter Duhm with his experiment of a 'culture crystal' in his 'site office'. The thesis is: for the sake of love the human being should first leave love alone, because it so incurably mixed up with corruption; first of all man and woman should unconditionally find themselves, and live their sexuality beyond the follower-dependency-fear of loss, and all moralistic sentimentality. In other words they should communicate with each other through the fifth chakra instead of the heart.

But shouldn't the cold have *preceded* the warmth? I sense here the great distance at which no-longer-clinging monads appear at first to stand opposed to each other, more egocentric than ever. There is hardly any communion – they forbid it to each other. There is a critical watchfulness while embracing. In this love-school a secret asceticism is noticeable. Must the path to the self lead away from the magic of *Eros*? For then we remain driven out of the female epoch, out of the condition of being embraced – no integration[14]. To take this magic up with us implies that we drop spiritual egoism, the performance-trip of the yogic mountain climber, and demands that we not attempt to reach anything, not even 'sanctity'.

Certainly however, the coldness must have *its hour*, and it could be important to be more on the alert about falling into embraces. Only when we also risk the cold, thinks Sam Keen:

May we hope for the fulfilment of that promise which fleetingly opened itself up to us in the kingdom of the heart. Before we storm the peak, we must be cleansed of poisoned illusions, projections, and defence mechanisms which determine our personality, the ego, and the socially conditioned self. We must bring our secret thoughts to expression... A kind of striptease takes place in the course of which superfluous self-imagings, roles, and conditioned reactions are scrutinised and removed. The personality shrinks as we seek behind the mask for our real face. [This search] becomes an indispensable adventure in a world encouraging everything external. To save face, to be able to hold one's own in a circle of acquaintances, to make something 'good', to be in line with public opinion – these things are the actual signs of the sickness from which our society suffers.

As far as the purification of all our adaptive lies is concerned, according to the old teaching, the voice-box constitutes:

...quite a special physio-symbolical seat of this form of consciousness. That which once was taken in uncritically must now be 'chewed' and actively broken down, if it is to be digested. Suppressed words and feelings must gain expression. The judgments – or rather the prejudices – which we have allowed to reach our mouths must be swallowed back. Creep to the cross and eat your words. Take back what you have said. The words that have passed through our teeth contain our whole judgment. They reveal our projections. What Peter says about Paul tells us more about Peter than about Paul.

When consciousness reaches the level of the fifth chakra, its main task consists in the reabsorbing of projections. In Tantric body mythology the fiery energy of the third chakra – the wildness of the warrior – has to be used for the destruction of the ego-fortress. Aggression, rage, and cunning, which we once used for defence against the environment, must now be directed against our own defence mechanisms. Our strength must serve to destroy our paranoia.

This will suffice for quotations from Sam Keen[15]. Is not this the path which leads to the next gate, to the 'Kingdom of Light', the objective view? We can only be objective, identifying the world with ourselves to the extent that we are not dominated by our immediate interests, projections, and prejudices.

What is the purpose of meditation? Meditation is the most all-embracing name for the techniques of purification, for the widest variety of paths of *inner* action, that is, the *changing of the inner world*[16]. Then it is unavoidable that our inner world should function as an automaton, a robot controlled by the outside world – which we have created.

This is not to say that work and meditation necessarily fall apart, or be separated in time. Work can be mindful and meditation doesn't have only to be sitting in Zazen. Meditation is a method used to achieve awareness of our action, whether this action be work, or loving, or feeling, or thinking – for our thinking is mostly without awareness, but 'the mill clatters by the rushing stream'.

The reason why we don't know what we are doing is not only because the horizon of our knowledge is intrinsically limited, but also because we allow our bio-computer to go on running as it was originally programmed. For this reason Graf Dürckheim has entitled a book *Every Day as Practice*, which makes the meaning of meditation especially understandable – as a technique of freedom, a technique of liberation from all unconscious alien determination.

Meditation primarily opposes the uninterrupted across-the-board daily thought-practice: namely to describe 'reality', 'unavoidable circumstances', in such a way that we have our dependency and comfortable excuses confirmed, and that nothing else would have been acceptable – with 'people as they in fact are'. The plaintive ego says: let us first get rid of threats, insults, frustrations – instead of leashing our fears, vanities and needs. But we came into the world in such a form, and have been so imprinted and conditioned, that we can *always* expect a danger, a humiliation, or a loss, and we react to this with security politics, with jealousy, and with annuity provisions. If we behave in this way and want to go on doing so, we create and reproduce the conditions which master us.

To be a path of purification, of becoming aware, of changing the inner world, of inner freedom, is the real purpose of what we ordinarily regard as meditation. But in truth this ordinary concept of meditation is only its forecourt – be it sitting in Zazen, dynamic meditation (yoga positions, breathing exercises, dance), up to bioenergetic and holistic therapeutic processes such as rebirthing and many others. While it is not true that there is no purification without these procedures, they are nevertheless tested openers and accelerators, and they are especially oriented toward a crucial point: as a rule we are not at all in possession of ourselves and do not have our forces of origin ready, so we must first centre ourselves, bring our energies back from activities under alien control, come to ourselves.

What is the significance of the simplest exercise such as observation of breathing for twenty minutes? During the first five minutes I count breaths on completion of breathing in and breathing out. During the second five minutes I count breathing cycles before completion. During the third five minutes I follow the breath during its whole long route through my body. In the last five minutes I concentrate completely on the coming in and going out of the breath through my nostrils.

When else do we pay attention even once to that basic life process which is easiest of access to our attention and which contains in itself the entire wisdom of evolution? In addition, concentration on this process has as its primary purpose the switching off of the noisy mill in our heads which repeats the judgments and prejudices of yesterday, so that the spirit of making a new start, which is so necessary to us, cannot even arise. For a twenty-minute duration, provided our head stays with the counting and observing, we do not project, and we are disconnected from corruption by the outside world. At the same time there lies in meditative practices a distancing, a de-identification from the ego-level – for this is the most extensive inner agency of alien determination, the more so if it operates unreflectedly.

And then, with regular practice, we feel more strength in us, which says of itself: *Look, I make all things new*. We feel ourselves to be part of that power rather than cut off from it, and we feel released from our unhappy consciousness. Also for brief periods we achieve the objective view, with the sixth chakra, the 'third eye' of self-knowledge, which comes to the help of purification. If we make it a rule to sit regularly, meditation makes us – even outside the practice hour – receptive of the universal language, of the whole *not-ego* – especially once we are clear how much *unmade being* outweighs beingness made by us.

Meditation is not asking and praying to a god, but coming back to the divine within ourselves. In the words of Hölderlin: "Only those who are themselves divine believe in the divine". Meditation, in its double function of purification and of preparing the ground for it, is the most far-reaching technique of autonomy, especially when, supported by its gains, *we act in the world*. This autonomy is not something handed to us from outside, a consequence of social arrangements, but is their source.

Free human beings will establish the kind of institutions suited to them. Under our conditions, where it is not hunger and sickness which destroy the physical basis for takeoff, we only deceive ourselves if we refer to the unfavourable nature of circumstances. Our circumstances are more favourable than they ever were. The Megamachine is all-powerful – *and* it is a disaster which we ourselves set up, and continually affirm, by telling ourselves people couldn't live without it.

Hanging on, as we do, to the 'animal', 'profane', vital level, and still involved in our struggle for self-assertion, we are not only unable to stop the Megamachine, but are compelled to push ahead with it. It is our true god, or rather our false god, the precipitation of our collective dead spirit. On the spiritual level, from heart through purification up to the objective look, we are (with) the divine. The masters have always said –

and here, in spite of being committed to patriarchy, they did not err –
the good society depends upon stabilising our existence at the spiritual level.
Meister Eckhart meant this when he spoke of the 'soul city', as the place
where Christ could be born in us. Buddha would add: the place where
he is already born, but not yet recognised, not activated, and hence
often depicted as less than he is.

Intellectuals, even more than the people, are inclined to regard
spirituality as unpolitical. They are frightfully ignorant, even about the
foundations of our own culture. And still more ignorant are those who
forget, when faced with the evil which unavoidably rises when we
embark on the work of purification, that people like Hitler are an effect
and not a cause. The black spirit is the perverted white one.

In one way or another the deepest social effects have proceeded from
enlightened people. Out of the mostly Rembrandt-like light-dark of
their spirits they have given form to cultures during their formative
periods, naturally in contact with those segments of consciousness of all
members of the community who came out to meet them. It is a complete
misunderstanding of people at home in this spiritual dimension to
suggest that they have to carry out extra politics 'alongside' such a
praxis. This is because their basic position includes the most extensive
political concept thinkable, and thus does not exclude appropriate
political action.

Unpolitical sages are people who have too small a picture of the
world, inside as well as outside. From the evolutionary point of view
meditation is not there only to generate psychological states and euphoric feelings. It serves the most political purpose conceivable today, of
liberation from ego-perspective and self-will, and liberation for rescuing
action, for building the culture anew, and for the transformation of
institutions.

Most representative of the turn-around which *homo occidentalis*
should make, is that anticipated in the life of Johann Gottlieb Fichte.
Fichte was *the* philosopher of the world-conquering ego, and from this
extreme he broke through to an opposite position which is identical
with that of Lao Tzu. I could also say that his is the western logic of
breakthrough, of the struggle to exit from the body of the mother,
pushed to the extreme. He had his fill, to excess, of the triumph of
victory, and so at last reached the ocean – as also did Beethoven in his
late Great Fugue.

Wilhelm Weischedel[17] has given us a wonderful picture of this arrival
at the position of Lao Tzu by the late Fichte: Fichte, whom he addresses
as *the* philosopher of freedom, is said to have discovered that if freedom
is not to annihilate itself, it cannot remain boundlessly absolute. Freedom would perish if it were to find no primal limits. The human being

is not a pure absolute, he is also a finite being.

> *For Fichte finiteness is most visible in the fact that the ego must assume that other entities like itself exist outside itself... The point of departure is no longer the isolated ego, but the community of free beings, the 'kingdom of minds'. Yet even this limiting of freedom by other people is not sufficient to banish the dangers therein, that the ego makes itself absolute...*

In truth freedom existed for Fichte only as already-determined – indeed from its *foundation*, one might almost say freedom is *determined* by the cosmic law or spirit of evolution. In the origin of freedom there reigned a deeper necessity. And for this reason:

> *Whoever goes back to the foundation of freedom must leave freedom behind. Freedom must transform itself to the mere hint of its origin. It must take upon itself the destruction of its self-power, in order to bring about the appearance of the true living reality, the foundation. It is 'the fate that can never be taken away from finiteness: that only through death can it win through to life. What is mortal must die, and nothing frees it from the power of its being'. 'The ego must be totally annihilated'. The late Fichte sees this as the most urgent task for the human being, particularly in view of his contemporary situation, which he calls the age of total selfishness.*

It is enormously significant that in the case of Fichte this position *presupposes* the transition through the affirmation of ego, through this essentially western achievement of the extremest ego-strength. On this basis Weischedel continues:

> *If the human being takes upon himself this radical killing of arbitrariness, he gets beyond himself. He who renounces in an ultimate sense the absoluteness of freedom discovers that it did not create itself. He glimpses the true absolute in the foundation of his self: the godhead. If 'the human being through the highest freedom renounces and loses his own freedom and independence, he will participate in the one true divine being'. In the place of the absolute ego steps the absolute God* (who, to Fichte, can in no way be distinguished from the Tao – R.B.). *This is the great and decisive turning point in the thought of Fichte. 'God alone exists, and outside him is nothing', he can now say. The human being however is nothing in his own right; what he is essentially, is 'existence and revelation of God...' 'To live in God is to be free in him...'*

The human being, who from this vantage-point is an organ of creation, would fulfil the conditions of the categorical imperative: his behaviour could actually be the measure of a general law-giving. Certainly he would no longer be political in the conventional sense, he would stand beyond the ancient *polis* and the modern mass-republic, he would stand above all political and social organisations, although he could continue to participate in them – and even in a special way. He would not conceive of the whole anthropologically, from the human-social stand-point, but cosmocentrically, biocentrically, theocentrically, to society, toward a socialisation in tune with being, toward a meditatively-led human culture.

My own Journey

To conclude this chapter I will touch upon my own experience with spiritual practice – by which I mean spiritual practice in the narrower sense, because the Communist Party, which I joined at the age of seventeen, was also a church, and was for me at the beginning more than the Christian church, and the spirits of Hölderlin, Fichte, and Beethoven were with me. In my circle in the fifties we disputed about communist matters like monks disputing over the concept of God.

For me the first benefits of psychoanalysis came at the beginning of the seventies from a couple of texts of Wilhelm Reich which had found their way into East Germany. I learnt that one's own most intimate frustrations, conflicts, inhibitions and entanglements are merely varia-tions of a problem situation which makes us all unhappy, or at least hinders us from enjoying life freely, from being *there*, from feeling the world, other people and nature. To some extent just reading and thinking were liberating, simply coming into contact with one's own biographical material. Also encouragement radiated from Reich to say *yes* to one's own sensuality, and to drop a few of the more life-hostile moralities which intellectually I didn't believe, but which nevertheless still controlled me unconsciously.

Even though Reich's argument was strictly materialistic and anti-mythical, I could detect in them the religious underground of *Eros*. He was also quite compatible with Lao Tzu, although admittedly in the East German editions, the mystic and the practitioner of yoga were pretty well concealed. I missed the reference to breathing meditation as a means of making contact with the *Tao*, as I read:

> *Without being occupied, and holding myself on the one,*
> *can the soul still distract itself?*
> *Accumulating the power of breathing, becoming pliant,*
> *can one not turn back to childhood?*
> *The glance cleansed by the look of the deep –*
> *can one not become free from impurity?*

I had my first intensive experience of meditation in the Johannishof in the Black Forest, which belongs to Count Dürckheim's *Rütte*. Dürckheim calls his path initiatory (introductory) therapy. But what is meant is healing in the widest sense, through which personal harmony is re-established and one's own inner self-image made purer and more visible. In those days it was a set of exercises, an 'enlightenment intensive', designed in this spirit and clothed in the forms of Zen Buddhism, under the leadership of Karin Reese.

The only theme for a whole week was the *ko-an* "Who am I?" (In Zen the *ko-an* are a paradoxical sayings aimed at throwing the person back upon himself). This was surrounded and punctuated by a few bodily exercises called *Arica*, and a few readings, walks, meditations and household duties carried out with awareness and rigidly prescribed. During the first three days the disciplinary exercises consisted of concentrating on this question, during ten periods of forty minutes each. Outside this ritual, and also during the simple meals, silence was required, with the holding to a sort of poverty-and-chastity vow.

At the beginning of each of the thirty rounds one elected anew one's partner, and every five minutes at the sound of a bell, alternating, one asked again the question of him or her, *"who are you?"* The question was pursued, but it wasn't necessary to speak or answer. It was sufficient to be confronted by the question. Early in the morning and after lunch came a self-description of one's bodily condition. It was repeatedly pointed out that the task was not reflection and discussion, so much as a declaration of one's own personal being, of existence itself.

Three or four of us were driven to temporary outbursts by this confrontation, and my first reaction was that I did not need to scream out any such grief. I was sorry for the others. It was not there, but only later, that I realised that my own repressions were more secure, that I had a shirt of chain-mail round my innermost kernel instead of heavy sheet metal armour around my external skin, that rattles more easily. It remained more difficult to make me insecure than the others. But I no longer feel that this was an advantage.

In the centre of things remained this question, which in the course of the first day seemed to me more and more stupid, even though I was able to see the purpose of the exercise. The question seemed silly for me personally, even though it was occasionally fun to say things about myself which normally I would have never put into words or even clearly thought out. What others said was more interesting and sometimes fascinating, and even more exciting was the silent union which established itself among certain people (not with all). Compared with my first impressions of them, and even compared with the experiences of the first round, many people changed completely, beyond all external recognition, in the direction of greater beauty and nobler being. And this in spite of the fact that many self-revelations might have been those of dismaying ugliness.

It really was a purification which took place. An older woman, who on the first day appeared to be altogether tied up in her neurosis, spoke straight from her being by the third day. On the second day she had cried terribly. She said she had always known she had *chosen* her behaviour, that with all earnestness she was acting, that she played a role of weakness, and that this was because of her powerlessness to get through to those close to her in any other way. No talk-therapist had brought her to this realisation. The *ko-an* itself and the multiplicity of 'mirrors' and self-revelations of her partners had led her.

For me the talk on the second and third day became ever more meaningful. On the one hand: how little of what I spoke out belongs to me alone, how little of myself was in the characteristics I revealed! How much of myself I recognised in what others said about themselves! On the other hand: what cannot be revealed is the most important, and is again not particularly specific to the individual. Dismayed, I recognised how much will-to-power had driven me to resist the conditions in East Germany, and how much it was bound up with my desire for woman, which in my childhood and youth had long been unsatisfied.

But the most rewarding thing, which I noticed with growing amazement and joy, was how the inner stream of life grew broader and stronger. I experienced it as I had done when, seventeen years old, I listened to Beethoven's Concerto in E flat major, and it sent shivers through me. In the house, silent messages reached me from the others, and in the woods messages from the trees.

On the fourth day, when the thirty sessions had already been concluded, there was a conversation about the ecological crisis, which, in this politically non-homogeneous circle, could not possibly have taken place at an earlier time. On a number of occasions on the last few days of that week I didn't *think*, so much as *see*, that in all people there is clearly a level of being where all are one, even among those whose spirits have little in common – a level which otherwise is perceptible in the communion of friendship and love. Society *does not* have to be *based* on differences and, taken with a grain of salt, each one of us could live intimately with *any* human being, if we and everybody else could gain access to this communal originary source.

It was also striking in how short a time people who were previously strange to each other can get into a higher state together. Naturally much of this is lost again, when they all move away and return to their various everyday routines. I asked myself, why is daily life, why are weeks, months, years, not lived and patterned by such means and with such festivals? Why do I travel in Germany and the world at large as a political wandering preacher, instead of setting up a place like this?

After achieving a certain distance from the event and from the euphoric mood, I could see all the more clearly how pure one's *own* character must be, and what it would mean to create a fully valid *social and cultural* character in Germany, in Europe. And also the old perfectionism had still not completely left me: the high-school students' anxiety about failing, and the melancholy and shy part of my potential, are still not so far behind me as I would like.

Let us begin to form this collective sovereignty! It is easy to formulate a political programme – but up to now it has always turned out that among the supporters were people whose characters function in exactly the opposite way. Yet, intellectual communication and understanding become easy if we know each other as whole human beings. Unavoidably, holistic politics must remain a hollow phrase without a practice of integration and meditation. Let us bring together, purify, and make precise the human substance with which we would be able to carry out that programme, when the hour strikes.

NOTES

(1) Ken Wilber gives a clear overview of this in his book *No Boundary, Eastern and Western Approaches to Personal Growth*, (Boulder: Shambhala, 1979) pp15-29.

(2) But Asia, at least the India of the Upanishads, does not necessarily talk in a different way. A few words from Tagore's *Sadhana*: "This longing of the human being for self-realisation is what leads him to seek wealth and power. But he must learn... that the highest human revelation is God's revelation within him." "For the human being, true misery consists in the fact that he has not quite succeeded in expressing his actual being, that the attempt is clouded by his ego and lost in his own wishes and desires" (p60f). "At first glance it looks as if freedom for the human being was that through which he receives unlimited possibilities to satisfy and aggrandise his self. But history teaches us differently. The carriers of revelation were always those who led a life of self-sacrifice." (Let us express this less like martyrdom, like a life of service: the fact that one might condemn service has to do with the projected character of what is served and with the inauthentic, artificial character of the engagement, and does not affect the principle of service at all). "We can observe our self in two different forms of appearance. We see the self which spreads itself around, and the self which transcends itself and in so doing reveals its true meaning" (p105). The more we base ourselves on that within us, becoming at one with all people, the more our existential individuality comes out.

(3) *Yoga der Erkenntnis, des Wissens* – also see the book with the same title by Vivekananda, *Jnana Yoga – Der Pfad der Erkenntnis*, (Freiburg: 1977), the English language version of which is *Vedanta Philosophy – Lectures of Jnana Yoga*, (Vedanta Soc, New York: 1907).

(4) Niklas Luhmann, *Liebe als Passion, zur Kodierung von Intimität* (Frankfurt: 1982), p208.

(5) *Ibid*, p46.

(6) *Ibid*, p198.

(7) Events in today's Soviet Union must remain totally incomprehensible – for all who primarily want to comprehend them sociologically, and who therefore want to know where party apparatus, state apparatus, the generality, and the state security service stand in the struggle for *perestroika* (even though nothing might be achieved with concepts of class). But here it is *consciousness-factions* which are fighting, whose carriers cannot be identified by their position in the apparatuses. One is not for or against Gorbachev because one belongs to the military, although the interests specially bound up with it might modulate. Basically it is a world-wide constellation. Thus everywhere a certain type of person – irrespective of his or her concrete social situation – is counting on Gorbachev as the bearer of hope of the interest of humanity. [This footnote was written in 1988, but has equally applied to President Yeltsin of Russia more recently, and might well apply beyond his time – ed.]

(8) To be exact I should have shown this strong arrow as splitting in two lower down, because it doesn't only transpose itself via rational insight. In spite of all analytical perception of exterministic symptoms, it is in most cases these which release the readiness for transformation. It is rather the other way about. The symptoms of crisis give welcome arguments for embarking on the self-experience, giving in to the desire for self-encounter over the objection of anxieties.

(9) Joachim Ernst Berendt, in two chapters of his meta-politically oriented book *Das dritte Ohr – The Third Ear*, called "Why women have higher voices" and "Hearing is feminine" – has pulled together many illuminating things about the feminine basis of culture, which we must go through again. Berendt makes it rationally clear why it is that in the process of integration we have to deal extensively with mental activities of an a-rational (not irrational) sort. One of the most important paths along my curved arrow is the path of hearing, our most receptive sense, the path of sound and music, as also of the spoken *Logos* of the original word. The arts in their original function as a means to intensified self-experience and world transformation must most certainly be regained.

(10) Tarthang Tulku, *Raum, Zeit, und Erkenntnis; Aufbruch zu neuen Dimensionen der Erfahrung von Welt und Wirklichkeit*, second edition of the special issue, 1986. In English, this is: Tarthang Tulku, *Dimensions of Thought: Current Explorations in Time, Space and Knowledge* (Dharma Pubs, Berkeley: 1980).

(11) Lao tzu, 13th saying.

(12) *Ibid*, 69th Saying.

(13) *Ibid*, 30th Saying.

(14) *Ibid*. 30th Saying.

(15) Sam Keen, *Königreiche der Liebe, die sieben Stufen der Ekstase* (Basel: 1986), pp98,99,114.

(16) See in this connection Reinhard Täube, *Innere Erfahrung und Gesellschaft. Klassischer Yoga – Indische Mystik. Beiträge zur Alternativkultur oder: Die Lotosblüte bekommt Stacheln*; copies of this dissertation can be obtained from the author at Stückhof, 3589 Knüllwald, Germany.

(17) See the Fichte essay in Wilhelm Weischedel, *34 grosse Philosophen in Alltag und Denken. Die philosophische Hinter-treppe* (München: 1980).

14. Axioms of a Path of Salvation

Today the language of science has captured the concept of the *axiom*. Ever since axioms came to be mathematical propositions from which all other possible statements in a theory can be derived, elegance has demanded that no more propositions than necessary shall be called axioms.

I shall use the word in its original sense. To the ancient Greeks an *axiom* was a basic proposition of *value* and *importance* which doesn't need proof, because it is self-evident. I hope the following summarising propositions will have something of this self-evident character.

I. The Opportunity

"To be (exterminated) or not to be" – suicide or spiritual rebirth – has become the present reality for humanity. A many-millionfold leap into a new mode of consciousness is its only chance. The ecological crisis is a unique occasion for making such a leap – which was already our task without it. And where else should this leap take place but in Europe, the cradle of this culture which has now turned suicidal?

Transformation – a deep change of consciousness, a new integration of human natural powers – is the basic process of our epoch. We are trying to widen and perfect our self-awareness in order to free ourselves of the conditioning of our birth and socialisation. This also involves the creation of 'a new heaven and a new earth', which means a new loving relationship between humans and the earth, between man and woman.

Cultures are based on deep structures in human consciousness. We can call these deep structures neutral *cosmologies*. Traditionally they are called 'religions'. The reference is to structures of consciousness which are coupled to the original basic equipment of our genotype, to our anthropological nucleus. A new culture presupposes a new structure of consciousness, which is what we mean by a 'new religion'.

In a similar way to what happened in the Mediterranean empire of the Romans, those forces are already perceptible in the western, Atlantic Metropolis today, creating a new and higher mode of consciousness, from which point the culture can be grounded anew.

II. Inner Enlightenment

This time there will clearly not be a new concept of God, detailed and precisely defined; no new idolisable anthropomorphic form. The spirit, it now appears, comes not from above but from within. This always was a given with our genotype – an aspect of evolution, of its inner guiding light. It is the implicit ordering aspect of our nature, of nature enfolded within us, whether we know it or not. Yet to the extent that we do not know it and do not ground our civilisation upon conscious communion with it – not all of us participate in it and are united because of it, and we differentiate among ourselves according to our individual genotypes – to this extent we will disturb the balance of nature because our knowledge and action would be focused on limited objectives.

The path of salvation begins with comprehending the crisis of civilisation in its essence, in its full depth and its pitiless lack of prospects. The material forces of inertia are monstrous and without historical example. It is as if we were to attempt to rescue ourselves from a shipwreck with tons of lead attached to our feet. Far too much New Age optimism – we travel to all kinds of workshops in a Mercedes or by plane – deliberately forgets the contemptuous mass-factor underneath. In this way it is easier not to notice the shadow of the cross that lies over everything.

We have experienced the ineffectiveness of environmental cosmetics and the macabre character of ecological-indulgence trade. We have an idea of the one fatal context which determines the whole inner milieu of our social body. It is also clear that we are encountering something very old, although in a new way: that the doom was always with us. But we still prefer not to look at what it really is, but rather to the outside and to others, rather than to ourselves, guilty and responsible for it as we are. The rate at which we consume is untenable. In order to see that we *must* reduce this, the logic of self-extermination needs to be brought out into broad daylight, otherwise the motivation will be insufficient to bring about the needed spiritual mutation. For this mutation must be bound up with a renunciation of our current lifestyle – otherwise transformation remains a private pleasure.

In the meantime all our acquired self-assertive habits of living, and the political games that go with them, are incompatible with our true life-interests. And yet it is not the bottomlessly-evil things that we do which are resulting in the ecological crisis. We are destroying ourselves with our *normality*. The earth can no longer put up with 'people as they actually are'. The calamity is a feature of the whole system. Only a modest attachment to any one of our finest achievements quickly results in the realisation that *everything* must remain unchanged if this single bloom is not to be lost. And how often do we feel we would rather die than renounce *any* well-earned achievement of civilisation – even in imagination? *What* then shall be saved – our worldly ego or our world? This *makes the difference* between death and life – today not just spiritually, but physically also.

III. Salvation Is Possible

We need to recognise what our fate would be if the Megamachine were to continue to run away with us – for we do not need to perish. *"If"*, as Lewis Mumford says,

> *human culture in fact arises, develops, and renews itself through fresh activities in the mind, it may be modified and transformed by the same processes. What the human mind has created, it can also destroy...*
>
> *I have found by personal experience that it is far easier to detach oneself from the system and to make a selective use of its facilities than the promoters of the affluent society would have their docile subjects believe. Though no complete escape from the ongoing power-system is possible, least of all through mass violence, the changes that will restore autonomy and initiative to the human person all lie within the province of each human soul, once it is roused. Nothing could be more damaging to the myth of the machine, and to the dehumanised social order it has brought into existence, than a steady withdrawal of interest, a slowing down of tempo, a stoppage of senseless routines and mindless acts*[1].

Thus trust in the purposes, goals, and plans of the organisation gives way to the feeling: *we have no idea what we're doing, we cannot be responsible for **anything***. Nobody who works in the honeycomb of the Megamachine can still carry out their daily duties with a good conscience. It would be ridiculous to want to talk oneself out of this on the grounds that one's small low-level function, taken in isolation or superficially modified, is not harmful. No man can serve two masters.

Only personal encounters and argumentations taking place many thousandfold, and particularly encounters with one's own machine-adapted ego, can be decisive for the Turn-around. The dividing lines are to be found not so much *between* people, as within them, and the split of consciousness in bailing out and defecting, in betrayal and slowing up of institutional activities, is the first and most important step. Confrontation belongs as a component of this, for whoever is willing to risk intimate talk can bring forward life and love, and push back death and power. Then, not just the pictures we have of each other will change, but emphases will also shift. The army of blue and white overalls proceeds into disintegration.

IV. To Know What Is No Longer Sufficient

We like comforting self-deceptions even if they cost us whole week-ends, not to speak of smaller indulgences. Those who have recognised the danger need the right feelings of hopelessness – they need to know what is futile, so that they do not waste their strength in ineffective or counter-productive activities. *There is no path to salvation along with the symptoms*, and whoever wakes up to a superficial awareness of them no longer deserves praise. Further, to the heart of things! The only thing that leads to the path of salvation is to pull oneself back from the Megamachine and its nodal points of power, and to have recognised the dissent around it. 'Let the dead bury their dead.'

Those who have always been proud of their thinking are usually even more biased. *All* ideologies of the bourgeois age – even the 'illegitimate' ones like anarchism, feminism and ecologism – are, as caused by the will-to-power of the bourgeois individual, at least inadequate. The three ideologies just named do indeed denounce power and its misuse, and they also give a few hints as to how *concentrations* of power could be avoided. But, because of the impulses it receives from the depths of personality, the will-to-power cannot be limited politically, except in the case where it is first culturally and spiritually limited. In particular, from birth on, children could be treated in a different way from that which they get in a performance-oriented society. They need a form of isolation from the world as it currently stands, like the little Parsifal. The utopias which are linked with ideologies all expect that even in a new situation we shall 'look for a state which is suited to us' – one which confirms us in our old prejudices and fosters our old way of behaving. All our traditional ideas of the state are ego-crutches and claims for or against power, and we must bid them farewell.

V. The Dead-End of Countervailing Force

The forces of transformation should not primarily want to have direct (and still mostly negative and protesting) influence on the rulers and the power apparatus, but should rather want to influence people's *consciousness*, regardless of their class.

Energies to put pressure on the political realm could concern themselves with real problems, starting with exterministic challenges, and withdraw forces from 'normal' businesses which reproduce the Megamachine. Sabotage is admittedly a possibility for articulating one's own transition to new positions, and pointing out the contradictions in the Megamachine, but it does not yet point the way to salvation, and even leads to new strategies for 'hardening', directing energies to the points of penetration.

We need to recognise that models of the form of *Lord of the Rings* –

final-struggle fantasies about 'white' against 'black' power-magic – rest on projection, and are fundamentally false and damaging to the ecological cause. We could pay much more attention to the impotence than to the power of the apparatus. It is naively unaware to assume that our rulers loom evilly over the world with the reins in their hands – which in reality direct them more compellingly than us – as long as they are living by the same rules of the game which directs us. There is no other positive possibility than the attempt to save the opponent along with ourselves, to 'embrace the wolf'. Whenever we omit to reach out in this way, we must put up with what happens. The more time we win for the work of transformation among *accessible* people, beginning with ourselves, the more probable it is that biophile energy, averse to nature, will intervene between the exterministic finger and the release button.

It follows that it is quite impossible to get the better of the Megamachine and the logic of destruction by force. Terror trains the mechanisms of the state of emergency, and cooperates fundamentally with exterminism, not just tactically. It confirms the moral and technical principles of the spiral of death, and is incidentally parallel with the New Age science fiction rubbish in the cinemas, where that which needs to be eradicated between two souls is continually externalised in Mephistophelian fashion and dualistically personified.

Even so, 'countervailing force' from anti-imperialistic terrorism of the Red Army Faction to the eco-terrorism of the 'revolutionary home worker' will grow more intense. In this process, Left and Right profiles will overlap. Terrorism is now an unavoidable symptom which points to the failure of the state in its primary function, and to the collapse of its legitimacy. *Governments lead, develop, and control their populations into downfall.* For people who have recognised the situation clearly, the only earnest alternative to countervailing force lies in a spiritual path of salvation.

VI. The Key

Self-destruction is the result of our success in mastering nature. The product of the exploitation has accumulated at particular nodal points: science, technology, capital, and state – including the military, mass media, schools, and health services. They are coupled to a single central power, which commits us to its course, yet is nourished by nothing except our living energy, and is dependent on our loyalty. Evolved as a top parasite which pursues its vital interests, we discover now that our psyche is an appendage of the Megamachine, which seeks to hold us firmly in this lost position.

What sort of immediate purposes are these? On their behalf we stop our psyche achieving its proper role, which is to be an organ of unity of human and *Bios*, or at least to uphold our own unity as body-soul-mind. Clearly these purposes go far beyond the securing of daily bread. They are our compensatory self-definitions, our ego-identities, which became ever more important the higher the cultural pyramid succeeded in growing. We have become more and more of a *nothing* in the face of the world machine which we have made. The termite queen is everything – as long as we fail to decide otherwise and accept certain risks concerning our ego-driven self-image.

The strengthening of our true self is the key to breaking up the Megamachine. We can do something in order to rediscover the original natural person in ourselves – the unique genotype – to reanimate it and to grow into the responsibility which falls to it. It is said that it does not wholly depend on us, and that something has to come to us 'from the other side' – grace. But charging this field of consciousness does require a contribution from us. Grace does not come to a society of depressive junkies. Even a moderate-sized concept of freedom could help!

VII. What Is Real?

Since the logic of self-extermination is a consequence of an anthropological dilemma, it can only be overcome from this root.

> *No outward tinkering will improve this overpowered civilisation, now plainly in the final and fossilised stage of its materialisation: nothing will produce an effective change but the fresh transformation that has already begun in the human mind[2].*

The essence of the human being, which includes his entire relation to the world, cannot be regarded as marginal. On the path of salvation, it is the root to which we must return, and the place from which we can begin anew.

At the present time a great split is happening concerning the concept of reality. Political realities, military realities, economic realities, everyday realities, and the corresponding opposite traits – how real are they in fact? *If* the 'material existence' of the human being determines his consciousness, and if this is the most important thing with which we have to reckon, then the point of no return has long been passed. If that realism which is based on 'laws of history' or statistical probability is accepted, there is no salvation.

There is something which we must needs regard as more real than technical or even social structures. It is true that a different society would make a more benign use of science and technology, but this different society presupposes a different polarity of the human spirit. The given structure of consciousness, in which the ego-intellect has our true self in tow, was bound to lead to the Megamachine. Resentments which are inseparable from this type of mental-social organisation are part of the problem, not the solution.

What we need now is not Christians or Buddhists, but a few million people like Jesus or Buddha. Each single man or woman who to some degree has been able to develop the spirit of the coming age, the spirit of *homo integralis*, has only a limited capacity and area of influence. What is needed is a 'critical mass' of individuals who are in process of transforming themselves. Up to now there has always been too few of them. Whether or not they are elites, things depend on precisely those people who feel themselves being spoken to when Jesus says: *you are the salt of the earth, you are the light of the world.* To hear this call is not arrogance so much as the first step on the path of emulation.

VIII. To Become Receptive

But aren't we stumbling about in the fog? Our heart may demand that where a logic of self-extermination is at work, a logic of salvation should also be working – 'everything is within us'. Here nothing is of any help unless we concern ourselves with its nature and direction: unless we bring to bear the human possibilities in body, soul, and spirit – thinkingly, feelingfully and meditatively. We can do nothing except make ourselves receptive to the demands of the natural balance, and to the possibilities of fitting into it again – which means actively correcting the current position and practices.

We need to resist the continuous temptation to do concrete things (actionism) – anti-this and anti-that – at least to the extent necessary to ensure that strength, time and means remain available to us for the essential task, making progress along the inner path to a new basic position. Without contact with the origin of the thrust to catastrophe and also of the forces of salvation, politics can only prolong the crisis and make it worse.

Even at the deeper levels of the exterministic thrust, direct access can still be inadequate. To experience a *lived* readiness to leave the industrial system behind us, to renounce monetaristic freedom, to give up Olympic competition and expansive self-fulfilment, to open up to others on the far side of ego-imposed constraints, and finally to say farewell to the temptation to make a name for oneself – all these things taken collectively lead to the threshold. Only by letting go of all the holy cows of our cultural identity can we win the spontaneity necessary for a new form and gesture of human solidarity.

IX. The Imperative of Happiness

It is not individualising which will vanish, but the *individualism* which is worried about its identity. We are not accomplishing the communion which would end the war of man against man, the competition of patriarchal egos. We even approach the issue of our intrinsically natural person from a position of competitive scarcity, not from one of plenty. We lack confirmation precisely because we don't allow ourselves to overflow. It is the anxious compulsion to compensate for this that gives our culture its unpeaceful character. The withdrawal from the Megamachine will only succeed as a withdrawal towards one's own centre, and our arrival there. This is what Einstein's words refer to when he says that it is not the atom bomb which is the problem, but the human heart. Only he who is sufficient unto himself, so that all that is necessary flows toward him, can stop being a hunter.

The human being who wants to find his own centre cannot dispense with the other person: as mirror, but more, as friend, but more, as beloved one, but more, as helper in reaching the godhead. This finding of balance between dependency and freedom, needfulness and self-sufficiency, is the ultimately inescapable task for culture. In the experience that "Hell is other people", as Sartre said, appears the core of the tragedy of individuality. We fear ourselves in the other, for ultimately we have to be at one with our opposite number, before we recognise ourselves in everything else.

For this reason the healing of the core of the culture depends upon whether it is possible to make secure the communion from love and to love. This would make unnecessary a great deal of compensatory drive to external action. It would be *the* shift of centre of gravity if, in our relations to others, for whose sake we alter the world, love would dominate instead of war – power, competition, mistrust. Except that it is impossible to arrange the world in a way which suits our ego *as it is*. It can only be arranged in this way if *we* ourselves, each man and woman of us, without presupposing the love culture as a condition, transcend the ego-centre, to learn to be ourselves from within ourselves.

This re-ordering of individuality is the path. It is not the elements of human existence which change, but the way they work together, the direction of their movement, and the *tonus* of the energy. Unhappy consciousness is the normal state of the rational (left-brain-centred) ego. It is melancholy instead of joyous. Out of the right hemisphere, whence from ancient times 'the gods' spoke, a different temperament comes into us – if only we allow it to speak – a positive one which can mobilise quite different energies. Of course, the customary depression feeds on itself.

If we want a good society, it is necessary to attain to a happier consciousness. We don't get to the root of things unless we learn to act from originary trust instead of defensiveness. We can go back to this source so frequently and extensively blocked up, and we must take care of it. We can only be *right* if we are happy. Acting purely from a *sense of duty* we will only take actions of such a kind that we once again disturb the harmony of the world: from Confucius to Kant we find only postponement of the fate hanging over us, only postponement of the solution, only new barriers against happiness. The turning-about of the heart must first of all be an opening of the heart. What is required is social techniques which develop our ability to love.

X. The Axis of the Path

Because the human being can only begin with him/herself and not with the world, with the centre and not with the periphery, meditation is the axis of the path to salvation – meditation as inner action in the whole multiplicity of possibilities. Everything in which we become *absorbed* becomes meditation, not least the communion of love. It can also be work, which we complete according to our nature, with all our soul. Meditation leads into our psychic inner space, from which alone the new culture can proceed. It can recondition us to make us able to reconnect our most mundane daily affairs with the implicit 'holy' order.

Meditation is the innermost of all the methods of experiencing the self now being practised, and which also will prevail, even if here and there overgrown by commercialisation and trivialisation. The spiritual renewal in this one world humanity of today transcends all church boundaries and all dogmas. Behind all differences of paths and formulas one truth shines out. The law of human existence itself designates the point at which these paths meet. We are dealing with a social praxis which takes back from left-brained intellect, still indispensable, the leadership of the historical process which it had usurped. This tool gained functional autonomy and, by means of the Megamachine, has access to a factor of positive feedback, so that precisely by its excessive activity, by its intrusion into the overall regulation, it reproduces itself ever more extensively. Perhaps this is the last form of the classical problem which was treated under the name of alienation.

The cardinal problem, then, is the stimulation of the right-brain functions for the purpose of subordinating the intellect to this more fundamental and higher regulation. Meditation is the royal road to salvation, and its dissemination throughout the whole society, and not least through its still-exterministic elites, is the primary political strategy.

XI. Journey Within

Our consciousness stands at the boundary between the inner and the outer world. Up to now the human being has perfected his knowledge and ability to make changes in the outer world, as was latent in the logic of evolution – the eye looks outward, not inward. The *objective observer* of what is outside converts to the *witness* of the inner world. Getting to know the inner world and acting on it turns out to be an ultimately enjoyable process, especially when, as in the 1970s and 80s, the ascetic obsession climbing to higher consciousness has been overcome.

From two points of view the journey within is the key to practical answers to alienation caused by the Megamachine. Where we have up to now given our energy to the Megamachine, we now withdraw from it the best and most motivated part, do not renew it so vehemently, tending rather to let it starve. And at the same time we alter the relationship of forces between our slave and patient nature on the one hand and our free, surplus energies on the other.

Politics as power-acquisition within the Megamachine remains a path of slavery and betrayal of our firstborn. We can leave the reforming wholly to those who are still satisfied to want to postpone the collapse of the apparatus of civilisation. In this they will anyhow do all they can.

We have another work to do. Truly ecological politics takes the indirect path, which in truth is more direct, because the psyche is the source of social evils, and social healing. Every time we busy ourselves with the preservation of something, we will remain aware that the problem here can be negotiated to a certain extent, but that it is in general insoluble.

XII. Politics of Salvation: Basic Attitudes

1.   On the path to salvation a new spiritual authority will gradually form itself. I call it an *Invisible Church*, which stands open to all, and to which all belong with that part of their consciousness which is free for the new world. It exists as a horizontal, multilateral network. It forbids itself all direct or indirect constitution as a commanding social or political power. The eco-spiritual movement does not aim at immediate success, nor at numerical growth, but builds on the radiation of everything which is true to life, biophile, loving, done with total commitment, which arises in it. Intensity and quality, awareness and beauty, draw out more of those qualities in people who are attracted to them.

Absolutely, power may only be employed 'negatively' in an ecological politics of salvation, only for limiting mischief and preventing it from getting the upper hand. It cannot set positive goals, but can at most be a subsidiary support for them. No tyranny, however well-meaning, could create a good and healthy society. As necessary as selective and well-aimed single eco-dictatorial measures may be, the bottleneck is not in the preparation of laws and in carrying them out, but in the preparation of souls. Over the short or the long run, the area which can be filled institutionally and administratively will depend on the amount of inner space freed up from ego-control and waiting for restructuring.

2.   Whoever has recognised the truth about the ecological crisis, the logic of self-extermination, and the path and politics of salvation, gives it out as pure wine. There are enough people who do not dare to do this because they do not know or do not want to know this truth. Whoever first asks whether s/he will be understood or accepted has not accepted the whole truth.

> *In fact, the problem of how to transmit our ecological reasoning to those whom we wish to influence, in what seems to us to be an ecologically-good direction is itself an ecological problem...*
>
> *I believe that... our greatest (ecological) need is the propagation of these ideas... If this estimate is correct, then the ecological ideas implicit in our plans are more important than the plans themselves, and it would be foolish to sacrifice these ideas on the altar of pragmatism. It will not in the long run pay to 'sell' the plans by superficial* ad hominem *arguments which conceal or contradict deeper insight.* (Gregory Bateson)[3]

In the customary minimal-consensus and 'people-fetching' politics, politicking oriented to power-winning is always manifest. Yet deep in their hearts people know the hour has struck, and they could be 'fetched' from quite a different place. What is at issue is whether we want to speak as functionaries-to-electors or as people-to-people. We need mass media and primarily television as the instrument of this eleventh-hour enlightenment. It is part of our doom that we keep a Satanic church in the media – and defend it from the Left, because censorship against violence-thrillers could also be applied to critical essays and documentaries. Many of those who worship violence and triviality would immediately retreat, if the media would clearly accept its obligation to serve communication among ourselves about our situation, and to widen access to the practice and practitioners of spiritual self-change.

3.   Eco-politics begins with the decision to recognise the apocalyptic analysis and the direction of salvation as correct, and in practice orients itself accordingly – whoever will not 'rule according to the Sermon on the Mount' cannot expect to be counted as an adherent to eco-politics. If all we ask is what is best and most feasible *within* the customary structure of consciousness and institutions, we can never arrive at an ecological politics of salvation.

Eco-politics propagates the *long-term, general and fundamental* interests of the human-and-earth-system *Gaia,* and it organises the spiritual accumulation of strength around this 'right-brain' basic position. It can seize hold of the majority of society all the sooner now, since there is already a multiplicity of destructive factors such that the long and the short term have merged into one. The house is already burning, and the first thing must be to protect and save the living. Despair about the fact that nothing is happening, together with the insight that the consciousness-structure in the old institutions is useless, is almost by itself sufficient to cause a Turn-around.

4.   A politics of salvation cannot be negotiated among representatives and lobbies of *special* interests, and it cannot be made capable of compromises. Since the regulation of special interests and their struggle for apportionment is the main activity of democratic institutions, compromises are inadequate for the main task of today's state. Interests of life must have absolute priority, and this needs to be guaranteed by means of institutional renewal.

After a determination of the necessary steps, there can and must be negotiation and decision concerning a fair adjustment. Privileged possessions, firmly bound up with the logic of self-extermination, may not be proliferated, but also may not be attacked in a spirit of social resentment. They will not survive the general collapse of civilisation, and thus possessions should thus be invested in the salvation. People like us need to choose to stand the test of becoming capable of releasing ourselves from a life-model which, although dangerous for life, is still comfortable and offers compensations for the mainly-psychological injuries and frustrations already directly experienced. Whoever asks about immediate advantages or disadvantages, and casts his eyes politically first in that direction, wondering whether 'the opponent' might or might not be winning something, will become more and more his own enemy.

5.   For its salvation, society under the spell of the industrial Megamachine needs to be newly-institutionalised. Neither the structure of consciousness nor the political constitution can any longer afford to be selfishly-oriented, as in the principle of the bourgeois constitution. The western world has not institutionalised the general good, but a state of siege, in which it was placed by the addictive character of needs. We need not wonder why there has been a totalitarian reaction. As long as the expansive tendency is not limited by human beings themselves, the law will have to forbid ever more. But it can only do this if the law-making process itself is not the victim of the lobbyism of special interests. Friends of the *status quo* reminisce on the freedom of the individual, but they seem to have in mind juridical persons like corporations.

6.   The sovereign capacity to set one's own life and behaviour to rights shall by necessity be decentralised to the greatest possible extent. For each group or organisation developing the new consciousness this sovereignty will need as far as possible to already be achieved, before it is granted protection by the society at large. Then from here on the idea of bringing about unilateral military and industrial disarmament may be dealt with at the still-decisive level of the nation-state. As one of the richest and ecologically most threatened peoples, we Germans have special reasons for being in the lead.

Inner sovereignty also presupposes a claim on outer sovereignty, for a solitary opting-out of the structures of disaster. Predictions about the reactions of friends and enemies are in vain – all they will do is indicate whatever is feared or hoped for at any particular time. We simply have to get on with it, and at the same time press for the kind of supranational and world-wide functions which are necessary for the restabilising of the system *Gaia*. These are the kind of problems which could not be solved in the interests and with the methods of the old ruling powers.

7.   In countries such as Germany there is no lack of material possibilities, and taking advantage of these is fully justified to renounce a model which is pressing on the rest of humanity. In any case the path to salvation does not primarily open itself from the economy or social questions, not even from national interests – or from the international level, or the interests of the external proletariat. It does not make sense to nominate oneself *here* as representative of the damned of this earth in the Third World, and then to want to single out their problems *there* for solution, rather than wanting to replace the model in the Metropolis which is throwing the whole world into calamity.

8.   Land, tools, buildings, and money – here in our 'advanced' countries all these things will be available as soon as the pattern of the alternative reveals itself. The traditional policy, favoured by the Left, of redistribution for the benefit of the Metropolitan lower classes and marginal groups, remains part of our crime against the rest of humanity and a contribution to our own calamity. It is clear that a spiritually-obligated social authority concerned with justice and the protection of the weakest will exert pressure. Even so we shouldn't forget that the 'poor whites' in the Metropolis are not by any means the last cases, and they live near enough to the safety-nerve of power to be able to press on it and to stand up for themselves as soon as they get organised. Ecological politics may exert itself for special interests only in such a way that it defends the general interest at the same time: whoever injures social justice cripples the process of salvation.

What spiritual and material resources can be obtained from the diagonal of destruction is decisive. The new consciousness particularly takes hold in the privileged circles of our society. It is similar to what Augustine once said about membership in the City of God: many are actually outside who meant to be inside, and many who appear to stand outside are in reality inside. Also, when we run up against economic boundaries, it is mostly boundaries of spiritual influence which are manifesting themselves, and these may also be connected with our own sectarianism. What it all depends on is: true encounter with others, friendship and love, beauty and order in surroundings, wisdom and culture in handling conflicts – and all these depend only to a limited extent on material standards, once we achieve a certain distance from our habits.

9.   Principles of a new culture:

- priority given to the originary cycles and rhythms of life, not to development and progress. Technology and techniques will exist and evolve – for the new cultural context 'the bicycle must be invented for the second time' – but this evolution must be tied to the cycle of eternal return. More happiness is possible only when we make less history;

- we may comprehend our interests by looking from the whole to the part rather than from the part to the whole, and express this also in our institutions. To quote Montesquieu:

    If I knew of something useful to me and injurious to my family I would banish it from my mind. If I knew of something useful to my family but not to my country, I would seek to forget it. If I knew something useful to my country and harmful for Europe, or useful to Europe and harmful for humanity, I would regard it as a crime[4].

- we want to extend this thought to all sentient beings, to all life, to the earth in general. Nothing may happen which could disturb the balance of the earth, or which could injure plants, animals, and children (later generations);

- if all this is taken seriously, we can only live in a state of unconditional disarmament, and we will need to cut back our industrial civilisation far enough so that no species can be lost; we can avoid exploiting animals and making them suffer; we can renounce most large-scale processing of materials, take no part in tourism, avoid driving automobiles, make minimal use of medicaments, avoid participating in money circulation through banks, pursue no positivistic science, and so on;

- in addition we need to stop treating the economy as an overarching realm of being which is of supreme importance for social life. Economy and ecology *in general* must be brought into relation with each other: an industrial-capitalistic social economy is incurable. It is necessary to pull back together the life-process, which at present is fragmenting into so many commercialised functional areas. All basic reproduction functions – nourishment, housing, handiwork, education and health agencies should be re-integrated back into the local context (communal and communitarian) where they belong. Land, tools, houses and working people need to unify again in 'second-order tribes', families by choice.

- We can only survive on the earth if we adopt a life-style of voluntary simplicity and frugal beauty based on a subsistence economy – and then only if we limit our numbers. This *contractive* life-style is also necessary if our distance from the objects of our action, desiring, and thinking are once again to grow smaller, for in contact lies the truth. The super-complex mass society can only be a realm of organised irresponsibility;

- those who decide to leave behind the Empire and its colonial consensus create for themselves a supporting and unifying network, in which are nodal points of greater concentration. After individuation, and consequent decay of all natural social groupings, penetrating right into the core family unit, a new social synthesis can best come into existence by a union, reached by elective affinity, of new small living circles and larger 'second-order tribes'. The new institutions will primarily have the goal of permitting the full development of all those human potentials which are latent in the polarity of erotic and spiritual energies;

- to the extent that we build up germ-cells of the ORDINE NUOVO, our efforts will lose their apparently private and arbitrary character. A new morality can be rooted only in the regulation of those every-day conflicts in which individualities get tangled. We will not, as has been the case in many living communities of the last few decades, continually criticise and analyse each other, and yet we will find an effective form for mutually evolving ourselves, for cutting back our self-centred, ego-constricted and power-oriented tendencies, dramatisations, and games. A certain amount of ritualising of the handling of conflict will be necessary;

- the capacity for life of new communities depends upon having a common vision and upon daily affairs centred on a spiritual practice in which *Eros*, *Logos* and work can be reconciled and elevated. The schedule of daily life in all higher cultures has built itself up starting with the Sabbath. So will it be once again in the new culture – or it will never come into existence.

NOTES

(1) Lewis Mumford, *The Myth of the Machine*, vol 2, *The Pentagon of Power* (New York: Harcourt, Brace, Jovanovich, 1970), pp421 & 433.

(2) Mumford, *op cit*, p434.

(3) Gregory Bateson, *Steps to an Ecology of Mind* (New York: Ballantyne Books, 1972), pp504-505.

(4) Montesquieu, *Cahiers, 1716-1755* (Paris: Grasset, 1941), p9f. English translation quoted in Gebser *op cit*, p419.

Part Four:

CATALYSING THE ECOLOGICAL TURN-AROUND

Part Four

CHALLENGING THE
ECOLOGICAL
LOOK-AROUND

15. Prelude to the ecological turn-around

Once Again, About the Divine State

This last section of the book concurs with the spiritual-political idea which has already been followed, and which is latent in Hegel, Hölderlin, Schelling and Marx: of an *Invisible Church*, a worldwide *communion of saints* directed to humanity's inner, secular and transcendent elements. This creative achievement of organising the excess of consciousness into a benign social power, overarching and limiting all particular powers and interests, is now demanded of western civilisation – not a copy of the old Communist Party, which was so gravely incriminated by the circumstances of its birth, but a pendant, nearer to the original idea of the restitution of a human instrument to embody the divine state.

Without such an instrument 'transcending the party level' it is impossible to lift the state out of the present situation, in which it is mixed up with economic special interests. Since the bankruptcy and decline of the Church resulting from the power-struggle between Pope and Emperor in the high Middle Ages, this goal, this ideal, has no longer had an institutional anchor. The individual pocket-compass is too weak.

If one grasps the order-creating challenge which resides in the ecological crisis, it is clear that it requires such a strong authority for society as a whole, such a mighty sphere of law, that the appropriate solution will be justified, possible and lasting only if its institutions stand in the light of a new *Civitas Dei* (divine civil order). Otherwise, pushed by the proliferation of immediate special interests, law and authority will unavoidably have their centre of gravity in the *Megamachine*. The secularised state cannot possibly derive such an authority from within itself.

With the Soviet Communist Party *over* the state and over all social special interests, a political structure using Lenin's approach could have emerged in the former Soviet Union which, *in principle*, could have led beyond the world of warring special interests and sovereign states. Only an institutional structure in which the fundamental, long-term and general interests actually have preponderance can possibly set up a regulative system which could limit our access to nature, for the sake of ecological survival or wisdom.

Since it is true that economic special interests do not predominate in all social formations, it is also thinkable to find an institutional counter-weight to them. But in our western societies a situation is *given* in which private and corporate-profit interests could establish themselves *in the state itself*, so that it is virtually constituted as a mediating mechanism *between* these special interests. The money-changers are allowed to haggle not just in the outer court of the temple, but in the Holy of Holies itself.

Let us for the moment take the Soviet structure as an ideal type, as if it had not been the overgrown bureaucracy and state apparatus which it in practice became. In this case a Communist Party *can* potentially be the organ of 'reasonable egoism' for humanity. The rest depends on how the party would work internally and in communication with society. Will that which they called *intra-party* (within the party) de-mocracy proceed from words to reality?

Intra-party democracy means essentially freedom of discussion under the umbrella of an ultimately-spiritual consensus about human nature. What this presupposes, or appears to have in view, is the taking-away of power from the party *apparatus*, or better, its subordination. This would be in order to ensure that all functionaries maintain the organisa-tional framework for domination-free communication-communion about highest principles and goals, and about the general business of society.

So the path would be an intensive process of intra-party enlighten-ment, which would take place in parallel to the same process taking place among the people. For the party boundaries would need to be open, permeable to that part of consciousness which belongs to this dialectical consensus-building. On the other hand genuine *glasnost* (gov-ernmental openness) would offer sufficient constitutional guarantees to mass-communication to enable it to transmit the best the human being can do, at the current level of evolution, in contributing to a 'divine plan'. *Transparency* – this is a concept in the field of light.

In a period of re-founding of a culture, institutions preferably repres-ent something higher than the average consciousness of their time and country, and create free space for the mass-unfolding of the subjective forces they release. In particular their level depends upon the consciousness-rank of the governing minority under whose leadership they are created, and the consensus for the principle of the revolution which is under way. They are culture-creating to the extent that they enable the whole polity to raise itself to a new stage. They grant to people a more noble, harmonious form, and they permit the wellsprings of the genotype, the *conditio humana*, to flow, so that society can rise to the challenges which inevitably occur.

Even if in a contrary and paradoxical fashion, institutions mirror the climb of human beings to a new level of awareness. For example, the Athenian ostracism-democracy certainly did not – seen for itself – stand above the old theocracy with which, to its disadvantage, Plato compared it. But it gave much more play to the unfolding of individualities than did the divine monarchy. Once a new form of individuality has become general, the institutional problem presents itself in a different form.

People can then assemble themselves *above* the whole pyramid of division of labour and administration, in order to decide on the general course and the mode of social life. Whether single individuals then work for a time 'above', 'below', or 'in the middle' of the pyramid becomes a secondary matter, because they are not subordinated to these positions – no longer reduced to roles or even castes. In my *Alternative* I wrote directly along these lines: "How is an 'assembly' of the whole society possible, so that all individuals can decide *over* their reproduction process? This is the cardinal question for socialist democracy"[1].

In the late 1980s in the Soviet Union '*perestroika*' (restructuring) suggested just this idea. A number of advanced individuals, though certainly not the whole society, assembled with a disposition to dominance-free discussion about the general issues at the peak of the historical process, after access had been opened *in principle* to the mass media and freedom had been given to exchange arguments in collectives and associations.

The *problem* of mediation – of how every unreasonable egoism rooted in immediate, short-term and special interests can be insightfully over-come – is with us in all structural changes in society. But we have no agency concerned with *general* interests. The highest legitimation – through general elections – is achieved through office-seeking parties and politicians shamelessly bowing and scraping before precisely these immediate, short-term and special interests. Even the citizens them-selves are dragged back against their wills to the darkest places in their souls. In view of the ecological crisis it is a scandal that most elections are frequently between two 'popular' parties, which are slaves to the lowest denominator of material selfishness amongst citizens, and to the political selfishness of their matadors.

Or am I mistaken, incorrectly failing to notice that parliamentarism could offer the *possibility* of making the general good of humanity and the balance of *Gaia* into our guiding thread? The only formal oppor-tunity would consist of the setting up of an upper house, let us say – in contrast to a House of Lords – a 'House of the Lord'. The immediate, short-term and special interests must be represented; but it is no longer tolerable that the representation of *these* interests should *dominate* the field institutionally, and that fundamental, long-term and general interests should receive only secondary consideration.

Earlier in the book, in a footnote, I mentioned Timothy Leary's neurological Tarot. Curiously, but not coincidentally, his *Game of Life* offers a revealing parallel to this political material. Of the 24 stages of evolution equalling 24 cards of his game, the first 12 correspond to our average consciousness, and the other 12 to higher consciousness. At the last position of the first dozen stands the Tarot card *Justice*, and it symbolises for Leary 'centralised religious socialism' as a typical social pattern of the twentieth century, and not just in the former Soviet Union. Characteristic for people of this phase is said to be 'insectoid socialisation' and 'beehive-consciousness'.

Concerning the overcoming of this constitution, it is relevant what Leary has to say about his card 17, which belongs to the second dozen and thus represents a higher consciousness. We are concerned here with the Tarot card *The Lightning-struck Tower*. Firstly it refers to the individual mind, but we can also see it as referring to the brain of the social collective, its institutional apparatus and its communicative processes.

Leary informs us that the Hebrew letter *Pe*, with the meaning 'the penetration of thy words brings light', belongs to the broken tower as 'stage manager of reality' – as principle of communication. At this stage the brain takes over the responsibility for its own functioning and thus becomes capable of selective new programming. According to the Tarot card picture both cerebral hemispheres are set free:

> The primitive tarot card shows a stylised tower with people living in it, the top of which is broken away. The top refers to the head, to the structure of the beehive. A bolt of lightning has struck the top of the head and set the building on fire. Two human figures with astonished, vacant expressions of face are hovering or falling down. It is certainly a card of bewilderment. The tower represents the spiritual structure of the beehive, which is being blown up by radioactive substances[2].

So much for Leary. This fits the atmosphere in Moscow after Gorbachev's *perestroika* and the rise of Yeltsin, which in this sense can be understood as 'neuro-political'. This reminds one of the pharaoh Akhenaton and his queen Nefertiti[3].

It is of course of the greatest interest how the problems of the social beehive present themselves, and how they are dealt with, *if* the institutional sphere is the expression of a truly human sphere. Yet with Leary a government at the level of 'The Tower' *precedes* the opening of the heart, the evolution of the capacity for love.

While one may regard this excursion into neurological Tarot as more or less enlightening as far as Moscow reforms are concerned, I at least see in it a pointer to what is my main concern in this book: that *the only conceivable politics of salvation will be a politics of consciousness*. It is of course insufficient to ascertain a ladder of brain-structures, or consciousness-switching circuits, however illuminating this may be. Leary's model offers *one* point of access to better understanding of history as psychodynamics. But it is not brain-classes which make history, but human beings, each of whom participates potentially in all the stages.

As far as the Communist Party as 'stage manager of reality' is concerned, my main criticism was that it had become corrupt, had abandoned its perspective, had no longer measured up to its task, had yielded to the special interests of its functionaries, and had indeed systematically allowed state and party officials to hold sinecure positions and become – as they were called in the Chinese 'Cultural Revolution' – 'capitalists of power'. It would never have occurred to Lenin to be the first to reach into the communal pot to get the larger portion, but it did occur to his successors.

It is not unthinkable that the Communist Party and its socio-political system could have fallen into line *from within*, according to an ethics of responsibility like that advocated by Max Weber, and especially that it could spiritualise. Gorbachev came too late, inadvertently precipitating the downfall of the party. In reality the Communist Party as initiated by Marx and then by Lenin was created in this perspective, admittedly materialistically-encased and abbreviated, because Christian spirituality was politically totally bankrupt. The rebirth of substance, which was latent in the idea of the 'Kingdom of God', began with this idea of an association for general human emancipation.

The essence of this was better formulated two hundred years ago in 1799 by Novalis than I would be able to do it. In that year he was looking at a new political spirituality, and wrote his essay *Christianity or Europe*[4].

When Novalis says 'Europe' we can now look at the entire world, and when he speaks of Christianity, we can imagine something like the 'community of saints of all peoples', an association which is nothing less than the upward-striving essence of humanity. Novalis' formulation is perhaps more contemporary now than it was in the time when he gave it expression, writing of the beginning of the decay of the old authorities:

What was initially personal hatred against the Catholic faith gradually transformed itself into hatred of the Bible, of the Christian faith, and finally against religion itself. More yet, hate against religion extended itself very naturally and logically to all objects of enthusiasm, branded as heretical fantasy and feeling, ethics and the love of art, future and prehistory; it placed the human being as a natural being with necessity at the top and turned the endless creative music of the universe into the uniform clatter of an enormous mill, driven by it and swimming on it, a mill in itself, without a building master and miller – in fact, a genuine perpetual motion, self-milling mill.

The time of the resurrection has come, and precisely the occurrences that appeared to be directed against its animation and threatened to complete its downfall, have become favourable signs of its regeneration. This can in no way be doubtful to a historical mentality. True anarchy is the procreative element of religion. Out of the annihilation of everything positive it lifts up its glorious head as a new world founder. The human being spontaneously climbs up toward heaven when nothing binds him any more, the higher organs step spontaneously out of the general uniform mixture and complete disintegration of all human talents and forces as the original kernel of earthly formation...

Peacefully and unbiased, the genuine observer might look at the new state-upheaving times. Does not the state-upheaver look rather like Sisyphus to him? Just as he balances it on the peak, the heavy load rolls down again on the other side. It will never stay on the top unless an attraction toward heaven holds it hovering there. All your supports are too weak, if your state retains the tendency to move earthward. But if you couple it through a higher desire to the high places of Heaven, give it a connection to the universe, then you have a never-tiring spring in it and your exertions will be richly repaid!

It is impossible that earthly forces should achieve balance by themselves – a third element that is at the same time both earthly and supernatural can alone accomplish this task. No peace can be made among the quarrelling powers, all peace is only illusion, only an armistice; from the standpoint of the cabinets, of the common consciousness, no unification is thinkable.

Who knows whether we have had enough war, but it will never stop if one doesn't reach for the palm branch, which alone a spiritual power can present. Blood will flow over Europe until the nations became aware of their terrible insanity which is driving them around in circles and, touched by holy music and rendered gentle, step before former altars colourfully mixed together...

Do not the nations have everything from the human being – except his heart? – his holy organ?

Where is that old, dear, only true faith in the rule of God on earth, where is that heavenly trust of human beings towards each other..?

Novalis demands a new, old "church without regard for national boundaries, which takes all souls into its lap who are thirsty for the supernatural, and which would gladly be the mediator between the old and the new world". "Then nobody would protest any more against Christian and secular coercion, for the essence of the Church will be genuine freedom, and all necessary reforms will be carried on under its leadership as peaceful and formal state procedures".

Yes, we must create for ourselves this saving authority, world-wide, but we need to begin with ourselves. The new social power will exist first as an inner design and then as an association of spirits, before the new reformation also embraces the state.

In a certain passage in *The New View of Things* Biedenkopf writes: "The free society is based on the uniqueness of human beings and their ultimately personal responsibility in face of an authority which lies outside themselves and outside human society"[5]. As a phrase something like this is to be found in the constitutions of a great many 'Christian' countries.

At issue here is a closer understanding of what the concept of the godhead means and intends to express today (and also what 'outside' means, and what it does not mean). If our society is innately expansionistic, the political energy needed to set limits to it cannot possibly be won from the political sphere alone[6]. What orientation do we have for the spiritual energies which we want to take in? Here we are thrown back upon a discussion of the subjectivity of salvation. On this forefield minds will separate from each other or find each other.

Rohrmoser Educates the 'Sovereigns of This World'

I shall shift my attention from Kurt Biedenkopf to Günter Rohrmoser, a philosopher usually assigned to the right wing of moderate politics, because he portrays his position in a rather fundamentalist manner. Once again, I shall not pay attention to the Left-Right model, which is unusable. To the extent that Rohrmoser is really a fundamentalist, I find myself closer to him spiritually than to Biedenkopf.

For while between Biedenkopf and me there is still a grey area in our descriptions of the state of the world – *is it or is it not really apocalyptic?*! – between Rohrmoser and me this point is fully clear. He too sees the holistic, fundamental character of the crisis and politically articulates it in such a manner that no half-measures should be tolerated any more. But I can find no basis in his thought for the way in which he still thinks that the current economy and ecology can be reconciled. It would really be a cheap trick to cover the nakedness of the capital-driven Mega-machine behind the platitude that in all historical periods economy *must* adapt itself ecologically, and has *more or less done so*(!). The fact is that whole cultures have laid waste their environments – at a time, now gone, when they were just localised accidents.

Also he cannot *spiritually* justify the way in which he spoke out earlier on behalf of rearmament with new missiles. For since the self-continuing logic of the arms race is obvious, it should follow unambiguously from his insight that the catastrophe is a result of the *power-logic* of reason, of its innate will-to-control, that "one must make the first move to stop it" (Franz Alt). The totalitarianism of the 'enemy', which is so very much involved with the foundations of our culture and represents its projection, is a wretched argument when one compares it with the scenario of threatening total catastrophe. How can we block things at the primary level on account of an aversion arising on a derived, secondary level? Isn't it high time to renounce *philosophically* this idea that we are threatened?

Günter Rohrmoser protects himself against such a demand by taking the precaution of demanding *time* for the Turn-around: he thinks we ought to reverse the maxim of Marx's Feuerbach thesis. "It is important first to interpret the world before we change it. As long as we have not understood the new situation in which the world finds itself, we ought to protect it from any change with a total claim and goal-directedness"[7].

He and I can agree as far as interpretation and new understanding is concerned: only when the reflection demands additional time, we must remind ourselves that meanwhile the world *will be changed*, or more precisely, annihilated. Imprisoned in the Megamachine, knowledge and tools *are* incessantly working against the "conservation-imperative of the human species" (Rohrmoser). Would an attempt to stop this spiral of death, by means of an unlimited moratorium until understanding catches up, be so impermissably 'total(itarian)?' Shouldn't such a general pause at least first be risked in thought?

The price (in loss of time) of the inconsistency becomes clear when Rohrmoser appeals to the old institutions which are prisoners to the logic of self-extermination. They are supposed to complete a commission for which the capacity in them has evidently died. How shall we achieve a new configuration if we don't want to risk making any break – including also breaks with friends who just want to carry on living as before – or any transition through moments or sectors of chaos?

Very correctly, Rohrmoser reminds us of the Two-Realm Teachings of *Civitas Dei* and *Civitas Terrena* – as if church and state, *as they were*, at the end of the Middle Ages, could still offer a spiritual authority capable of rescuing human substance. He is admittedly well acquainted with the idea that the murderous power struggle between popes and emperors had removed the last square mile of unpolluted ground for any later exercising of the divine right of kings. Otherwise science-technology-capital would never have become free for their uninhibited plunder-trip.

All conservatives make the same mistake: they expect the burnt-out hulls strewn along the path of humanity's past to resurrect themselves and continue their original content. If I see a church of Assisi rising up I'll revise my opinion! But even here it would be better to rely on a new birth out of the living spirit, because new churches of Assisi would come to nothing without new Francises who are prepared to go all the way in breaking with institutions, something which the original Francis of Assisi did not see himself compelled to do.

The ideas of the general good and *Civitas Dei* can only be preserved if the corruptly-constructed party state and the churches as they really exist are *in principle* abandoned. After all, Augustine declared breaking with imperial Rome a condition for *Civitas Dei*. What is there to suggest that we are not in a situation which just as compellingly demands that we break away from the modern Metropolis?

The question of the church is even more important than the question of the state, because it has to do with the basic religious consensus of the west: *this* is in question. It is correct to embark first on a theological discussion instead of discussing politics. We will reach more easy agreement about *Civitas Terrena* (the earthly order) if we have first reached an understanding about *Civitas Dei*: whether or not we must begin anew at the beginning?! If the godhead, if the moral idea has been regained, the concept of the state will fall 'correctly' into place again.

Even today one can encounter the godhead within the church, because it is at least a step aside. But dogma and hierarchy distract from the living Christ and a living Mary, in whom the difference between heavenly and earthly love were cancelled, can unfold itself with only great difficulty. What would the words of Christ following the Sermon on the Mount mean today: "I come not to abolish but to fulfil"? What would it mean to tear down the temple and build it anew?

In any circle where people reckon with the existence of something nameless and holy, there is always some tendency toward all those things which, in our culture, have been arranged around the figure of Christ. Precisely in those areas where he is special there should be no need for apology or protection in the face of other paths. Our unfilled cathedrals should open their inner space for the meeting of all paths to the godhead, and to all suitable practices. But taking the existing condition of our churches as they are, we cannot expect more than non-disturbance of what comes together ecumenically.

If one makes the appeal, *without* characterising the situation as *radical*, that politics in times of deep crisis must be guided by religion – the Christian religion is implied here – then one is today regarded as a

Pharisee or a scribe *opposing* the New Covenant. The values of the Christian church did not lead out of what Thucydides called the dilemma of the struggle for dominance and for freedom. Rohrmoser is in reality pleading for a legitimate power-politics of the old type, not because it is exactly what he wants, but because he doesn't think things through fundamentally to the end.

The ecological turning-point depends mostly on *correct* conservatism. Since a salvation movement must in fact save, and this means also preserving the substance of evolved European individuality and subjectivity, it can only come out of the depths of inner historic space. In this case a politics of salvation would have the soul of the people on its side. And if this is achieved I can imagine an overwhelming acceptance for the necessary measures, achievable in relatively few years, so that the obstructing forces, however powerful they may be, will be pushed back to passive resistance. Why could it not happen one day in every large bank, that members of the board should discover that there are more important things than finance, and that it is not compatible with human dignity to be just a functionary serving the flow of money?

The values we are concerned with can only be saved if we resolve to bring about a revolutionary renewal of the institutional structure, thereby latching on to the strongest political-psychological predispositions of our people. Governments today are unable to find an answer to the ecological crisis – and yet, in spite of all their bad experiences, people of democratic countries have retained a feeling that there *must* be an authority for the common weal, although it must be a worthy one with genuine authority – of a kind which current parliaments cannot provide, since their members are under all kinds of obligations, though not to their consciences. Let parliaments for the moment stay as they are, in order that special interests, since they exist, can continue to be bargained with; but let us create an additional authority for the general interest, a form of genuinely overarching presidency – though later we must be more concrete.

Without a powerful, overarching authority, bourgeois democracy is in no way the guarantor but much more the exhaust system of individual autonomy. It is a constitution which is adequate for the race for unlimited capital accumulation. There *are* alternatives for securing freedom of opinion and even of joint control of general affairs, which lie in the direction of a new, well-considered 'tribal constitution' for the whole of humanity, as well as for all its 'tribes'.

The new solution must first of all be regularly advocated by a competent personage; for only in a personified form will it be perceptible to the majority of people. Since the structure at whose leading edge this figure could appear does not exist, the demand must first express itself as a movement-supported candidacy for a different condition of the state. The charismatic portrayal must avoid shying back in face of the foreseeable outbreaks of hatred coming from structurally-conservative forces. The prophecy must be publicly risked. Perhaps there is also the possibility of a double-candidacy of an inspired politician still in line with the realism of the democratic structure, and a political prophet. Both would need to have a conservative cut of personality but a non-authoritarian character[8]. People could learn again that charisma is a power which is beyond good and evil and challenges us, individually and collectively, to think about purification.

This following of charismatic leaders has its difficulties. After all, in a country like Germany, it was always one and the same people throughout history that gave first to its dukes and later to its kings a place on their shield; that threw itself into a millennial movement (1000 AD) in the upswing to the high Middle Ages; that expected from its emperors not only territorial peace but also the Peace of God; that later rose up under Thomas Müntzer against the old order, to gain more from the Reformation than just a new state church; that rose up in 1813, in 1848 and then against the regional princes who no longer had any imperial qualities, so that a republic should grow more worthy than the divine right of kings; that in 1870/71 bubbled with enthusiasm behind Bismarck for the illusion of a new empire; and around 1933 behind Hitler, once again for the idea of a *Reich*.

In Russia it now appears that Stalinism was the larval stage of a new great beginning, possibly dawning now. We Germans are more thoroughly wrecked, so politically our form must be wholly born anew. Even so there is a continuity to the contemporary Green, ecological movement reaching back at least to the youth-inspired beginning of this century, to the *Hohenmeissner*, as a reaction to monetary industrialism, and the history of it has something to do with the polarity of Green and brown, which is characteristic of the German social movement in the twentieth century.

In Germany, our mistake was that we refused to question the *power* which stood *behind* the brown fascist movement, which was simply vitality itself – admittedly already disposed and channelled toward catastrophe by the concrete historical situation. But that was then: authoritarianism and resentment are now weaker and self-insight is stronger. Hardly anything can lead away from fascism more effectively than the therapeutic and spiritual movement, because it works on aggressions and resentment, makes them conscious, and reduces them.

Something better can result from those same energies which then were disposed to bring about catastrophe, and even from the disposition toward the *Teutonic furore*, if they are exposed to consciousness and so brought under control. There is no more objectionable thought than that of a new 1933! Yet precisely this can save us. The *ecopax* movement *is* the first German people's movement since the Nazi movement. It has to redeem Hitler too – the psychological tendency through which he, though weakened, is still in us – as Russia is now redeeming Stalin, without making a devil of him, without excusing him, and with all reverence for sacrifices made under his influence. The economic miracle of the 1950s-80s again almost transformed the West Germans into a 'people without space', even more real and intensive. But this time the energy is mainly directed inward, even if only because there is no longer any external boundary which really yields or appears to be yielding.

Let us admit: parliamentary democracy will not survive the ecological crisis unchanged, because democracy cannot stop the crisis. There must be a better way, and especially one that is free from the use of force for adapting institutions to the challenge. Whether this is possible or not depends upon the conscious consensus for such a transition, including a conscious working-up and mastering of history. The energy which in Germany could run in the direction of a new Hitlerism needs to be re-arranged towards a better perspective on investing the power. Each nation has its own ghosts to deal with, and this is Germany's ghost.

NOTES

(1) Rudolf Bahro, *The Alternative in Eastern Europe*, (London: Verso, 1978), p437.

(2) Leary, p156ff.

(3) Without doubt it was the original Akhenaton who first demonstrated that with the breakthrough to this stage one is actually *consumed* with insight and is unable to make or preserve a state. The king was the victim of the euphoria of his nervous system, and his attention was so distracted, both internally and externally, from the realities of power politics, that he – although himself terroristic in the establishment of the new sun cult – at least opened the way to catastrophe. Anyway this at that time completely new stage of consciousness first emerged on the basis of unstable nervous systems, even from phenomena of degeneration and decadence. This was no different in the case of the later Roman Caesar Heliogabulus, and there is no purpose at all in damning these figures on the one hand for pragmatic-political or even narrow-minded moralistic reasons, or on the other hand in praising them for their psychic breakthrough. If it occurred at the imperial level responsible for the beehive, it had to be tragic, because the entire intermediate structure to several stages down socially was almost completely missing, while in the mind of the outstanding individual it was fragile enough. But today such achievements of the nervous system can be occasions for an integrated structure and the peak of a solid pyramid of 'consciousness castes', both in the individual and in the society.

(4) To be found for example in: *Deutscher Geist: Ein Lesebuch aus zwei Jahrhunderten*, Vol 1, (Frankfurt 1982).

(5) Kurt H Biedenkopf, *Die neue Sicht der Dinge, Plädöyer für eine freiheitliche Wirtschafts- und Sozialordning*, (Munchen, Zürich, 1985), p211.

(6) Biedenkopf also refers to the churches, but doesn't go as far as the question, which really lies quite close, of what the foundation of their new green posture is – in fact a most unsolid one! The Christian-western picture of God, which became the foundation for our later science and technology, has been crafted as genuinely expansionistic. Otherwise we would not have had a Crusader church at the first high point of our civilisation, and would not stand today in face of the self-made last judgment. Hence this tradition in its never-revised official shape offers no position for taking action against the unleashed powers of science, technology, and capital, which indeed had emerged from it in a necessary fashion. Jesus, contemplating 'his' church, could only renew the idea of tearing the temple down in order to build it anew.

(7) Günter Rohrmoser, *Krise der politischen Kultur*, (Mainz: 1983), p330.

(8) I designate the figures as masculine, because what we are immediately concerned with is the creation of a state-related ecological order to stop the Megamachine. In the meantime women also take a more influential part in these still patriarchal functions which nevertheless – although absolutely nothing is to be said against their participation, they too have to go at least partly through this – is not their own domain. This is much more the renewal of the culture, something which goes much deeper. Naturally it wouldn't do any harm if political offices of the conventional sort, for the sake of this deep transformation, were to have feminine-minded incumbents, which does not necessarily mean that they should be occupied by women. At issue here is much more the strengthening of the social influence of the feminine mode of behaviour, than such things as quota allocations for women in functions belonging to the Megamachine.

16. Overcoming Ecological Crisis

An Emperor's Dream

A long time ago I was gripped by Franz Werfel's novel *The Forty Days of Musa Dagh*. He gives an account of something which really occurred.

During the second year of World War I a community of Armenian farmers numbering perhaps five thousand, which had settled on the Syrian coast, decided not to allow itself to be driven into the desert and annihilated by the Young Turk government without offering resistance. The Young Turks treated the Armenians in just as criminal a way as the Nazis were later to treat the Jews. They withdrew to the *Musa Dagh*, the mountain of Moses, and there withstood three Turkish attacks until, after forty days, and at the last minute, they were rescued by a French naval detachment.

Parables are never literally valid. This was a conscious campaign of extermination, and while the logic of self-extermination of currently-accepted economics and politics is inherent, such incidents are an unintended though accepted side-effect. Nevertheless I am forced to compare the latter with the atmosphere of the withdrawal from the villages and the far-reaching social change which the conservative Armenian farmers took upon themselves, because they no longer possessed any alternative to perishing. It is not a question of an *ideal*, but of the worthiest imaginable mastering of an emergency situation on the part of a community which could still be surveyed as a whole, and which was in no way seeking new goals.

The community of the seven Armenian villages was small enough to permit a solution without recourse to terror, although not without coercion in the face of private egoisms. The large majority was indeed unprepared for the change. Almost to the end, when it was already completely useless, those who were previously better off and even rich defended their old property-status at least symbolically, even though all provisions and especially the herds of sheep, by which status was measured, had had to be communalised. The social structure changes itself according to the situation, even though within the limits of the all-too-human. A new hierarchy formed itself, that of a war tribe. Only few of them had a sufficient distance from their ordinary roles to enable them to step beyond what they normally did. But two of these had that certain charisma which enabled them to be the soul of a resistance. Without them the Armenian farm people, more prepared for long-suffering than a western people would be, would not have roused themselves up.

One of these was Gabriel Bagradian. After more than twenty years as a Paris intellectual, he returned home with his French wife, initially just to take care of business matters after the death of his elder brother. As an artillery officer Bagradian had participated in a Turkish field expedition in the Balkans. When he saw the disaster coming, he made an inventory of the terrain of the mountain homeland and studied all the resources of the villages before the farmers had begun to be seriously worried. Thus when the hour of danger came he had a plan of defence worked out and could offer a perspective to his people. He, in effect still a stranger, became the unchallenged war-king of the tribe.

The other is Ter Haigasun, the orthodox chief priest of the communities, a skeptical man who was to experience some miraculous events on the mountain, some saving coincidences which nevertheless seemed to be more than coincidences. When the Turkish expulsion order came, he called a popular assembly together in the garden of Bagradian's house. He did not open the proceedings with a comforting, rousing or resigned speech – he did not allow any illusions that the people would survive this test, but told them the bitter truth in its entirety, that nobody would survive this time, and even said that there was little prospect of a dignified death. In this light the people decided in favour of *Musa Dagh*, although a minority, grouped round a different pastor, decided not to resist the evil. Ter Haiġasun was not only their spiritual shepherd and moral judge, but became the supreme head of the people and finally, because the elected council came to grief on account of the vanities of a few important members, he became an involuntary dictator without personal despotism.

Something similar to this epic may be the best we can await, unless we act earlier – as if in the moment of the acutest danger. These Armenians stood in the kind of situation of which it is said in Schiller's *Wallenstein*, the people knew far better what to do in a situation of hated coercion than in one of a difficult choice.

The subjectivity of salvation leads to the dream of a saving social power constituted out of it. After all it wants to 'find the state which is suited to it'. Here 'state' is used in the old and comprehensive Platonic sense, meaning the institutional constitution of the social body, grounded in morality. I think that now we need to be naive enough to examine the problems of social power once again from the point of view of their archaic substance, from the archetype of the problem of the prince or hero.

In earlier times people placed such authorities as the war-king and the priest in opposition to each other, without being completely aware of the part played by their own projection. Now it is up to us to construct into a social authority our own imperial nature, a nature which, in full public consciousness of the process, must not alienate itself. A people which is only half-way aware of itself and its situation may perhaps project a preceptor, but not a Hitler. It requires much more than the ordinary level of regressive mother-complexes and father-complexes – it requires mass-obsession, rigidity and resentment, for the rat-catcher to gain entrance to the stage instead of the preceptor.

These things have little to do with 'above' and 'below', but a great deal with the way in which a social movement is today more than ever composed of individuals capable of awareness of how it gets its consensus, or through which representative pattern or group this consensus communicates itself, and of how capable of communication and communion this medium is. Certainly a new solution for the whole of society can only be worked beyond that structure of consciousness in which authority and subordination mutually corrupt each other.

Even if impulses for a Turn-around movement will hardly emerge from the old structures, they nevertheless *can* come from people who are still bound up in them. A leading politician, who fundamentally wants to change something, has personally no more basic problem than any other critical spirit, and there is no other criterion here than the consistency and integrity of the person concerned. If s/he comes from 'above', then he must leave behind his or her identification with power; if s/he comes from 'below', so also with his or her identification with being oppressed.

Both a tyrant and a slave are hidden within each person (along with disguises and paradoxes), and the two figures correspond with each other in the individual and the social body. Even the reformatory constellation is affected by this. But a solution to the ecological crisis depends very much on how strong, and in how many individuals, is the self-responsible middle ground between the two precarious poles. Whether or not there will be terror will not be decided by future despots nor by our warning about this, but by the strength or weakness of the alternative structure of consciousness, on which basis a convincing general solution is worked out and proposed, around which a movement can form and organise itself.

If such a new crystallisation is missing, while no community obligation to the existing order has a compelling strength, people can only proceed from the basis of their immediate, short-term, and private interests, so that all that remains in common is resentments and anti-attitudes – such was the social basis for the devastation which broke out in the former Yugoslavia in the early 1990s. If, on the contrary, the vision of a new order exists, and if its design is already visible, then an association of the best individual efforts could result. Most people are fully capable of rising up to their fundamental, long-term and general interests. Admittedly the atmosphere will be determined in this or that case by very different characters, according to whom it will be our evil or our good spirits that take the middle of the stage.

The basic decision to 'moor the boat to the bank' can only be made when the entire population is ready – ready at least in its deeper layers – to support it. Those individuals who form the privileged decision-making elite of our current society must re-orient their compasses to find something different from that property-usurping and world-circumnavigating behaviour which is so typical for our culture. But how is this to happen without an institutional framework which meets with it and rewards such behaviour? For centuries our entire political system has rested on the principle that 'the whole takes care of itself' if each person takes care of his or her private interests.

Here in Germany after 1945 this uncommitted individualism has been legitimated up to the hilt by our transatlantic cousins, who have had more practice in using it. In such a situation, just networking the forces dedicated to an ecological Turn-around is not enough; over and beyond this the new emerging whole needs a strong, visible symbol. And it is only human nature to expect that this symbol will come in the form of a human being who pre-embodies the new constitution. It could also be a group of humans. In any case it is time to get rid of that anti-personalism which complies so nicely with our individual narcissism: 'no power for anybody', and above all 'no prominence for anybody'. For me the words of Hölderlin express a higher attitude: "But if one person is fully human, is not he more than hundreds who are only partly human?"

The task of bringing our social existence back into line with the balance of nature, and of arranging for it to be contractive and centripe-tal, focusing economically on householding rather than on enterprise, means that the medium will need to have a strongly feminine accent. For breaking through this mass of civilisatory concrete strong charis-matic forces will be needed. The requisite capacity, latent in the core of the human being, will reveal itself in all those who participate in the movement; for something of it is always liberated if people take even one step to free themselves from the spider's web of dependency and interest-politics. Whoever makes the assumption that charismatic po-tency is incompatible with enlightenment and critical ability helps to reproduce a constellation in which such a false polarity can manifest itself again.

The political, institutional aspect of such a Turn-around movement cannot be better grasped than through the imaginary figure of the 'hero of an ecological turning-point'. For the European north-south axis as a whole, this archetype can best be visualised in an emperor's dream. As we picture to ourselves the experience of our failure with the purely secular state constitution, together with the experience of the *godhead in ourselves*, this imperial authority also takes its place *within ourselves*, not *over* us.

The question concerning a 'hero' for a saving transformation is independent of the fact that fears and hopes, varying from day to day, link themselves up with it. The psychological resistance which arises to oppose personal leadership can justify itself in Germany on account of the negative experience of the National Socialist period, and must thereby presuppose that the psychopath at the head of a great people discloses more about himself than about the people. Even now Hitler is the great excuse of those who fear their own subordination.

Where everything is fully structured, an outstanding representative may be superfluous, although the monarchistic impact can enhance the creativity of a society as it interacts with its situation. But in times of deep crisis it mostly comes to such a projection, and attention should focus on the *quality* of this projection – primarily on the character and intellectual integrity of those who vote. In Germany the projection has long had the form of an emperor's dream together with the corresponding idea of a *Reich*. If, last time, 'precisely he' came, in the form of Hitler, this tells us a great deal about the actual social and spiritual constitution of the Germans in the first half of the twentieth century, which one way or another would have created for itself an appropriate expression.

Antonio Gramsci, referring back to Machiavelli, has thought of the modern Communist Party as the (collective) hero of a transformation. Earlier Schiller in his *Wallenstein* struggled with the same theme. I have already spoken about Plato's *Republic*. In India the emperor Ashoka sought to govern with the world-conception of Buddha. In Britain the fallible myth-hero Arthur was set in contrast to the sage Merlin. In China for 2,500 years, and into the struggles of the Mao Tse-tung era, the Confucian and Taoist conceptions of a lordly and a non-lordly sage stood opposite to each other as 'hero' images. The contents differed, but all the time we were concerned with more than class-interest. The rhetorical theme confirmed itself as a necessary authority *in* the individual, so that one could just about say: the appearance of the true hero is only the complement of the empty place within us, of that intraindividual space in which we do not measure up to the categorical imperative.

As long as we project at all, personalising is fully normal, and to refuse it is merely a repression which will in some way avenge itself. It is only western individualism which here fears so much the *tyrant*, because paradoxically they belong together: the neglected whole appears in this *misshapen* form. In Asia the succession of state forms in the west described by Plato – from the (theocratic) monarchy through aristocracy (or oligarchy) to democracy, which in its degeneracy led to mob rule, which then brings about tyranny, so that this then evolves into the original monarchy – did not happen in comparable form. For this reason Lao Tzu, who from our perspective appears anarchistic, didn't have any problem in envisaging the social whole as governed by a kingly sage, in a manner totally different from the despotism to which, in face of the furies of private interests, Plato saw himself driven.

For Lao Tzu, the emperor was responsible for taking care of the *harmony* of the world, which means on no account disturbing it through intervention. Earlier, I quoted his concept of the human constitution, according to which somebody would be suited to be 'master of the world', because it seemed to me to be exemplary for the goal-direction according to which a contemporary 'hero of the ecological Turn-around' would act, and indeed intervene, because he would find that the balance has already been deeply disturbed. But with Lao Tzu one does not find this fundamental 'separation of powers', as it has developed with us, between 'true' and 'superficial' politics, and which derives from distinguishing between spiritual and secular order – a distinction which he himself would have regarded as ultimately *not* in order. In the Taoist state conception, social power is both holy and profane at the same time: they are two aspects of a polar unity, and may not be torn apart from each other.

Naturally personalising is primarily an aid to breathing life into the proposed idea of order. The *form* of the state is in my eyes not a measure of value in itself. I do not believe in any intrinsically-best constitution, such as for example representative democracy. Certainly it corresponds best to the modern European form of individuality and the corresponding type of civilisation which spread out all over the world. But this form of constitution – however much there may remain something substantial in it to preserve – has become questionable. *In that representative democracy appears to make it empirically impossible to define anew the general good, it is unsuitable for a situation in which society must transcend its own nature.*

It was always a question of a fitting, good and just order of the whole, or in Christian language 'theocracy' – which appeared in many versions,

from science to the environmental police, on purely humanitarian grounds, and in the course of doing so a large number of honourable motives will be exploited and perverted. We will yet be thankful for the police, because they will postpone murder and homicide among those who are predisposed to fight for survival. And the most important thing we should notice: all this follows *not* from perfidious conspiracies among a ruling minority, but simply from the existence of the Megamachine and the hazards it causes, which we indirectly endorse as long as we want to rebuild it instead of pulling it down.

Anti-industrial resentments are much weaker now than they were sixty years ago, because the blessings of industrialism are so widely spread around that they have become the foundation of the security of the political regime with which the Megamachine has provided itself. It is basically accepted. It is for this reason that, as soon as the system as a whole has adapted itself to 'environmental protection', the immediate panic-reactions will refer back to the murderous 'side effects' of the Megamachine, not its core principles.

Clearly, supported by traditional 'social' movements, there will be no system-changes. Political struggles have a system-conformist function – at issue is merely the realm of stability between inner peace and world market effectiveness. Neither of the two main industrial powers, capital and labour, will break the basic agreement. Any partisanship for one of the two sides confirms the rules of the game of the industrial disaster.

No genuine motivational strength emerges any more from this whole normality. Organised selfishness has lost all moral status. The players of the special interests are beginning to appear contemptuous. Even the party-political 'carriers of hope', will, in the epoch which has begun, never have anything more than the happiness of an electoral episode, because the deception of offering leadership rooted in the old structure, will be exposed ever more quickly.

What we normally understand by politics is simply not political enough. Politics is mere *politicking*, and becomes more and more a part of the problem instead of its solution. In fact, all that counts now is what people can offer in order to make a new start spiritually and practically. Only when enough people do this, giving out signals of readiness for a Turn-around, will something happen institutionally which breaks the disastrous continuity.

Seen as such, leadership is not a command function, but the communication process in which the creative elements of a grouping meet together to illuminate the path and goal of their initiative. In the ideal case this communication embraces the whole of society. In this case leadership does not come from outside, but from within, and is much more readily *in front* than *above*. Since the state is also the shadow of individualism and egoism, all it can do is recede if the form of individuality which it complements diminishes. The striving for power cannot either be domesticated or overcome by rulers, but only in the *human being*.

In reality we have to ask about conditions with which the human being overtaxes him/herself in adapting to the civilised world, instead of adapting this civilised world to him/herself. Even more important than convivial tools is a convivial social order, a political constitution on the human scale. With the ecological crisis we will become aware of how closely the danger we are in is bound up with elementary contradictions of human nature, which can indeed be institutionally strengthened (for better or worse), but ultimately have not been caused by these structures – it is much more likely the other way about. To proceed in a truly fundamentalist manner means to seek for a new solution to these basic problems. The tempo of our devastating history does not appear to allow us either the time or the peace for this.

So we see ourselves facing the following dilemma: in order to keep any future option open at all, something must happen to stop the Megamachine. This is inconceivable except through a command. But with the highest probability this would only lead us to 'solutions' which once again strengthen the final cause of the catastrophe – its subjective drives which lead into an anxious and greedy subordination. But couldn't the question be: after we have claimed for ourselves the dignity of queens or kings, how is a tyranny which operates out of a mentality of 'divine right' possible? The first thing which kings and queens have to learn has always been: order yourself.

Transcending Oneself

For nonconformist militants, a comradely *discussion* with ordinary politicians is an affront – which has to be endured. For this it is mainly necessary to overcome negativity born of inferiority complexes and feelings of weakness.

The *ecopax* movement has given accented expression to a change in the *Zeitgeist* (spirit of the time), in the collective psyche. Deep cultural currents are stronger than all special power interests. However exploitative may be the attitude they take to it, power interests have to take account of the spirit of the time. Such was the case in the falling of the Iron Curtain. Apart from this it is improbable that a mass society in ecological crisis would stay on the rails, if its whole regular superstructure blocks. It would also be expensive, not just materially. Our society needs an institutional structure for the orderly withdrawal from the dead-end mode of progress which, promising happiness through industrial mass-production, is more and more revealing itself as a failure.

A social movement cannot directly bring about such a new constitution. Yet the more intensively it is present in general consciousness, the more it would work to this end. However, this presupposes that it does not allow itself to be bound up in the old structure round-the-clock. It works by preparing an *atmosphere* in the country. This comes about through a radical clarification of the situation (the true meaning of the Greek word *apocalypse*), through compromise-free criticism of those half-measures and evasions through which those who are politically responsible seek to sneak away and also many 'victims' who do not want to recognise themselves as *accomplices*. Furthermore, it happens as we start living out the subjectivity of salvation as the starting point of a different politics – and do it in such a way that the rest of society notices the pull radiating from communitarian nodal-points in the network of the new culture of love.

Now, in this end section, I turn once again to Kurt Biedenkopf, in that I acknowledge that he has at least touched upon all the important points. He says directly that we are "not in the same way essentially *dependent*" upon the *present* organisation of the legal political order "as the passengers of the Titanic in their ship on the high seas. At least within limits we can 'get off'. At times when the functioning capability of political installations is on the decline, people are able to help themselves"[1]. Only when a reciprocity exists between autonomous changes 'below' and a consistent reform-impulse 'above' does a sufficient gradient come into existence. But what is now already possible are spiritual preparations which do not rest upon a distinction between 'below' and 'above', but on a horizontal network of relations between equally-striving people.

Indeed, the social-legal order must no longer be determined by the state and by other, less-authorised actual powers. Right must come *before* might. Otherwise the 'rectification of concepts' (Confucius' basic demand as political adviser, also central for Biedenkopf[2]) would only bring a stabilising and upgrading of the condition of the state whose foundations are at variance with ORDO, the new order. Nothing else is worthwhile – because nothing else is more able to save us than the attempt to 'rectify concepts' *right down to their foundations*, to arrange society *from the ground up* according to the Tao, the original-natural run of things, and so to exert our spirit that it is capable of completing the circle. This does not mean wanting to restore something old: it means to satisfy, here and now, at the most fundamental level of existence, our innate conformity with natural law.

When a collision occurs between culture and nature, culture must be set right by rebuilding it from bottom to top, on penalty of its total collapse. Confucian exertions on behalf of good morals in a badly-ordered world, to bring moral regeneration in a power-apparatus, are no longer enough, if they ever were. It can be a wonderful adventure to bring ancient motivations into play again at the level of awareness which is possible today. In doing this we will not fall back into barbarism, since we already know too much for this to happen. *There could scarcely be a harder test for our capacity for consciousness than the ecological crisis.* It will no longer be this or that motive which is put to the test, but *motivation* as a whole.

We must rediscover our roots as well as cultivate higher up in the tree of our knowledge, our *Logos*. Even in the spiritual area, tearing down and building anew is possible. And doing this is more rational when it is foundations and piles that we are concerned with. This does not require that we throw away modes of questioning and differentiating which have already shown themselves as fruitful. It is possible to take a new approach to the matter, for we are not *forced* to be constrained by the foundations of the earlier building.

The ecological crisis not only compels us to perceive the everlasting within changing forms – it offers also the joyful opportunity for clearing away all the flotsam and jetsam accumulated during the course of history. "Law and justice are inherited, like an eternal sickness". How many things there are which were originally right, and which in time have not simply become false, but also wrongly integrated!

In view of this challenge there is probably no more difficult question than that of the function of the state for a humanity which is growing together in a world-embracing way. The European solution, which begins with the *Magna Carta Libertatis*, and ends in general Napoleonism, has been tried and found wanting.

Our national and legal constitution (I don't mean primarily the written text) is, *taken as a whole* the adequate expression of a society which saws away at the evolutionary branch on which it is sitting. It is absolutely unsuited for survival, even for the next fifty years. The unsuitability resides in structures far more fundamental than those which usually become visible or undergo subliminal changes – so that all we need to do is wait.

Naturally the question of the (residual) legitimacy of the state cannot be brought up from the point of view of bourgeois resentment, but only from that of a critic of the *entire* consciousness-structure of society, which expresses itself in institutions *as well as* in the attitudes of single individuals. Biedenkopf complains that 'inner sovereignty' will be handed over to the "anarchy of the interest gang"[3]. "The struggle over the distribution of social resources, purchasing power, property, power and control has become the decisive basic principle"[4].

And he sees that the evil is deep-seated: "Even the economic and social-political structures, which have their roots in the ground of the industrial revolution, continued to be stamped by the experience of expansion. Growth is a part of their structural inheritance"[5]. "The drive to growth *can* only be overcome if the group-egoistic dynamics of social segments can be caught and directed again toward the goals of the whole"[6]. Yes, and again yes! The problem of our time, the crisis of legitimacy, consists in the fact "that a growing number of people sees our society as existentially threatened by dangers which emanate from *the existing structures and institutions of the society and the state...* The 'expansive society' overtaxes its legal order as well"[7].

It is clear that Biedenkopf does not see the degeneration of the essence of parliamentary democracy in the reduction of the struggle of special interests (even though it arose with industrialism?!). And this in spite of the fact that some 'interest gangs' are to be found who could buy whole countries. And the most powerful of all do not even have to participate in the struggle, because their influence is already built in in advance.

Every reformer begins with an appeal to management colleagues, reminding them of the principles they hold, which are upheld verbally though long since disavowed in deed. He says to them that they will condemn themselves to ruin if they do not rouse themselves for re-generation. From a certain point, the majority will realise first unconsciously, and shortly thereafter consciously, that for the sake of their own survival they must sacrifice their accustomed institutional protections. But then there will also be found a leader to 'new shores'. The strength of the conservative reformer is that he does not turn against institution as such, *but against these unfit ones*, because he is *for* competent institutions, and in this is united with the *common sense* of the people. But then he must reach out far enough to find these competent institutions!

Not even Biedenkopf realises the true size of the task. Are not economic interventionism and the underlying struggle for distribution mere epi-phenomena? For to take up the sword scratches only the external skin of *homo conquistador*. We do not need interventions, but *one* intervention package, such that the Megamachine stops – at least for a large moment of reflection!

Can we and dare we really risk envisaging an enormous despotism to create and maintain a measure of order? The market must be limited to really necessary exchanges beyond the locality. We *must* ration what we eat and consume, and we *must* limit our numbers. This is not a call for regulation 'starting tomorrow morning', but a demand that we *recognise a principle*. The ecological crisis casts such very serious doubt on the world situation, and especially on all forces having a great influence on and priority in it, that there may be a possibility of forcing back even the most powerful special interests, and for clearing the way to give prior passage to fundamental needs which, for all of us, result from the *conditio humana* and from the need of the whole to thrive.

In summarising, I wish to lengthen Biedenkopf's lines a little, certainly taking some of them beyond the provisionally-intended horizon.

Firstly. ORDO as starting point means that economic evolution may no longer be left to itself, but must be subordinated to a social, a *de facto* moral rule, to a *picture of humanity* (which should be newly painted, as was last done at the time of the Renaissance). The anonymous and autonomous dominion of the economy over human life-processes must be eliminated, and everything standing in the way of this must be altered. *As long as the economy has the state, the law, morality and human beings as its functionaries, all hope of salvation is in vain.* We must appeal from the entirety of human existence in order to regulate (subordinate) the economy.

Secondly. As in the case of no other politician who has expressed himself consistently, for Biedenkopf the most dangerous characteristic of western civilisation stands in the centre of attention: its internally-unlimited material expansivity. So it is a project which concentratedly focuses on limiting the dynamics of accumulation, and on removing the tension from the drive which pushes people in the old direction.

Thirdly. Interest groups, at the centre of the struggle for the re-distribution of goods, play a disastrous role – if not as the main driving force, dominating society and economy altogether, then nevertheless as mechanisms and reinforcers. In order to restore the 'inner sovereignty' of the state and its capacity to serve the whole, it must look around for new social strength and power which can stand up to organised special interests. Since the body of the state as a whole is addicted to growth, and its personnel has been attacked by the virus of corruption in general, Biedenkopf has in fact pointed out the vacant area in which a new institutionalisation must take place. This can only be achieved with the people, not by some party or other, nor even by the public itself. It requires a plebiscite in the grand style, both to mobilise the population *and* to win the constitutional assignment.

Fourthly. Something which in my opinion is more important than the political tug-of-war for the national treasury: Biedenkopf seeks a means originating in the human situation, for defusing the struggles for distribution. Dependence upon an incorruptible, super-complex whole would seek to lower thresholds of social anxiety, yet it would tend to heat up struggles for position. People ought to be able to get back for themselves at least a part of what they produce for existence, instead of nourishing bureaucracy with their contributions. Shortening of working hours and a basic social insurance would primarily widen the scope for individual initiative, in that people can determine their lives anew.

Fifthly. Biedenkopf sees increasingly sovereign small living circles as a new centre of the social order. They could build themselves up from the residual nuclear family to larger units ('second-order tribes'). This can only avoid being a dream if they also become the new cells of the economic evolution. As soon as they want to join, the people must get the land and the tools necessary for their basic requirements into their own hands. Industrial production and infrastructures must be understood as subsidiary to this and be fitted in accordingly. A new subsistence and personal economy comes into existence as the core of a contractual mode of production. Modern technological knowledge will function in quite a different way if it arises from and is used by such social entities. Small-scale production can be productive today, especially when the development is organised around convivial tools.

Sixthly. Biedenkopf heads for a Green-transformation policy by means of a popular majority. Sub-cultures frequently express in a more radical way the crisis of the whole, but no new whole will crystallise around them. He offers a reference-point where radical and off-centre positions, which for the moment are unavoidably in the minority, can meet together with the normality. For me the tense lines of cleavage cut across the traditional social and political camps. Our customary political squabbles and safeguards are unbelievably small-minded and irresponsible. All down the line the parties are fighting a false battle, which can only mean that they are false parties, directly opposed to the necessity for an understanding of our drama and a path to salvation. It is not just this or that policy, but the political system as a whole which is functioning falsely: it is the *whole formation* made by capital *and* work, Right *and* Left of the rich western countries which has become a Titanic steaming hell-for-leather toward the iceberg.

All that is interesting now is whatever is suitable for 'mooring the boat to the bank', stopping the machines – and as a precaution starting the lifeboats. Those having the 'new view of things' – supposing they really have it – will become increasingly clear that tomorrow they belong together, wherever they have come from. Why not go together openly now, why not form a new social body? One behaves subversively just by paying no attention to the customary material, and conversely one behaves conformingly by playing along in the old orders of battle.

The greatest problem which I see consists in the temptation to see the *conditio humana* as culturally Eurocentric, and the whole as bounded by the *nation*. We can no longer be saved by any inner reconciliation conditioned by that monopolistic position which the white man has assumed for centuries. We drag everyone along with us against the limits of nature, by means of the material standard for which others everywhere strive. The embattled situation of whites in South Africa can, from the social point of view be the paradigm for our situation tomorrow. The rest of humanity can simply no longer tolerate our model untransformed[8].

NOTES

(1) Kurt H Biedenkopf, *Die neue Sicht der Dinge, Plädöyer für eine freiheitliche Wirtschafts- und Sozialordning* (München, Zurich: 1985), p223.

(2) *Ibid*, p102ff.

(3) *Ibid*, p189.

(4) *Ibid*, p209.

(5) *Ibid*, p157.

(6) *Ibid, p201.*

(7) *Ibid*, p202.

(8) I find it dangerous when Richard von Weizsäcker, who sees the gigantic shears, nevertheless regards the path of our civilisation as "an irreversible world-civilisatory evolution" (*Spiegel* 12-1986). It is indeed this, if we don't make a turn-around, and to the general misfortune, on a scale for which there will be no example. The domestic environmental crisis is in reality the smallest, if also the most immediately effective occasion for drawing the small living circles in such a way into the middle of an ecological turn-around project as I have indicated, certainly going beyond Biedenkopf's permission. Incidentally, even a Wilhelm Röpke was of the opinion that towns of more than 50-60,000 inhabitants, gently stated, are not good places and should gradually be reduced in numbers. For the first time in world history we could stride consciously and preventively towards such fundamental changes in our culture.

17. The Matrix of the Political Turn-Around

Two Great Coalitions: the Triple Arrangement of Metropolitan Interests

I have already quoted how one of our greatest enlighteners, Montesquieu, wanted to deal with the problem of the imperial Metropolitan consensus, which we have just touched upon. Just as in the first centuries AD the poorest freeman was privileged – if he were fortunate enough to be a Roman citizen, and thus bound into the consensus of the Metropolis – so in the same way every citizen of an affluent democratic country is also privileged. We could afford World Wars I and II and still be able to play, passports in hand, the role of world citizen first class wherever we go. Against this background, let us repeat once again the words of the great Frenchman:

> *If I knew of something useful to me and injurious to my family I would banish it from my mind. If I knew of something useful to my family but not to my country, I would seek to forget it. If I knew something useful to my country and harmful for Europe, or useful to Europe and harmful for humanity, I would regard it as a crime.*

According to this criterion our entire Metropolitan *status quo* is a crime without parallel. The Euro-American model has become a burden to the world, and fortunately at last also for us as well.

The collapse of the imperial consensus began with the *ecopax* movement. We are now also beginning to understand that 'Rome' is no longer worthy of being defended – at least not in its existing cultural pattern and political constitution. And unlike then, not even barbarian hordes now stand *ante portas* (outside the gates). Only we ourselves can free ourselves, in order to bring about the necessary transformation. We could hardly have a more favourable international situation than the present one. The formerly-competing Eastern Bloc itself has put the question almost in the same way that we must put it on our agenda – except that, while emulating their willingness to make changes, we will have no existent socio-economic system to adopt or emulate. There is a convergence of the new thinking.

But how is a majority to come out of this, which is ready to go to the roots of the ecological crisis? Here we are dealing with a particular psychological shift and new orientation in the political consensus, which has been underway since the 1960s, has manifested itself as 'Green' since the 1970s, and has been gaining in tempo since the catastrophe of Chernobyl. The idea of a politics of the ecological turning-point can naturally only spread itself among those who are ready, at the cost of their own comfort, to look the reality of world destruction in the eye and then acknowledge themselves as *contributory causes*. It is true that others are also victims, even those who promote the exterministic project. But it depends mostly on those who recognise themselves as contributory *agents*, and are no longer willing to bear this responsibility.

The actual sounding-boards of the signs of disaster are certainly *women*. But to achieve a breakthrough requires that the significantly thicker skin of the technocratic elite should also be made uncomfortable. This is a matter of personal conversion, case by case, until there occurs a mass-splitting of these exterministic monks, something which is now visibly preparing itself. At the present time the consensus for a politics of salvation is already rallying itself in very many responsible heads, even if the 'concentration per head' is not yet sufficient to bring about an individual or even corporate crystallisation. In order to avoid any misunderstanding: even though I am speaking about very many heads, I am speaking about a minority, yet it is a qualified minority, which will soon be in a position to rouse the inert bulk of the bureaucratic and technocratic red-tape worms in the silos of offices, command centres, and institutes.

Planning measures won't be enough – a new general structure must come. To propose a politics of the ecological turning-point is to propose a new state, indeed to conceive the state anew. I have already said that we must first free the sphere of law and the state from the context of the Megamachine, if there is to be any chance of getting at the material foundation, the material dynamics of the diagonal of destruction. If society is more and more endangered by the course of militarising, large-scale technology and mass-production, the will-to-life of the population drives a wedge between the existing apparatus of the state, which is formally committed to protection against damage, and the capitalistic techno-structure, the Megamachine in the narrower sense.

What is needed is to move the regulatory functions of the whole society, alienated in the great ellipse of 'society as Megamachine', into the small circle, where they will be dependent on the living spirit and will be accessible to a permanent re-determination of content made by a free decision of the general public. This move requires that the proposal for an ecological politics of salvation is efficiently manifested, spreads consensus around itself, and finally achieves hegemony in the social atmosphere. Then the real powers will yield, adapt and even seek to climb on to the bandwagon; and the old political parties, should they survive, will vie for the chance to execute the political Turn-around. The crux really doesn't lie 'above', the crux lies in the consensus which present chancellors and presidents represent, more than those of us like to admit, who see the masses as victims of malevolent seduction. The *people* must re-learn their lessons to be worthy of other representatives.

In criticising the dominant institutions, it is therefore not they which are the target, but people who are still identified with them and not yet sufficiently distanced from them – and also those in responsible positions in the whole power-complex of science-technology-capital and state. The receptivity is directly connected to how inwardly sensitive, how open for personal experience the various characters are. The decisive factor for the tempo of the regrouping would be for all those awareness-particles, already moving on new paths and catapulted out, to create a new focus out of these particles themselves. The question is to what extent people will choose to put their idealisim into practice, while for the moment even in their own families, they are still in a minority. Nevertheless, they will already have achieved a moral legitimacy, leading towards a fresh social integration in a new context.

We speak of 'new social movements', which often emerged from a reforming of older attitudes of protest still tied to the polarisation-schemes of bourgeois society. There exists today a 'new' pacifism, a 'new' nature-protection, a 'new' animal-protection, in which what is new comes from the overall context of the general transformation, which has also transferred a lot of new blood to the traditional commitments. Animal protectors, for example, can suddenly find themselves in a psychic confrontation with the entire political and psychological *status quo*, because this includes abattoirs, feed-lots, and mass animal-experimentation.

In the political field, the Greens wanted to be a foundation on the opposite shore. Others were the eco-institutes, eco-societies, eco-circles and eco-associations which have formed themselves in so many places. Still others are alternative projects of various sorts. In my opinion, those that reach furthest are the communitarian associations which undertake to build anew the entire context of daily life, on the far side of the Megamachine.

Wholly different, and nevertheless comparable to the development in the nature-protection sector of bourgeois society, the older spiritual circles are moving into the context of the new age – they often remain socially totally bound into the *status quo*, yet they are more or less anticipated. In the final analysis communitarian societies, planning their everyday working and living around an undogmatic spiritual vision and practice, will be the farthest-reaching and most stable initiatives.

All these are institutions of the new age, and it is altogether characteristic for the radical change in which we find ourselves, how many people 'do the splits' – try to get a footing in a trial fashion, with one leg in the new, while remaining in the old culture with the leg they are standing on. But in this way many people prepare for a shift in the centre of gravity, and then the energy-flow turns around in an enduring way. There then occurs a diversion of economic-financial energies, out of the old and into the new structures. These streamlets could not avoid being falsely evaluated if one were to compare them quantitatively with the mass-flows of the regular economy, because the new material cultural context must turn out to be 'cheaper' by a factor of ten and allow room for animals, plants, earth, water, air and fire to resume once again their own evolutionary direction.

Against this background of a shift of psychological forces, and with the aid of a last diagram, I want to deal with the problem of power. I call it the *matrix of the political Turn-around*. I will not yet speak of the salvation government, but look first at the tension-field in which the new social power gradually forms itself. And even this does not lead immediately into the power-politically 'ultimate' problem of building new institutions. It leads to the question of a salvation *movement*, which alone can humanly support a salvation *government* and limit it in its function. The last chapter will be dedicated exclusively to the salvation government.

The matrix of the political Turn-around refers schematically, with the rectangular block in the middle (divided into three parts), to the *totality of politically-relevant consciousness in a Metropolitan country which has been ecologically battered*, as is the case with countries like Germany. The matrix links on to the dynamics of the social movement for pulling out of the industrial system. It concerns the political struggle over the detaching of society from the diagonal of destruction, from the exterminism of the Megamachine, which manifests itself in the state (etatism) and in the economy (economism). And its goal is in the direction of that rainbow society which begins with the piles on the other shore.

The *horizontal* of the matrix is the conventional dimension of the political struggle between 'Left' and 'Right', between 'progress' and 'reaction' on the ground of the bourgeois society, which has shown itself to be in conformity with the overall character of the capitalistic formation. Salvation in face of the ecological crisis is not possible through a

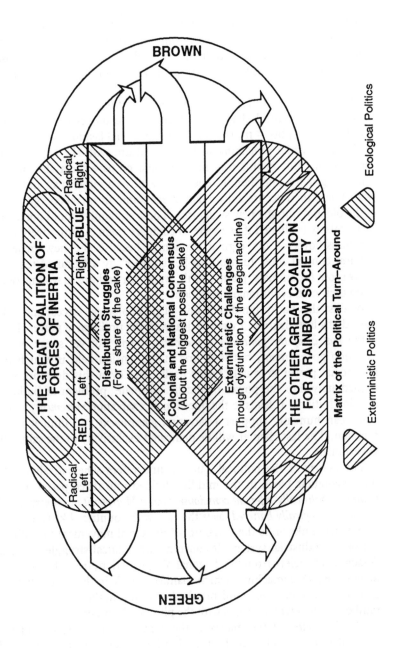

BROWN

THE GREAT COALITION OF
FORCES OF INERTIA

Radical
Left | RED | Left | Right | BLUE | Radical
Right

Distribution Struggles
(For a share of the cake)

Colonial and National Consensus
(About the biggest possible cake)

Exterministic Challenges
(Through dysfunction of the megamachine)

THE OTHER GREAT COALITION
FOR A RAINBOW SOCIETY

GREEN

Matrix of the Political Turn-Around

Exterministic Politics

Ecological Politics

power-struggle between the old political fronts, which runs parallel with the axis of destruction, and may even be identical with it. 'Etatist' Red and 'Economistic' Blue are not alternatives, but partial aspects of a false whole. The Nazi movement was already correct in its attempt to overcome this battle order.

Salvation is in no way possible through forces which follow *any sort of* special interests prescribed by the logic of the bourgeois society, and which make their actions dependent on how this logic would affect their power position. *All* of them are interested in the preservation of the common basis of life, but only *secondarily*! Since we know how normal that is it becomes all the more clear how much we need a cultural *mass-movement* in order to unlearn the patriarchal ego.

The *vertical* dimension of the matrix is the *movement* by which our whole social body is gripped and which tends in the direction of 'Green', or rather of 'rainbow'. Here the forces of inertia anchored in the hitherto-existing apparatus and the forces for ecological change stand opposed. Naturally, in reality we have a mixed situation over the entire political field of consciousness, and hardly anybody occupies only some 'official' place which might be ascribed to him (or her). There is hardly anybody who cannot feel the split in the world running through his or her own breast. This is precisely what is advantageous in the situation, for it permits a non-antagonistic *form* of the argument, a subordination of the hate-elements under the love-elements of the process of Turn-around. While for the moment institutions are stationary, it is nevertheless unthinkable that they would not be dragged along an inch or two, even before their indispensable collective reformation.

I first arrived at this orientation of an Other Great Coalition in 1980 after the foundation day of the Green Party, and in preparation for a First Socialist Conference in Kassel. In those days I was not yet free from the desire to subordinate the Green perspective to the Red one I had brought with me. I wanted to make comprehensible to the radical Left, that Green would settle into a new political topography running *diagonally* through the old party camps on the Right-Left axis. I said to the Left, that in times of all-embracing crises in civilisation one would have to deal less with class parties than with 'historical parties', with a political-psychological division (also generational) into *progressive, conservative* and *reactionary* forces. To change the world ('progressive'); to leave everything as it is with minor improvements ('conservative'); to turn the clock back ('reactionary'): these three positions would then become party-constitutional, and would weigh more heavily than class-interests, which would run parallel. But:

Admittedly even the customary concepts for characterising those 'historical

*parties' appear strangely turned around, because we need a world change
in opposition to much of what, up to now, was called* progress, *because
we must restore some things which have been historically lost. Thus the
'historical parties' now actually reduce themselves to two: one, habituated
to privilege and enjoyment of power, wants everything to carry on as it has
done up to now. One could call it the bloc of forces for perseverance, for
inertia. Sluggish forward movement on the already-established track...
The other 'party', the reforming bloc – and here somebody had the good
idea..., to quote the wise Sicilian aristocrat Lampedusa – "roll everything
over radically, so that everything stays as it is". This conservatively-
intoned aphorism is extremely useful inasfar as it characterises the way
many people who form the Green movement now are motivated. We can
count on it, that in the case of a radical rolling-over not everything would
remain altogether like it is*[1].

Against this background, I spoke of the One and the Other Great
Coalition. Theoretically this concealed a departure from left-wing political theory – with its centrality of class struggle and 'taking account of
environmental problems' – and the sociological schematic and materialism. Whoever is in a position to observe the situation here from outside
can no longer consider Metropolitan workers as a potentially revolutionary, world-freeing class, and he will also be skeptical about what
concerns the workers for multinationals in third world countries *in their
characteristics as a class*. One can be convinced that capitalism must go,
but it will not disappear on account of the struggle between wage labour
and capital.

On the contrary, what still remains from the social questions of the
19th century pushes exclusively in the direction of perfecting wealthy
bourgeois existence. The only concern is with the distribution of seats
on the Megamachine. One does not need to close ones eyes to the
internal injustices, to the ever-recurring 'new poverty' and 'new social
question' – the dominating forces themselves see to it on the grounds of
good 'social security' that such explosives are held below critical mass.
Every internal social-political solution will be shifted to the 'damned of
this earth', to the 'external proletariat'. How big the cake is which the
imperial centre can squeeze out of the world market, and how it secures
its political dominance in this way, is more important than share-
segments, for the underprivileged, the poor free people of the Atlantic
empire.

Let us assume that the rectangle in the middle of the matrix is the
totality of politically-significant social energy, political interest and
awareness of the population in a Metropolitan country – how then is this
field differentiated in the vertical direction? The division into three

which I have drawn and labelled in the rectangle is schematic and without regard for weighting. Otherwise the middle part would have to be much more extensive compared to the other two hatched areas. In the distribution-battles for money, power and influence it is just as dominant as it is in compromises over environmental politics.

Naturally the three elements of my scheme are also present in the structure of consciousness of each individual. The scheme is not meant to be corporative. Each single man or woman participates, and will have his or her options somewhere on the Left-Right horizontal. The various individuals and collectives (for example, corporate ones) distinguish themselves from each other in the configuration and weighting of the three areas of interest, and their manner of handling them. Just on this basis occurs the new polarisation between ecological and exterministic politics – according to which edge, the lower or the upper, from which we approach the whole puzzle.

Indeed, in a wide sense all interests meet together in the decision about consensus, which gets its accent from the imperial situation, but which must not remain trapped in it indefinitely. It is really decisive from which edge all this is integrated into the functioning ability and viability of the whole. Does the old Great Coalition of Forces of Inertia dominate, or is the Other Great Coalition already determining things in the direction of an ecological Turn-around? Each man or woman has opportunities of integrating into both variants, so that the affair is not forced to come out as a fifty-fifty constellation but, at least in theory, could decide one hundred percent for a new structure, in which old elements of consensus can then find their appropriate place.

The two triangles, placed on each edge, are intended to symbolise this structure problem – one for the hitherto-existing exterministic politics, and the other for the ecological politics of salvation. Exterministic politics does not ignore the environment, it treats it 'only' as a dependent variable. An ecological politics will not ignore the struggle for distribution. In reality the point is not any predetermined grouping into important and less important things, but the integration of these into each perspective.

However – here comes the exciting part – this spiritual regrouping does not take place merely as an unnoticeable diffusion of individuals who are isolated from each other. Society is not atomised to *this* extent, and it also does not function only through institutional channels. If this were the case, the play of life would exist no more. *Within* the tripartite rectangle the socio-political field is seen at rest, and the movement on the vertical axis, the re-accenting of countless particles of consciousness, is more implied than symbolised. But this rectangle is 'surrounded' by more definite political forces which specialise themselves in order to articulate various interests:

Above from extreme Left to extreme Right is the spectrum of political parties and associations which constitute the democracy of fighters over distribution; their location is on the diagonal of destruction (see diagrams in chapter one), and the result of their actions is exterministic politics.

Below – here reality creates itself in movements, yet we are dealing with an extensive unmanifested tendency which is already powerful – the new social alliance for a politics of salvation, its emerging institutions, the body of the ecological turning-point.

Left and Right are the forces of movement which feel themselves repelled by the regular political sphere and the dysfunctions of industrialism. It is not 'Red', but the polarity of 'Green' and 'Brown' which is characteristic of forces which would like to evade the Megamachine. The arrows leading out of the rectangle, Left to Green and Right to Brown, indicate from where and in which direction forces of movement push off, among them the retarding forces – social forces in the Green, and in the Brown, national resentments which flow back into the politics of extermination. As can be seen, my approach is schematic: as yet only around half of the energy of social movement goes in the direction of the Other Great Coalition, and around only a third of the energy of social movement is truly directed to the ecological crisis.

What is important with the Green movement we more or less know, or at least think we know, while foreigners won't leave us in peace because of the suspicion that it couldn't be true that Germans or other Metropolitan peoples suddenly have a popular movement directed to saving the *earth*, a movement devoid of any sprinkling of Brown. One cannot demand of the distant observer that s/he will already regard the Left-Green movement as the final political expression of a European ecological Turn-around[2]. I shall return to the problem of Left-Green politics later in this chapter. But it seems to me to be important to look into the Brown problem. I will not do this exhaustively, but I must indicate my attitude to it, because it is significant for my general political perspective.

At a Green Party meeting in Hamburg in 1984 I was not well understood, for good reasons, because I said that the Greens rose up in very much the same way as the Nazis once did. I will document, in a digression, what I said there about this.

All the time in left-wing circles the Brown ghost gets painted on the wall but it is always said "it has absolutely nothing to do with us". This is too simple and rather dangerous. Works by Hannah Arendt, Walter Laqueur, Jacques Ellul[3], and Carl Jung's *Wotan-Aufsatz*[4] point in the same direction. After the outcry at the Green Party meeting, and superficial press reports, there was no discussion of my opinion concerning this theme. The potato was too hot.

An excursion into Green and Brown
This is an edited quote from my speech at the Hamburg conference.

Even in the Green Party we cannot seriously believe that the great machine which pushes us ever more to the wall can be stopped by anything else but an insurrection. It is not a reformist time, but a reformation time that is beginning. There is a small difference here, for the Reformation includes something which Engels once called the most radical fact of German history: the great German Peasant's War. There was not just Luther. There was also Thomas Müntzer. He had led people into battle under the rainbow flag, at the front an invisible peasant-Christ, after the masters had left no other choice but rebellion. The peasants were vanquished.

It is written that he who lives by the sword will perish by the sword. Well, next time do different and better. But we must be Müntzer-like, not of the soft-living flesh of Luther, not an eco-liberal Paul's Church party, that bows and scrapes before representative democracy in the way that the late Bismarck-liberals did in 1848/49 before the constituted monarchy. For to them, the people, the wild oafs, were only permitted to speak when well dosed. First there were meetings like the unlawful assemblies around Behaim Hans in Niklashausen – but then they had something more than we did: their naive vision of the Kingdom of God. As has been said, these were just early disorganised squalls. The storm has yet to come.

Nowadays there is a 'data-processing' of a kind the masters didn't think about. People see death of forests, dioxin, low-flying planes, pollution of ground water, allergic diseases, experimenting with animals – in each case we are dealing with the whole thing and it all belongs together. The population is beginning to sum things up, to understand what it has already suspected for some years: that in the daily horror-announcements a single total catastrophe is announcing itself, and it has one deeper cause, even if not an altogether simple one. The person who understands the deep layers of the logic of self-extermination would also have a better understanding of the character of the one salvation movement which is coming.

I must speak about the relationship between the ecopax movement and fascism, but differently from what you might expect. Seen formally and structurally, movement, state, and society stand opposed to each other today in a very similar way to how they stood in the Weimar Republic, and Greens are rising up in a similar pattern to the Nazi party. In order to come out of it well this time – in order that the people's rising shall be non-violent – the Greens must not get lost. If they let themselves be co-

opted, then when the storm reaches its greatest strength and the waves reach their full height, they will be just one more system-party – there would be no better way to prepare the civil war and dictatorship which would follow hard upon it.

But there's more to say about this, particularly about the fact that the movement for peaceful transition needs a different structure from the one a political party needs, one that works from within; we do not want to set the fox to watch the chickens of a new culture. It may be only a political branch which in the decisive moment occupies the opposition, so that the machine of the state is paralysed, by a movement which allows nothing to come out of the barracks, after having split the soldiers right up into the ranks of the officers. Novotny, at the end of 1967, called in the army and security forces – and they didn't come because they were split.

A politics that clears away the giant chemical concerns, for example, clears away with them the job as access to life support... Let us begin building up a self-sustaining society independent of jobs with corporations and the European Community Agrarian Market – and make this *our positive project and main direction.*

The human being does not live to produce. The fact that we do a great deal of producing is exactly the cause of our downfall. I would like to speak about that, and about why the Other Republic needs to be primarily an association of communities – living communities with God or Goddess in the middle. And I would like to add a few words about the fundamentalistic alliance, the network we should build up across the entire land, at the back of all party and movement structures, and conceived as going far beyond the present circle to all sensitive nonconformists in all social and political camps. The fundamentalists all still see everything as rooted in a different reality which we all possess within us, but is daily covered over. The race with the apocalypse can only be won if this becomes a great time of faith, where the living spirit is poured equally over all.

Only from there can politics be newly grounded, so that it is not led back into the old vicious circle – politics of salvation comes only from there. Contrary to all appearances, ecological politics means: away with the safety belt, away with all the armament we are carrying. Then we shall live. Then also everything becomes possible politically. The idol is wobbling already. And he will fall.

Out of My Hamburg Papers

At the level of social movements in Germany since the turn of the century, Green has been the opposite pole to Brown. In the Greens today character-structures prevail which are non-authoritarian and more flexible in the form of its resentment than the Brown movement.

The two wars which Germany started have initiated a spiritual up-heaval, which in the post-war generations gradually bore fruit. The moral harvest of Germany's defeat is now at hand. Also the flight forward in military and industrial changes has superseded remaining aggressive potentials. And the economic miracle *happened* – Germans won this third war, and while the victory has now become stale, there is a cushion of satisfaction – that others are worse off. In sum, an al-together different situation than in 'Weimar' in the 1920s. Nowadays, resentment expresses itself defensively, especially in evil hatred of foreigners. There is no fascistic *movement*, but there is an *ecopax* move-ment which develops in the direction of freedom from violence, of reconciliation with the international outside world, and with nature.

Yet there are aspects where the contrast between Green and Brown can reproduce itself within the *ecopax* movement, and does so. We are not through with the old story, in that the mechanisms of alienation and atomising of the individual are still at work. It can endanger us through our alternative power mania. The struggle for position can only keep the more sensitive ones away from the party, giving them no influence on its internal political culture. Thus the influx of people who want to be led and carried by a mass movement will be promoted.

As far as the content and procedural forms of Green politics are concerned, we might like to stand as fundamentalists or as realists diametrically opposite to each other, but we can promote the realisation of power as a result of our confrontation. We could set things up so that what becomes of the Greens is something which, from the point of view of grass-roots democracy, we want to avoid: the embryo of the next state machine, the candidate for the dreaded eco-dictatorship.

In the case of an actual outbreak of catastrophe even the mob portion in general consciousness would understand itself as 'Green'. Until then there ought to be a good deal more than political structures around which an alternative can crystallise. One and the same person can, in a situation of emergency, behave in very different ways, according to which of the forces within him are addressed. To do preparatory work here is so enormously important, because in view of the ecological crisis we cannot denounce the awakening in people as 'nationalist-racist'. We must seriously open our doors to this ambivalence, we must not repress it and explain it away as non-existent.

We must look in the mirror at ourselves and at the Green movement without prejudice – it is really the first German popular movement since the twenties, and it is a formally-similar confrontation, as in the case of the Nazis, with a failing party system. We are not just a party of the Left, even though it looks like it. The Left-National or National-Neutralist view of things is false – this has to do with power-political thinking that looks to state subjects. The historical trend will be decided in the underground of the soul. It is very important that the minority with the initiative does not obscure its own contour for the sake of temporary advantages and alliances.

What nonsense to want to win back lost identities, bourgeois, national, nationalist-racist, ethnic, as if all these led toward love and life. The national and ethnic liberation movements are all victims to the Empire in this respect. If we, here in one of the core areas of the Empire, wanted to start caring for the ETA- and IRA-mentalities, the result would be a head-stand *against* the Basques and *against* the Irish. If, on the other hand, we were to pass over to the task of dissolving the Empire from within, taking the pressure away, people everywhere on earth would gain the freedom to raise themselves *above* their traditional identities. We should certainly not participate in the *repression* of old elements of identity. This must be brought into the daylight of our individual and general consciousness.

What successfully attacks the state is something original and natural, and for this reason insisting on monopoly of power won't help, not this time. In olden times political representatives and oppressors of society have always been made answerable for the relation to nature – things like earthquakes or bad harvests questioned the legitimacy of power. Even today ministers must rush as quickly as possible to the site where a natural catastrophe occurs.

But what now, when such natural catastrophes are ever more frequently home-made by humans themselves, when they are called into existence by just those structures which should be protecting society from harm? Today the state represents the negative, suicidal part of the general interest. It stands for those necrophile mental forces in all of us. It is a strengthening of the life-hostile tendencies which are innate within our whole civilisation. Unavoidably, for the state is *its institution*. Humans must make new their institutions out of different realms of their psyche, realms where they want life. Since the rational level of our existence is almost completely occupied by the alienated rationality of the Megamachine, since we ourselves have allowed our reason to be instrumentalised, so that it deals with the dialectics of technology instead of with life, we need an injection from the depths. We need to renew our institutions, and we can only do this ourselves. We mustn't give in to disappointment and the urge for revenge. The energies breaking forth do not want to be tamed, but cultivated anew.

How a millennary movement can be led, or can lead itself, and with what organs: *that* is the question. Something of this sort is coming up for discussion because the *ecopax* movement *is* a millennary movement for the founding of a new culture. Where humanity seeks to begin anew, a thousand-year kingdom is frequently the goal: for Marx the *Age of Freedom*, for Hölderlin the *Kingdom of God*. If it is asserted that nothing more could come out of the *ecopax* movement but an uprising bringing such disastrous changes as have happened before, in revolutionary situations, that would then once again be a victory for a Hitler. Be very clear about it, the *ecopax* movement is an attempt to solve a very similar problem in the next wave-trough of the capitalistic iron heel. *Things can and must go differently this time.* The more conscious we are and the clearer it becomes to each one of us, that we can fall away from the true task and degenerate, thinking "I have resolved to become a politician" – so much the better will be the people we can call upon, who will come to meet us.

Whereas in the past this movement acted externally and power-materialistically, expansively and aggressively, the *ecopax* movement makes a turn inward. It tends to avoid projecting the danger outward, seeking it rather in the inner workings of its own culture. Thus have prophets of Israel in the Old Testament explained external threats by the fact that the Jews themselves had turned away from God. This is a great example for us. For the sake of our own bodily and spiritual welfare, and even for our survival, we must in this crisis move forward into unilateral disarmament of our civilisation, not join the Empire as a counter-force.

The Greens have no idea what they are doing when they let themselves be co-opted. And the bourgeois society also has no idea what harm it is doing itself if it co-opts us. Bourgeois society risks everything if it co-opts us – just because it cannot tolerate the small risk that we represent when we are outside the gates.

Do we not sense the buildup of an earthquake in the depths, a human quake? Woe, if the volcano erupts and there is no consistent political force to make possible a constructive character to the inner upheaval! Nuclear bombs and power stations touch life only abstractly. Meanwhile the potential for crisis – not just an economic one – is more all-embracing and goes deeper than at any time before. The people are in the process of figuring things out, and going though unemployment, breakup of professional identifications, the many-sided threat of the technological revolution – all this comes together to make an emotional readiness to attempt something wholly different. If the breakthrough of the mentally-repressed meets with the predictable situation in which the issue is survival rather than the good life, then we would have a frightful transition into ecological civil war and after it, dictatorship.

In a fortunate constellation, society has created in the *ecopax* movement an organ for forestalling this hour of extremest crisis, in two different ways: firstly, by fully applying all possible brakes, in order to bring about the greatest possible effect. And secondly through timely cultural support for the uprising of the people, both spiritually and materially. The preservation of the Green party as an uncompromised instrument of mediation is a subordinate, but important aspect of this cultural task. This is why alternative power-mania stands out so clearly with the Greens. It is no accident that, in this greed, satisfied by rising up to political power, there are formal similarities to the events in the rise of the Nazi party and movement.

When an uprising comes, if the Greens are already used up or reckoned as part the unrescuable old institutional complex, the masses, without structure, will have to get on with the job of wrecking whatever is wrecking them. There are now three kinds of possibilities. Sensing their approach, one can break out into hysterical cries of warning. One can be so narrow-mindedly concerned over this leached-out party, that for the sheer noise of the ringing of bells one doesn't even anticipate the nature of the jungle into which everyone is plummeting. And finally, one can prepare oneself to ride the tiger, being at least critically aware of one's own fantasies of omnipotence, so that one is not carried away by them. To this end one must be in alliance with one's truest, deepest concerns and must not want to censor one's will-to-life. We must not throw away the baby with the bathwater.

One must love the tiger, in order that the animal only annihilates what it must annihilate: the life-hostile structure which has become dominant in our overall society, and not the human substance which is trapped in it. It must not devour any people. In short: one must want and prepare for non-violent uprising, if one does not want a civil war.

All this is risky. But the millennarian movement this time has a character like never before.

To What End Is the Nazi Comparison Necessary?

Parliamentarism as the anti-fascistic minimum. The trap is not the parliamentarism *debate*, but *parliament*. *Why* is it a trap for us, while it clearly wasn't one for the Nazi movement and party? Since *because* the Nazis were anti-parliamentarian and unconditionally hostile to the system – *we must not be*. We do indeed regard parliament as an anti-fascistic triumph! We have indeed accepted the idea that it would be 'totalitarian' to place this thing in question as being part of the whole exterministic institutional complex. And *for this reason* bourgeois liberals draw us over into their camp. Right from the beginning we have not seen ourselves as sovereign, but as a reform movement within the Empire.

There was not just the Nazi *party*. Here lies the deepest motive for my attempt to put ourselves in relation to the Nazi movement. We cannot reduce the Nazi *movement* to the imperial instrument which the Nazi *party* afterwards was: behind this *also* stood – as is said by Armin von Gleich – "a widespread criticism, supported by immediate raw experience, of conurbation, mechanisation, rationalisation and the putting of everything into a scientific mould". "This criticism", Gleich continues, "could not be accepted by a German Communist Party, resting on technical progress and rational enlightenment".

Immediately after the arrival of the Greens in Parliament in Bonn, I pointed to the slope we were letting ourselves get on to[5]. Or rather, I used the image of a transmission-mechanism. The whole system is turning, then comes its giant gear-wheel, the state, then its intermediate drive-wheel the parliament, and next the small gear-wheel the political parties, which then pass the drive right down to the grass roots. All this repeats itself again in local parliaments. Had we not thought we would be able to build a counter-slope, a counter-transmission? Shouldn't the two turning moments meet each other in parliament so that we could make the Megamachine splutter, even if we couldn't immediately block it? Had we thought we wanted to oil it anew?

The decisive question is, what re-evaluation must we undertake if we are to counter the slope of total-system-parliament, in order to bring benefit to the full unfolding of the consciousness movement in the country, and to limit power's room in which to move or manoeuvre? We must begin to create new realities and new institutions. Are we to perfect the allied democracy or blow it up?

Green and Brown – two poles of one *movement.* If we want to mobilise, then we must demand of ourselves that we keep the Green-Brown social polarity fully conscious. We are not free of the other pole, the Brown one. If we are unclear, unconscious, then no Green measures will be effective without Brown tendencies being able to climb on the bandwagon. If we want to be responsible, the demand on us is *to risk a concept of the movement which distinguishes between Left and Right, not from the beginning, but always.*

We must think of the movement as an ellipse whose axis has two poles, Brown and Green. In itself Brown is not less radical, but radical in a different sense from Green. By any reckoning there is no more stupid strategy for handling the opposite pole than fear of contact driven by our own defence mechanisms, and the denial of its presence in our own psychic constitution. On the contrary we have everything to gain if we make use of *our* minority Brown components as antennae to open up to us, via the corresponding positions in the opposite pole, an access to the Green components there – and they are certainly present! We can set ourselves the task of associating with the opposite pole, and on this basis of setting its energy free and reprogramming it. The condition here is that we leave aside our own pharisee characteristics, make use of self-understanding in order to uncover the other position and be able to disarm it, under conditions of non-discrimination. The mistake lies in not seeing the Green-Brown polarity as inside the *one* phenomenon, 'social movement'. The postulate that there are two social movements, one Green and one Brown, doesn't assume the 'necessary' place for an independent, consistent Brown movement opposite to us.

We must discard the past-fixated anxiety which governs our fear, for that which we continually fear repeats itself *now* in Germany and most similar countries in the world. We must acknowledge that we have once again almost the same existential problems to which the Nazi movement reacted after World War I, but now under incomparably more advantageous conditions, and more radically than then. On the basis of the ultimate interests of life the darkest, most 'totalitarian' eco-dictatorship can be grounded. If we also want this in our own countries, all we need to do is, with the aid of real-political cosmetics, let the wagon proceed further to the point where, all too suddenly, it falls over, because the centre of gravity of the load had become too high.

Awareness of the power problem. The warning I wanted to give in Hamburg was truly not *about the Greens* – I wanted to warn the *Greens themselves*. I had three things in mind. Firstly, we should know about it. Secondly, we should exploit it consciously (instead of unconsciously, ashamed and dishonestly). But then thirdly we should deal unreservedly, with pain-releasing openness, not only with the *colour*, but with the *substance* of the power problem in our project.

So, in Green parties, two things are likely to happen, which also happened in the 1920s to that very different, dark social revolutionary movement. Firstly, dispossession of the movement through the party. Secondly, political access to power by the party, so that the Green cultural revolution will take place just as little as the Brown one did then. This is what I mean by Green restoration of the Empire, analogous to that of the Browns then. In all probability we shall neither have to set up concentration camps nor persecute Jews or foreigners, nor even make war – but who knows what we shall do as alternatives to these things! If we are not ready and capable of timely interruption of our development, for a pause for reflection, we might well have the repetition of something old...

Eco-socialism Is Still Exterminism

In a Metropolitan land standing in the centre of the white Empire, national resentment can only lead to a situation where the water of the movement is led back to the mill of the state. If Turn-around really gets going deeply among the people, it will generate in the movement many opportunities and needs for making good. It will then be necessary to climb helpfully down into the darkness of the past, in order to fight with the dragon where he sits and has his territory. In some versions St George doesn't kill the dragon, but chains him, in order to open to his energies a different channel from the one used up to now.

With respect to 'social politics' and 'social work' in the Metropolis, the Left may simply not know what it is doing. The dismantling of the Megamachine requires a just distribution of the burden of change, and thus a certain amount of conventional interest-group politics. Because the dismantling will affect millions of jobs and life-planning, it can only be accomplished by means of an all-embracing social outline plan. In this sense I can agree with Oscar Lafontaine when he writes: "Whoever demands the switching off of whole industrial plants, but wastes no words on the further fate of workers who are employed there, is not behaving ecologically..."[6]. Such a person would quite simply never reach such a goal.

What I don't know is whether, in Lafontaine's eyes, anything really counts as an alternative which does not envisage creating for the affected workers other jobs *within* the industrial system. If I take Lafontaine's statement in its full context, I am more able to predict that with his 'ethics of responsibility' he will not achieve even the first step towards an ecological Turn-around. In its context, it comes after another sentence in which the whole seems like an unintended self-parody: "But the necessary changes must take place without great social disruptions. Whoever demands the switching off of whole industrial plants, but wastes no words on the further fate of the workers who are employed there, is not behaving ecologically, because he is not behaving with solidarity". And then he prioritises the old 'power question' (unions versus entrepreneurs) *before* the necessity of 'ecological reconstruction', and makes everything dependent upon the merry-go-round of the struggle for distribution, and upon the maintenance of the living standard of the richest lower class in the world – dependent upon safeguarding the *accustomed form* of living-standard.

The highlight of Lafontaine's argumentation comes with the introduction of the concept of *solidarity*. To make *ecology* dependent on *solidarity* presupposes that ecology is being treated only as a conversion question – and thus to erase its principal content. But the ecological crisis means we must stop giving social comfort priority over natural balances.

And apart from this basic problem, do I or do I not have the moral right to demand the switching off of all nuclear power stations, even if I carry no social plan for those who are employed there? For the possessors of jobs, for whom I should display solidarity, it is established in advance that they do *not* have to be impoverished – indeed they have something to gain, if their routine collapses for truly existential reasons. The entire concern for the concept of ecology is degraded if in the end it is subordinated to a demand for solidarity – which is reduced to the demand for justice among us travellers in the boat heading for the waterfall.

Nobody will voluntarily want to provoke social disruptions if the consequence is that human energies would be used up on old fronts instead of flowing into the restructuring of conditions. But then, the earth does not compromise with us. The whole undertaking of our welfare society is an arrangement which is absolutely lacking in solidarity. Unlike Lafontaine, *Biedenkopf* gives priority to ecological reconstruction, then wanting "to hold altercations, conflicts, strife, and emergency as low as possible during the period of transition"[7].

It is one thing to take seriously social safety and distributive justice problems from the point of view of an ecological politics of salvation: it is a different thing to seek compromises with the political representatives of the opposite project. There is a tendency in such quarrels not to deal with the concrete issues themselves, but to let them become weapons in a conceptual confrontation.

Nowhere in economic theory was Georgescu-Roegen's statement, that economy and ecology are dramatically irreconcilable, refuted or even challenged. To reconcile ecology with economy, without subordinating economy, means the reverse: to want to subordinate ecology. The top parasite wants to go on eating as if everything which he has recently learnt about the finiteness of the earth were nevertheless not true – because it is unthinkable that the human being would set aside his own interests, habits and comforts.

Eco-socialists are resistant to enduring this obvious contradiction. First, they must always do good to somebody, and they simply don't want to notice that this is something *they* are trapped in. They hang on to this role, into which the ego has escaped – the whole affair remains *politically* both false and non-genuine, even if real feeling resonates within it. They are also a part of the ecological crisis, being pastoral and social workers in this secular Protestantism which both supports and spoils the whole *ecopax* movement. It is regarded as 'inhuman' to reveal to people that in truth they *want* the bomb, nuclear power stations, mass-production and dioxin, because they don't believe they are able to renounce military and industrial armament. This is the humanity about which Jung said, "that word *human*, which sounds so beautiful, when really understood, signifies nothing beautiful, nothing virtuous, nothing intelligent, but just low-grade mediocrity"[8]. It is there for *self-protection*, and it won't save us. It is only the push which gives us a chance.

The contradiction will only be overcome through a struggle in one's own consciousness, which cannot but be crippled if 'occupying powers' represent the organisational apparatuses.

Since the industrial formation as a *whole* is the problem, the antagonism of industrial classes is secondary in relation to it, and the interests of wage-workers play the same life-hostile role *everywhere*. We have seen in the past the disaster which emanates permanently from industrial work, because it pulled the ground out from under the feet of the agricultural majority of traditional societies, and is doing so still. The myth of the world historical mission of the proletariat is proving itself true only in the world's exterministic Turn-around. The accumulation of capital and wage-labour are both the same exterministic process.

In the 19th century, when Marxism and the workers' movement began – implicitly Eurocentric, nationalistic, and colonialistic – one could simply disregard the fact that at home there was something more going on than the struggle over produced wealth and the political upward struggle of the modern plebeians, the second industrial class. This something more was the consensus that the progress of science and technology are the condition of general emancipation. On this basis the inner struggle between bourgeoisie and proletariat ought to decide the fate of mankind. *Concerning industrialism the opponents were at one*, so that together they could mock the handful of defeated romantics who opposed themselves to the iron stream.

The idea of the proletarian revolution was that the social spectrum in the middle, between the two antagonistic classes, would break apart. National cohesion was disastrously underestimated. Admittedly Marx and Engels, then Rosa Luxembourg and Lenin, had run against the imperialistic corruption of the proletarian *avant-garde* of humanity. Rosa Luxembourg had already ascertained that the functioning of the Metropolitan process of reproduction, and the moderation or exacerbation of the social struggle, depended upon the inclusion of ever-new 'peripheries' in capitalist exploitation.

Even if the *national* consensus can break up at times of military defeat or crises resulting from disaster, the *colonial* consensus of *homo occidentalis* has hitherto proved unchallengeable. The overwhelming majority, at least up to 1989, regarded the West as the best of all possible worlds. Every European worker can appear as a colonial master, or if necessary as a popular educator. All 'development helpers' (*ie* members of, for example, the Peace Corps) are agents of influence, and decoys for the diagonal of destruction.

To make the economic interests of the Metropolitan lower classes the *starting point* for a politics, and to demand well-paid *jobs* in the industrial system, after the world-historical mission of the proletariat has gone overboard, the socialist Left has become morally bankrupt – a manifestation of their collective selfishness. They want to make politics at any price, in order not to have to change themselves, in order not to fall into personal nothingness. Around this has crystallised a lot of small-mindedness, self-pity and intellectual laziness. This whole mentality fixes human consciousness where the expansionistic thrust arises.

People of the trade union Left speak mainly about their own power-claims or role-wishes, capable of debating for days – hopelessly shut within the horizon of capital logic – about the interests of those dependent on wages and those who are unemployed, without reminding themselves that the entire formation, within which they want promotion, spells disaster for humankind and all non-human life. They are seeking ways of staying within instead of ways out.

All old concepts of shop-steward democracy and self-government are just as conformist. In no way do they have *human beings* as the centre of attention, but workers as *producers* – not to speak of the illusion that the planetary techno-structure could ever be self-governing from below. The way everything revolves around economy, and around the interests of production and producers, only shows how characters are trapped in the industrial-capitalist *formation*. With industrial production at the centre-point of our world-view, we have the perpetuation of wage-labour, goods-fetishism and object-alienation with us in our baggage, along with all their life-hostile consequences.

In 1983 the German Greens spoke of *environment and work* (in that order), while in the new draft 'reconstruction programme' for industrial society they say *work and environment*. It makes in truth *no* essential difference, because in both cases 'environment' is thought of as a variable to be 'protected' – but otherwise as a dependent variable of the industrial system. He who assiduously tries to prove that environmental protection creates jobs and then writes that nothing should happen which goes against the interests of wage-workers, should as a matter of integrity drop the prefix '*eco*'.

NOTES

(1) Rudolf Bahro, *Elemente einer neuen Politik: Zum Verhältnis von Ökologie und Sozialismus* (Berlin: 1980), p126ff.

(2) In connection with a dialogue-meeting between Greens and Conservatives organised by Alexander Langer in Bozen, at which among others both Italian communists and South Tyrolean "black" people's party representatives took part, the "Tageszeitung" (on April 15th, 1987) asked Herbert Gruhl, the original co-founder of the German Greens, whether there his green-conservative wish-project was being resurrected.

Gruhl: Yes, it was doubtless my wish-project. Naturally we have lost ten years in which then this position hasn't been recognised. The situation has become more difficult in so far as, unfortunately, the Greens have to a great extent failed to win the ear of conservative and Christian circles. People there tune out when they hear something coming from a Green direction. That is the sad thing, that the Greens have come into a classical situation of suspicion as being socialists, a taint which they won't find it easy to remove. On the other side conservative-bourgeois forces see things more sharply as a result of the events of Chernobyl and Basel (Gruhl means the pollution of the Rhine on account of the Sandoz fire – R. B.). From this comes a positive development for even yet getting the ear of the conservatives. But the Greens can't do this, the task must fall to others. Either by a party like the Ecological Democratic Party (founded by Gruhl after he left the Greens – R. B.) or by other public paths.

Tageszeitung: Let us assume this works, what does it mean for the ODP?

Gruhl: If there is to be a big influence on politics by ecologists, this must take place from two directions, one from the left side, that is from the Greens, and one from the right, the ODP. Only then could one expect to bring about a defection of voters from the CDU/CSU and also the FDP, that a second opposition block would be created. Only then would there be possibilities of other coalitions, also with the SDP. Up to now the appearance of the Greens has been a boomerang. Votes were taken from the SDP and the right block, which hardened up, was strengthened. For this reason the right wing must now be canvassed.

Tageszeitung: Are developments in the CDU imaginable which could advance the cause of such a debate?

Gruhl: That is at the moment altogether unimaginable. Since my departure the situation is, I could almost say, un-changed. This confirms me that I could not have remained in the CDU. Nothing at all has moved. The only person who attempts to bring ecological discussion into the CDU, Kurt Biedenkopf, is completely isolated and losing the influence that he once had. On the other hand the outlook isn't all that bad. There will certainly be more environmental catastrophes. The frustration of people at being repeatedly lied to by Kohl, Strauss, and others, his its limits. This cannot be pushed too far. People like Wallmann (the first environmental minister from the CDU in Bonn, lately minister-president in Hesse – R. B.) cannot stand there and say they want to save the environment, and at the same time push through exactly the opposite using all legal measures.

Tageszeitung: After the red-green debacle in Hesse, does the black-green theme come on to the agenda?

Gruhl: It is urgently necessary that the same diffusiveness which exists between the SPD and the Greens should also make itself felt in the C-parties. Then we can achieve different divisions in the middle, different majorities, but not before."

(3) Jacques Ellul, *Von der Revolution zur Revolte* (Hamburg: 1974), p150ff.

(4) see p192ff in *The C G Jung Reader* by Franz Alt.

(5) Rudolf Bahro, *Pfeiler am anderen Ufer. Beiträge zur Politik der Grünen von Hagen bis Karlsruhe*, offprint from the periodical *Befreiung*, (Berlin: 1984), p58.

(6) Oskar Lafontaine, *Der andere Fortschritt* (Hamburg: 1985), p195.

(7) Biedenkopf, *op cit*, p45.

(8) Franz Alt, ed, *Das C. G. Jung Lesebuch* (Olten: 1983), p189.

18. Breaking the Imperial consensus

From Where Does the Imperial Consensus Break?

Any interest-representing politics which anyone, whether Left or Right, can make presupposes the imperial consensus. We are all 'Roman citizens'. The way of thinking of trade unions functions in an actively imperial fashion, even if from an internal standpoint it may appear altogether legitimate.

In spite of the pressure of competition from Japan and some 'marginal countries' there is no threat here either of a collapse of the internal socioeconomic structures or of foreign relations. The ship won't founder even on the dangerous reefs of unemployment, the stressing of the welfare state or the indebtedness of the third world. The long-term tendency to European decline in the face of Japan, and China behind it, is a different kind of thing. It is related to the slacking off of the psychological-cultural drives which have supported the European expansion.

For quite a while Metropolitan society will be able to tolerate the alienation which, even with economic progress, has been continually increasing – in spite of the consequences for psychological health. In particular we shouldn't believe that unemployment will break up the consensus. As long as the influx from the world market remains big enough to finance the minimum existence, unemployment will be politically almost unnoticeable.

Only the threat coming from the ecological crisis and nuclear militarism can disturb the inner peace, and endanger the overwhelming consensus resting on identification with the 'democratic industrial society'. I say 'endanger', no more, because people are much too willing to be distracted. It is possible, for example, to ascribe the scandal of poisoned fish in a river to the failure of a helpless environmental minister who, if involved in the matter, is clearly himself to blame. The problem not in the environmental minister, nor to his inadequate resources and capabilities. How much longer are we going to be content with just measuring faster and more accurately? The problem is not in the spilling of cyanide, but in the *existence* of the production of poisons on far too big a scale. The only

288

person who has really understood the situation recognises the most fundamental of crimes, the increasing of the basic load with which we block the remaining ways out.

The majority of the population in no way remains spiritually motionless. Potentially we stand at the threshold. Shall we, just at the moment when we are the ultimate victors of history, distance ourselves from those *achievements* thanks to which we have 'never had it so good?' Naturally this presupposes that the benefit was only undisturbed comfort, rather than an animated 'freedom *for* something'. A population whose majority had won *this* freedom and now felt threatened, would concern itself much more radically both with the ecological, social and political rehabilitation of its polity.

Thus we have a fluid situation which even now would probably admit of a different politics, if the institutional and mass communication channels were not blocked by the traditional power and property interests. Anti-imperialism and anti-capitalism, to which especially eco-socialists attach moral value, are worse than empty words in this position, which doesn't take the imperial consensus into account, but accepts and cultivates it as the matrix of the whole political game between Left and Right.

People are referred not to new priorities, but to the old party profiles. What is brought into the centre of attention is not the question of how we can push ourselves away from the diagonal of destruction, but the alternatives to Red and Blue.

People haven't begun to understand that the idea of assembling 'Green people' around some social-democratic reform politician directly contradicts the real task (in USA they did the same thing rallying behind Clinton in the *topos* of Democrat versus Republican). It is not just tactically short-sighted – inasmuch as a politics of ecological Turnaround and disarmament cannot be achieved with a majority of little over 50%. What is worse is that the population will be sorted into false groupings: domestic political blocs stabilise which simply are not alternatives. By using customary methods of capturing voters, the subject of a politics of salvation won't be advanced by even a millimetre.

With the idea of the 'majority against the Right', Red-Green is just the most recent variant of a left-wing laziness and cowardice in thinking. The real interests which stand behind it have become historically almost weightless.

No 'majority against the Right' will end the arms race, stop the Megamachine, free the damned of this earth from the weight of the 'good life' in Washington, London, Paris, Zurich, and Frankfurt, or even relieve them, or set limits to our Satanism against animals and plants. The Roman lower classes never broke the foreign policy, the colonial, imperial consensus, and never forgot the supply and defence interests of the Metropolis. This is even more true today, where the differential is incomparably greater.

In opposition to the Marxian conviction that workers are not a class of bourgeois society, but stand antagonistically outside it, social democracy has learnt from politicians that the workers belong to it, they want to belong to it, and they want to overcome their class situation to vanishing point. Accordingly they no longer set themselves the task of using the struggle over distribution to dynamite the consensus of bourgeois society. They would much rather maintain and perfect this consensus. They strive for the complete integration of the Metropolis. Imperial, colonial and national interests are taken for granted. They are simply the outer side of the *Pax Atlantica*.

The issue is always the size of the cake and the securing of the channels of supply, and therefore of preventive defence – and only later of the size of different people's shares and of the nicely-calculated domestic political struggle. Since those who are wage-dependent are the dependent variable in the capitalistic formation, their readiness to run risks is less than that of those in the 'bourgeois' camp. Their interests are more readily vulnerable, they can stand less disruption, no sacrifice, and no bets on winnings which can only be collected the day after tomorrow.

The Green minister in Hessen (Jöschka Fischer) once issued a brochure concerning how it would be possible "through reasonable measures of economy, which would entail no sacrifice of comfort", to lower the consumption of drinking water. There would of course be problems of procurement, and there would be damage to nature caused by the procurement. It was then stated that the rate of water consumption since 1930 had *increased fifteen times*. The proposals were then to reduce consumption by 40 per cent. They are all reasonable. Now, every government will recommend something similar. But what is the message on the cover? "*Hessen becomes Green*: through the sparing use of drinking water". The truth is: "If you follow this advice, Hessen will turn into a desert more slowly". The function of this kind of Green politics consists of pushing the imperial consensus together again at the place where it is actually breaking apart.

In this spirit the Ministry of Environment in Hessen also planned a symposium, "Hessen as site for the chemical industry – perspectives on low-risk chemical manufacture". It is only because the consensus is *indeed* falling apart, that nothing we can do is any use. Even though it was not the intention, such a conference nevertheless strengthens the subliminal despair.

Is it thinkable that such a conference takes as its point of departure recognises that chemical mass-production is incompatible with the fabric of life? The Green Ministry of Environment of Hessen was propagating the logic of self-extermination, while claiming to be saving something.

How Does the Imperial Consensus Break?
I see seven different possibilities of dealing with the imperial consensus in the ecological crisis. They should be named, although I do not want to involve myself with all of them:

- *the* restorative, *which from the point of view of the balancing-out of struggles over distribution, repeatedly makes it secure by doing the necessary minimum of environmental protection (official environmental cosmetics);*
- *the* reformistic, *which would like to lure people out of it bit by bit, without them really noticing it (Red-Green realpolitik, with concealed fundamentalist intention);*
- *the* radical-conservative, *which wants to pull it straight moralistically and by means of economic planning;*
- *the* Left-radical *(New Left), which approaches it in a hostile manner from the standpoint of the external proletariat;*
- *the* terroristic, *which, operating from the same standpoint, wants to terrorise it into insecurity;*
- *the* radical-ecological, *which would like to break it open with reasonable and human-egoistic arguments (which can also pass over into terrorism).*
- *the* spiritual-fundamentalistic, *which would like to dissolve it from within.*

I saw years ago that German social democracy had reached the end, *historically*, so that I never had a Red-Green perspective, even though there were times when a transient tactical combination seemed possible. I did not clarify this then, because I found myself involved in a personal crisis due to my evolution along with the Greens, which I had co-founded. In 1984 I was overtaken once again by my oldest political identity anxiety: at all costs not to wind up in the other camp! Should I have helped to furnish the 'system' with yet another new party, innovative for its purposes? While I was inwardly not yet freed from the party project, I was anxious about getting lost, along with the Greens, in the 'system', of 'being devoured', of 'landing in the swamp'. Superficially I laughed over all these formulations, but they got to me even so.

Apart from the dichotomy of 'we and 'they', which today is extremely inappropriate, and which goes into every socialist education from the ground up, I saw – very ego-involved – that we wanted to share in governing and administering the White Empire, we wanted to take the state along with us, functioning as it does as the instrument of the logic of self-extermination both inside and outside. My emotion also had something to do with the memory of Ulrike Meinhof. The more I saw the Greens falling behind, the more I felt myself politically thrown on to the null position from which she jumped off into her desperate terrorism.

The problem was how to act politically when one sees oneself spiritually in the following situation, which was *to this extent* also mine:

> *After the claims to legitimacy of parliamentary democracy and the liberal-constitutional state had been successfully destroyed by Marxist, neo-Marxist, anarchistic and cultural-revolutionary ideological criticism, the only political perception which remained was of a society which behaves like an incorporated association for the organised exploitation of nature, with the promise of a continuous raising of the material standard of life, potentially for all its members[1].*

This is still *dominant* today – at any rate according to a quantitative way of looking at things. Whoever has never pushed forward to the point of view of Ulrike Meinhof about the imperial consensus, or has not fallen back from it for safety's sake, does not, I believe, fully comprehend the question. The entire power debate is rather at too low a level: nothing is happening except exchanging old and well known arguments. Politically, on the basis of practicality, non-violence cannot be justified. For terror is an existential, spiritual option, whatever its quality. Politicking doesn't reach that far. A political party without a spiritual basis can only take things to a certain level of opportunism. Fundamentalist opposition or imperial consensus is the central political issue, and its solution depends on the *trans-political* character of the fundamentalist opposition.

But then certainly a new point of access offers itself, and that is trust in the fundamental realities and needs of human existence itself. This trust is also the precondition for another point of access to problems of imperialism and fascism which I propose. For the eco-sociological approach appears to me superficial and devoid of prospects.

Up to now a ruthless analysis of the aggravating alternatives could run as follows: either we have this unbearable established party or we have terrorism. The ecological crisis resolves the dilemma. In the ecological crisis, imperialism, which has the tacit assent of the majority in the Metropolis, strikes back at its centre, at its own point of departure, and for this reason there is a splitting in the imperial consensus.

Corresponding parts in each individual consciousness, which until now have had to remain atomised and impotent because they were unable to find any social expression, finally get organised through the strike-back.

According to the ethics of emergency as Hans Jonas has outlined it, the ecological turning-point shall "protect..." for the human being "the intactness of his world and his being against the excesses of his power"[2]. This is the formulation of an *inner* contradiction.

At the same time someone like Hans Jonas would find it difficult to deny any of the facts which outraged Ulrike Meinhof and drove her to act. Exterminism includes everything which moved her: the impoverishment of half of mankind, the annihilation of people's self-determination, and the military, bureaucratic or commercial crushing of any resistance to the Megamachine.

The perspective of an ecological politics of salvation in the Metropolis depends on how quickly the majority becomes clear that it must liquidate the Empire in its own interest, and create a substitute for the imperial supply-base and the capital-driven Megamachine. In Rome even the Christian opposition was not ready to let go of the benefit of imperialism until the fourth century with Augustine (a good hundred years earlier, Tertullian, with the same demand, was still looked on as a sectarian). With this slow rhythm we would be too late.

The New Left had already taken its departure from the crisis of *civilisation* and the industrial-capitalistic *total formation* in the Metropoles, but had not yet fitted the economic scheme to the *world scale*. Where the internal proletariat had fallen away, the external proletariat should now carry on the fight. The New Left analyses were still based on Marxian paradigms. They drew their last spark of life from the hope that 'development' could still get into the hands of the 'correct' radical Left, and everything could turn out emancipatingly well. Anti-imperialistic, anti-colonial revolutions with their aim of catching up with and overtaking the West continually had this despotic, bureaucratic perspective.

The New Left ought to have recognised that anti-imperialism wasn't anti-imperial enough. It did not happen, and the result was the panic-stricken concept of a guerrilla war in the Metropoles. It had directly counterproductive effects – mental and politico-military re-armament deep into civil society. In addition the city guerrilla was culturally in conformity with the system of coercion: "War to the war" is a battle-cry which reveals the necrophile, exterministic motivation of its representatives. It is no coincidence that it comes so easily to the real powers to exploit the guerrilla. The paranoia of powerlessness is greater than the paranoia of power. The ecological dimension will attract the corresponding psychological potential more than the anti-imperialistic one.

Yet this will not be a path of salvation. The New Left was thus hopelessly delivered into the hands of the imperial consensus, because they possessed little access to the people and are perceived as cultural foreign bodies.

Anti-communism was a defence-mechanism of *homo occidentalis*, who has to fear the counter-strike of the whole non-European world challenged by him. The radical Left of the post-war period identified itself with the anti-colonial liberation struggle (Algeria, Vietnam, *etc*), or with China, Cuba, *etc*. That is, it appeared as an advance post of the *external* proletariat and its *hostility to the system* was perceived by the society in this sense. In addition the attitude of this radical Left appeared as a luxury product, for it shared to a great extent the privileged initial position of the Metropolitan middle and upper-class heritage.

Where, in this generation without a traditional background, should that feeling of collective responsibility, of responsibility for the *local* whole, indispensable for an oppositional hegemony, come from? For the time being the ultimate possibility was the collective responsibility for everything suppressed, persecuted, injured and battered down. After the defeat of the student uprisings of 1968, for many people Green could only be another welcome weapon against the hated power and the majority supporting it.

On the other side the regular prejudices are waiting, eager for corroboration that one dare not 'under any circumstances' be Green. This factor was stronger than the great Green theme. Thus it was that the Greens couldn't achieve much beyond their initial impulse. Now, as impulse, they are almost a thing of the past, and entirely a thing of the past as far as possible social synthesis is concerned. A different, non-party political solution is needed in order to create the institutional basis for an ecological politics of salvation. Political parties divide the people, or strengthen already existing lines of division – while the conservation of the earth *is* a community task and relegates to second rank all special interests.

From a psychological point of view, people in the Metropoles are not more firmly stuck in the habits, prejudices, obviousnesses of their culture than are other people. The actual trap is the privileges which they enjoy. No specially scandalous or evil intention stands behind the imperial, exploitative character of our style of life. In Germany today the imperial consensus does not express itself in a particularly aggressive manner – in spite of fascist tendencies which are once again on the rise, and which are increasingly spreading among the younger generation. As far as the material standard is concerned, it is simply an enormous advantage to live here, and one naturally does not like to be reminded of its *unjustifiability*. It is the things which are all too human which are killing us.

Apart from our efficiency there is nothing specifically German about this. The specific impenitence of the post-war Germans has on the whole been rather a welcome epiphenomenon for the next generation. Here indeed was a specific scandal! Not quite so anti-authoritarian as we thought, we sat firmly on the moral button. But outrage about other people does not amount to a project for oneself. It was theoretically consistent to declare war not only on the state, but equally on bourgeois society. In fact the basis of the imperial consensus is the deep identification with the *whole step-structure of that logic of self-extermination*. The question is how we want to respond to this.

It is too simple a stunt to entrench ourselves in the Cartesian ego with a machine pistol, and intellectually to batter down the *whole* reality of the Metropolis, solely from the point of view of its *structure*, which as a whole *is* false. Ulrike's last view of things is an extreme case of the European cosmology, a quintessence of the lethal-nihilistic male Logos, which can just as easily get power over the female mind. A politics of revenge and death can itself only be a sign of the apocalypse, and whoever practises it is its accompanying demon.

The psychology of terrorism, which in the face of exterministic legality 'permits itself everything', can only be spiritually understood, because in a society which has fallen into the logic of self-destruction there is no longer any legitimate authority which could otherwise judge it. The public prosecutor counts for nothing. Terrorism can only be rejected and dismissed by the loving conscience. And since in ultimate matters no single individual standpoint carries through to the end, we need a reconstruction of the Godhead. A new value-system with transpersonal validity must erect itself on the crisis itself. What humanity has spiritually acquired in its best moments will appear once again. Nothing will come through which smells of moralistic restoration.

The new value-system will be born out of the spiritual exertions, ego-experiences and intuitions of those who do not fear to look into the abyss, and do not need a guarantee of survival or a scapegoat in the event of destruction. The imperial consensus breaks up on the exterministic dysfunctions of the Megamachine, but does not collapse due to this alone. That we have a chance at all is thanks to those who are ready to transform themselves, to leave behind the accustomed life and to make a new start.

Since the final question of how the political energy for a new order shall come together can best be treated in the thought-style of Antonio Gramsci, in the following chapter I shall use the phrase which he coined, ORDINE NUOVO[3].

If I emphasise the spiritual foundation in the chapter title, it is in order to bring something forward which is intrinsically self-evident. There is no culture without a spiritual foundation, however much we may want to deny it. The European cosmology is also a spiritual foundation, which has been up to now valid, or at least dominant in our very limited Christian western civilisation. Thus the thesis of the last chapter is that building up a new culture begins with the spiritual foundation and must be consciously approached with this in mind. The first thing to do is bring about a change in subjectivity[4].

I have indicated where this must lead in the axioms of a path of salvation.

Now let us turn to the character of a salvation movement, in order to produce a draft of a salvation government, and to discuss it.

NOTES

(1) Günter Rohrmoser, *Krise der politischen Kultur* (Mainz: 1983), p255ff.

(2) Hans Jonas, *Das Prinzip der Verantwortung* (Frankfurt: 1949), p9.

(3) I will not be scared off by the fact that today a neo-fascist group in Italy uses the same name. We will have to be dealing anyhow more and more with *such* demands for or offers of order, should we not achieve at the right time a constitution which is adequate for a basic change of direction. Otherwise the crisis in civilisation will become so acute that it will drive us to an emergency condition. The affinity for fascist "solutions" expresses in an already impaired way the need for an order which will control the anonymous powers of annihilation. Now the new ecological dimension adds itself to the social threats which we were able to thrust into third world (as also with the threat of war by means of our nuclear deterrence – now our wars are fought there 'conventionally'). Whoever does not have a new order in mind, or merely the wreckage of an old recipe for one, should quit getting excited about pro-fascist resentment in society.

(4) More could be added. There are also other access points, similar but yet different, for example Hubertus Mynarek's book about ecological religion. I also want to mention Alan Bleakley's *Fruits of the Moon Tree* (Gateway Books, 1987) – the return of the goddess will be one of the basic features of the new constitution of the soul, because it is a precondition for a new understanding between man and woman beyond patriarchy and the Amazonian fight against it.

19. ORDINE NUOVO
on a Spiritual Foundation

The Utopia of a Salvation Movement

If we want to re-settle society at a place where the gap between civilisation and nature can close itself, and if we can agree what the subjectivity of salvation consists of, the question still remains as to what the movement of change would look like. The political names Green and Brown, which in reality are only tendencies in the broad field of social interests, say very little about the appropriate consciousness issues involved, because in these we are concerned with objective and surface phenomena.

What particularly interests me is the *one* movement toward a rainbow society. This movement may encompass the polarity between Green and Brown political tendencies without basing itself on it or cultivating it. How the movement will articulate itself politically, in the context of the struggle among social interests which will accompany consensus-regrouping, is something which I shall only attempt to answer at the end[1].

Here we are concerned about the carriers of this movement. Ecological politics of salvation is a derived function of all the forces which want to abandon the diagonal of destruction, and with it the Empire of the white man. To one degree or another almost every man or woman participates in this exodus, except that in the case of most people it is still something private. The energies of all those who want to convey their alternative intentions through the old institutions are mostly consumed by those who wish to maintain to secure the old logic. For many reasons – often inadequate insight into the logic of self-extermination – there is much too little recognition that institutions belong to the core inventory of the Megamachine and thus are the fox which is set to guard the chickens. The logic of salvation, if it were to come to power, would completely reorganise their functioning, and in the process they would be correspondingly restructured.

Now is the time when an attracting opposite pole is forming itself for all the 'particles' (not always whole individuals, but often, so to speak, partial persons) which are thrown out or who struggle out of the

previous context. The actual psychological driving force standing behind the re-grouping and power flow-direction in the political Turn-
around, which decisively influencing the political-social field of forces
from 'below', must also be manifested in reality. Then the whole
process will greatly accelerate. Meanwhile reading the signs at a social
and political level would only be assessed falsely.

Structural conservatives are ever and again surprised by how strongly
the wind blows in their faces, while election results still seem to indicate
stability. And the traditional Left in its sociologically-grounded defeatism is mistaken in a very similar way. The objective spirit – even if it has
not found itself in new structures – works from the depths of evolution.
From there it weaves the 'living garment of the Godhead' ever anew. It
is from there also that the new political paradigm gets its authority, one
from which the old powers of the science-technology-capital-state complex are increasingly unable to withdraw. The pressure of evolution
knocks on the doors of the psyche from within, and then we see,
surprised again and again, scenes like that of Paul on the road to
Damascus.

If I speak of the *utopia* of a salvation movement, and of the *idea* of a
salvation government, it is because I am trying to do justice to two
things. Concerning the first of these, "the human being infinitely
transcends humanity" (Pascal). Thus the *movement* itself must 'count
back' from the *goal*, the *ideal* of an order which is just to nature and
humanly dignified. The utopian vision belongs to the conditions of
existence of the new order! Where the movement is everything and the
goal nothing – as in the famous Bernstein sentence – there is in the end
no movement, but at best a purposeless changing, leading nobody
knows where.

A salvation *government* is, in contrast, a limited project. It can be
constructed rationally, and in principle it can be *done now*, as soon as it
becomes accepted as an idea. And because the necessity of doing it is
increasing rapidly, so is the possibility of doing it. This new government cannot create an order, but shall secure the ground on which the
order can arise. On the other hand the movement is seeking fulfilment,
is aiming at arriving at a certain place. And it must be in existence in
advance of the government and the state.

There is no period of transformation possible without the state. Yet
the quality of the movement, the subjectivity or vision that arises within
it, and how it organises itself, are decisive for the transformation and for
the *serving* character of the institutions. The movement is above all the
process in which the vision of salvation comes into existence. And it is
the matrix for the sovereign body of transformation. So much for the
first thing.

The second and most important point immediately *transcends salvation*. In the foreground it is only necessary to ensure that life continues. But if in reality salvation depends upon the leap into another consciousness, into another experiential, mental and spiritual mode of awareness, this ascent becomes an autonomous motive. 'Survival' is in any case the formula with the Brown accent; *if* we *must survive at all costs*, then we must set up an eco-dictatorship as soon as possible. But from the point of view of the *ecopax* movement as a consciousness movement, social life is only 'good' when it offers a framework within which we can exhaust our human potential, and win all the knowledge about life concealed within our souls. When and how shall we succeed in organising and *patterning* our communal social life so that it puts us on the *path*, transforming our whole life into a process of initiation?!

How many people, frequently women, identify themselves with the 'stages' poem of Hermann Hesse! It contains a call not only for individual growth, but also for a social structuring of *opportunities*. We have created a 'Great Society' and at the same time such small families, ultimately one-person households. But out of the extremest individual isolation the reconstruction is now beginning, which we must seek to drive forward as far as the great tribe, in the spirit of the spiral and recovery at a higher level.

It seems to me that to take up Tantric and Indian initiation praxes and rituals from two sides guides us in the direction of the creation of an integral cultural pattern, and also in the direction of solving the problem of the Megamachine: because we will no longer need overproduction, wanting only to make what is necessary, because we will have a better use for our energies – the building up of a culture of love bound together with nature and sinking its roots in her secrets. This culture of love will properly climb up from below, from the contact senses of touch, smell and taste, up into hearing, seeing, feeling and thinking.

This is the true utopia for which the ecological crisis is the great opportunity. And above all *for this reason* it would be worthwhile to stop the Megamachine and the spiral of death. The logic of salvation requires an intervention, not according to questions of survival, but according to questions of *life*, according to the potential of human life for exploring, thinking, planning and carrying things out.

Cleavage Among the Exterministic Monks

The great cleavage in consciousness runs diagonally across the old political and philosophical fronts and unfolds itself according to threats and dysfunctions, through the middle of many sensitive heads and troubled hearts. The challenge of the *Silent Spring* (the title of one of the first books about the dying-off of species) thrusts directly into those strata of our being where we still intuitively know that the human being will vanish along with trees and animals – and that the less deeply the older and archaic modes of perception are buried within us, the more strongly we react. This is also the reason why women, less governed by isolated intelligence than men in general and career men in particular, react in a more elementary way to the spiral of death.

Between the minority which has already embarked experimentally on the task of building a new culture and these predominantly female states of consciousness in the people, the psychology of the official elite is the main arena of spiritual-cultural debate. Many people here have become much more insecure than one would guess from their public behaviour, which is still role-conforming. For example, many doctors have recently moved away from being unwilling slaves of the pharmaceutical industry, and suffer more intensely than earlier from inhuman mass-production activity from the many people who call for their help – from the unwholesomeness of a healing routine which, because of its situation, does not heal at all!

Shouldn't it be the privileged people of this exterministic civilisation who bemoan the fact that, plugged into the hunt for profit and status, they are losing their lives? Lives in which they believe they must fight their way up in the ranks, to the summit, or at least hold the place they have achieved in climbing the pyramid? The jet-set high-life is the exact renunciation of the adventure of the soul. How much longer will we keep on with it?

Today the management of the Megamachine is carried out by scientifically educated people. And the scientists in the narrower sense, the descendants of Christian monks, differentiated out into the natural and intellectual sciences, are the ones who are most sensitive to the basic crisis of the whole undertaking which rests on their work – in a polar manner to the 'witches' of today. Today a greater schizophrenia cannot be found anywhere than amongst 'egg-heads', and in their beehives. There, out of the sum-total of conflicts of conscience and antinomies, something is brewing that finds a parallel in the cleavage among the monks of the Middle Ages in response to the Reformation (see Eco's *The Name of the Rose*). The new reformation is already under way. Einstein already signalled its beginning.

Because science is not only a search for truth, but also a bread-winning profession and religious totem, there is a considerable confusion associated with it about the nature of the internal crisis. It is committed researchers, not dim-witted faculty-idiots, who are torn apart among each other and within themselves, concerning whether they want to perfect science, or whether they should give it up – it is an institution of the Devil removing humans further from their true destination and from their happiness, not least in the personal life of their ascetic, inhibited and armoured adepts.

On the basis of Descartes' *Discourse on Method,* modern *science* cannot be saved – so that the *scientists* must save themselves by renouncing their roles as secular priests and becoming integrated human beings, undergoing a transformation which most would initially reject as being 'brainwashing' or 'hocus-pocus'. Alternative expertise still remains stuck in *eco-modernism* – one of the main causes of the recapturing and spoiling of the Greens[2]. As Julian Jaynes has shown, it is unavoidably the case, that science cannot but miss the Godhead because it arose in a situation of loss of contact, alienation and splitting off from the whole, and established itself on the basis of this psychological disaster[3]. Every time we get a little nearer the truth we get even further from it.

I am not talking about someone like Goethe, who as a researcher was no scientist. I am not talking about knowledge, about awareness in general, but about science as a psychological and sociological institution which is the quintessence of the patriarchal spirit. I speak about a science which, as in the case of biology, built up all its researches on the torture of living beings, taken over by people like Bacon from the persecution of witches, and which still represses the scandal.

We shall only come to a non-exterministic objectivity by means of a different subjectivity. This is the path which has been taken by researchers associated with the new age: their concepts have changed because they themselves have changed, or they have brought a sensitivity into science – with which they had to misbehave. *De facto* they take things from that point at which Meister Eckhart sought contact with all knowledge, in that he found the *Logos* in the depths of his own consciousness and recognised himself as one end of a world axis whose other pole lay even beyond the great God of the Middle Ages.

The issue is not whether this or that judgment about reality is in itself true or false. It is rather that our basic way of behaving, sanctified in science, is always first to want to change something external – now even against the exterministic dysfunctions of the Empire. In this way we can only achieve a deferment of the judgment of doom imposed over us, because we leave untouched the thrust of the catastrophe and even move ourselves forward in its direction. Theoretical science at least tends to oppose itself to the continued application of its earlier conclusions. Here the belief-struggle within this modern priesthood is going on fairly openly, because in the fundamental disciplines intuition out of the right-brain is required.

In science, more than in the military field, the proposition is valid that 'one must begin to stop' – to say we must abandon the production of exterministic knowledge. Here the general strike against continuing in the old way must begin, flowing from the insight *that the given general structure of knowledge in the field of attraction of the Megamachine will convert into an element of the spiral of death.* Whoever wants to remain professionally defined as a scientist (physicist, biologist *etc*), in reality defines himself as exterministic.

Now is the time to say that *firstly I am life, I am a feeling being, I am a human* – and thus must take part in the Turn-around movement which will bring about the social basis for a new human knowledge. To generate further knowledge focused on the *exhaustible* and *exploitable* uses of the earth, while the social constitution and the underlying structure of consciousness remains unchanged – this is criminal in the deepest sense, which the Greeks associated with the word *hubris.* These laboratories are the forebrain of the Megamachine. It is from *there* that the impulse must be withdrawn. It is *there* that a mass refusal is due, and particularly on the part of leading people. They must throw down the towel and set out on the journey within, in order to get to the right 'place' for a praxis which serves life. From there they can integrate anew the particles of knowledge which have been collected up to now.

Where we're getting to is a kind of *double rule in social consciousness.* The *existing* consciousness split must be brought to the surface: it still smoulders under the etiquette of institutes and management corridors, rather a crippling, uncreative schizophrenia without votes. Here 'splitting instead of reconciliation' is valid, for there is no other way from the old to the new consensus except through a split. In their early years the Greens offered a small foretaste of this double rule – there was no conventional position any more, never mind how authoritatively represented, which they wouldn't have disputed! And in this case the schizophrenia was fruitful and had perspective. This double rule could be the eve of the reformation, of an open mass-confrontation within the scientific and managerial elites.

Naturally men (and a few women), exist subliminally in each of their beehives in a philosophical clinch, and still the old and new frontlines are often in inextricable confusion. Men/women have not yet 'sorted themselves anew'. But still the work is not blocked. Still the strike against doing things in the old way has not yet begun. Even proto-Greens behave everywhere as if *they* did not know that the scandal lies not in the defects of the system, but in its *existence* and its still relatively efficient functioning. Schools educate in the exterministic perspective, even when something different and much more important comes across out of the hearts of many teachers.

I speak about schools and I have also spoken about the health system, because these areas are most easily accessible to people in general. But the split among the elites will not come to a halt in front of the managerial suites of the Chase Manhattan Bank or of the car and armaments concerns; not with the leaders in cancer research with their wretched animal experimentation (which fails even by their own standards); not at the official cadres of administrations and ministries; and not at the military, who plan and carry out 'defence' or 'peacekeeping' as self-annihilation.

This is not the old ball-game between conservatives and social-liberals; it is not merely a debate about modernising the customary practices of expansion and exploitation. People will be more frequently facing the question, not of whether they should change their way of being bankers, captains in economics, scientists, public officials, doctors, officers, or teachers, but the question of whether they should carry on with these things at all. It will come to the point where the careerists of carrying-on will lose the greater part of their strength in defensive struggle against moral and spiritual erosion. *That is the way it should be.* The smart new arrivals which management schools love so much will ever more frequently have reason to suspect sabotage in the higher ranks of the firm, to discover that there is too little pazzazz in the activity of profit-making.

The whole model is beginning to run out. The expansionistic impulse is used up. The European soul would like to find peace, or if this is not possible, at least to transpose its adventure playground. A new cultural and indeed spiritual hegemony is rising. The hour of the 'idealists' is coming – idealists who raise the demand for a *spiritually-determined reaction* to the challenge of the crisis of civilisation. They are now already stronger than they know. For an atmospheric power radiates from an individual's alignment to a reality which is different from the technical intellect, the 'kingdom of this world' – especially if it is consciously radiated and shown in one's bearing.

The forces of inertia have nothing of equal weight with which to oppose it. The independence and firmness of stance, which will be needed when the struggle becomes open, depend on self-awareness, inner strength. Will you take the risk of openly standing by something which, for the most part, you have already believed for a long time, instead of just showing those obligatory cynicisms which long ago ceased making a scratch on the *status quo*?

The men and women of the new orientation will soon create for themselves stronger social backings, beyond tactical alliances for or against this or that, for new life-contexts with a minimum of social safety beyond the Megamachine, and offer to single fighters the reference point of a common spiritual home. Interest-representations of the trade union type are no longer sufficient, and are only good for keeping open margins to move in, and opening up new margins. Their logic of behaviour still refers to the old paradigm.

People must join together everywhere *for* projects of Megamachine-exit and Turn-around, and work communally at constituting both society and their own persons anew. In order to clarify the perspective for this, to stabilise spirit and feelings for the journey into the open and the unestablished, a sort of order-building of a new type will be needed. In the following paragraphs, I shall describe these two figures of the salvation movement.

Grass-roots communities of the ORDINE NUOVO

The new order exists first of all in heads and hearts, in the unsatisfied wishes of human beings. Right at the beginning it may not be more than the undefined vanishing-point at which negative experiences with the *status quo* run together. Thus that empty place comes into existence which only a new order will be able to fill up. Meanwhile the old system will seek to cheat its way through with the aid of auxiliary structures, which in time will be recognised as increasingly incompatible with the old constitutional spirit. Only then comes the hour of revolution, of reformation.

To be more precise: this basic transformation will first of all be visualised by organised minorities, who for practical purposes will draft a new politics. This can be nothing less than a politics of salvation, which first makes its appearance as an alternative draft. A new social beginning must be posited, which shows that humans do not need a job in large-scale industry or bureaucracy to maintain their lives.

The most important thing is to locate places at which a reconstruction of God can take place. The last chance for our existence and emancipation lies in our being able to free ourselves from the patterns of the old culture, and to risk again an appeal to the Godhead. *"When two or three are gathered together in my name, there shall I be"*. When Beethoven, in 1821, dedicated his E major Sonata opus 109 to Maximiliane, daughter of his beloved friend Antonie von Brentano, he wrote: "The spirit which holds together the better people on this earthly sphere is speaking to you now". We must make such holding-together more concrete, in order to permit the basis of the new age to rise up within us.

The social organising function must be built anew, developing around meditative self-change. In emphasising this point, I do not consider federations associated with consciousness-growth to be the sole embryos of a new society. There will also be other life-contexts of various kinds. Hitherto 'profane' projects will spontaneously turn more inward. In all this there is nothing which can be prescribed. We can try rather to imagine what sort of a manifold, networked archipelago will arise from the partial chaos resulting from the break-up of the Megamachine.

The impulse for the new institutionalising can come negatively from catastrophes, but positively only from such new beginnings. We cannot count on a self-regeneration of the existing apparatus, since it is so much an extension of the Megamachine. It is conceivable that it would adapt to a considerable extent, just in order not to lose all initiative. But for this the new social forces will not be needed, because there are always plenty of reformistic *realos*.

We should not place our own organisations antagonistically opposite to the apparatus, for all that will happen is that we will be infected. We must build it mainly 'backstage', as support for the new contexts of life, as their internal organs, without excluding a many-fold contact in all social areas which are receptive.

Since the change affects the foundations, what is up for decision is rather more than a political revolution. Thus the decisive thread in its preparation is not a political one, yet ever more clearly a spiritually-motivated culture-revolutionary Turn-around movement.

In general a social movement is a consciousness concept. When one speaks of a movement, what is being indicated is those parts of our psychological energy neither absorbed by the reproduction of the *status quo* nor used up on compensatory activities. For this I have earlier coined the expression 'surplus consciousness', a concealed potency which can be actualised in each human being. A constituting praxis is needed, which begins with regular meetings and then strengthens its emancipatory tendencies through invocation, exchange, association and active mixing in with the social process[4].

Grass-roots communities of the ORDINE NUOVO – in the form of a network of like-minded and like-feeling people everywhere, in nodal points of communitarian life – will be the first existential form of the new culture. *Germs* there are in plenty – all the partial defence movements, the various communitarian projects, the extensive therapeutic and spiritual scene – and even Greens, however conventional their politics is.

But this is for the most part a culture of leisure-time and weekends, so that the centre of gravity for the participants is *de facto* still with the Megamachine. For example, so many teachers are engaged – enough for hundreds of free schools. And in the therapeutic and spiritual area, political orientation is lacking. The spiritual adepts and communants are not candidates for a politics of salvation, or a salvation government. Politics is left to those who must be regarded as least qualified for it. The political and spiritual wing share individualistic narrow-mindedness, often springing from a lack of understanding that total-itarianism gets its start precisely from the atomising and *anomie* which the Megamachine engenders.

The real alternative, which in a crisis would first show itself from its unfavourable side, is whether, after the crisis, isolated units should be clothed in the form of a sub-culture, or whether we, bearing our social capacities in mind, associate together and create crystallising seeds of sufficient strength to be on offer to the entire old society. For *utopia* does not mean papers and yet more papers – it means designs and projects within one's own daily life, and in cooperation with others, placing previously-existing ties at risk, and opening ourselves to a multiplicity of new encounters.

Beyond the relatively accidental and non-committing week-ends and workshops, the subjectivity of salvation can only stabilise and manifest itself socially if we base our life-contexts on it, and bring into it the experts who, still members of the bourgeois society, charge money for their services (and within reason must do so because the structure has not yet changed). In short, the new subjectivity has to risk itself to everyday life and must concern itself with giving beauty, a ritual frame-work and a spiritual centre to the daily business of living together. Ultimately it is only in real contexts that we can learn to communicate more deeply with each other, to bring our wishes into it, to live out our needs *and* set limits to them. Only in this way can the gestures and form of the new culture emerge.

The real association, that living circle which is initially small, claims at the time to be a 'culture crystal'[5]: a whole new society in a nutshell. It does not grow according to external criteria, but from directing inner energy on to society, and from its spiritual project, which must span the whole earth.

Modesty is required of us if we are correctly to estimate our *practical* range, and if we are not to fall into perfectionism and doctrinairism – if we are to tolerate the tension between *is* and *ought* or *want*, and to face the possibility of concrete disaster and failure. But not so much that we attempt less than is necessary for humanity. The single community can strive to live self-reliantly, so that it can picture to itself the possibility that the whole species could be organised in analogous cells, responsible for *Gaia* – having an appropriate contact with the world of animals, plants and minerals, and with the original elements of earth, water, air and fire.

Beneath the surface the need for such associations is widespread, fruitful for the theme of individual-community-society. There is a res-onating basis handed down by tradition. Everything depends on what we do with this.

The world-wide Invisible Church

In the widest sense the trans-national Turn-around movement as a whole is the catalyst of the ecological turning-point; belonging to it *by their natures* are all those segments of consciousness, social and political energy-factors, moving in the direction of the other edge, the Other Great Coalition – in that they reach out beyond narrow and selfish identifications. But here the difference between consciousness and awareness (*Bewusstsein* and *Bewusstheit*), between being-in-itself and being-for-itself in the moving spirit, plays a very important role.

We are concerned with an awareness which doesn't set itself *against* those elements which are unenlightened as to its task, but which wants to integrate *everything*. We are concerned with the being-in-and-for-itself of these forces of consciousness in movement. That is what they meant in those days when they conspired – Hegel, Hölderlin, and Schelling – for reason, freedom and the invisible church, in the direction of the slogan 'Kingdom of God'.

In this joining together of reason with *freedom*, Europe has created a new access to the *topoi* of 'church' and 'theocracy'. In this way, by bringing the conscious individuality into the depths of its self, the 'communion of saints' can become an *invisible* church, a free, non-hierarchical union. At least in intent, this was present in the idea of the Communist Party as a 'fighting union of the like-minded' – when it was still not joined to the changeling of 'democratic centralism', to plaster over the enormous gaps between consciousness of revolutionary purpose and true transparency and self-insight, which I have called the *subjectivity of salvation*.

The worst thing about the dark phase the Communist Party idea has had to endure in its recent journey through the shadow-kingdom of the western Metropolis, was the *hypocrisy* of emancipation. Lenin had clearly said, here will only be created the *foundations* of socialism and the real freedom. He spoke of dictatorship over the working class and did not disguise that the ban on fractions within the party could make even the communists into party-slaves. But later the attempt was made to shamelessly announce what was desired, as if it were already attained.

The Italian princess Vittoria Alliata, as she pursued her female identity in the Orient in the 1970s, interviewed the Druse leader Kamal Jumblatt, head of the Lebanese Socialist Progress Party and carrier of the Lenin Prize[6]. What he said is impressive mainly because of the black-white uprightness with which he gives his view of reality, and therefore that of the rescue-prince. He speaks in the presence of his followers.

Monsieur Jumblatt, who are the Druses?

The Druses are the heirs of ancient – Egyptian and Greek – wisdom, mixed with a certain Muslim gnosticism. They have 5,000 years of history behind them, since the human being has been human and has sought the truth about the perfect unity of the cosmos. Their religion is not some popular religion or other, but an esoteric secret teaching, a philosophical and moral wisdom, the ontological search for the pure being of the world.

But what value ranking does religion have today, Monsieur Jumblatt?

If all religions of the world today are going through a great crisis, it is because the human being is searching for a universal credo.

The Church is running away from itself in the attempt to be modern to the masses: in the place of divine grace it places the grace of the masses. But it is utopian to believe that the masses could become conscious of the serious problems which threaten them. Just as it is utopian to believe in a rule by the people, in a democratic representation, all things which presuppose a real distinction between good and evil – something which the masses are altogether incapable of.

The masses want to eat well, they want to have radio, television, automobile, and every other comfort; they want wealth, and like the rich, they are only the miserable slaves of money. Only a genuine elite can renew the world: individuals who recognise the high mission of evolution and do not allow themselves to be blinded by the mythos of money, progress, democracy, and socialism; people with a keen understanding, who elevate themselves to a non-self-serving view of things, in the knowledge that happiness is something inward, having nothing to do with the heaping up of things, and that society must be created for people and not people for society...

Jumblatt continues questioningly:

Who will be the hero who will rise someday and begin the turn-around? And what sort of a person must he be?

What is necessary is a man possessing a sense of justice, charity, and courage. He would have to be a dictator, in order to carry out reforms of which democratic systems no longer offer any hope. The masses are composed of individuals who differ from each other in respect of their past karmas; for many of them, thinking is very difficult, and only few understand the deeper meaning of life. Equality is an absurdity...

But are you not the leader of the Lebanese Left?

My striving is directed toward equality in poverty. If all were to become rich, this would be a terrible catastrophe. As Jesus Christ said, one cannot serve both God and Mammon at the same time. What I support is a truly human communism, the only one which can call a halt to this devilish process which is destroying the world. What Marx did not understand was that, since his needs are limited, the human being should only have access to limited means for their satisfaction...

Even at that time Jumblatt had seen the ideological opening in the then Soviet Union, because he had antennae for the strong left-sided or right-brained potential there. He mentioned, as an indicator: "Already, parapsychological studies in the USSR have taken a great forward jump, and further diminished the interpretive poverty of historical materialism..."

If one speaks intimately with western politicians and politically-involved people, their democratism appears hypocritical. Almost all of them share their assessment of the 'masses' – and brief observation of the way they publicly deal with the masses in election battles makes clear how they stake everything on appealing to people's stupidity, short-sightedness, security-mentality, dog-in-the-manger attitude, vindictiveness, greediness and subordination, in order to exploit them and keep them alive.

A different perspective from Jumblatt's reveals itself only in the line of development of western *spirituality* – which is still unredeemed if one examines the bright side of individualistic western cosmology. If it is the ideal goal of the western design to found a 'republic of kings' (and queens!)[7], kings and queens are already an apostasy of human determination, for these figures imply militarism and subordination, the 'pitiable boasting of robbers' which Lao Tzu apostrophised. In Hölderlin's *Oak Trees* he demanded that they should *wake up* into his 'invisible church' and his 'Kingdom of God'.

There was a community designed at that time in Tübingen, which was to have arisen on the basis of individuality. They certainly didn't assume that all subordination could instantly be overcome, but their community was *on the way* from the old order and lodge concept, esoteric and 'white magical', to the new order, a socially-open community which erects no great barriers to admission. Thus this dichotomy between the 'initiated' and the 'masses' softened up, and the leader and dictator was partially dissolved in a collective which *in principle* included every last one, detotalised – the dictatorial affected only critical areas and aspects of behaviour where individual selfishness injured the general welfare.

If – in the Asian idiom – *all* already 'are Buddha', then nobody has to remain excluded or 'steal weeping away'.

The idea was structurally arranged in exactly the way which Marx, Lenin and Gramsci followed, with their concept of the 'proletarian' Communist Party as the new sovereign, the collective intellectual.

Certainly, this latter formulation, shaped by the highly sensitive Gramsci, discloses that the vision was rationalistic, abstractionistic and intellectually narrowed; in addition women were included only as equals or 'like men'. The concept of reason was not directed toward the integration of *all* subjective forces of being, not toward *individuation*, not toward *love*. Those in Tübingen had a broader access. It was also characteristic that Lenin, in his concept of the party, opposed spontaneity of awareness as the thing to be overcome.

With his criticism of spontaneity, Lenin had certainly not wanted to reject impulsivity – as one could suppose from his words. This criticism was rather directed against the social forces of inertia, against habitually working along the lines of the *status quo*, even in the movement bringing in the new epoch. But already, on account of the rationalistic framing of awareness, on account of its revolutionary-utilitarian narrowing-down, the impulsivity, the living aspect of spirit, was then indeed ascetically strangled.

Lenin did not refer to Hölderlin and Schelling, but directly to Hegel – yet here not to the glowing young man of the *Phenomenology of Spirit*, but to the system-coagulated *Science of Logic*. With Rosa Luxembourg, Karl Leibknecht, Antonio Gramsci and even Leo Trotsky, the idea of the party was a broader and deeper river. Even so, Lenin's breakthrough was no coincidence. The four people just mentioned were in the widest sense Leninist, even Rosa, although she was always accused of 'spontanism', because she felt that the rigidity of the Leninist concept was fatal for the workers' *movement*.

What remained of Lenin's Marxist-Hegelian concept, in the latter days of the Soviet Union, with the words *glasnost* (transparency, the opening up of proceedings) and new thinking – is his key word *awareness, awareness, awareness!* in *glasnost* the whole original richness of the idea could again flow in anew.

In the Tübinger triumvirate of the time of the French Revolution, the quintessence of an endeavour of many thousands of years was present. In order to get to reality this stream had to break through canyons and then stand up to the toils of the plains. Even Hölderlin himself, in his *Hyperion*, the terror of the French Revolution before his eyes, allows his heroes to complain about the illusion that one could found an Elysium with a band of robbers.

The question remains, whether humanity needs an organ like the 'Communist Party' or rather the 'Invisible Church', in order to be able to attain, in reason and in freedom, the 'kingdom of God' on earth. This is not a specifically Russian or Bolshevist question (the Russian Revolution was an event in humanity as a whole, as the Chinese Revolution also was), but the basic question of western civilisation itself, from Plato to Augustine, to Joachim di Fiore, to Thomas Müntzer, through the centuries of the bourgeois revolution into the century of the 'proletarian' revolution.

In western Europe we had a wonderful formula for modern theocracy, and what the system must incarnate, found by this Joachim di Fiore. He found it at the moment the Pope and Emperor Friedrich II were preparing for the last attempt to destroy the foundations of the Augustinian conception of the *Civitas Dei* as the kingdom of Christ, in that they showed humanity, through their struggle for world-domination, that the important thing was not salvation, but power.

Shortly before this the illuminated monk stepped forward in Calabria. Joachim had the vision of three kingdoms following one after the other. The first kingdom was the Kingdom of the Father, the jealous God of Israel, the kingdom of the Old Testament. Control from above. The second kingdom was the Kingdom of the Son, of Christ as the brotherly guru, the Kingdom of the New Testament. The third kingdom that Joachim saw coming was the Kingdom of the Holy Spirit, which should be poured out *equally over all*. This was Whitsun Kingdom, the principle of a mystical democracy. *They wouldn't have to seek consensus about the general good – they would have it.*

Joachim's vision fell like seed-corn into the ground. The Franciscans – their persecuted wing – continued with the idea. It influenced Eckhart, Müntzer and classical philosophy and poetry in the whole of Europe. Its conscious rebirth in contemporary communism has been completed by Ernst Bloch. But with Marx began the *restoration* of the old idea of theocracy, on a new level, even though patriarchal for a last time, and still too collectivistic.

We are only now able to see what an invention that was, this system with the Party as a spiritual authority in disguised form at the top. With this Party idea of Marx and then with Lenin's praxis ('awareness versus spontaneity') – after the church of the theocratic idea had collapsed – the substance in it, at first disguised, returns again for humanity. In any case, 'proletariat' for Marx was not the true working class, but rather a name for a new kind of 'communion of saints', advantageously introduced in a purely secular manner. 'Workers' were those who carried the mission of world history. And what was the mission? What, ultimately, does general emancipation mean? It is a liberation which cannot be thought without spiritual consequences, without discovering and experiencing the *divinity in ourselves*.

This communist beginning was, so to speak, a trick of history. Incidentally, communism in the 16th century was still spiritual, as again it was in France during the 19th century. They knew, like Thomas Müntzer, leader of the peasants, that above the theme of social justice a higher octave resonated. Nowadays we have reached a point where the *enlightened*, the bourgeois *liberated* people, want again to communicate with the godhead and also must do so.

Now the international 'proletarian' Communist Party is not enough. Now it is the chrysalis which will be broken open (in the once-Soviet East), or the evolutionary precursor which will be succeeded (in the West). On its heels comes a worldwide Invisible Church, syncretistic at first – in which things first mix which later will join together, but the approaches converge. At the end of *The Phenomenon of Man*, Teilhard de Chardin has called the convergence-point of spirit around the noösphere enclosing the planet, the Omega Point!

I already see ten thousand people who belong to the trans-party association with a greater or smaller number of threads from their hearts. Perhaps '*Invisible Community*' would be nearer to the facts than 'Invisible Church'. There is quite an analogy to what was meant right at the beginning of Christianity by the 'Communion of Saints' and also with that 'fighting association of like-minded people' which communists and anarchists originally had in mind. Or would we rather speak of an open order? I am convinced that the idea of the federation is timely.

If we want to, we can all be members of this latest church, this new 'communion of saints'. Access in any case is open. There is no lodge magic, no initiation rite, even if there may be an initiation of a kind which today would hardly be esoteric – the introduction by a specific person or group. Initiation as a ritual is lightly repressive. Today the process which Carl Jung called *individuation* is the appropriate initiation, because it is precisely not a question of growing up into the traditional culture, but of the second birth of the adult into another one.

What is necessary is not 'initiation' into some sort of psi secrets, even if available, but that as many people as possible dedicate themselves to a task, an assignment which transcends them, and in the face of which one's own condition is no longer so decisive. Very many psychological turbulences, in their expression and power to take over, are due to the lack of binding and fully responsible engagement.

It is an open conspiracy, and we can only wish that the membership expresses itself in a committed manner – for example in the form of reception which we prepare for each other – and that the solidarity would express itself in a natural and unconcealed way. In particular we need more communism in our world-wide network than in the Gospel according to St. Luke, according to which they 'had everything in common'. If it were really to come to a complete de-bureaucratising of the communists in 'really-existing socialism', to a withdrawal of the parties from the machine of state, and to a spiritualising of their programmatics and praxis... I won't complete the sentence, because the happy turn which history at the end of the twentieth century could take is almost unthinkable.

But for the coming-into-existence of this association, we must consciously do something at all levels of social communication (local, regional, national, continental, world-wide) and in all groups, toward disciplined and substantive cooperation. We need a permanent 'meeting of the ways', and we need mission, 'inner mission', especially at home. As Christ, according to Matthew, said in the Sermon on the Mount: "A city set on a hill cannot be hid. Nor do men light a lamp and put it under a bushel, but on a stand, and it gives light to all in the house". Above all, it will be in daily practice where the subjectivity of salvation forms itself, to be this light.

Religious Totalitarianism?

There will probably be an outcry: at the end of the modern period and after the shipwrecked Brown millennarism, are we to have the Green utopia of a new Reformation, the founding anew of monasteries, an invisible church? And are we to take up again the perspective of theocracy, the Holy Empire? I can't help it, this is the light in which I see the ecological crisis. But, in one last excursion, I will gladly respond to this outcry.

Since my imprisonment on account of *The Alternative*, nothing affected me more than a four-week stay in the commune of Baghwan Shree Rajneesh in Oregon, which has since been dissolved. And how many people took offence! How many people worried about my reputation! And how many people fully understood the personal issues which must have been concealed by it all! In any case, I had no problem with that.

Since I think it is a pity that the experiment carried within itself the seeds of such a rapid self-destruction, I'll say a few words about it. Perhaps it would be smart of me not to call to mind that in 1983 Rajneeshpuram appeared to me to be the most important place in the world, even though I was struck by a number of things which I hoped would be corrected. Meanwhile the commune was an experiment at just that psycho-spiritual 'place' where it had to be undertaken: at the location of that split, that world-tear in ourselves; it was a commune aimed at that small circle in which community and society can coincide with each other again on the far side of the great modern ellipse. What happens at such a place is, even in view of the unsatisfactory outcome, incomparably much more important and instructive than the new revolution, for example of the Red-Green used-water circulating pump. Even then I didn't exclude the idea that Rajneeshpuram would fail, but my attitude didn't depend on this. At the time when they were regarding what I was saying as in error, I asked the Greens in return whether they seriously believed that parliament, into which we had just moved, was a more important place?

Where then was the defect – for otherwise the experiment would not have exploded so unexpectedly – in the inner design which Baghwan Shree Rajneesh himself represented? On the subjective side it must have been that the enlightened one deceived himself about his own claim to power, as if there had not been one. It is insane to treat a large society of several thousand people, who have already committed to a path, as if the power aspect were altogether non-existent, or at least irrelevant. Rajneeshpuram has made *ad absurdum* the popular spiritual short-circuit which says that the political realm is unreal and can therefore be forgotten. It was nothing but politics which blew up the commune from within.

Baghwan did not want to carry the responsibility for his creation, which he had set up in such a way that it was bound to derail, in that the Sannyasins were prevented by a high psychological barrier from accepting responsibility from their side. The problem does not lie in the strange terror itself, but in a previous agreement over the *exemption* of responsibility for all social affairs. The *structure* which Baghwan had set up ought to have been so devised as to show experimentally when the will-to-power is racing unstoppably. Every check was institutionally excluded. Himself inaccessible, he had set up a representative office with full power, which in addition could refer to him as an unreachable authority of concealed wisdom. He permitted a devotional religion to be grounded which was not at all what he wanted. In this way at least he provided evidence that in and for itself illumination implies no *social* competence, no *social* assignment, and no *social* structure: not *a priori*.

In Rajneeshpuram all the problems which were discounted and left out of consideration came in again through the back door, including also those of Baghwan's half-vulgar Marxist and half pro-capitalist development-ideology for poor countries, expressed in his book *Beware Socialism*. Otherwise the parades of cars wouldn't have happened. No spiritual qualification gives permission to play fast and loose in ethical and political matters with the content of the forces brought to life by consciousness-evolution between two world epochs. Even the rich man perhaps needs a guru at moments, but not a 'guru of the rich man', as Baghwan only half-ironically characterised himself.

But with what vehemence, in what pure culture, in what compression of time and space the precise central problem, the power problem, broke out: that emphasises what the experiment by any reckoning was worth. It seems to me to have been demonstrated that it would be more fruitful not to allege that the ego would vanish soon and that anybody may be an 'empty bamboo tube' of the universe.

Morris Berman, referring to Gregory Bateson, has raised the question in more detail as to whether his 'Learning III' – a spiritual transformation in which the teacher-pupil relationship is in play – must unavoidably lead to totalitarian social structures[8]. I am certain that this does not have to be the case. But then it is, however, necessary to realise when thinking about social structures, that the power-willing ego can 'survive' right into the most beautiful states of enlightenment.

Here Steiner's idea of three parts is excellent: the social (economic) and the legal (political) life must, vis-a-vis the spiritual life, be relatively autonomous, and bindingly regulated on the basis of consensus against any arbitrariness, all the more so on a perspective aiming at 'theocracy!' In a clean meditative climate it should be possible to distinguish clearly between mainly ego-concerned negative resentment and criticism oriented by the 'world-self', so that the latter cannot immediately be discriminated against out of precaution, as an evasive manoeuvre.

We must hold two things firmly separate from each other: here the purely personal relation between two people, of whom one may be a spiritual master and the other his pupil, and there the social organisation. Holding separate, however, does not have to mean opposition. The person who is awake *cannot* ask the person who is sleeping if he wants to be awakened. But what a misuse of this idea to use it for the building up of a town, and to delegate the awakening to other sleeping people. A small group can experiment differently from a big one. Rajneeshpuram was already a small *society*, and it didn't get its due. 'Democracy' among the thirteen of the Last Supper is nonsense – but even the history of the Apostles is not free of despotic overtones.

On the other hand: the more the Megamachine itself establishes its universalistic despotism – here is Huxley's *Brave New World* of 'benign' controls, and the Orwellian dictatorship of *Big Brother* – the more threateningly anxious spirits paint the precise totalitarian danger. Subliminally, many people had so much trouble with Baghwan Shree Rajneesh, that they worried about the few thousand westerners voluntarily assembled in Rajneeshpuram and other centres and their self-determination, as if the kingdom of evil were suddenly to lie there, and as if the horror of the suicide commune of Jonestown were no longer just one more bubble on the swamp of this decadent civilisation, but its very heart. Yet even the worst thinkable developments in Rajneeshpuram would have added little to the apocalyptic things which the United States has to offer in its streets.

There is here a common precondition shared by the sect preachers and the left-wing 'emancipators': their firm belief in the seducibility of the small man and woman, whom they would much rather still have under their own pastoral competence. There exists that caretaker belief in the inability of the human being to put an end to his subordination by his own efforts. According to some obsessive ideas, even John gave up his own autonomy when he attached himself to Jesus. According to these ideas the pluralism of special interests, blind to the whole, should be protected 'critical-rationally' against sombre theocrats, from Plato to Hegel. Any general view, any comprehensive order, is at all costs to be avoided, especially for the Left-critical individual!

On account of the threatening Baghwan-type 'dictatorship by friend-liness' paranoia breaks out directly. In view of the way you see him, is it possible that Baghwan is your own shadow?! That are you perhaps not anxious about your Cartesian fortress, perhaps preventively defending the collected substance of your existence?

Just because there is a readiness to throw around one's neck the authority of a super-father, we cannot possibly prohibit ourselves from reflecting upon a spiritual practice which would support a Turn-around, and upon a state and social catalyst of ecological transform-ation. So much has been said about the conditions which suggest a fall back into the old conformism. But nothing is more suited to upholding these conditions than the defeatism of our late-Roman intelligentsia. On the long view, individuality will stand up to things this time. Now is exactly the hour of the newly-emerging spirituality, but first we are experiencing its testing.

The lesson of Rajneeshpuram is drastic, but on the whole the experi-ment 'failed successfully' and in the end did not confirm the fears. It is clear that we cannot escape from the polarity between our individuality and our participation in the whole. He for whom the politics of the whole is *nothing but* suspicious is cooperating mentally with the next incorrect choice for a central position, a choice of fear concerning the weakness of the ego. Yet in all this our individuality is suffering; wishing and also hoping to find the condition of being at one, in the unseparatedness, the individual nothingness, the assumption into an existential whole.

Since we have a culture characterised by a high degree of separateness – one which absolutises the pole of individuality and finiteness – it is easy to believe in just turning it around: either isolation or regression. Does it have to be this way? Shouldn't we try to accept the polarity and regard it as *the* theme of the culture? We urgently need access to the 'universalistic' pole, without throwing away the baby (individuality) with the bath water (ego-dominance). And we must find a social consti-tution which furthers the balance of our consciousness-tendencies, and *in this way* determines the centre of gravity so that we don't fall out of the human role, on the trip which our existence now signifies.

Teilhard de Chardin, in his *The Phenomenon of Man*, in reference to national socialism and communism, points at the political question as follows:

We have 'mass movements' – no longer the hordes streaming down from the forests of the north or the steppes of Asia, but 'the Million', scientifically assembled. The Million in rank and file on the parade ground; the Million standardised in the factory; the Million motorised – and all this only ending up with Communism and National Socialism and the most ghastly fetters. So we get the crystal instead of the cell; the ant-hill instead of brotherhood. Instead of the upsurge of consciousness which we expected, it is mechanisation that seems to emerge inevitably from totalisation...

In the presence of such a profound perversion of the rules of noögenesis (the evolution of spirit in the human), I hold that our reaction should not be one of despair but of determination to re-examine ourselves. When an energy runs amok, the engineer, far from questioning the power itself, simply works out his calculations afresh to see how it can be brought better under control. Monstrous as it is, is not modern totalitarianism really the distortion of something magnificent, and thus quite near to the truth?[9]

And Teilhard sets his hope on the person and the forces of personality-building, and on the tendency of the personal to converge – for the Universe itself is personal and person-building. He speaks of that "irresistible instinct in our hearts which leads us towards unity whenever and in whatever direction our passions are stirred"[10].

If it is correct that cultures have religious foundations, a new culture cannot be based on the principle that 'religion is a private matter' – a principle which emerged from the break-up of Christianity in the late Middle Ages. As in the case of the state, where apparatus false from the ground up is defended by the principle of a binding order, so that order itself would appear to be suspect, we bump into the misunderstanding that the 'freedom of the children of God' is threatened when this bourgeois-individualistic principle is called into question. In addition the word 'religion' is irritating because its meaning has been deformed by the church. As far as I can see, in the tendency of the various paths to meet each other, something has begun which will permit a new cosmology to come into existence *without* extinguishing that which is special and individual.

In our modern epistemology *after* Kant, it is now established that we cannot really know about all those things which we really *are*. But rationalism only permits us to use the abstract intellect, which in itself is *one* useful instrument beyond good and evil. But this discursive instrument gives us no access to the *wisdom* of nature. At the same time it is completely obvious that the human being and nature are adapted to each other. The question as to how we can know anything at all is, alongside its cleverness, completely stupid because "all things in the divine constitution answer each other"[11]. We can only make use of this fact that we let our awareness arise from the other pole of our psyche, the opposite pole to that of the intellect. Then the entire implicit order back to the beginning of life can become inwardly present to us.

Perhaps it will not be possible for us to learn again to experience the primitive shudder of awe, to the degree that it could lead us or hold us in check. Perhaps we need an ethic of renunciation based once again on rational purpose and knowledge about the recent backfiring of our use of power. But if such an ethic is to work against the otherwise-unchecked heroic-strategic thrust, the best we can hope for is a periodical trembling of the hand and a delay of the forward march. A basically ecclesiastical moralism which, because it grew up on account of an immanent corruption which it was unable to stop, would be insufficient now.

The extreme European confrontation between intellect and body, human being and earth, and between male and female souls, is a problem which cannot be solved (alone) through abstract thought. What we are dealing with is the anxiety-determined *physiology* of the psyche, and for this reason anxiety is more powerful in our culture than in other cultures, because the law of Nemesis belongs to the implicit order. We have intervened, injured, disturbed and destroyed more *forcefully*, and must therefore arm ourselves *all the more* against the recoil.

The more we learn about all the things which we do not *necessarily* have to be, the more sensitive we become for that which is truly natural and socially necessary. De-identifying and re-sensitising are to a great extent the same thing. What we gain at first is, of course, not the Great Freedom, but awareness of our many entrapments and dependencies, in relation to our neighbour as well as to the whole.

The manner in which we speak about the demands of the ego-task often obscures the essential point. Let us imagine various Buddhas – say Lao Tzu, Christ, Buddha himself – and it is then immediately clear *that they have brought out their individual genotype* to the extremest degree, cleansed of the accretionary defensive-ego structures which did not correspond with their intrinsic image. The '*self*', which is set up in opposition to this ego, contains as an aspect of itself the content of the *individual* genotype with which we are born, and which is given along with this whole meditatively-accessible reservoir of evolutionary experience and belongingness.

In times of tranquil evolution and stable culture it is less urgent to go back to the unformed, pliable basic substance of our existence, although it was always good when 'saints' existed who carried on immediate contact with it. But where the tradition fails and when the culture becomes exterministic, as it has done now, there lies in this contact the decisive and promising reserve for renewal and regeneration. With this contact we are not going back to some earlier *state* of culture or even of nature, but are accessing here-and-now our *natural capacity, potency and pliability.*

All this means that we do not have to see the transformation as a struggle between separated *objective* forces of light and darkness. It is more likely that there will be just as much transformation as individuals themselves transform. The implicit order will not give instructions through a new quasi-ecclesiastical or state authority, to pull back from the Megamachine and to build new small alternative republics. The spirit will rather take its path of diffusion from person to person. Without millions of individual decisions, even an imaginable 'ideal' eco-tyranny set up 'to prevent the worst', could achieve nothing. A strong state could prevent *some* things, but neither a state nor a theocracy can furnish a new cultural beginning.

The greatest chance of avoiding a religious totalitarianism, or total-itarianism of any kind, will be precisely in the possession of those who fear it least, and can therefore risk trust in the spiritual, and in them-selves, and who can trust whomever may be their neighbour. The left in particular should bring to their mind a specific aspect of Lenin's failure, for nothing good has come from the proposition, 'trust is good, control is better'. Popular wisdom has always known about the phenomenon of resonance: what one shouts to the forest echoes back. What are the powers of the soul on which we want to build?

NOTES

(1) We are of course tempted the whole time to want to give this priority, to get it done. It would nevertheless be the greatest mistake, once again to fail to find the patience for the decisive forecourt and not to want to have the time to build up the new structure of consciousness from within. Politics is immediately and always a power play, even if an alternative one, by means of which 'the struggle is carried on over domination and freedom.' It can only be subordinated through a process of spiritual purification – not perfectionistic, but as a continuous priority – in the sense of the conscious raising up to the level demanded of true human behaviour. This purification is the first priority of an ethics of responsibility. The conjuring up of the 'danger of fascism' even by the lightest knock on non-rational motives is mainly the expression of this impatience and the enlightened Pharisee mentality which belongs to it: 'Lord, I thank thee, that I am not like other people, who have aggressive, coercive, and

sadistic motives.' But: in the case of any direct political game which evades inwardness and self-experience in the dimensions of power and the capacity for love, things go relatively unfavourably, because the fascistoid tendencies then have a greater chance. In spite of time pressure due to the ecological crisis, we need 'unhurried urgency.' The urgency to get things done politically is anyhow partly neurotically conditioned, less objectively based than admitted. Who is happy to see himself in the dark mirror?

(2) Whether the issue is decentralised energy production, benign chemistry, or substitutes for experimentation with animals – alternative experts have only in the rarest cases freed themselves from the code of the age of science, from that basic posture which Heidegger calls the 'western forgetting of being.' Rather they are helping to save this code by demonstrating the unscientific nature of their opponents, and behaving, in this time of transformation, as if all that had to be done was once again to replace one scientific paradigm by another. These alternative experts are most transparent on the peace question, where many of them don't even want to know that the criticism of this or that weapons system does not touch the peace question at all. From the 'defensives' invented by alternatives to, in the case of the Greens, the much loved social' defence – what window-dressing! In addition the U.S. troops should vanish as far as possible, but the German federal armed forces shall be 'armed in a different way.' The U.S. withdrawal would soon happen anyhow if the west European peoples would make it clear that they no longer want to be defended in a military way. But it is still friends of peace, who speak to the people's 'legitimate security interests,' who participate most keenly of all in threat analysis and themselves investigate the situation of the enemy. Today we do not need any more studies of factual militarism in order to make the case that we must literally live without *any* armament. But those people to whom the need for the renunciation of force and defence in this sense would be obvious, dispute the qualification of being experts.

(3) Jaynes shows that the social process which leads into the urban civilisation and regal despotism changes *social communication* to such a degree that the hitherto cooperative effect of the working of our two halves of the cerebral cortex was disturbed in a persisting manner. The 'bicameral mind' breaks down. The left cerebral hemisphere in which we can localise the conceptual, discursive, part extracting intellect, takes over one-sidedly the conduct of business. The right cerebral hemisphere, which is the organ of our intuitive, body-soul mediating knowledge of evolution, that is the trusting communion with the whole, becomes extensively subordinated, suppressed, left undeveloped through lack of use, and turned into an expression of dull discontent. From this hemisphere in archaic times the Logos of evolution guided us unconsciously, then in the magic period it overarched our powerful specific intervention, and in the mythical time counteracted by means of divine voices our already constituted mighty ego. As afterwards we have then used our tools and finally the Megamachine for the purpose of strengthening our intellectual function, *one* function of our complex psyche, by means of ever renewed positive feedback, so for the first time we have built up the coupling of abstract performance of our left hemisphere, the joining together of concepts, to an objective power which further strengthens the lack of balance in our brain functioning. Rational society is firmly locked in the vicious circle of rationalism. Science arises because through it the need exists to reconstruct that whole, *additively, discursively, partial truth by partial truth, step by step,* to which we have

extensively lost intuitive access (still more, we have so discriminated against those people, especially women, who have not or not so totally been dragged into the new one-sidedness, that the intuitions which *still* arise could be laughed away as fancies and superstitions – everything 'unenlightened' counted ultimately as inferior and stupid). Thus stands above this science from the beginning the motto, 'you will never succeed.' It cannot replace the lost voices of the gods, and the godhead, instead of revealing itself more and more, conceals itself most thoroughly. Jaynes reminds us of the mystical ambitions of a Newton, which from a historical point of view got horribly wrecked on positivism. This book by Jaynes should most certainly be translated into German. [Julian Jaynes, *The Origin of Consciousness in the Breakdown of the Bicameral Mind* (Boston: Houghton Mifflin, 1976), p467.]

(4) Revolutionary parties which understand themselves to be, to a greater or lesser extent, 'parties in statu nascendi,' (as was the case with the German Greens at the time the party was being born), are in the ideal case aspects and organs, 'political arms' of the movement (I was a member of the Greens so long as I saw them primarily in this role). On the other hand the movement can be invaded from the side oriented to the old system, an exemplary case being the National Socialists, although in this case the national socialistic element, which was much more oriented to the state rather than the people, especially invites it.

(5) As Dieter Duhm calls it in his *Aufbruch zur neuen Kultur.*

(6) Vittoria Alliata, *Harem. Die Freiheit hinter dem Schleier* (Frankfurt, Berlin: 1984), p44ff.

(7) Hölderlin in his poem 'The Oak Trees:'
'But you, you masters! stand, like a race of Titans
In the tamer world and belong only to yourselves and Heaven,
Which nourished and reared you, and the Earth, which bore you.
None of you has yet gone to the school of humans,
And you thrust your way happy and free, from the powerful root,
Together rise up and, like the eagle the booty, grasp space
With mighty arms, and against the clouds a sunny crown
Clear and large, is for you prepared.
Each of you is a world, you live like the stars of heaven
Each a god, in free community together.'

And Shelley, as if to continue this, in his *Prometheus Unbound*:
... thrones were kingless, and men walked
One with the other, even as spirits do,
None fawned, none trampled; hate, disdain, or fear,
Self-love or self-contempt, on human brows
No more inscribed, ... none with eager fear
Gazed in another's eye of cold command...
None, with firm sneer, trod out in his own heart
The sparks of love and hope till there remained
Those bitter ashes, a soul self-consumed...
... the Man remains, –
Sceptreless, free, uncircumscribed, – but man:
Equal, unclassed, tribeless and nationless,
Exempt from awe, worship, degree, the King
Over himself; just, gentle, wise, – but man: . .
                    [Act III lines 131 – 197]

(8) See the chapter 'The Politics of Consciousness' in Morris Berman, *The Re-enchantment of the World* (Ithaca: Cornell University Press, 1981).

(9) Teilhard de Chardin, *The Phenomenon of Man* (New York: Harper and Brothers, 1959), pp256-257.

(10) *Ibid*, p266.

(11) Adelgundis Führkötter OSB, in her biography of the enlightened woman in: *Die grossen Deutschen*, vol. 5 (Gütersloh: 1978), p45.

20. Salvation Government

The Idea of a Salvation Government

Now, over the long haul, we can create a large number of communes and other small living circles, and there is probably no better way to create the foundations of a new culture. We can also make more rapid progress than we did in the past, as in the case of the 'transition from slavery to feudalism' in Italian late antiquity.

Nevertheless we shall still be too late if nothing else happens, and we wait until a majority of the population spontaneously shifts to an order capable of survival. We can demand whichever democracy we like: liberal, socialist, grass-roots or committee democracy – the people who would save and even free themselves with it are stuck much too deeply in the habits and prejudices which lie in the logic of self-extermination.

Thus we find ourselves in an altogether paradoxical situation with our criticism of the state. Doesn't the basic evil of the logic of power lie embedded in its mere existence right from the beginning? Is not politics as a power-related, state-related behaviour the ultimate and oldest cause of the evil? Is it possible that there could be an ecological *politics*, a peace *politics*?

Is it not a self-contradiction, to speak of a non-violent politics? There is indeed a difference between a greedy and a relaxed grip, between a conquering and a protecting power-impulse. Not all cats are grey, but they are all cats and thus are opposed to mice.

Is it then a correct precondition, is it a part of the implicit ORDER, *that there must be* a state, a power monopoly, an Institute of War both for domestic and foreign affairs? If this *was* unavoidable – *is* it unavoidable now, and must it *remain* unavoidable? If it is conditioned by the complexity of large societies, perhaps there shouldn't be any large societies? Or perhaps we haven't mastered the problem of managing large societies? Perhaps the evolution and existence of the state illustrates an inadequacy, an un-ORDERLINESS of human nature, of the human spirit?

Now, in spite of all of this, and since there is no other instrument in sight, we must count on the principle of ordering of the state to halt the spiral of death. It belongs both to the reality of the situation into which we have got ourselves, and also to the way out of it.

In this case the most important responsibility-problem both for the politician and also for the political human being is to de-identify himself from the state, from the *desire* for the state, from the *desire* for power-politics, from playing cat-and-mouse with other people, and from treating the earth, plants and animals as tokens in this game. What we need, if we want to hold free the space and time needed for building a different culture, is a good, strong and rigorous popular government, a parental-lovable government, which actively organises consent for the necessary measures.

I say 'government'; more exactly, and using old fashioned language, I could have spoken of a *'regimen'*. For what is meant by 'government' is not just the executive alone, but the institutions of salvation in their totality. Whoever, coming out of the Other Great Coalition, would apply as candidate for the office of president or chancellor would have to appear on television and make something like the following declaration:

> *According to all the information we possess, it is all too probable that we must reckon with a world-wide collapse of the ecosystem which will occur during the lifetime of the middle and younger generation, not even waiting for the youngest generation. In our country – and beginning probably on the coasts and rivers – its occurrence will be especially dramatic.*
>
> *The resulting attempt to save one's situation will lead to a frightful struggle of all against all. Perhaps we could call in our military to keep order for a time and especially to secure supplies from outside. But the latter is by no means certain, because weapons are spreading rapidly. In twenty years there will be far more nuclear-armed countries than there are today, and also a nuclear terrorism. And we know how vulnerable our complex infrastructures are.*
>
> *If we want to avoid this, we must meet the danger now, while we still have a braking distance which might just be sufficient. Admittedly nobody can say what exactly is the degree of irreversible damage which can never more be made good – no exterminated species can be resurrected. But let us reach agreement on a plan as to how we can prevent the ultimate overloading, and with it the collapse of the biosphere and the atmosphere! This is possible, if we pull our reason together and rein in our egoism.*
>
> *The main idea is that we must lower the basic load which our civilisation is imposing on the earth, by a factor of ten to one. This must happen worldwide – it is a problem for all the industrially-developed lands together, who must act together. Correct. But we know from disarmament negotiations that taking the path of prior negotiation does not work. Only some help could be expected from what we may call unilateral industrial*

disarmament.

This *is the country which will begin the politics of salvation – in the hope that gradually other countries would pull with us, and that possibly developing countries would put the brake on their industrialising and turn back – but we must not be dependent upon their following our example. None of the risks which, according to conventional criteria, we would be running (currency devaluation, loss in face of the competition etc) is decisive. We will see in detail what will happen to us, and find solutions at the time. In any case it isn't just us that the ecological crisis is pressuring.*

What does it mean to 'lower the basic load?' Let us be clear about this: the basic load is the product of the number of people per unit area of earth surface, and the level of demand per person. At least in view of today's usual level of demand per person, the population is too big, and especially in the developed countries, where one *human being inflicts far more damage than s/he does in poorer countries.*

We all agree that there are too many people in the world. But we must begin with ourselves. There are too many Germans in Germany, too many Americans in America. Our territory cannot stand our daily average use of energy, 150 to 160 kilowatt hours per person. Let us then at least accept reduction in the number of births; naturally also population movements caused by the metropolitan industrial system must stop, for they only cause problems and solve none.

And then the lowering of the basic load affects our material basic needs for food, clothing, housing, education and health, and also the need for (military) security, for mobility and communication, and for pleasure and development. As a consequence of big organisations, big technology, transport systems determined by world markets and a security-fixated psychology, we satisfy these needs at the cost of a disproportionately high expenditure. We 'solve' the problems resulting from this – not least of all that of protecting the environment – by making ever new inroads into the non-renewable resources of the planet. But since this process is structurally-determined – that is, granted the given pattern of civilisation it is insoluble – we must make basic changes in the structure itself.

This becomes especially clear when we look at the things we must abolish – because without far-reaching structural changes there would then only remain a miserable torso of the industrial Megamachine, from which would come nothing but frustration. What, then, must clearly disappear? Obviously nuclear energy production. But we must also give up the private automobile, extensively abandon truck and special vehicle traffic, and close most airports. Naturally the wheels of the military must also stop turning. Chemical mass-production and automobile production must be cut back, and we must abolish the arms industry completely.

There will always be accidents with atom, chemistry, technology and the technical sciences in general, not to speak of the harmful consequences of 'normal' mass-production which are discovered too late. We can no longer permit ourselves these inhumanly large standards of operation. No solution is any good in which the human being may not fail any more.

Which way can we go, if industrial jobs are to be abolished in this way, and we have to make do mainly with the mineral, agricultural, and atmospheric resources which we can still find in our own land? We then must remind ourselves that the human being was not always cut off from the nourishing earth and the tools of his work – cut off not only by distance but also by property-relations.

In spite of the density of its settlement, the land in our country is still sufficient for us to meet our own needs by biological cultivation, especially if we cut back on the eating of meat. We could nourish ourselves by the work of our hands.

For tools, containers, storage and dwellings, small industry is easily sufficient, provided we limit the production of basic provisions to the immediate neighbourhood – say to a transport-radius of 25-30 kilometres. If we concentrate our intelligence on a convivial technology of the order of 'small is beautiful', the result could be a highly-productive system of tools demanding not more than four hours per day for material reproduction.

Everything depends on readiness for a form of existence organised locally around the commune and the living community. The division of work would essentially be built up anew from there. In the centre of things however would stand not work, but life, the inter-personal traffic of a high, love-filled culture, where the values of being stand above the values of having.

It is not necessary now to paint all this in great detail, in order perhaps to tempt with pretty pictures. More important is that a political strength and a political will forms, such that the appearance of a candidate for president or chancellor of the kind just described is realistically imaginable. Once this is granted, there are many roads to Rome, and we will have the means. If we liquidate big business and go to work in a planned way, there will remain in the end a considerable mass of assets of bankrupt resources, which can be invested in the new beginning.

An essential step would be to allocate the right to the usufruct of a thousand square metres of agricultural land (whether or not it is immediately put to use) to each adult member of the society, and a supplementary amount to mothers for their children, without regard for property-ownership in land. A fee for using the land should then be nationally established. A true majority will could solve the habit- and power-problems associated with all this.

Another essential step would be to make available long-term credit for starting up in wholly new life-contexts, which individuals can then combine in order to create for themselves a basis of self-reliance, that is of communitarian self-sufficiency with a humanity-wide cultural horizon. The first thing which would then reveal itself is that the bottleneck for such a reorganisation would lie not in material, but in psychological resources.

So the immediate thing to do is to make ourselves familiar with the idea of a communitarian moving-together, and gradually start looking around for other people, families and groups, with whom we could risk the adventure of a different life. The sooner the process of sounding out closer relationships begins, the more solidly one can grow into it. Naturally, many intermediate stages are possible. There are also numerous people in the country – many of whom hitherto individualists – who have gained a range of experience as to how a loving group climate comes into existence, and how conflicts can be solved in a dignified and effective way, and more advantageous for evolution. But such people must leave behind them their roles of therapist or counsellor and move in totally.

This whole social re-grouping cannot and should not be engineered by the government, even if it be the best of all possible options. The government should create only the legal framework for the transformation, and make help available in face of the catastrophe coming from our previous civilisation, holding time and space free for this purpose.

The changes will be unpleasant – but most unpleasant if they only 'avoid the worst', without bringing about a new beginning. Voting for such a government or for such a chancellor is like the act of setting the alarm clock in the evening, because the next morning you have to get up when it goes off – which is usually sooner than you would like to. Whoever has good reasons for getting up early, whoever must get up early, will not only set the alarm clock, but will also obey it on the following morning, and will resist the temptation to turn it off and continue sleeping.

We need a final revision of the idea of the state, going beyond the Marxian concept of a transition from mastery-over-people to the management of things. General human emancipation will only lead to the end of dominance if it is also a liberation from selfishness and the need for possessions. *This brings the practice of spiritual liberation into the centre of the social project.* Thus, politically, the idea of theocracy becomes once again topical – at least in its substance. This signifies less if God is regarded as an aspect of the individual human or the human group, than if, as is customary, God is understood as a totem pole or as a patriarchal idol.

To Augustine even this theocracy was not yet the highest, not yet the kingdom of Christ. And later for Joachim di Fiore even the Kingdom of Christ was not yet enough, for Christ had still to dissolve himself into the commune of illuminated women and men, all living equally close to divinity. So this ultimate revision of the idea of the state is a restitution. Here we must re-establish something which indeed was never realised, but which has been more adequately thought out than it ever was in the rationalistic modern period. This period was a falling-off to the extent that in its emancipating progress it failed to preserve so many things which should never have been filtered out.

The modern period has made sure that the idea of theocracy must be mediated by the *political* and *social* autonomy of the individual and its institutional guarantee. Precisely out of this achievement of the bourgeois era, and in spite of all its problems, grew the possibility that the dilemma of the state could still be solved from within. Theocracy is no longer the same thing, and can no longer fall back into totalitarianism, so long as individual autonomy is really part of the constitution of the individual.

But to what extent is it part of the constitution of the individual? Up to now the human being has needed a whole supporting framework (from rites and customs to morality and law), in the face of which as a rule he had not seen himself as autonomous. Then he began to emancipate himself from all this and became anti-authoritarian, sometimes without doing justice to social necessities, and without internalising them sufficiently and granting them a new validity from within.

Now our enlightened, individualistic, anthropocentric, sociocentric praxis has confronted us with the earthly *totality of nature*, upon which we are *more strongly dependent* than our forefathers were upon the *conditioned near nature*, from which in time they could break free. Precisely *our* ancestors had chosen this war-and-wander-solution – what lies nearer to us now than to conquer the cosmos, ridiculous and hostile to pleasure as it would be? Instead of this, since we are higher above the same point on the spiral at which our ancestors stood, we must give ourselves anew an unchallengeable, holy order coming from *Gaia*, the earth, and the cosmos, this time at the level of individuation. Adolescent projects like Star Wars then disappear of their own accord.

At this point all the original problems which humans ever initially sought to solve become newly acute and topical. This is because the human being of the post-industrial era must *exist* in such a way that s/he no longer disturbs the natural order. We must either have Platonic guardians, or each of us must be his own keeper. The either/or of Biedenkopf (change institutions *or* people) must dissolve of its own accord, so that we secure institutionally a *path of initiation for all* into the knowledge and secrets of human existence, and into the possibilities and limits given to it by the planetary context.

However, in our transition we run repeatedly into the problem of the means by which we could remedy our social condition, far out of balance as it is: it is the problem of a healing tyranny. Not only on behalf of the state but also of science people very readily say that the wound can only be healed by the weapon that inflicted it. But the sword will only be antiseptic if it is used completely selflessly – and also in a way which avoids the destructive methods which we usually use to discipline people and investigate nature.

We are not concerned with the sword, but with ourselves. More than 1,500 years ago an unknown Chinese wrote this verse:

I have bought myself a sword five feet long
and hung it on the middle beam.
I often caress it, and with more tenderness,
than I ever gave to the body of a girl.[1]

This is the way it is with our forces and powers. They are impregnated with our need for self-defence, our narcissism and our pride. And when someone is certain of being the Samurai who 'no longer exists' when his sword dances, we may doubt it. A sword never danced in the Origin.

Could a *group* of people overcome the gap which separates every 'king of the finite world', and every queen too, from the original Great Order? Could we combine our purity and our selflessness and not let our impurities and selfishnesses get into the act when we resolve to do something? How could we make ourselves so aware that we are transparent to each other in the divine, the human and the all-too-human?

We cannot ask soon enough how weak we may still be *realpolitically*, because the moment of action decides who we really are: this shapes the new order which we can create. Just for this reason the subjectivity of salvation has political primacy.

Politics of Emergency or Politics of Salvation?
Basically, we cannot meet the crisis of civilisation with the existing constitution of political life, which is made for struggles on the diagonal of destruction. By the nature of its structure it is trapped in exterminism. Meanwhile we have seen that the confrontation between the Megamachine state and the protest and resistance minority of the counter-culture does not bring breakthrough. Repeatedly, old motives of conflict struggle with each other in the foreground on both sides, and the repetition of rituals of dispute in the media suggests defeatism rather than hope. Usually these struggles show the problem, not the solution.

Meanwhile we move further into the situation of acute ecological emergency. This means the collapse of the world-city structure, which at first will be fought off with more Megamachine structure. The essence of this situation will be the shortage of all the basics of life. At the last minute there will be a chaotic and murderous assault on the shrinking agrarian foundations. Physical need is often the most effective teacher, but it will occur too late for us to be able to make good use of our insights.

The capitalistic European social order has not broken up on account of its inner injustice, because it has been able to compensate for this through its world-dominion. There was always the carrot as well as the stick. If our system continues to follow this logic of avoidance *via* colonialism (we colonialise with almost all our socially-recognised activities), it could be able to avoid inner collapse for a generation longer, because although the ultimate limits have already been reached, they have not definitively struck back.

We have organised ourselves economically in such a way that only physical limits can halt the accumulation. But if we don't make a halt sooner, we shall bring things to the point where outer peripheries break up first – in that we continue to make use of our superior power to push things away, in the meantime selling to the world even our patents – there will finally be a catastrophe frightful in its extent.

Naturally, because nothing else will work, we will then have an emergency government, without western democracy raising objections, and this will make the general situation worse, in that to an even greater degree people will be turned into *objects*. Such an emergency government, introduced and accepted without any particular gnashing of teeth, will be the final expression of our spiritual failure to give ourselves new institutions adequate to the challenge. Customarily emergency governments call themselves 'juntas of national deliverance' or something like that, and up to now there are even exceptional cases where, with such a junta, things can be carried on a bit longer, until the next crash. But on account of the acute ecological emergency there will hardly be such chances.

Now, a government would still be possible which could justify the name of salvation, and not simply misuse it for its opposite, on the principle of Orwellian double-think. We must manage to drop our compartmentalisation and our prejudices, prejudices which locate us on the left-right axis, and constitute our surplus consciousness (that part of our spirit with which we want to carry responsibility) into *one* 'sovereign of the ecological turning point'. On all levels and in all areas influential people will come forward, or people will acquire influence, who are in favour of the same change: 'to moor the boat on the bank' and decide to carry out the necessary new institutionalising.

Representatives of the *status quo* seem to themselves to be progressive when they get 'philosophical' about whether one should not give consideration to the popular mood. And even those who have 'actually' understood it excuse themselves in front of their colleagues, saying that they are only concerned about stability, about the best of the old whole which must be protected from decay. Just as long as nobody gets the suspicion that a 'philosophical' politician could be rendered ill-at-ease in himself or on account of the subject matter – instead of being ill at ease professionally and on behalf of the political culture, when the police are called in.

There will be no tomorrow if we stay with regular institutions which do nothing except give in unwillingly to the 'popular mood'. Naturally, if the majority really wanted an ecological turn-about government, it would get one in a relatively short time. But it behaves like our Goethe formerly did, who wasn't able to wish for upheavals which would change the country. Even so, whether people in themselves already know or want to know it clearly, want to demand it or not – *politics* is still legitimate only if it undertakes what is necessary in order to set the logic of self-extermination *en bloc* out of action – to stop the Megamachine and create a substitute for its supply-functions.

No politics of salvation is possible with the creeping approach of the usual sort of adaptive party-political reformist circles. Society can only be *led* out of the ecological crisis. However much it stands in opposition to the individualistic basic tendency of western emancipation-ideology, the change in course demands that there really be government. This presupposes a stronger consensus than can be achieved by party election – it demands a completely different political culture. The words 'salvation government' stand as a metaphor for the whole new institutional system that we need, not just for the executive; it is not a title that overnight could be hung on a government of the present type.

Every complex organism has a leading function, however it may be arranged and perceived. In reality the only leading function of our society is that which is practised anonymously by the logic of capital, the market mechanism and the reproduction needs of the Megamachine. If we ask about the leading function for the requisite systematic transformation, we find an empty place. The people are meanwhile ready to accept far-reaching ecological saving measures, if they are represented by legitimate authority. But nothing of the sort is being proposed – on the contrary, official mediocrity continues to serve the prejudices which the masses themselves no longer like.

As for the Left and Green opposition, before we start repeating slogans whose general meaning is 'no power for nobody', we should first admit that already we are demanding calculated eco-dictatorial measures from the matadors of the *old* order – in spite of our anti-authoritarian ideology, we see ourselves as depending on the state. Protest and resistance are nothing but an attempt to put the existing apparatus under pressure. Does our behaviour really mean, as Brecht says, that *"we want no other masters but none"*?

Or perhaps, is it really such a salvation government, or a regular social power, which we wish would march in against the logic of self-extermination, against the disastrous economic mechanism of destruction? The idea of wanting to stop the catastrophe without a corresponding institutional system at all levels of social life, does not need to be seriously discussed. The only choice we have is whether we want to further the functioning capacity of such a system by opposition pressure 'from above', 'from within', or 'from outside'.

But can this ever work with an unwilling apparatus? Mustn't it come to the point where the forces of transformation penetrate right through and renew the whole institutional system? The demand that the Greens should 'assume responsibility' is grotesque, because the Greens would be seduced into taking responsibility within the old institutional system, which is to put the fox in charge of the chickens.

As far as the existing relationship of forces in the country is concerned, people would have nothing to fear from a true salvation government. It would not rearrange anything to their disadvantage, although naturally the installed mechanism for passing the load downwards would not readily stop functioning. Yet only for monopolistic 'legal entities', mainly the great economic corporations, would ecologically-motivated interventions add something to the power-monopoly of the state.

They will cry 'stop thief!' – the actual sources of totalitarianism *are* in fact the capital intensive large-scale technologies of production, data processing and research. When interventions slow up or obstruct these powers, corporations will in actual fact serve to protect individual freedom of movement. The matter will resolve itself around concrete measures for limiting the use of energy and the rate of material throughput, of orders of magnitude and variety of production, of emissions and volumes of garbage. Schiller has written about Solon's remission of debt in ancient Athens:

> *This edict was by any reckoning a violent attack on property, but the extremity of emergency of the state made a violent step necessary. It was the lesser of two evils, because the social class which suffered from it was far smaller than the one which was made happy by it*[2].

Yet the old institutional system is obviously so very much wedded to exterminism that it doesn't permit itself to be used as an emergency brake. It demonstrates that society needs an instrument for a real ecological Turn-around, for which this old system is unsuitable, independently of the qualification and energy of its functionaries. No government which could be constituted on the present 'place' of the state could be anything but a bad emergency government.

Instead of this we need a regimen such as the Jews had for the exodus from Egypt. For Schiller, the central question is how the higher historical principle can be conveyed in a popular manner, without the spirit completely escaping while doing so. Thomas Mann sketches the *motive* of tyranny, without which such a social reformation is not imaginable – he shows that mystical democracy must for a while remain a utopia, *as long as* this communication problem exists, *as long as* a continually-inadequate religious-political education, biased by the arrogance of the 'educator', shows merely that the spirit is not yet 'poured out over everything'.

It is nonsense to treat as unchangeable the polarity of an emergency government on one end of a political scale and a salvation government on the other – a scale on which one can envisage social power in relation to the ecological crisis, and then want to decide normatively what should be 'rejected' from the point of view of a democratic individualism. In reality this means treating behaviour as a matter of taste, overlooking just that factor with which the possibility of breaking out of exterminism or totalitarianism emerges. It will be totalitarian, eco-dictatorial, or whatever we want to call it, just *to the extent* to which the individual omits to bring him/herself up to the level of the historical challenge. Normal human behaviour is enough to ensure that it's all up, or that the situation ends in a destructive catastrophe – as *every* revolution and counter-revolution in European history has done up to now.

S/he who grasps this and then decides to be a responsible person, does not need a repressive government, and will not provoke the emergence of one. S/he will introduce government into our psychological household at the same rank of importance with which s/he introduces serious intentions of self-development for the coming year. This government would be *selectively* repressive, suppressing *specific* bad old habits. To do the same thing at the collective, social level has always been the function of new, higher institutions. If the purpose of these were overlaid by distortions stronger than the intended ideal, if we were always 'closer than we were in the beginning', the reason lies in the small degree of development of the general awareness.

Authoritarian repression can only occur when the social field of consciousness tears apart into that antagonistic progress where the pioneers of today are always the exploiters of tomorrow. In the West the suppression has institutionally retreated somewhat into the background, only because the disciplining of the majority is taken care of by 'dictating facts'. If, without spiritual progress, we were only to win back the control over our reproduction, private arbitrariness would return with it.

It is improbable that we shall make it either by pure emergency government or by pure salvation government. But the balance-point between the two will depend upon how responsibly we are ready to live. More than ever, we get the government we deserve. If we orient ourselves actively and awarely toward a salvation government, we will earn a better one than we would by continuing the unproductive, and frequently counter-productive, struggle against an emergency government. For in doing this, we are anyway only fighting off mere epiphenomena.

In the most favourable case 'salvation government' means *just as much* 'dosed out revolution from above' as we have to accept on the basis of carefully-deliberated interest. 'Dosed out' refers to the possibility of restraining regular violence by constitutional means *through* an appropriately-timed new institutionalising. We can think of this as a 'division of the state into two', and can on one side establish that realm for which the existing constitution remains valid, and on the other side we can create a 'state above the state', which is the institutional sluice-gate into the new order, and receives overlapping powers for maintenance requirements.

Politics of Salvation and Democracy

Early in 1985 I gave a lecture on the outline of this book. After having an intensive personal discussion with him over supper, Günter Rohrmoser said in his lecture on the following morning, that my idea of fundamental opposition and millionfold turn-around into a new order is "very clearly directed to the overcoming of the parliamentary-democratic system and the total social-political order of the Federal Republic of Germany'[3]. That is correct, so long as it is not presented as the main purpose, and as a purpose in itself.

I reject a *disorder* which guarantees progress toward ecological catastrophe and is constitutionally unsuited to avoid total destruction of society. For the rest, what Goethe's *Alba* says for freedom is valid also for democracy: a beautiful word, if you understand it properly. Up to now our parliamentary-democratic system reliably prevents really important things from ever coming to the table. It is an enormous distraction manoeuvre away from anything essential. What it has been entrusted to do has yet to happen – so let it happen now!

Rohrmoser then continued, saying that for me it is "not permitted, in view of the threatening catastrophic challenges, to glance at the successes of our history", which means I am "ready, for the sake of rescuing humanity, to treat everything as disposable, including the constitutional state and parliamentary democracy". Now, these two statements, which he here joined by 'which is to say that', are not identical for me. I acknowledge the second, adding to it that to treat something as disposable does not mean to reject or even throw it away *in and for itself*, but for the moment just to remove taboos from it.

What I mean in particular is that *no* achievement of our civilisation may now have a veto right against changes necessary for life, because exterminism is a sickness of the *whole* social organism; democracy and the money-economy are intimately associated, and whoever wants to see *specific* organisations preserved at any price is simply blocking any basic institutional change, and as a rule wants just this. The principle of the constitutional state *can* be preserved within the framework of constitutions quite different from ours; apart from this, in the European Enlightenment, the right to revolution was acknowledged again and again, and this means a transient breaking with the law in order to establish a higher law.

I am not at all suggesting that we should no longer examine and evaluate our achievements. Our society has far too little consciousness of history, far too little love of former cultural achievements. Unfortunately we understand *achievement* to be the dead deposit rather than the living spirit and its undischarged potential, which must still manifest itself.

But then Rohrmoser gave confirmation on the previously-quoted sentence: "If it is really a question... of the last chance which is now due, of the radical Turn-around, which will preserve humanity from the otherwise unavoidable self-extermination, then naturally the reference to respecting majority rule, to the principle of the constitutional state, is no longer any argument". Why always this identification of principles with *this* constitution, this *constitutional reality*?

I find our current constitutional reality, a counting-democracy which has not progressed a step beyond the Athenian ostracism-court, to be exceedingly shabby[4]. For the ecological turning-point we need a *more and more intensive* consensus than would ever come together for some 'people's party' or other, and for this reason we need a different mechanism from the demagogic interest-war between parties on the unmoored boat.

Rohrmoser concluded, "We must be clear about the essential tension which exists between such an apocalypse in the inner world, the proclamation of it, and the survival-chances of free democracy". Here he leaves it pretty unclear whether he is actually diagnosing the real apocalypse or not. It is possible to understand the sentence as meaning that the announcement of an apocalypse in the inner world is an ideology (mine) and not a state of affairs.

At this point Rohrmoser, like the leftist warners, evades totalitarian solutions and withdraws into a denunciatory undertone. His lecture is at least concerned to make the post-war political achievements of the West Germans, not even their own, into a precondition for a discussion about the human crisis. It is a classical process of indirect apologetics. It addresses itself to the Philistine in every one of us, who puts up with the greater risk because he is scared of the lesser risk.

'Liberal democracy' could desperately need to die in its current limited and corrupted form, compromised by the exploitation of the whole world, so that the principle it was intended to embody could be born again – beyond the capitalistic society in which it is a *consequence* of the market-logic oriented to unlimited appropriation. Liberal democracy came into the world at least as disguised as communism. It is a luxury of the rich ruling peoples, a fruit of the Metropolitan power-position, which makes the Imperial consensus possible – for it is this which supports liberal democracy, and which is its foundation.

The cultural renewal, which is the essence of the salvation movement, will mean a new thrust in the direction of individualisation and individuation, and will create a much wider and more solid foundation for making the autonomy of the person valid for the general will, the goal-direction of social synthesis. Instead of mechanistic parliamentary democracy, which reduces individuality to the charm of a lottery dice, it will give a new mode of consensus-building from the collectivity of our psychological forces, under the leadership of intuition, and under the integration of rationality.

The Indians with their small tribes and their medicine wheels have practised something which could now be for us a very essential procedure by which the great tribe of humanity could come to an understanding of its path and its goal, and regulate its conflicts in a manner tolerable both for society and the natural order. It is not possible to be serious about staying with a political system in which the act of election to party-parliament every four years counts as the highest expression of political co-determination.

I will gladly carry on, giving my vote now and again, if in the meantime we are building something new which would give more meaning to the old arrangements. As far as the institutional aspect is concerned, it is not a question of abolitions – not as the first order of business. The important thing is those *additional acquisitions* which would put society in the position to express its higher needs – those of the spiritual, truly human consciousness which are accumulating everywhere, and, in our institutionally-selfish system, are quite unable to achieve expression.

The crux of such conservative philosophers as Rohrmoser, and such conservative politicians as Biedenkopf, is their basically pessimistic concept of human nature. If they believed in the possibility of an anthropological revolution, an institutional re-forming would not appear to them as a threatening risk so much as a chance for salvation. It is neither necessary nor desirable to repress the risk. It is the attitude we take which is the parting of the ways, whether we begin with the opportunity or with the risk.

The Institutions of Salvation

What I will now develop means a changing of the constitution. And yet that is the unessential formal side of it. The entire text up to now has been developing the idea that the existing constitution is inadequate to meet the challenge of the ecological crisis, because of the foundations of the crisis, which are bound up with exterminism. In his theory of democracy, Macpherson has shown that the market mechanism and the dominance of market morality were established *earlier* than the corresponding constitutions, and are thus a *derivatives* of the economism which regulates modern European history.

A constitution which was made for the purpose of guaranteeing capital a legally free path for unbounded appropriation and exploitation, and to be a guarantee for its expansionistic accumulation, cannot possibly be taken as a counter-argument, when it is a question of measures to be taken to stop this very economic process. The constitution would anyhow only change itself *jointly*. This can happen quite legally and is even possible under conditions safeguarding formal continuity, if the will is there.

Seen from the point of view of method, constitutional reform could be sufficient. In terms of function and content it would then be a revolution even if the context stays as it is and the institutional structure of the state is not changed. But then the putting of new wine into old wineskins would cause so much stress that they would burst of their own accord. In this case it would be better if the conservative, conservationist lawyers would themselves attend to the providing of new wineskins.

Just as in the past, when bourgeois society was first established, the legal system came *later*, so also this time the new social need will first of all establish itself in the face of the obsolete legal system. The analogous cunning of reason will manifest itself spontaneously. Since it is first of all a question of principle, I am not interested in legal and process details. What interests me is solely the actual function of the constitution in the course of time. And since the whole system which it conceals is failing, no court will be able to rescue the legal foundations on which, *de facto*, it rests.

The decisive point is the demand for a subordination of the economy to the sphere of law, which is *not* itself primarily derived from the economy. This has already been demanded by Ordo-liberalism in an bashful kind of way. The masters of the economy can scream all they want about the evils of planned economy – we need a planned economy, of dimensions quite different from those of the small-minded interventionistic one, about which they have been complaining. Society must rigorously deny to the economy – and science – whole fields of expansion. It must reverse the burden of proof in all matters of investment, research, product innovation and of the licensed re-sale of 'approved' products. Only where the suspicion of harmfulness is refuted can a green light be given or allowed.

Where should those forces come from which could push something like this through politically? To rein in the economy and *effectively* to place a sphere of law above it is only possible for a popular movement which verges on a popular uprising. The decision would be made or reflected in that field which is the province of the trade union: the defence of jobs must be given up, and very thoroughly – the *process of investment* is politically covered by the interests of the 'employees' as the dependent second industrial class. Capital invests in the socio-political aspect, in Metropolitan stability, not for the sake of profit, but for the sake of 'creating work'. The process cannot proceed in any other way than through those who depend on wages, for they *are even more involved* with the general logic of capital accumulation, and the functioning of the economic situation.

The idea of jobs must itself fall. The idea of wage-dependent work as access to the means of life, the idea of the industrial working class must also fall. As Gustav Landauer said at the beginning of the century, to walk out of capitalism means to walk out of the factory. People must be unified again with the earth and with the tools necessary to cultivate it.

This question will be decided not at the level of national and economic central powers, but in the life-designs of the 'people affected'. "Slave, who shall free you?" – this means de-identification with the roles of worker and employee. The solution to the land question depends on this. It must be solved as soon as necessary because the fires in the parasitical big industry will go out. No interests of ownership or speculation will be able to stand in face of the mass pressure which will then result. A legally-correct solution will be found – there is no shortage of proposals.

There is no shortage of land and material means. The shortage is of alternative life-designs. In a Left-Green discussion meeting in Bremen, where the closing of a dockyard had put thousands out of work, I suggested the rhetorical question, *why don't 300 of the 3,000 people affected orient themselves with their families to a communitarian solution?* Why not buy back approximately half an acre per person, in order not to become 'farmers' there, but to put themselves on their own feet for basic needs?

Where should the means for this come from? If perhaps 20 of the imagined 300 from the 3,000 people affected actually did the suggested experiment of throwing together what they had accumulated in houses, cars, life insurance and savings accounts, plus what would come to them in redundancy payments (five-figure amounts), plus the amount they would get from the dole, plus what could be got as subsidy by exerting appropriate pressure, in order to get hold of the land? All this together would be enough for a significantly more magnificent new beginning than alternative drop-outs put up with!

It is not true at all that it would fail for lack of material resources. Yet I don't know of a single person who has been sacked who would have canvassed even timidly for such an idea. And even the most en-lightened, the most green representatives and leaders of the workers didn't even dream of raising such a question, let alone of placing themselves at the head of such a project, of such a change of conscious-ness. No, they appealed as always to the social-democratic local digni-taries, and from sheer anxiety the rosy father of the city state of Bremen received a couple of votes more than usual: get us subsidies, so that, in opposition to the workers in other, poorer lands, we can continue to dump our ships on the world market, or create for us new and different jobs, but please, only for the navy here or elsewhere.

Is it, or is it not clear, what is missing here? That a re-orientation of life-perspective is impending? That it is a question of the deep-psychological and religious foundations of human existence? The people affected, when things get serious, still trust capital and state very much more than themselves, their work colleagues and their neigh-bours. There may be a little defensive solidarity, but to count for the rest of life on the fact that a couple of dozen or a couple of hundred other people in a similar situation could join together and *replace* the whole regular security system, by building up an intact living-circle of cooperative work, mutual help and support – simply unthinkable! Only an extreme emergency could bring that about.

Or equally a long-term, exemplary work, an exemplary good life, in order to soften up and replace those automatisms by which the majority lets itself be ruled. Both together is the most probable. A mass-withdrawal from the market, from the world market, the building up of a local private economy for the satisfying of basic needs, or at least the lion's share of them, will be unavoidable. But this idea must be intensively carried into society. The necessary new construction of a whole society can only succeed through a renewal of its spiritual foundations, namely through existential new decisions about the design of one's own life, through the distancing from the whole value-system of have-have-competition, and through the regaining of psycho-physical sensitivity and openness toward life.

Now I am referring back again to the diagram of chapter 17, of splitting off from the origin. In order to put ourselves in the position to end the institutional dominance of the economy over society, we must pull back the legal and political authorities which are extremely alienated from the living spirit, and which have moved high up into the large ellipse, back into the lower small circle. In the new 'place', we must arrange and equip institutions according to the spirit of the Turn-around movement, which expresses itself most clearly in the invisible church – in such a way that they serve the fundamental rebuilding of civilisation, and can amputate from the economy every veto-right against the requirements of the natural balance.

It is decisive that these institutions should serve *not* the existing infrastructure, but its lasting changes. So they may not be dependent on the actual powers of the Megamachine, but must be constituted far away from it. They must virtually live by the principle 'my kingdom is not of this world'; they must be spiritually conceived 'outside the gates of the Empire' and powerfully anchored there. Then they could be supported by a popular movement which abandons the Empire ever more consciously and in ever greater numbers.

The new institutions will not be set up opposite to the Megamachine in its own field, and will not be concerned to think up a better alternative solution to *its* problems – it will not be there to benefit its regeneration. They will rather give expression to the forces pulling out of the industrial system, and form its social pattern, which will become that of the entire society of the future.

The perspective is that of a system of tribal councils built one upon the other in a hierarchical arrangement from the locality to the world level. I have said that humanity will organise itself into 'second order tribes' and will be, as a whole, like a single tribe. Human beings cannot permit themselves to be regulated by producers – or by consumers – or by any other special interests. The addition of such different advisory systems merely gives expression to the fact that we take for granted the separation of different spheres of life from each other, and that we do not believe in the reunification of the social life-process. The idiotic division of work, forced by our false scientific logic, must be corrected and extensively reduced, because it contradicts human nature, its dignity and its power to communicate.

Tribal councils were originally 'ecological councils', in that right from the start they emanated from the *Great* Tribe, including the whole of nature and built on it. They had a considerable capacity to keep humans and nature intuitively in balance, and thus to secure the 'eternal' perspective for the community as a whole. We now need a world government which fulfils the same function. What we can have first is a national institution of this character which, obliged to hold to the axioms of the path of salvation, operates on the assumption that the interests of its own people can be satisfied in a way which does not contradict the interests of other peoples.

Formally the initial solution can more or less be based on the British arrangement of upper house and lower house. Admittedly the British Upper House is a residuum, like the British Royal House. Even so in these residuums the royal and aristocratic principles of obligation to the general good are acknowledged. What we need now is a fully earnest restitution of these principles.

We do not create a 'House of Lords', but rather – to introduce it by a meaningful play of words – a 'House of the Lord'. According to an old saying, the voice of the people is the voice of God – a saying which has hardly ever been justified, because people must be conditioned to it in the appropriate way. But the voice of an upper house of a society which wants to regain ecological balance must be the voice of divinity – which today can be adequately expressed only if a certain feminine preponderance can be assured in the new institution.

Since divinity is the equivalent of nature, this means that in this upper house all questions must be treated from the point of view of the total earthly natural context, inclusive of cosmic influences. There is no representation of special interests, except only in a deliberative and reflected manner. The upper house may hear representatives of social interests, but may not have them in its ranks. In other words: the delegates sent to this general council are expected to disregard their own special interests and those of their districts or professional fields in everyday social life. This will be guaranteed by a practice of purification which stands at the centrepoint of legislative work.

However, what must be specially represented in this upper house, and for which there must be elected delegates, is the interests and rights of all those aspects of nature which cannot create a human social power. In this upper house earth, water, air and fire; and stones, plants and animals, must have a seat and a voice, and be represented by lawyers who ritually identify themselves with them. The only human group in the domestic population which should be represented in this way is the children.

In addition, minorities of ethnic groups in the country, and guests (newcomers, immigrants and those claiming asylum) should belong to it. Especially in countries with Imperial histories, it can be arranged that the voices of the dependent and exploited rest of humanity are obliged to be heard. Through the obligation to consensus and the veto right of each represented aspect, the fundamental, long term and general interests get priority in the social decision-making process.

This upper house would not replace existing parliaments, but would be the higher institution which gives it its framework, and sets the scale and limits to the struggle between social interests. It would determine the themes of referenda and formulate the alternatives which shall be voted on. Beyond this it would propose candidates for the presidency or for an elected monarch – perhaps for a seven year term – (roughly as in France or the United States), so that the entire population may then vote.

The president does not symbolise the state, but the whole community – less a 'civil bourgeois society' than one of God's peoples. He nominates the chancellor as the first servant of the general will and defends the government put together by this under regard for the party-proportions in parliament – meanwhile governments obliged to parties and party fractions will have ceased to exist.

The government has the task – supported, should the need arise, by constitutional jurisdiction – to coordinate the wills of the parties and interest groups as they express themselves in the lower house, and bring them into accord with the guidelines from the upper house, which are given with unchallengeable authority by other agencies.

What is intended will be perhaps clearer if we imagine how we could arrive at such a constitution, and if we remind ourselves that it could only emerge from a salvation movement, and can only be a realisation of it. Out of the movement, and especially out of its body as invisible church, the germinal form of a later regular upper house would be created, namely an Ecological Council, which would act as such an authority and in this way acquire a growing public authority.

This Ecological Council would distinguish itself from 'citizen parliaments' in that it seeks to make the voice of divinity audible. An example of this is perhaps the great Indian medicine wheel. In order to collect experiences in the use of it, we are led to the geste and mode of a human council republic, which could direct itself by such 'wheels' built one above the other.

The Ecological Council, which the upper house anticipates and exercises, is primarily a spiritual-political authority which takes influence along the lines of the axioms of a path of salvation, in that it turns to the insight-capability of the human being as a 'citizen of two worlds'. Representatives of all traditions and all philosophical and political camps sit together there. They do not see themselves as representatives of faculties in opposition to each other, but as bringing to expression and integration all the non-human and non-Metropolitan interests which the future upper house, the 'House of the Divinity' should safeguard.

Thus the Ecological Council becomes the reference-point for all consciousness groups ready to appear in the population, and can lend a conscious and directed character to the transformation pressure. And especially it can give extra strength to the ecological and spiritual awareness that is making itself felt everywhere.

The invisible church, when it comes to new-institutionalising, remains also the real organ for articulation and interpretation of divinity. As stated, it works according to the principle of the 'city on the hill' and the 'light on the bushel' – solely by its radiance, its spiritual authority. Its concrete function is to practise and maintain the ongoing and highest possible differentiated awareness of the general necessities of human existence, our responsibility for the whole of nature, and our further ascent toward freedom, truth and beauty.

The Will to Power – Whence and What For?

A salvation government can only come true, can only be what it should be – an institution with a healing effect – if it is created out of a salvation movement, with a purified, responsible subjectivity. The new and changed institutions are only an earnest project to the extent that we develop and affirm them as elements within our consciousness. Whoever takes a critical attitude to the idea from the start is altogether right in fearing social power, in fact any form of government, but contributes at the same time to their repressive character.

All warnings about despotism, all of this subjectivism about 'no power for nobody', always make the assumption that power is alien and hostile and that we are potentially subordinated to it, that we ourselves are not powerful and have no power. But all this is not true. Special power-formations exist because we do not establish ourselves as fully responsible *zoon politikon* (Aristotle's definition of the human as a political animal). Why does society disintegrate into a philosopher-king, a caste of guardians, and the common people? Because we *permit* ourselves to fall apart into such roles and don't really demand that we be *also* 'guardian', and *also* 'king'. For then these roles would fall away, and they wouldn't be reified and fetishised.

The mentality of the western Left – which on principle has hardened in a negative posture to authority, an adolescent posture of *no* toward father persisting until their own hair has grown white – no longer stands up to criticism. Indeed, in the perverse world of capitalistic modernity, power has been understood as the capacity for exploiting other people, to be above them and to outlive them. But in the ecological crisis this perversion blows itself sky high with its own hands. Thus power can once again be understood as creative potential, as our own creative power, in the inward unfolding of human body-soul-spirit.

The important thing is to develop the will into responsible participation in social power, and to develop the design of the ecological turning-point and its institutions in this sense. S/he who is a candidate for the Ecological Council, the Presidency and the Chancellorship will need to have realised the whole truth. This truth includes that the human species must rationally regulate its social sphere, because otherwise it will overthrow the natural balance and annihilate individuality. So we need a new-institutionalising, even if it is not a question of survival: one which is appropriate to the Great Order and to the human being at its present emergent level.

NOTES

(1) *Chrysanthemen im Spiegel. Klassische chinesische Dichtungen*, published, translated from the Chinese, and put into poetic form by Ernst Schwarz (Berlin: 1969) p167. ·

(2) Friedrich Schiller, *Werke*, v. 2, Special Edition, Die Tempel Klassiker, p887.

(3) Günter Rohrmoser, *Hohenheimer Protokolle* (Stuttgart: Jochen Gieraths, Academy of the Diocese of Rottenburg, 1985), p61.

(4) Robert von Ranke-Graves, *Die weisse Göttin. Sprache des Mythos* (Berlin: 1981), p578.

Bibliography

Literature quoted, mentioned, or made use of

Adorno, Theodor W. and Walter Benjamin. *Integration und Desintegration*. Hannover: 1976.

Alliata, Vittoria. *Harem, die Freiheit hinter dem Schleier*. Frankfurt, Berlin: 1984.

Alt, Franz. *Frieden ist möglich, die Politik der Bergpredigt*. München: 1983; *Peace is Possible: the Politics of the Sermon on the Mount*, Schocken, New York, 1985.

Amery, Carl. *Natur als Politik, die ökologische Chance des Menschen*. Reinbek: 1980.

Amrito (Jan Foudraine). *Bhagwan, Krishnamurti, C G Jung und die Psychotherapie*. Essen: 1983.

Anders, Günther. *Endzeit und Zeitwende, Gedanken über die atomare Situation*. München: 1972. See p24ff. 'Über Verantwortung heute,' especially pp35-40.

Die Antiquiertheit des Menschen, über die Seele im Zeitalter der zweiten industriellen Revolution. 2nd ed. München: 1956. See 'Die Welt als Phantom und Matritze, philosophische Betrachtungen über Rundfunk und Fernsehen.'

Andreas Salome, Lou. *Friedrich Nietzsche in seinen Werken*. Frankfurt: 1983; *Nietzsche*, Black Swan, Redding Ridge, 1988.

Arendt, Hannah. *Elemente und Ursprunge totaler Herrschaft*. Vols 1-3. Berlin: 1975.

Bäschlin, Daniel Lukas. *Der aufhaltsame Zwang - Sinn und Wege des Widerstands gegen Kernenergie*. München: 1981

Bahro, Rudolf. *The Alternative in Eastern Europe*. London: Verso, 1981. *Ich werde meinen Weg fortsetzen, eine Dokumentation*. 2nd edn, enlarged. Köln, Frankfurt: 1977.

Plädoyer für schöpferische Initiative, zur Kritik von Arbeitsbedingungen im real existierenden Sozialismus. Köln: 1980.

...die nicht mit den Wölfen h ulen, das Beispiel Beethoven und sieben Gedichte. Köln, Frankfurt: 1979.

Elemente einer neuen Politik, zum Verhältnis von Ökologie und Sozialismus. Berlin: 1980; *Socialism and Survival*, Heretic, Lon don, 1988.

Wahnsinn mit Methode. Über die Logik der Blockkonfrontation, die Friedensbewegung, die Sowjetunion und die DKP. Berlin: 1982.

Pfeiler am anderen Ufer, Beiträge zur Politik der Grünen von Hagen bis Karlsruhe. Special edition of the newspaper *Befreiung*, Berlin: 1984.

From Red to Green, Interviews with New Left Review. London: Verso, 1984.

Bahro, Foudraine, Fromm, Holl. *Radikalität im Heiligenschein, zur Wiederentdeckung der Spiritualitat in der modernen Gesellschaft*. Berlin: 1984.

Bartsch, Günter. *Die sozialen Sonderbewegungen - Satelliten oder Eigenmodelle - Trotzkismus, Ratedemokratie, Religiöse Sozialismus, Sociale Dreigliederung, die Freisozialen*. Hannover, Marburg o.J.

Bastial, Till. *Nach den Baumen stirbt der Mensch, von der Umweltverschmutzung zur Weltkatastrophe*. Frankfurt: 1984.

Bateson, Gregory. *Steps to an Ecology of Mind*. New York: Ballantyne, 1972.

Bauer, Wolfgang. *China und die Hoffnung auf Glück; Paradiese, Utopien, Idealvorstellungen in der Geistesgeschichte Chinas*. München: 1974; *China and the Search for Happiness - Recurring Themes in 4,000 Years of Chinese Cultural History*, Seabury, New York, 1976.

Bechmann, Armin. *Landbau-Wende, gesunde Landwirtschaft - gesunde Ernährung*.

Frankfurt: 1987.

Berendt, Joachim-Ernst. *Nada Brahma, die Welt ist Klang.* Frankfurt: 1983; *The World is Sound, Nada Brahma: Music and the Land scape of Consciousness,* Destiny, New York, 1991. *Das dritte Ohr, vom Hören der Welt.* Reinbek: 1985.

Berman, Morris. *Reenchantment of the World.* Ithaca: Cornell University Press, 1981.

Bhagwan Shree Rajneesh. *Intelligenz des Herzens.* Berlin: 1979.

Biedenkopf, Kurt H. *Die neue Sicht der Dinge, Plädöyer für eine freiheitliche Wirtschafts- und Socialordnung.* München, Zürich: 1985.

Bille-De Mot, Eléonore. *Die Revolution des Pharao Echnaton.* München: 1965.

Binswanger/Geissberger/Ginsburg (publishers). *Wege aus der Wohlstandsfalle: Der NAWU Report; Strategien gegen Arbeitslosigkeit und Umweltkrise.* Frankfurt: 1979.

Binswanger, Hans Christoph. *Geld und Magie, Deutung und Kritik der modernen Wirtschaft.* Stuttgart: 1985.

Bleakley, Alan. *Fruits of the Moon Tree,* Gateway, Bath: 1987.

Bleibtreu-Ehrenberg, Gisela. *Der Weibmann, kultische Geschlechtswechsel im Schamanismus, eine Studie zu Transvestition und Transsexualität bei Naturvölkern.* Frankfurt: 1984.

Bloch, Ernst. *Das Prinzip Hoffnung.* Vols 1-3. Frankfurt: 1959; *The Principle of Hope,* MIT Press, Cambridge, MA, 1986.

Bödeker, Johanna. *Liquiditäts-Äquivalenz von Angebot und Nachfrage.* Hannover: Gesellschaft für Sozialproblem-Forschung, 1962.

Bohm, David. *Wholeness and the Implicate Order.* London: 1980.

Bookchin, Murray. *The Limits of the City.* New York: Colophon, 1974. *The Ecology of Freedom.* Palo Alto: Cheshire, 1982. *Hierarchie und Herrschaft.* Berlin: 1981.

Brecht, Bertolt. *Hundert Gedichte 1918-1950.* Berlin: 1951. *Leben des Galilei.* Berlin, Weimar: 1964. *Prosa.* Vol IV, 'Me-ti, Buch der Wendungen.' Berlin, Weimar: 1975.

Breuer, Georg. *Der sogannante Mensch, was wir mit Tieren gemeinsam haben, und was nicht.* München: 1981; *Sociobiology and*

the Human Dimension, Cambridge Univ Press, Cambridge & New York, 1983.

Brinton Perera, Sylvia. *Der Weg zur Göttin der Tiefe, die Erlösung der dunklen Schwester; eine Initiation für Frauen.* Interlaken: 1985.

Burkhardt, Hans. *Verlorene Wirklichkeit, vom Elend der Ideologien.* München, Berlin, 1980.

Canetti, Elias. *Masse und Macht.* Hamburg: Sonderausgabe, 1984.

Capra, Fritjof. *The Turning Point, Science, Society, and the Rising Culture.* New York: Simon and Schuster, 1982.

Castaneda, Carlos. *The Second Ring of Power.* New York: Simon and Schuster, 1977.

Caudwell, Christopher. *Illusion und Wirklichkeit. Eine Studie über die Grundlagen der Poesie.* Dresden: 1966; *Illusion and Reality: a study in the sources of Poetry,* Macmillan, London, 1937.

Chrysanthemen im Spiegel, klassische chinesische Dichtungen. Translated, put in verse form, and published by Ernst Schwarz. Berlin: 1969.

Daly, Mary. *Gyn/Ecology, the Metaethics of Radical Feminism.* Boston: Beacon, 1978.

Der Ochs und sein Hirte, Zengeschichte aus dem alten China. Pfullingen: 1981.

Ditfurth, Hoimar van. *So lasst uns denn ein Apfelbäumchen pflanzen, es ist so weit.* Hamburg, Zürich: 1985.

Djilas, Milovan. *Die unvollkommene Gesellschaft, jenseits der »Neuen Klasse«.* Wien, München, Zürich: 1969.

Dürckheim, Karlfried Graf. *Der Alltag als Übung.* Bern, Stuttgart, Wien: 1980; *The Way of Transformation - Daily Life as Spiritual Exercise,* Unwin, London, 1980.

Duhm, Dieter. *Aufbruch zur neuen Kultur, von der Verweigerung zur Neugestaltung; Umrisse einer okologischen und menschlichen Alternative.* München: 1982.

Eccles, John C and Hans Zeier. *Gehirn und Geist.* München, Zürich: 1980.

Eckhart, Meister Eckhart. *Vom Wunder der Seele.* Stuttgart: Friedrich Alfred Schmitt Noerr, 1977.

Eckhart. *Meister Eckharts Mystische Schriften.* Translated by Gustav Landauer. Wetzlar: 1978.

Ehrlich, Paul, and Anne Ehrlich. *Der lautlose Tod der Pflanzen und Tiere, was tun wir und was können wir tun?* Frankfurt: n.d.

Eliade, Mircea. *The Myth of the Eternal Return, or Cosmos and History.* Princeton: Princeton University Press, 1954.
Yoga. New York: Pantheon, 1958.
A History of Religious Beliefs and Ideas. 3 vols. Chicago: University of Chicago Press, 1978-85.

Ellul, Jacques. *De la revolution aux revoltes.* Paris: Calmann Levy, 1972.

Erikson, Erik H. *Kindheit und Gesellschaft.* Stuttgart: 1987.

Eschenbach, Wolfram von. *Parzival.* Essen, Stuttgart: 1985.

Eucken, Walter. *Die Grundlagen der Nationalökonomie.* Berlin, Göttingen, Heidelberg: 1959; *The Foundations of Economics, History and Theory in the Analysis of Economic Reality,* Hodge, London, 1950.

Falk, Richard. *The End of World Order, Essays on Normative International Relations.* New York, London: 1983.

Fenske, Mertens, Reinhard, Rosen. *Geschichte der politischen Ideen, von Homer bis zur Gegenwart.* Königstein/Taunus: 1981.

Fernbach, David. *The Spiral Path, a Gay Contribution to Human Survival.* Boston: 1981.

Fetscher, Iring. *Überlebensbedingungen der Menschheit, zur Dialektik des Fortschritts.* München: 1980.

Fromm, Erich. *Escape From Freedom.* New York: Rinehart, 1941.
The Anatomy of Human Destructiveness. New York: Holt, Rinehart and Winston, 1973.
On Disobedience and Other Essays. New York: Seaburg, 1981.

Führkötter, Adelgundis. »Hildegard von Bingen«, in *Die Grossen Deutschen.* Deutsche Biographie vol 5. Gütersloh: 1978; *The Miniatures from the Books of Scivias - Know the Ways of St Hildegard of Bingen, from the Illuminated Rupertsberg Codex,* Turnhout, Belgium, 1977

Galtung, Johan. *Self-Reliance, Beiträge zu einer alternativen Entwicklungsstrategie.* München: Mir A. Ferdowski, 1983.
Strukturelle Gewalt, Beiträge zur Friedens- und Konfliktforschung. Reinbek: 1975. Various manuscripts which are either unpublished or available to the author only in photocopied form.

Garaudy, Roger. *Gott ist tot, eine Studie über Hegel.* Berlin: 1965.
Aufruf an die Lebenden. Darmstadt,

Neuwied: 1981.
Il est encore temps de vivre, voici comment. Paris: 1980.

Gebser, Jean. *The Ever Present Origin.* Athens: Ohio University Press, 1984. (A translation of *Ursprung und Gegenwart,* 2 vols. Stuttgart: Deutsche Verlags-Anstalt, 1949, 1953, by Noel Barstad with Algis Mickunas).

Gehlen, Arnold. *Der Mensch, seine Natur und seine Stellung in der Welt.* Wiesbaden: 1986; *Man, His Nature and Place in the World,* Columbia Univ Press, New York, 1988.

Georgescu-Roegen, Nicholas. *The Entropy Law and the Economic Process.* Cambridge, Mass: Harvard University Press, 1971.
Energy and Economic Myths, Institutional and Analytical Economic Essays. New York: Pergamon, 1976.

Gloger, Bruno. *Kaiser, Gott und Teufel, Friedrich II. von Hohenstaufen in Geschichte und Sage.* Berlin: 1970.

Glotz, Peter. *Die Arbeit der Zuspitzung, Über die Organisation einer regierungsfähigen Linken.* Berlin: 1984.

Goethe, Johann Wolfgang. *Die Wahlverwandtschaften.* Berlin Edition vol. 12. Berlin: 1963; *The Sufferings of Young Werther, and Elective Affinities,* Continuum, New York, 1990.

Göttner-Abendroth, Heide. *Die Göttin und ihr Heros.* München: 1984.

Goldschmidt, Harry. *Franz Schubert, ein Lebensbild.* Leipzig: 1962.
Um die unsterbliche Geliebte, eine Bestandsaufnahme. Beethoven-Studien 2. Leipzig: 1977.

Gramsci, Antonio. *Philosophie der Praxis, eine Auswahl.* Translated and published by Christian Riechers. 1967.

Grof, Stanislaw. *Beyond the Brain; Birth, Death and Transcendence in Psychotherapy.* Albany: State University of New York Press, 1985.

Gruhl, Herbert. *Das irdische Gleichgewicht, Ökologie unseres Daseins.* Düsseldorf: 1982.

Guardini, Romano. *Ein Gedenkbuch mit einer Auswahl aus seinem Werk.* Leipzig: Werner Becker, 1969.

Heer, Friedrich. *Das Wagnis der schöpferischen Vernunft.* Stuttgart, Berlin, Köln, Mainz: 1977.

Heinse, Wilhelm. *Ardinghello und die glückseligen Inseln.* Leipzig: 1973.

Hirsch, Fred. *Die sozialen Grenzen des Wachstums*. Reinbek: 1980.

Hölderlin, Friedrich. *Sämtliche Werke* (in one volume.) Leipzig: Friedrich Beissner, 1965.

Hochgesang, Michael. *Mythos und Logik im 20. Jahrhundert*. München: 1965.

Holl, Adolf. *Der letzte Christ, Franz von Assisi*. Berlin, Wien: 1982; *The Last Christian*, Doubleday, New York, 1980.

Hübner, Kurt. *Kritik der wissenschaftlichen Vernunft*. Freiburg, München: 1979; *Critique of Scientific Reason*, Chicago Univ Press, 1983.

Hunke, Sigrid. *Europas eigene Religion, der Glaube der Ketzer*. Bergisch Gladbach: 1983.

I Ching, or Book of Changes. Translated by Richard Wilhelm. London: 1951ff.

Illich, Ivan. *Tools for Conviviality*. New York: Harper, 1973.

Gender. New York: Pantheon, 1982.

Initiative Sozialistisches Forum Freiburg. *Diktatur der Freundlichkeit; Über Bhagwan, die kommende Psychokratie und Lieferanteneingänge zum wohltätigen Wahnsinn*. Freiburg: 1984.

Jänicke, Martin. *Wie das Industriesystem von seinen Missständen profitiert*. Opladen: 1979.

Jannberg, Judith. *Ich bin ich*. Frankfurt: 1984.

Jánossy, Franz. *Wie die Akkumulationslawine ins Rollen kam*. Berlin: 1979.

Jaynes, Julian. *The Origin of Consciousness in the Breakdown of the Bicameral Mind*. Boston: Houghton Mifflin, 1976.

Jonas, Hans. *The Imperative of Responsibility*. Chicago: University of Chicago Press, 1984.

Jung, C G. *Welt der Psyche*. München: 1981. *Das C G Jung Lesebuch*. Selected by Franz Alt. Olten: 1983.

Kakuska, Rainer, ed. *Andere Wirklichkeiten, die neue Konvergenz von Naturwissenschaften und spirituellen Traditionen*. München: 1985.

Kaltenmark, Max. *Lao-tzu und der Taoismus*. Frankfurt: 1981.

Kapp, William K. *Soziale Kosten der Marktwirtschaft*. Frankfurt: 1978.

and Fritz Vilmar. *Sozialisierung der Verluste, die sozialen Kosten eines privatwirtschaftlichen Systems*. München: 1972.

Keen, Sam. *The Passionate Life*. New York: Harper, 1983, Bath: Gateway, 1985.

To a Dancing God. New York: Harper, 1970.

Kitamura, Kazuyuki. *Japan - im Reich der mächtigen Frauen*. Berlin: 1985.

Kleist, Heinrich von. *Über das Marionettentheater*. Frankfurt: 1980; *About Marionettes*, Three Kings Press, Mindelheim, 1970.

Klix, Friedhart. *Information und Verhalten*. Berlin: 1971.

Erwachendes Denken, eine Entwicklungsgeschichte der menschlichen Intelligenz. Berlin: 1983.

Knipper, Udo. *Anthroposophie im Lichte indischer Weisheit*. Gladenbach: 1986.

Koestler, Arthur. *Der Mensch - Irrläufer der Evolution*. München: 1981.

Kohr, Leopold. *Das Ende der Grossen, zurück zum menschlichen Mass*. Wien: 1978.

Viele Wege, Paradigmen einer neuen Politik. München: Satish Kumar and Roswitha Henschel, 1985. See also their *Metapolitik*, 1985.

Kongtrul, Jamgon. *Das Licht der Gewissheit, mit einem Vorwort von Schögyam Trungpa*. Freiburg: 1979.

Krishna, Gopi and Carl Friedrich von Weizsäcker. *Biologische Basis religiöser Erfahrung*. München: 1968; *The Biological Basis of Religion and Genius*, Harper & Row, New York, 1972.

Krishna, Gopi. *Kundalini, Erweckung der geistigen Kraft im Menschen*. Berlin, München, Wien: 1985; *Kundalini, the Evolutionary Energy in Man*, Ramadhar, New Delhi, and Hopeman, 1967.

Kumar, Satish and Roswitha Henschel, eds. *Viele Wege, Paradigmen einer neuen Politik*. München: Satish and Henschel, 1985.

Lafontaine, Oskar. *Der andere Fortschritt*. Hamburg: 1985.

Langhans, Rainer. *Theoria diffusa aus Gesprächen mit drei Frauen*. Nördlingen: 1986.

Lao Tzu. *Tao teh Ching*. Translated and with a commentary by Richard Wilhelm. London, New York: 1977.

Lau-tse. *Daudedsching*. Translated from the Chinese by Ernst Schwarz. Leipzig: Ernst Schwarz, 1970.

Laqueur, Walter. *Die deutsche Jugendbewegung, eine historische Studie*. Köln: 1983.

Leary, Timothy. *The Game of Life, neurological Tarot*. San Francisco: 1984.

Lenin, W I. *Werke.* V. 38, Philosophical Notebooks, see among other things the Hegel excerpts 'Wissenschaft der Logik.' Berlin: 1964.

Lessing, Gotthold Ephraim. »Die Erziehung des Menschengeschlechts«, in *Triumph der Wahrheit, Gotthold Ephraim Lessing Mensch und Werk.* Berlin: 1951; *The Education of the Human Race,* C K Paul, London, 1880.

Liebknecht, Karl. *Studien über die Bewegungsgesetze der gesellschaftlichen Entwicklung.* Foreword by Ossip K. Flechtheim. Hamburg: Ossip K. Flechtheim, 1974.

Linse, Ulrich. *Ökopax und Anarchie, eine Geschichte der ökologischen Bewegungen in Deutschland.* München: 1986.

Luhmann, Niklas. *Liebe als Passion, zur Kodierung von Intimität.* Frankfurt: 1982; *Love as Passion: the Codification of Intimacy,* Harvard Univ Press, Cambridge MA, 1986.

Luxemburg, Rosa. *Gesammelte Werke.* Vol. 4, August 1914 to January 1919. Berlin: 1974.

Macpherson, Crawford B. *Democratic Theory, Essays in Retrieval.* Oxford: Clarendon, 1973.

Macy, Joanna Rogers. *Despair and Personal Power in the Nuclear Age.* Philadelphia: New Society, 1983.

Mann, Heinrich. *Henry, King of France.* 2 vols. New York: Knopf, 1937, 1939.

Margo, Anand (Mitsou Naslednikov). *Tantra - Weg der Ekstase, die Sexualität des neuen Menschen.* Schloss Wolfsbrunnen: 1982.

Marx, Karl. *Das Kapital.* Vol. 1. Berlin: 1957.
and Friedrich Engels. *Manifest der Kommunistischen Partei.* Marx-Engels Works, vol. 4. Berlin: 1959.

Mechtersheimer, Alfred. *Rüstung und Frieden, der Wiedersinn der Sicherheitspolitik.* München: 1982.

Meinhof, Ulrike. *Der Tod Ulrike Meinhofs, Bericht der Internationalen Untersuchungskommission.* 2d. ed. revised. Tübingen: 1979.

Meinhof, Ulrike Marie. *Die Würde des Menschen ist antastbar, Aufsätze und Polemiken.* Berlin: 1980.

Mensch, Gerhard. *Das technologische Patt, Innovationen überwinden die Depression.* Frankfurt: 1977; *Stalemate in Technology: Inno vations overcome the Depression,*

Ballinger, Cambridge MA, 1979.

Metz, Johann Baptist. *Unterbrechungen.* Gütersloh: 1981.

Metzger, Dorothea. *Copper in the World Economy.* New York, London: 1980.

Morris, William. *News From Nowhere.* London: Routledge and Kegan Paul, 1973.

Mowat, Farley. *Der Untergang der Arche Noah, vom Leiden der Tiere unter den Menschen.* Reinbek: 1987; *Sea of Slaughter,* Atlantic Monthly Press, 1984.

Müller, Rudolf Wolfgang. *Geist und Geld, zur Entstehungsgeschichte von Identitätsbewusstsein und Rationalität seit der Antike.* Frankfurt, New York: 1977.

Mumford, Lewis. *The Myth of the Machine; Vol 1, the Pentagon of Power; Vol 2, Technics and Human Development.* New York: Harcourt, Brace, 1964, 1966.
The Transformations of Man. London: George Allen and Unwin, 1957.
The City in History, Its Origins, Its Transformations, and Its Prospects. New York: Harcourt, Brace and World, 1961.

Musashi. *Das Buch der fünf Ringe.* München: 1983.

Mynarek, Hubertus. *Ökologische Religion, ein neues Verständnis der Natur.* München: 1986.

Naranjo, Claudio. *The Healing Journey, New Approaches to Consciousness.* New York: Pantheon, 1974.

Naslednikow: see Margo, Anand.

Negt, Oskar/Alexander Kluge. *Geschichte und Eigensinn.* Frankfurt: 1981.

Neumann, Erich. *The Great Mother, An Analysis of the Archetype.* New York: Pantheon, 1955.
Zur Psychologie des Weiblichen. Frankfurt: 1983.
Amor and Psyche, the Psychic Development of the Feminine. Princeton: Princeton University Press, 1956.
The Origins and History of Consciousness. Princeton: Princeton University Press, 1970. (A translation of *Ursprungsgeschichte des Bewusstseins.* Zürich: Rascher Verlag, 1949).
Depth Psychology and a New Ethic. New York: Harper, 1969.

Nolte, Hans-Heinrich. *Die eine Welt, Abriss der Geschichte des internationalen systems.* Hannover: 1982.

Novalis. *Dokumente seines Lebens und Sterbens.* Frankfurt: 1979.

Orthbandt, Eberhard. *Geschichte der grossen*

Philosophen, das Buch der philosophischen Denkmodelle. Hanau.

Otani, Yoshito. *Untergang eines Mythos*. Neu-Ulm: 1978.

Pascal, Blaise. *Geist und Herz, eine Auswahl aus dem Gesamtwerk*. Berlin: 1964.

Pilgrim, Volker Elis. *Dressur des Bösen, zur Kultur der Gewalt*. München: 1974.

Plack, Arno. *Die Gesellschaft und das Böse*. Frankfurt, Berlin, Wien: 1979.

Plato. *The Republic*. Leipzig: 1978. New York: Vintage, 1991.

Raith, Werner. *Das verlassene Imperium, über das Aussteigen des römischen Volkes aus der Geschichte*. Berlin.

Rammstedt, Otthein. *Soziale Bewegung*. Frankfurt: 1978.

Ranke-Graves, Robert von. *Die weisse Göttin, Sprache des Mythos*. Berlin: 1981.

Ravenscroft, Trevor. *The Spear of Destiny*. New York: Putnam, 1973.
Der Kelch des Schicksals, die Suche nach dem Gral. Basel: 1982.

Reich, Wilhelm. *The Murder of Christ*. New York: Simon and Schuster, 1953.
Äther, Gott und Teufel. Frankfurt: 1983.

Rilke, Rainer Maria. *Werke, Auswahl in zwei Bänden*. Leipzig: 1957.

Richter, Horst Eberhard. *Der Gotteskomplex*. Reinbek: 1979; *All Mighty - A Study of the God Complex in Western Man*, Hunter House, Claremont CA, 1984.

Rinser, Luise. *Mirjam*. Frankfurt: 1983.
Im Dunkeln singen, 1982-1985. Frankfurt: 1985.

Röpke, Wilhelm. *Civitas humana, Grundfragen der Gesellschafts- und Wirtschaftsreform*. Erlenbach, Zürich: 1949; *Civitas Humana: A Humane Order of Society*, (microfilm), Hodge, London, 1948.

Rohrmoser, Günter. *Krise der politischen Kultur*. Mainz: 1983.
»Technik und Zivilisationskritik zwischen Utopieverlust und Pessimismus«, in Hohenheimer Protokolle *Technik - Fortschritt in Verantwortung und Freiheit?* Stuttgart: Jochen Gieraths, Akademie der Diözese Rottenburg, 1985.

Rolland, Romain. *Beethoven, les grandes époques créatrices*. Paris: 1966. (The translation is from a partial publication of *Beethovens Meisterjahre*, Berlin: Verlag Rutten & Loenig); *Beethoven the Creator - The Great Creative Epochs*, Harper, New York, 1929.

Ruesch, Hans. *Nackte Herrscherin*. With the story »Nachruhm« by Manfred Kyber. München: das Manifest gegen Tierversuche, 1984.
Die Pharma Story, der grosse Schwindel. München: 1985.

Schaer, Bernhard. *Die Kraft des Regenbogens, spirituelle, ökologische und politische Modelle zur Vernetzung des Bewusstseins*. Wald: 1986.

Schiller, Friedrich. *Werke*. Vol 2, special edition, Die Tempel Klassiker, in which are »Die Sendung Moses« and »Die Gesetzgebung des Lykurgus und Solon«.

Schmidt, Alfred Ernst. Manuscripts received from him 1982/83 on the theme of the politics of salvation. (Address: Alfred-Mumbacher- Strasse 67B, 65 Mainz, Germany).

Schmölders, Günter. *Psychologie des Geldes*. München: 1982.

Schubart, Walter. *Religion und Eros*. München: 1978.

Schütt, Peter. *Der Wald stirbt an Stress*. München: 1984.

Schumacher, E. F. *Small Is Beautiful, Economics As If People mattered*. New York: Harper, 1973.

Schweppenhäuser, Hans Georg. *Das kranke Geld, Vorschläge für eine soziale Geldordnung von morgen*. Frankfurt: 1982.

Sève, Lucien. *Marxismus und Theorie der Personlichkeit*. Berlin: 1972.

Sheldrake, Rupert. *The New Science of Life*, London, Collins 1983. *Das schopferische Universum, die Theorie des morphogenetischen Feldes*. München, 1983.

Sik, Ota. *Humane Wirtschaftsdemokratie, ein dritter Weg*. Hamburg: 1979; *For a Human Democratic Democracy*, Praeger, New York, 1985.

Sohn-Rethel, Alfred. *Geistige und körperliche Arbeit, zur Theorie der gesellschaftlichen Synthesis*. Frankfurt: 1970; *Intellectual and Manual Labour: a Critique of Epistemology*, Humanities Press, Atlantic Highlands, NJ, 1978.

Sorge, Elga. *Religion und Frau, weibliche Spiritualität und Christentum*. Stuttgart, Berlin, Köln, Mainz: 1985.

Späth, Lothar. *Wende in die Zukunft, die Bundesrepublik auf dem Weg in die Informationsgesellschaft*. Reinbek: 1985; *Facing the Future: Germany Breaking New Ground*, Springer, New York, 1986.

Spangler, David. *Revelation, Birth of a New Age* – Findhorn 1978. *New Age - die Geburt eines Neuen Zeitalters, die Findhorn Community.* Kimratshofen: 1983.

Steiner, Rudolf. *The Renewal of the Social Organism.* Spring Valley, N.Y: Anthroposophic Press, 1985.

Strawe, Christoph. *Marxismus und Anthroposophie.* Stuttgart: 1986.

Suhr, Dieter. *Bewusstseinsverfassung und Gesellschaftsverfassung, über Hegel und Marx zu einer dialektischen Verfassungstheorie.* Berlin: 1975.

Täube, Reinhard. *Innere Erfahrung und Gesellschaft, klassischer Yoga - Indische Mystik; Beiträge zur Alternativkultur oder, Die Lotusblüte bekommt Stacheln.* Dissertation to be obtained from the author. Address; Stückhof, D-3589 Knullwald, Germany.

Tagore, Rabindranath. *Sadhana, the Realisation of Life,* New York: Macmillan, 1916.

Tamo, Ryoju. *Vertäut den Kahn.* Kamakura, Koshigoe 5-5-14, Japan.

Teilhard de Chardin, Pierre. *The Phenomenon of Man.* New York: Harper, 1959.

Thompson, Edward P, *et al. Exterminism and Cold War.* London: New Left Books, 1982.
The Making of the English Working Class. Harmondsworth: Penguin, 1968.
Writing by Candlelight. London: Merlin, 1980.

Thompson, William Irwin. *The Time Falling Bodies Take to Light; Mythology, Sexuality, and the Origins of Culture.* New York: St. Martins, 1981.
Pacific Shift. San Francisco: Sierra Club, 1985.

Thomson, George. *First Philosophers.* Atlantic Highlands, N.J: Humanities Press, n.d.

Thucydides. *History of the Peloponnesian War.* Harmondsworth: Penguin, 1954.

Toynbee, Arnold J. *A Study of History.* 6 vols. London: Oxford, 1951.

Tränen des Vaterlandes, deutsche Dichtung aus dem 16. und 17. Jahrhundert. A selection by Johannes R. Becher. Berlin: 1954.

Trevelyan, George. *A Vision of the Aquarian Age.* Bath: Gateway, 1994.

Tulku, Tarthang. *Raum, Zeit und Erkenntnis, Aufbruch zu neuen Dimensionen der Erfahrung von Welt und Wirklichkeit.* Second edition of the special issue of 1986.

Umbau der Industriegesellschaft, Programm zur Überwindung von Erwerbslosigkeit, Armut und Umweltzerstörung. (Draft). Bonn: Die Grünen, 1986.

Vanier, Jean. *Gemeinschaft, Ort der Versöhnung und des Festes.* Salzburg: 1983.

Vivekananda. *Jnana-Yoga, der Pfad der Erkenntnis.* Vol 1. Freiburg: 1977; *Vedanta Philosophy - Lectures of Jnana Yoga,* Vedanta Soc, New York, 1902-1907.

Weischedel, Wilhelm. *34 grosse Philosophen in Alltag und Denken, die philosophische Hintertreppe.* München: 1980.

Weizsäcker, Carl Friedrich von. *Die Einheit der Natur.* München: 1981; *The Unity of Nature,* New York, 1980.

Welskopf, Elisabeth Charlotte. *Probleme der Musse im alten Hellas.* Berlin: 1962.

Werfel, Franz. *The Forty Days of Musa Dagh.* New York: Modern Library, 1937.

White, Kenneth. *Das weisse Land, Essays.* München: 1984.

Widder, Erich. *Freude aus der Tiefe.* Linz, Wien, Passau: n. d.

Wiesenthal, Helmut. »Versorgung und Revolution, ein Rezensionsessay«. In the newspaper *Commune,* 12/1985.

Wilber, Ken. *Up From Eden, A Transpersonal View of Human Evolution.* Boulder: Shambhala, 1983.
No Boundary, East and West Approaches to Personal Growth. Boulder: Shambhala, 1981.

Wilder-Smith, Arthur Ernest. *Man's Origin, Man's Destiny.* Wheaton, Ill: Shaw, 1968.

Wilson, Robert Anton. *Prometheus Rising.* Phoenix: Falcon, 1983.

Ziegler, Wolfram. »Umweltschutz, Versuch einer Analyse«, Offprint from *Jahrbuch 1984 der Technischen Universität München,* pp305- 319, and »Am point of no return«, in *Ökologie,* 26/1984.

Zweig, Stefan. *Die Augen des ewigen Bruders.* Leipzig, No 349.

About the Author

Rudolf Bahro was born in 1935 in what later became East Germany. His father was a farm overseer and Rudolf gained a great deal of farm experience as a child and teenager. He joined the East German Communist Party in 1952 and became a leading Party intellectual, taking a left wing position which became increasingly displeasing to the Party apparatus.

Angered by the invasion of Czechoslovakia in 1968 he wrote, between 1972 and 1977, a fundamental critique of 'socialism as practised'. This was published in 1977 in West Germany as *The Alternative in Eastern Europe (Die Alternative: zur Kritik des real existierenden Sozialismus)*. Its publication was announced in an interview in an October 1977 issue of *Der Spiegel*. Bahro was at once arrested and sentenced to eight years in prison for 'publishing state secrets'.

He was released on October 11th 1979 under a general amnesty and left East Germany. In West Germany he joined the Green Party, becoming an intellectual leader of the 'fundamentalist' wing (the 'fundis'). Disappointed in the progress of the Greens, he left them in 1985 to become a freelance writer and educator.

In 1990 he was officially exonerated by the Supreme Court of East Germany, leading out of the reforms in the East and the reunification of Germany. Currently he is teaching in the Humbolt University of East Berlin, where he has ensured that every student studies basic ecology.

Index